T   D 1000

Regional History of England

General Editors: Barry Cunliffe and David Hey
For full details of the series, see pp. xiv–xvii

The South East from AD 1000

Peter Brandon and Brian Short

Longman
London and New York

Longman Group UK Limited
Longman House, Burnt Mill, Harlow,
Essex CM20 2JE, England
and Associated Companies throughout the World.

Published in the United States of America
by Longman Inc., New York

©Longman Group UK Limited 1990

First published 1990

British Library Cataloguing in Publication Data
Brandon Peter F.
 The South East from AD 1000. — (Regional history of England),
 1. South — East England, history
 I. Title II. Short, Brian, *1944–* III. Series 942.2

 ISBN 0–582–49246–7 CSD
 ISBN 0–582–49245–9 PPR

Library of Congress Cataloging-in-Publication Data
Brandon, Peter F., 1927–
 The South East from AD 1000 / Peter F. Brandon and Brian M. Short.
  p.   cm. — (Regional history of England)
 Bibliography: p.
 Includes index.
 ISBN 0–582–49246–7 — ISBN 0–582–49245–9 (pbk.) 1. Kent (England) — History. 2. Surrey (England) — History. 3. East Sussex (England) — History. 4. West Sussex (England) — History. 5. London (England) — History. 6. England — History, Local. I. Short, Brian M., 1944–
 II. Title. III. Title: South East from AD one thousand. IV. Series.
 DA670.K3B73   1988
 942—dc20   89–34441
                                              CIP

Set in Linotron 202 10/12 Sabon Roman
Produced by Longman Singapore Publishers (Pte) Ltd.
Printed in Singapore

Contents

List of Tables

List of Plates

x

List of Figures

xii

Acknowledgements

The authors and publishers would like to thank the following for their permission to use the illustrations in the text:

Archaeologia Cantiana (Plate 2.2); *Brighton Marina Company* (7.3); *The Trustees of the British Museum* (2.3, 2.5, 5.2, 6.1); *British Library* (5.9); *British Rail Pension Fund Works of Art Collection* (5.5); *the British Transport Museum* (6.11); *Chichester Cathedral Publications* (2.8); *Country Life* (6.10); *East Sussex County Council* (E.1); *English Heritage* (3.4); *Government Art Collection* (4.5); *Hastings Museum & Art Gallery* (5.10); *George Holleyman* (6.2); *Howard Grey* from *Omega and After: Bloomsbury and the Decorative Arts (Thames and Hudson)* (6.8); *London Transport Museum* (6.5); *Meridian Airmaps, Lancing* (1.1); *The National Maritime Museum, Greenwich* (2.6, 2.7); *National Library of Vienna* (5.4); *Painshill Park Trust* (5.6); *Parham Park Ltd* (4.1); *Edward Reeves* (1.2, 3.1, 4.3); *The Royal Blackheath Golf Club* (6.6); *Science & Engineering Research Council* (3.3); *Spink & Son Ltd* (5.1); *Surrey Archaeological Society* (4.1); *Sussex Rural Community Council* (1.3); *Times Newspapers* (7.1); *Tony Stone Worldwide Photolibrary* (6.4); *Victoria County History* (4.6); *Tapisserie de Bayeux* (2.1); *Weald & Downland Museum* (3.2).

General Preface

England cannot be divided satisfactorily into recognizable regions based on former kingdoms or principalities in the manner of France, Germany or Italy. Few of the Anglo-Saxon tribal divisions had much meaning in later times and from the eleventh century onwards England was a united country. English regional identities are imprecise and no firm boundaries can be drawn. In planning this series we have recognized that any attempt to define a region must be somewhat arbitrary, particularly in the Midlands, and that boundaries must be flexible. Even the South-West, which is surrounded on three sides by the sea, has no agreed border on the remaining side and in many ways, historically and culturally, the River Tamar divides the area into two. Likewise, the Pennines present a formidable barrier between the eastern and western counties on the Northern Borders; contrasts as much as similarities need to be emphasized here.

The concept of a region does not imply that the inhabitants had a similar experience of life, nor that they were all inward-looking. A Hull merchant might have more in common with his Dutch trading partner than with his fellow Yorkshireman who farmed a Pennine smallholding: a Roman soldier stationed for years on Hadrian's Wall probably had very different ethnic origins from a native farmer living on the Durham boulder clay. To differing degrees, everyone moved in an international climate of belief and opinion with common working practices and standards of living.

Yet regional differences were nonetheless real; even today a Yorkshireman may be readily distinguished from someone from the South East. Life in Lancashire and Cheshire has always been different from life in the Thames Valley. Even the East Midlands has a character that is subtly different from that of the West Midlands. People still feel that they belong to a particular region within England as a whole.

In writing these histories we have become aware how much regional identities may vary over time; moreover how a farming region, say, may not coincide with a region defined by its building styles or its dialect. We have dwelt upon the diversity that can be found within a region as well as upon common characteristics in order to illustrate the local peculiarities of provincial life. Yet despite all of these problems of definition, we feel that the time is ripe to attempt an ambitious scheme outlining the history of England's regions in twenty-one volumes. London has not been included – except for demonstrating the many ways in which it has influenced the provinces – for its history has been very different from that of the towns and rural parishes that are our principal concern.

In recent years an enormous amount of local research, both historical and archaeological, has deepened our understanding of the former concerns of ordinary men and women and has altered our perception of everyday life in the past in many significant ways, yet the results of this work are not widely known even within the regions themselves.

This series offers a synthesis of this new work from authors who have themselves been actively involved in local research and who are present in or former residents of the regions they describe.

Each region will be covered in two linked but independent volumes, the first covering the period up to AD 1000 and necessarily relying heavily on archaeological data, and the second bringing the story up to the present day. Only by taking a wide time-span and by studying continuity and change over many centuries do distinctive regional characteristics become clear.

This series portrays life as it was experienced by the great majority of the people of South Britain or England as it was to become. The twenty-one volumes will – it is hoped – substantially enrich our understanding of English history.

Barry Cunliffe
David Hey

A Regional History of England

General Editors: Barry Cunliffe (to AD 1000) and David Hey (from AD 1000)

The regionalization used in this series is illustrated on the map opposite.

* already published

1. The Northern Counties
2. The Lancashire/Cheshire Region
3. Yorkshire
4. The Severn Valley and West Midlands
5. The East Midlands
6. The South Midlands and the Upper Thames
7. The Eastern Counties
8. The South West
9. Wessex
10. The South East

Preface

This book is the outcome of two historical geographers working closely together whose field of research for many years has been the regional and local history of south-east England within its geographical context. We are agreed that if regional history is to have its own distinctive approach it must share the methods and ideals of Professor Everitt, as being concerned primarily with the ever-evolving interrelationships between people in essentially different types of local community, the unifying social imprint that this has stamped on local areas which the French call *pays*, and the attempt to elucidate questions of more general historical significance through the intensive study of the locale. We are also convinced that regions matter because they are positive forces, not merely recipients of 'national history localized'. The people within our region shaped a distinctive product – a *south-eastern* culture; a *south-eastern* feudalism, or a *south-eastern* capitalism – which may be very different from that experienced and ongoing in other regions.

In writing this book within the constraints of defects in our knowledge and limitations imposed on us by necessary selection, we have sought to portray the region 'in the round' by building outwards in scale from the infinitely varied matrix of localities within which regional consciousness and economy was sustained and fostered. For this reason the counties have rarely been our unit of reference, nor has any attempt been made to pass off the history of a village, town or tract of country as the 'truth' about the region. This standpoint has been facilitated by the appreciable degree of unity which the South East has ever evinced from the circumstances of it being for many centuries essentially a central forest waste within the more habitable fringes, so giving it a functional coherence which went, and continues to go, far towards the shaping of society on a regional basis.

On re-reading our text on concluding this book we are conscious that although the South East is well trodden land it still has its unexplored grounds, themes and periods. Much remains to be done to extend our knowledge of the lives of those successive inhabitants of the region's hills and valleys, downs and marshes, woodlands and heaths, and towns and coast. In attempting this synthesis we have been struck by the fact that although the old order changed at various junctures of history, there was nevertheless a strong underlying continuity of human life which appears to have undergone repeated cyclical growth and decay. Hopefully this will be seen as a strong vindication for writing this history.

Our debt to Professor Alan Everitt will be self-evident. We also desire to record with gratitude the late Professor S. W. Wooldridge whose scientific studies of the Weald sowed the seed of the idea of the South East as a composite unity in diversity, 'a region with a pattern . . . variations on a theme . . .', although we have been at pains to demonstrate that the physical environment of the South East was not wholly *given* but was effectively *made* as a reflection of human institutional structures.

This book could not have been written without the works of the several hundred scholars, past and present, whose publications are listed in the bibliography. We also wish to thank the undergraduate, postgraduate, and continuing education students, and the many colleagues within geography and history who have helped us to clarify thoughts and identify problems. Thanks are also due to archivists and librarians who have been of assistance, particularly those at the Institute of Historical Research, University of London, the University of Sussex, the London Library, the Society of Antiquaries of London, and the staffs of the various county record offices. Among those who have given us specific help are Joyce Crowe, Desmond Gunner, John Gurney, Alun Howkins, Willie Lamont, John Lowerson, David Martin, Anne McCormack, Alan Parton, Barry Reay, Francis Rose, Heather Warne, Christopher Whittick and Rendel Williams. Other help has been provided by Leila Burrell-Davis, Amanda Davey and Martin Wingfield. We are especially grateful to Susan Rowland, who drew the maps with such enthusiasm and meticulous care and to Ann Winser who compiled the index. The guidance of David Hey has been greatly appreciated.

Finally, our thanks go to our families and friends for their forbearance and support during the writing of this book.

Chapter 1

The Personality of South-East England

By whatever criteria it is studied or in whatever period it is viewed, the peninsula of South-East England formed by the Thames and English Channel ranks as one of the world's most important regions. Its strategic position between London, the largest population mass in England and its seat of government, wealth and patronage, and the Continental mainland has ever made it one of England's most advanced economies. Its human activities have thereby multiplied, quickened and expanded; and they have been precociously developed to bring it repeatedly into a pivotal position in national and international affairs. It is no accident that its regional exclusivity and local patriotism begins early with the simple account in Caesar's *Commentaries* based on his military campaigns of 55 and 54 BC of its advanced civilization and immense population contrasting with other areas of Britain; or that its landscape, by then so full of 'observables' and historical associations should have inspired William Lambarde to write in 1576 *A Perambulation of Kent*, the first of the county histories; or that organized cricket and football matches were being played on its village greens as early as the sixteenth century.

The extreme regional diversity within its overall geological framework of hills and vales is a consequence of the very gradual evolution of many different local landscapes and economies shaped by people of once rather different backgrounds, dialects and folklore, and developed at different rates and in different ways. These co-existed as complementary neighbouring *pays*. It is the very variety of these formerly distinctive lands and local cultures, together with their mutual dependence as conjoint and interacting environments through human agency, that constitutes the *genius loci* of the historic South East. The growing network of human relationships of the greatest possible variety complemented the natural diversity of the region, and these in turn were overlain by the other relationships emanating from London and the Continent. All this has meant that diversity in the South East is greater and more pervasive than in most other regions of comparable size. It is indeed a land full of presences, crowded in detail. To use Christopher

Marlowe's phrase, it had 'infinite riches in a little room'. This has been both a burden and an asset.

The South East is a good starting point from which to essay the universal in several respects. Ever since enthralling nineteenth-century geological discoveries, it has been a model for the decipherment of other parts of the Earth's surface (Jones, DKC 1980). Historically, the Interior Weald was the largest expanse of wild country cleared and settled for agriculture in England since Domesday (Plate 1.1). Although largely occupied by the Black Death in 1348, the uncompleted landscape was still undergoing a final phase of colonization in the sixteenth and early seventeenth centuries. This offers a classic example of human striving in a region difficult to tame and settle. To a quite unusual degree we can trace the evolution of the landscape and society by slow degrees over the course of centuries, and in particular, we are treated to the spectacle of the *becoming* of places. On account of the richness of historical associations, the region's human development can be clearly discerned in the intimate relations between local natural conditions and local material cultures of a society rooted in the land and with the bulk of its population either working the land or serving those who did, and the successively accelerating stages over the past 200 years in the dissolution of this traditional, rural, local and regional pattern of life.

The primary catalyst in the region's modern change up to its present post-industrial (and incipient post-agricultural) phase of civilization, when localized uniqueness is fast disappearing and much of the region has become a 'sort of undeclared National Park for the largest population group in Britain', has been the gigantic presence and international role of London whose unplanned sprawling mass became the basis of a new mode of human existence, the first and archetypal city of our modern age. This fundamental change of human habitat, which has had unforeseen effects upon social organization, habits of thought and the natural resources of the Earth, has inevitably brought a complete transformation in the outward aspect of the region within 40–50 miles of London, and the inward nature of its new society. For a countryside it has thus had an ample covering of asphalt and concrete. This can now be seen as the initial stage of a revolutionary way of living which is spreading the world over. Yet 'Megalopolis is still denied'. Since the Second World War people have been obliterating the yet-unbuilt green peninsula at an accelerating rate but it still remains true that the modern development has been contained to a great degree within the framework of roads, fields, farmlands and copses largely shaped more than 800 years ago by its then primitive pastoral society (Everitt 1986: 38).

The rapid and largely unplanned metropolitan growth has deeply affected the arts addressed to the imagination and the ways in which the countryside has been sensibly experienced and emotionally enjoyed. From tensions between the ideal and the real; between town and country; and between two other opposing forces operating in the region, the pull towards

Plate 1.1 An aerial view of the High Weald. To the medieval pioneer farmer the remaining forest was something to be conquered. A vivid impression of the wilderness subdued by the axe and the challenge of the pioneer's environment can be gained from this photograph of Wadhurst. Although the belts of timber (shaws) around the fields are in retreat, enough small, irregular and wood-bounded fields survive to convey the atmosphere of the medieval farming scene. Farming in these Interior conditions was nevertheless regarded by Arthur Young in the late eighteenth century as 'effectually a barbarism'.

the future and the pull towards the past, has burst over the last 200 years a new shaping cultural force as a remarkable efflorescence of regional literature, landscape painting, music, landscape design and domestic architecture, richer in relation to the countryside than that of possibly any other part of the globe. This literary invention of the South East as a cultural unit has fused nature and the spirit of man in the manner of the *jeu d'esprit* of Shakespeare's Duke:

Are not these woods
More free from peril than the envious Court?
. . . And this our life *exempt* from public *haunt*
Finds tongues in trees, books in sunny brooks,
Sermons in stones, and good in everything.
I would not change it
(*As You Like It*)

In general terms, the region of the South East largely corresponds with the natural region of softly rolling hills, streamlets, woodlands and heaths framed within the bordering rim of chalk downs referred to as the Weald after its once largest single topographical feature, the great tract of damp oakwood which extended across the intractable clays of the interior (Fig. 1.1). Surrounded on three sides by tidal water and with forest difficult of access, the region assumed in antiquity 'an isolation which more than counterbalanced the fragile civilisation along its outer margins' (Everitt 1976: 14). Conveyed with this sense of isolation and remoteness was the feeling of an island, with an island's abounding variety, self-containedness and self-sufficiency. Although such isolating influences have long been broken down, a feeling of insularity has still not been entirely lost in the remoter areas. This lingering feeling has been sustained in modern art and literature as an alternative 'resistant' world to London, an ideal, an Eldorado, or 'lost paradise', bounded by its chalk hills which protect and contain it.

In past times the rural economies within the South East diverged from each other for reasons some of which are physical and others economic and social, but all of which stem from a variety of responses to local environments by successive generations attempting to reorganize them to fit new purposes and ideologies. Relations between people are the cornerstones of relationships between regions. As some people flourish, as cultures change, and as political and economic pressures vary, so are regional structures and interactions affected. The structures of the regions were, and still are, dialectically linked with social, economic and political institutions, such that a change in any one of these will have repercussions on all the others. It is also important to remember that the people who lived in what we now call south-east England lived in environments created for the most part not by them, but by their predecessors, to fulfil needs of an earlier age than their own. They lived in landscapes largely not of their own creating, but which powerfully guided their lives, just as did the social, cultural and economic structures into which they were born. Some had the ability or good fortune to help shape and modify the structures of their lives. Most did not.

These developments occurred against a diverse geological background. Through the processes of geology and landscape evolution, South East England is moulded in a striking earth architecture, the chalk strata of the Chilterns dipping under London, running along the North Downs and re-appearing in the South Downs (the over-arch having been progressively

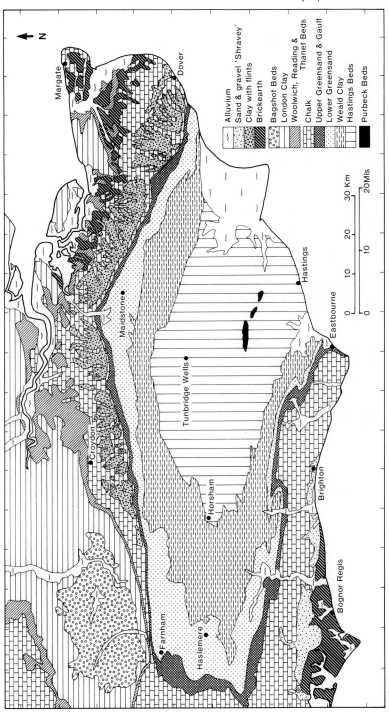

Figure 1.1 The geology of south-east England.

5

destroyed and re-shaped by the agency of rivers to expose the intervening Weald). The departed crest of the Weald is a denuded domed landscape comprising a great bowl of space between Lympne in Kent and Petersfield in Hampshire. Around its horizon, encircling hills afford panoramic views of unaccustomed grandeur in lowland England (Plate 1.2 and Fig. 1.2). Denudation of the dome has revealed a concentric outcrop pattern of sandstones and clays within the chalk rim. The geology is intricately varied around the margins of the Weald where steeply dipping and narrow formations have been exposed by erosion. Nowhere in Europe is there a region of similar size allowing the study of such a variety of rocks and a corresponding variety of plant, animal and human life. Writing of Kent, Garrad remarked that 'owing basically to the geological conditions, the nature of the soil probably varies more frequently and more abruptly than in other county of comparable size to produce an uncommon profusion and diversity' (Garrad 1954: 1–2). A similar comment could be made for Surrey and Sussex which are structurally similar. In many parts of the South East it is possible to encounter in a short walk almost every type of young sedimentary rock and mood of scenery within lowland England. Light and chalky downland soils contrast with deep loams and intractable clays with their stretches of oakwood; and water meadow, sandy heath, hop grounds and orchards, as well as arable and pasture fields, are all to be found.

This diversity of soils ranges over extremes of fertility and sterility that are reflected in differences of perception and which underline the caution needed in generalizing farming conditions over more than a few square miles. To the Elizabethan mind, the sight of cherry orchards, hop grounds, and the beautiful multi-coloured fields of north-east Kent made it the Garden of England, and a presentable imitation of Eden unparalleled in beauty anywhere in the world, a district already moulded by centuries of human use into the semblance of the then much-admired *champion*, cultivated open country. The trim parterres, regular paths and close-clipped box of its gardens also left an impression of general well-being, orderliness, proportion and abundance:

> O famous Kent
> What country hath this isle that can compare with thee

sings Michael Drayton (a Warwickshire man) in *Polyolbion* (1612)

This image of Kent as a terrestrial paradise was conceived along the London to Dover highway which is crowded with foreign impressions and those of newly-returned English travellers, quick to seize on the differences between this varied, small-scale landscape and that of the more coarse-grained and less-diversified landscape of northern France. This popular image of parts of the South East does not square with reality. The few travellers who penetrated into central and west Kent had quite a different story to tell. Their story was of poor land on dry chalk downs, sterile sands and wide belts of wet, stubborn clay. Although Kent contains in Romney Marsh and the Maidstone–Sittingbourne area some of the most fertile land in England,

Plate 1.2 The escarpment of the South Downs and the western antechamber of the Weald. From Lodge Hill, Ditchling the view encompasses the crest of the Downs stretching westwards to the wind-blown clump of beeches on Chanctonbury Ring. Blackdown, massively enclosing the western Weald, forms the distant view. Only a tight control on the residential development has saved such splendid downland settings.

these areas are of limited extent and the county as a whole 'is not *generally* fertile like such east midland counties as Leicestershire and Northamptonshire' (Everitt 1976: 5). Kent has a great deal of 'unrewarding and intractable land, and that intractability has always been one of the most important factors in the settlement history of the county' . . . and until satisfactory nineteenth-century underdrainage 'the difficulties of cultivation in Kent were more widespread and decisive in their effect than they are today, particularly in the heavy claylands of the Weald'.

These remarks may be applied even more vehemently in the case of Surrey and Sussex, where foul winter weather placed erratic but generally severe limits on the agricultural productivity of the clays. Much of Surrey has never been a very promising environment for agriculture and although Sussex was a great wool producer its cornlands have historically only been permanently successful on the rich soils of the coastal plain, which in turn corresponds closely to the North Kent loam belt. Surrey and Sussex owe much of their town-centred arcadian view of the cultural landscape to wide-eyed Londoners who painted, sketched, photographed and wrote in lyrical strains of a re-discovered Eden as a foil to the enormous and over-crowded metropolis. They appeared blessedly unaware that stamped over the most picturesque landscapes was a historic record of repeated agricultural failure and defeat, the consequence of adverse secular change and cyclical catastrophe. The significance of this 'poor land and poor living' of the south-eastern Interior in much of past time stems from the fact that the Weald covers about 40 per cent of the total area of the region. West Sussex is the most heavily wooded of all the English counties and Kent is not far behind. The problems of the small farm on difficult land are age-old in the agricultural history of the South East. Farming on the poorer lands had always involved hard work, worry, and the investment of precarious capital. According to clay farmers, theirs is a man's land, compared with the boy's on the chalk (Reid 1958).

The extreme diversity of soils is mainly the outcome of the special geological conditions which themselves make for exceptional variety. These differing soils are well displayed as they occur in a series of numerous strips or belts of country running approximately east and west in correspondence with the dominant geological outcrops (Fig. 1.1). The relationship between geology, farming, employment and landscape is by no means one of simple determinism. Nevertheless the soils have exerted a profound influence on agriculture, and it is impossible to divorce geology from any consideration of topography, rural settlement, agrarian history and vernacular architecture (Hall and Russell 1911: 1–15).

Several of these soil belts have for long offered especially good opportunities for tillage. The most important of these is the easily-worked stoneless Brickearth loam on the coastal plains of West Sussex and North Kent. This soil is akin to the continental loess of legendary fertility, and William Marshall judged the Sussex Coastal Plain to be the most valuable

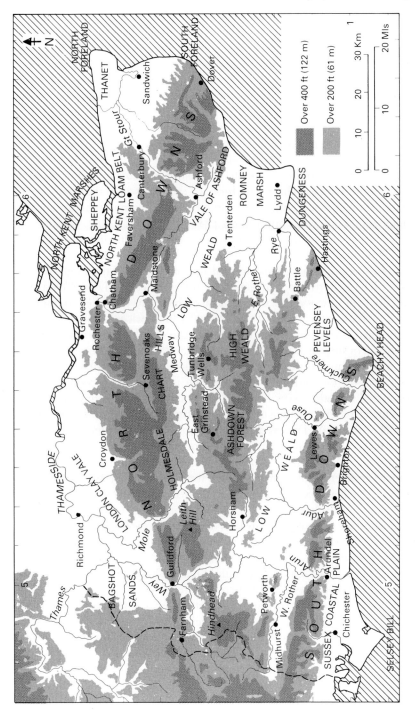

Figure 1.2 The South East region.

arable district in England (Marshall 1798, II: 239). Until recently this belt has always supported the wealthiest and most populous rural communities in the South East. It was devoted to sheep and corn husbandry, with hops and orchards on the Kent portion near London, on the basis of flexible rotations, reduced fallowing, and advanced cultivation techniques. Another fertile soil belt is that of the Romney Marsh and smaller alluvial tracts such as the Pevensey Levels and those of the Stour in Kent. For much of their history these areas have been under rich pastoral use on damp, unhealthy marshland, but when competently drained, they have been capable of supporting intensive arable crops. The final belt of rich soil is that of the Lower Chalk and Upper Greensand bench outcropping immediately below the chalk escarpment of the North and South Downs. The warm, forward crumbly soil of the 'malmstone' is in places stained black with vegetable mould and animal manure applied over millennia (Wooldridge and Linton 1933: 297–310).

At the other end of the soils spectrum there are belts of below-average fertility. The most notorious was the intractable Weald Clay, on its great horseshoe distribution wrapping around the hilly core of the High Weald. Destitute of base nutrients and generally intractable, the Low Weald was traditionally kept in woodland or poor grass which was ploughed to improve the sward or for corn in times of exceptionally high prices (Plate 1.3). These soils were tilled with great difficulty until the use of field drains in the 1840s, when removal of surplus water was 'as if the island were once more rising from the sea'. Arthur Young observed after travelling in France and all over England that he had never met with any clay like that in Sussex. A second clay type was associated with the heavy London clay outcrop mainly confined to north Surrey, which gave rise to some of the poorest agriculture in that county. Most of the soils of the chalk Downs are also naturally somewhat mediocre. There were sticky clays on the summits derived from the Clay-with-Flints; and the drier, flinty soils of the upper slopes which under modern conditions yield moderate to good crops of corn, but which were low-valued, stony arable land as seen in the medieval extents attached to *inquisitiones post mortem*. The best of the downland soils were probably the red loams lying on the lower flanks. Finally, around the outer edge of the Low Weald is the escarpment of the Lower Greensand on the Folkestone and Hythe beds which, except in Kent, gave rise to coarse, permeable sands and barren heathland (now largely wooded) rising to about 900 feet above sea level at Leith Hill and Hindhead. The subordinate Sandgate beds in West Sussex and Surrey are fertile.

Between these two extremes of soil fertility were those of more average utility to the farmer. These comprised the belt of marine gravels giving rise to light, stony soils on the northern edge of the Sussex Coastal Plain, improved and enclosed since the sixteenth century; and also the heavy Gault Clay exposure, mostly a very narrow tract abutting onto the Lower Greensand. Finally there was the High Weald, at the very centre of the region. Here Crowborough Beacon stands nearly 900 feet high, and sandy and silty soils gave rise to heathy

Plate 1.3 The waggoners. 'Slow progress laboured forward, then the check . . . ' (Sackville West 1946). From *The Times* picture page of the 1920s, this scene was almost certainly near Paddock Wood, Kent. Depicted here is a team of massive horses hauling oaks out of grudging, sticky Weald clay in winter. The waggon wheels have sunk into the sodden ground and the photographer has caught the horses at the precise moment when their combined exertions have moved the load. The combined work of sawyer, wheelwright, lumbermen and horses reflects the close relationship which formerly existed between the tree-clad Weald and its people.

wastes in St Leonards and Ashdown Forests. Further east the Forest Ridges presented more silts and clays, with the Wadhurst Clay, for example, being exposed in the deep, narrow valleys called ghylls. The best soils in the High Weald were generally under hops and mixed farming.

Professor Wooldridge long ago remarked that much of the interest and significance of these soil patterns lies in the contrasts between the centre and the fringes (Wooldridge and Goldring 1953: 2). Great as are the local differences in the soils within the region, the main forces that shaped the lives of the early settlers were the locations on warm, easily cultivable and seemingly inexhaustible soils in the coastal districts and lower river valleys on the one hand, and on the cold, heavy clays of the interior woodlands and its central and bordering heaths, with their variously arrested stages of development on the other. The inward-facing chalk holds back the former wilderness like a girdle, and broadly divides the South East into two distinct but harmonizing areas. Each had its different face, and supported its distinctive economies and rural cultures.

The basic distinction between these co-existing and reciprocal cultures is broadly coincident with the distinction between the Weald proper, as bounded by the outer edge of the Lower Greensand outcrop, and the Downs and their overlying tertiary rocks in West Sussex and Kent. The latter area would also include the scarpfoot zone at the base of the Downs. It is around this basic dichotomy of *Interior* and *Coastal Fringe* that much of the history of the South East can be woven. If there were processes which were ever drawing the two parts of the peninsula together into inter-connection, there were equally powerful forces as constantly dividing them. The various elements of the relationship were ever-changing because the most potent agency is the mutable factor of man, but the actual complementarity of the structural interplay of the two divisions or domains has never ended. In modern times it is arguably as important a distinction as ever before.

The geographical disparity and inter-dependence of the two divisions in the past, the one relatively advanced and the other comparatively backward, is reflected in divergent patterns of population distribution, states of economic development and technologies, rooted and determined by their respective social, economic and physical environments. The old-settled and relatively crowded parts of the South East were confined until the thirteenth century to the most easily cultivable soils of the Coastal Fringe. These areas had been stripped of their woodland cover in the Prehistoric period and by the eleventh century, when the colonization of the interior forest was under way, they already presented a palimpsest of the marks of people in stage after stage of occupation extending over millennia. An initial advantage had been secured, and this was to be reflected in a relatively high level of population and wealth for the Coastal Fringe. The long coastline, stretching from the mouth of the Thames around the North Foreland to Beachy Head and the creeks of the Eastern Hampshire Basin, was also a most important influence. Here there had been ease of initial access, rewarding loamy soils, and an axial position between Britain and the Continent. The export of surplus corn became critically important and coastal shipping, in the centuries before the railway, linked the area to London and major markets, so acting as a stimulus to specialization, productivity and innovation.

By contrast the forest hinterland was still the natural margin of most human life in the South East up to the eleventh century. The life of the inhabitants on the Coastal Fringe had a long-established rhythm revolving around the seasonal migration to summer wood pastures. When this era died away in the twelfth and thirteenth centuries a fresh reciprocity between the two divisions developed. Now the burgeoning wealden districts became the chief source of supply for migrant labour for the productive cornlands of the Coastal Fringe manors. The latter was one of the most naturally fertile and hence historically wealthy lands in Europe, the former one of the most difficult and unrewarding, a place where custom was strong and change-resistant, and hence notorious as a district where men's labours ground to a standstill in bad times for farming. It was also notorious for the difficulties and discomforts of travelling in winter and other wet periods. Without adequate roads, every commodity in the Weald had to be carried on foot or on horseback with results that were crippling for agriculture, and which condemned workers to severe under-employment or what was at best half-time farming. Because the costs of internal transport (despite the fact that nowhere was more than 30 miles from the sea) could exceed production costs or the sea freightage from channel ports all the way to London, marginal land was unprofitable when wages rose and/or when prices fell. There was little incentive to produce surpluses when the market was so hard to reach, except for animals which went to market on the hoof. The atrocious roads also help to explain why few great landowners wished to live permanently on their wealden estates. Infrequent homages were taken in the medieval period, often under the protection of armed guards, for law and order could at times be unenforceable. The forested Weald was thus an environment which could not be efficiently utilized by the more complex village communities under feudal regimes such as developed in the cereal-growing places of north-east Kent and the Sussex Coastal Plain. It is not an easy country to travel through, even now.

It will be argued in this volume that the Coastal Fringe communities achieved technological, commercial and socio-political dominance over those of the Interior. People within the Coastal Fringe acquired high levels of skills and capital within the hierarchy of occupations, which allowed the accumulation of a surplus and the consequent reinforcement of the primacy of the area through accumulated rewards. Such a concept is perhaps familiar to students of Development Theory, but is a less well-trodden path in the context of an English region, not to mention one in which core–periphery relations were manifest long before the advent of capitalism. In this study the 'core' is the Coastal Fringe, and the 'periphery' is the Interior, a curious geographical inversion, but one which will allow new insights to be brought to bear on regional history.

One such insight, which will be expanded throughout the text, is that the wealden Interior has been systematically exploited by the Coastal Fringe via a series of institutional relationships (Fig. 1.3). These institutions, which might include the multiple estate, the strip parish, the detached parish or manorial outlier, the Sussex Rape or the Kentish Lathe, manifestly pre-date the rise of capitalism, however that is defined. But their effect has been to allow the Coastal Fringe communities to make decisions in their own interests which directly affected the Weald. The latter has been under-developed, and this term will be used to describe that process by which one region comes to dominate and subdue another. The Interior is thus to be seen as consisting of a series of dependent economies, in which change is contingent upon decisions made elsewhere. Seen this way, many aspects of the development of agriculture, industry and towns in the South East can be seen as part of a longer-term structural pattern. And this structure can be seen to be equally emanating from human agency as well as physical endowment. The Weald is not merely 'poor' because its soils were inferior. It was poor because of human institutional structures, which siphoned off its wealth 'outwards and upwards' and gave little back in return.

Such regional relationships are not solely the result of economic structures. South East England has for centuries functioned as an exact counterpart of the political power of London and the Court, and of its lifestyles – the part-real, part-dream country of the London citizen, the landscape of the pastoral dream coming to life. The sheer immensity and shapelessness of London, arising from its over-rapid development due to its place as the hub of Empire, and its polluting and corroded atmosphere, created the need for refuge. To counteract their repressive urban environment and to make urban life endurable, the London middle classes annexed much of the countryside of the South East within reasonable reach of London termini as a playground, sanatorium, health resort, field laboratory and open-air studio all thrown into one.

Figure 1.3 The structure and mechanisms of dominance and dependence in south east England. The basic structure (top left) shows the regional variation between Coastal Fringe and Interior as used within this volume, and also the 'miniature interiors': those areas which partake of many of the characteristics of the Interior, whilst being located outside the Weald. Space precludes much discussion of these latter areas within this volume, but further research might usefully incorporate their idiosyncratic histories of development within the South East. The structure of dependency (top right) shows, by map and cross section, the dominance and dependency associated with geologies and areas of early and later settlement. The mechanisms whereby such dominance and dependency were exercised are portrayed (bottom left), and the final section (bottom right) attempts to show how such dominance and dependence has a strong temporal dimension, in that the manifestation of such dominance re-asserts itself in different ways at different periods of history (and indeed prehistory), from the prehistoric hill fort to the development of twentieth-century decisions about landscape protection and land for development.

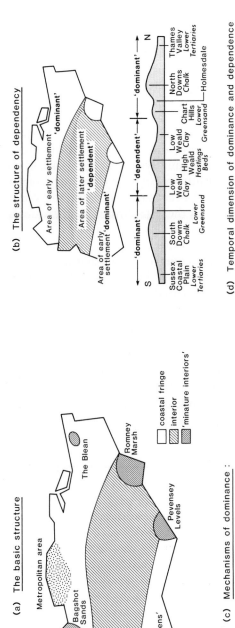

(a) The basic structure

Metropolitan area

The Blean

Romney Marsh

Pevensey Levels

Bagshot Sands

'The Mardens'

☐ coastal fringe
▨ interior
▦ miniature interiors'

(b) The structure of dependency

Area of early settlement 'dominant'

Area of later settlement 'dependent'

Area of early settlement 'dominant'

S — 'dominant' | 'dependent' | 'dominant' — N

Sussex Coastal Plain — Lower Tertiaries
South Downs Chalk
Lower Greensand
Low Weald Clay
High Weald — Hastings Beds
Low Weald Clay
Chart Hills — Lower Greensand
North Downs Chalk
Thames Valley Lower Tertiaries

Holmesdale

(c) Mechanisms of dominance :
advantages of the coastal fringe are institutionalised

Parish or manor with detatched outlier

Mother church with dependencies
mother church

Kentish lathe

• villa regalis

Strip parish

nucleated village •

fortified castle town •

Sussex rape

manor or home farm

Multiple estate

▨ Wealden and dependent part of spatial unit

(d) Temporal dimension of dominance and dependence

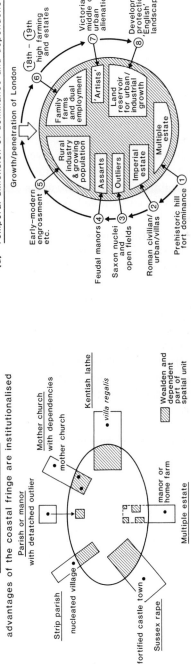

Growth/penetration of London

(18th – (19th) high farming and estates
⑥
⑦ Victorian middle class urban alienation
⑧ Development/ protection of 'English' landscapes

'Artists'
Land reservoir for urban/ industrial growth
Family farms and dual employment
Multiple estate

Rural industry & growing population
Assarts
Outliers
Imperial estate

⑤ Early-modern engrossment etc.
④ Feudal manors
③ Saxon nuclei and open fields
② Roman civilian/ urban/villas
① Prehistoric hill fort dominance

The rapid industrialization and urbanization of the later nineteenth and twentieth centuries accelerated this recognition but similar attitudes towards the region are deeply rooted. The perception of the South East as Arcadia and refuge has persisted over centuries. In its role as an alternative world to London it has long had a tolerance to deviant outsiders who felt that things were out of joint in the prevailing social order elsewhere, so that it always had a concomitant of social nonconformity of one kind or another, whether of oppressed peoples in the Middle Ages or earlier who took to the woods; seventeenth-century Levellers or more recent 'back-to-the-landers'. As early as the fifteenth century, nobles, squires, gentry and wealthy merchants chose residences in the accessible Kent and Surrey countrysides amidst parks, fields and pastures, rather than dwell permanently in London. Here was a direct contrast with prevailing customs on the European mainland, as travellers such as the Italian, Poggio, were quick to notice. By the sixteenth century the region's landed gentry included men whose forebears had tamed the wilderness but who themselves cultivated the higher nature as courtier, romantic and poet. From the 1750s the conviction spread in Georgian bourgeois circles that an existence alternately at the worldly centre of London and in the seclusion of a practical rural retreat was the essence of civilized life. This dualistic lifestyle has indeed remained a norm amongst the London elite.

With the growth of London, the South East has become a prime example of Raymond Williams' notion of an almost inverse relationship between the decline of farmscape as a working environment and its cultural importance as a source of rural ideology for urban needs (Williams 1975: 297). As the poorer lands collapsed into semi-dereliction with the importing of cheap corn, timber and livestock produce from the 1870s, so correspondingly they have been enhanced as places of recreation and interest. For at least 250 years the region has functioned as a kind of undeclared national park which has served the geologist, botanist, ecologist and geographer, the poet and writer, the artist, architect and landscape gardener each with an abundance of creative material. We have already indicated something of its special significance for the natural scientist. The region has also been one of the cradle-lands of the lyric, of modern domestic architecture, landscape gardening, the resurgence of English music, landscape painting and 'country writing'.

Such a set of human responses to 'the country way of life', set within particular 'historical moments' and arising from particular conjunctions of social, economic and political forces, has had many guises. It has included the very different, if overlapping, practices of the conscious attempt at a simpler existence (The Simple Life), daily commuting between metropolitan villages and the city, week-ending, retirement, pleasure-farming, solitary contemplation, country writing, the revival of rural arts and crafts, and myriad open-air leisure pursuits. These have created their own specific forms of human habitat. The list is long, but would include villadom, suburbia, shack plot-land communities, dormitory villages, garden cities, new towns, landscaped parks, 'wild' gardens and arboreta, model farms, estate villages, bungalow settlements, holiday camps, youth hostels, golf courses, tea shops, petrol filling stations and roadhouses. Old patterns of human settlement and lifestyles were thereby transformed, so virtually completing the destruction of the old regional locale by a 'coca-colaization' of landscape and its replacement by an 'earthly and largely alcoholic paradise'!

The creative emotional and recreational power in the South East is not, however, to be fully explained in terms of the intrinsic qualities of its scenery. A distinguishing feature of the region's contribution to the arts is that it represents a special type of thinker, writer and artist which could not have blossomed until the intellectual atmosphere was pervaded by the metropolitan imagination. The South East acquired a heightened charm from its contrast with the over-crowded metropolis on its border. The foil of London has made a tremendous difference to the perceived freshness of the air and the greenness of the grass.

It follows from this that those parts of the region which were most accessible to Londoners have made the most psychic impact. As previously noted, north Kent has long been fully in the public consciousness. It acquired such an accumulation of sentiment and historical association that neither Shakespeare nor any other sixteenth-century writer with historical leanings could even then write of it dispassionately. But for the most part, it was the Victorian Londoners, with their avid desire to read about and visit the countryside, who created the artistic South East. Before this time, much of the region could hardly be said to have existed in literature and the arts. Perhaps therefore, it was still too much a working countryside? There were large void areas in the imagination: the South Downs, the Ashdown Forest, the Leith Hill and Haslemere districts of Surrey. These districts were 'invented' for urban consumption by city-bred artists and writers. It is interesting to note that no Robin Hood figure ever roved the region, nor did poets people it with Orlandos or Rosalinds, and there are no folk tales of Oberons or Titanias such as frequented Sherwood and Arden in the imagination. Instead, the South East is associated with its own fascinating collection of literary characters in more modern guise such as Sturt's Bettesworth, Kipling's Old Hobden, Rupert Bear, Winnie the Pooh, the Starkadders of Cold Comfort Farm, and the Larkins of H. E. Bates.

Yet they equally celebrate the fulfilment of the good life and the estrangement of contemporary, civilized man from great cities, especially from London. In recent times, the region has become a prisoner of its own southern image, lodged inextricably in the media's file of stereotypes, with the enormous impact of 'country writing', landscape painting and advertising on people's choice of residential location and outdoor pursuits. The South East is the principal part of England where areas and places have been recognized as beautiful even to the point of destroying that beauty. Many parts have indeed become identified with the idea of England's despoliation, and one of the greatest of postwar regional problems has been the devising of planning controls and forms of environmental management to reconcile these human aspirations to the 'good life' with the conservation of the attractive environment which engendered it.

Chapter 2

The Early Middle Ages

The Pre-Conquest South East

When Domesday Book was being written the South East was already one of the longest-inhabited and most populous parts of England, with layer upon layer of inherited man-made features etched into the face of its varied countryside and townscape. Yet the exceptionally lengthy period of time of man's exploitation of the region, and hence of the very gradual evolution of the landscape, has only recently become apparent. By 1959 Lennard was sufficiently impressed by the complex process of Anglo-Saxon colonization to call Domesday England 'already an old country' (Lennard 1959: 1). A generation later, thanks to aerial photography and environmental archaeology, it is now recognized as an ancient one. The notion that the Anglo-Saxons were the makers of the South East has had to be discarded and the open and chequered landscape of coastal Kent and Sussex at the present day is now attributed to continuous agricultural colonization over at least four millennia. By the Bronze Age the bare downland scenery of Domesday shepherds had already come into being, with over-zealous eradication of forest, as also had the scrawny Surrey and Sussex heaths, where round barrows bury evidence of a once richer, more wooded environment. The management of coppice woodland, first recorded in the regional economy in Domesday Book, was until recently thought of as an eleventh-century innovation, but there is now reason to suspect that this type of managed woodland had evolved from the first century BC or even earlier. As for settlement and field systems, the low light of winter photography or crop marks in late summer reveal a palimpsest of an older population and system of agriculture repeatedly incorporated in the new (Taylor 1983: 104–6 and *passim*; Drewett, Rudling and Gardiner 1988). This evidence of a landscape long since begun would everywhere be more evident than it is had not prehistoric and Romano-British earthworks been needlessly destroyed during the past 25 years for the production of surplus food.

Recognition of the ancientness of the south-east landscape has led to a questioning of the traditional story of Anglo-Saxon settlement as one of gradual colonization against forest. Sawyer has argued that the 'rural resources of England were almost as fully exploited in the seventh century as they were in the eleventh' (Sawyer 1976: 1–2) and Taylor has speculated that an eighth-century Anglo-Saxon charter for Sussex gives details of land occupation not of recent origin but of two or more centuries earlier (Taylor 1983: 182). Whatever may be the outcome of the archaeological investigations which will be necessary to verify these speculations, the extent and nature of early settlement in the South East is not capable of simple generalization. The region comprised both early, developed parts and ones which were left in a primitive state until much later. In respect of Kent, such landscapes of contrasting development have been called 'landscapes of continuity' and 'landscapes of colonization', examples being north and east Kent on the one hand and the Kent Weald on the other (Everitt 1986: 2). In the former Everitt has indicated the numerous places and neighbourhoods where continuity of Jutish occupation with the Roman era seems likely. A similar depth of study does not exist for Surrey and Sussex and Everitt's concept could usefully be extended to the region as a whole which must have exhibited in the eleventh century a remarkable combination of advanced civilization on the anciently-settled arable of the Coastal Fringe, and the pioneer farming conditions then pertaining to the Interior woodland where some half a million acres of uncolonized (or de-colonized) woodland and marsh were subsequently reclaimed and settled in the 250 years after Domesday. This is a saga of man against the wild without parallel in medieval England.

As part of the Anglo-Saxon state, the region had a long and by no means inglorious history. Although one of the smallest, the once independent kingdom of Kent was a precocious and influential English state with law codes going back to the early seventh century. Here St Augustine landed and the two ancient sees of the county, Canterbury and Rochester, were both founded in the reign of King Ethelbert of Kent (d. 616) (Witney 1982: 3). From the latter part of the tenth century under the leadership of Archbishop Dunstan, there began a great period of activity in learning, literature and art. Christ Church, Canterbury in the reigns of Ethelred (978–1016) and Cnut (1016–1035) produced numerous illuminated manuscripts of the Gospels for religious institutions at home and abroad (Backhouse *et al* 1984). The county of Sussex quite corresponded to the self-contained kingdom of the South Saxons whose leader, Aelle, was briefly acknowledged as a single overlord, a *Bretwalda*, ruler of Britain. Owing its economic and cultural base to the narrow strip of downland and coastal plain, Sussex later lost its independence to the expanding kingdoms of Mercia and Wessex and was reduced to 'a worse state of slavery' behind its broad barrier of woodland and clay (Sawyer 1978: 43).

In the tenth century much of the South East appears to have been a relative backwater. It appears that Surrey, Sussex and Kent were normally administered by the great leaders of the West Saxon house. From the eleventh century the South East steadily grew politically and economically at the expense of its great rival region, Wessex, the base of the West Saxon dynasty. This new importance may be connected with the entry of early-eleventh century Danish armies into England through the South East. It was this threat that made Sandwich an assembly point of royal fleets in anticipation of the permanent federation of the Cinque Ports in the thirteenth century. This growing importance of the South East may also explain the remarkable rise to power of the family of Godwineson, whose vast landed wealth and influence in Sussex suggests a South Saxon origin. It is significant that their lands were particularly concentrated at strategic points controlling the English Channel and North Sea. Behind their rise to power lies the relative decline of Winchester, Wessex and Mercia, in the eleventh and later centuries and the re-orientation of English culture towards Normandy and Flanders (Williams 1981: 171–87; and Loyn 1982: 315–30).

The closest Sussex connection of the House of Godwin was with the port of Bosham. It was at Bosham that Swein Godwineson's ships lay in 1049 when he abducted and subsequently murdered his cousin, and from Bosham also Godwine, Swein and Tostig fled to Bruges in 1051. The Bayeux Tapestry shows the stone-built house at Bosham with a first-floor hall above an arcade along the front where Harold feasted before making his ill-fated journey to Normandy in 1064–5 which was to lead to his loss of the crown of England (Plate 2.1).

Other matter-of-fact representations of dwellings in the Tapestry throw light on contemporary building. The typical burgess's house, whether of wood or stone, had an undercroft containing his shop or workshop within a single arch opening to the street. Above was the living space (*sale*), probably divided into 'rooms' by the means of flimsy partitions or curtains. An additional room known as a solar with smaller window openings might occupy a second floor. In the Tapestry a balconied sale and solar house of this type is shown at Dover and another is shown without a solar but with carved wooden posts. Sussex peasants' huts are also depicted in the Tapestry with only a door opening in the façade and built of either plan-boards or shingles (Holmes 1959: 179–83).

The achievements of the Anglo-Saxon South East are not solely to be measured in terms of politics and culture. The fact that the coastal areas of Kent and Sussex appear to have been relatively densely settled for centuries implies that the land was being more competently farmed than the standard of the day. Numerous Anglo-Saxon charters attested that the Weald was pig-fattening and cattle-grazing country still in a pioneer condition. As to cultivation on the Coastal Fringe, the Anglo-Saxon charters are rarely detailed enough to give us a glimpse of Saxon farming and almost all other written records relating to Anglo-Saxon rural life have perished. Exceptionally, there is fragmentary information available for the archbishop's manor of Pagham, the Bishop of Chichester's manor of Selsey and Harold Godwin's manor of

Bosham, contiguous lordships possessed of huge tracts of the rich Sussex countryside. A corroborative clue to the relatively highly developed agriculture by the late eleventh century, probably in advance of farming generally, are the large renders of legumes made by the archbishop's estate of Pagham and to St Peter's of Winchester at Southease. In the thirteenth century the coastal demesnes of Sussex were intensively worked on the basis of soil-renewing rotations using extensively sown legumes. The scraps of evidence we are considering are not inconsistent with the conjecture that the basic elements of the high farming so amply recorded in the later middle ages had already been adopted in embryo before the Conquest (Brandon 1978: 11).

The wealth of the Coastal Fringe on the eve of the Norman Conquest is reflected in the proliferation of boroughs and mints. Apart from Canterbury, smaller mints were established at Guildford and Godalming in Surrey; at Chichester, Arundel, Steyning, Hastings and Pevensey in Sussex; and at Hythe, Sandwich, Old Romney, Dover and Rochester in Kent. This unusual number of mint towns is consistent with the location of the towns, most of which were ports, close to, if not generally within, the most active areas of later European commerce. These hints of a flourishing agriculture, commerce and a cash economy are some of the most direct witnesses we possess to the wealth and prosperity of the region in its last years under Saxon rule. The Flemish merchants who crossed the Channel in 1113 and brought 300 marks for the purchase of wool which they collected for shipment at Dover may well indicate a similar traffic a century earlier (Sawyer 1965: 162). By the eleventh century the towns were mostly developments of the fortified towns (*burhs*) founded in Alfred's reign and in that of his successor Edward in such a way that no villager was more than thirty miles away from a refuge from the Vikings. The rectilinear street plan of Chichester is typical of these early towns with its intra-mural streets running around the town walls, allowing the free access of garrison troops defending the town, the north–south streets, including the *Ceap* street, the main market of the town, the back lanes and larger peripheral blocks left as hedged areas (*hagae*) into which fugitives from the countryside could flee. As the towns grew in the tenth and eleventh centuries the *hagae* were gradually built over, as we can trace in Domesday Book. Some indication of the relative importance of towns in the reign of King Athelstan (d. 939) is the dismantlement of two of the former burhs, Burpham and Newenden which shrink to villages and the concentration of mints and moneyers at Canterbury, to which seven moneyers were allocated,

Plate 2.1 Earl Harold's hall, depicted in the Bayeux Tapestry. Harold feasts on the upper floor of his manor house at Bosham, adjacent to Bosham church, the centre of probably the most important and richest estate in late-Saxon Sussex, held originally by his father, Godwin. The men drink from horns and bowls, for which there is no earlier authentication before the twelfth century, apart from the Tapestry itself. Harold and his men have returned from hawking and hunting and are about to embark on the ill-fated voyage in 1064 which led to Harold's capture by Guy, count of Ponthieu, and to his alleged promise of support for William's claim to the throne of England (Wilson, D.M. 1985: 3, 4, 174–5).

Rochester three, Lewes two, and Hastings and Chichester one each (London was to have eight moneyers and Winchester six). Urban life was then, however, still disturbed by Viking marauders and this surprisingly resulted in the re-fortification of Cissbury, the Iron Age hill-fort, which was provided with a mint to service its market and refuge centre (Stewart 1978: 100). Despite this Lewes seems to have prospered with considerable overseas trade, for coins of two of its moneyers stamped LAE URB travelled as far as Rome (Hill 1978: 187). On the eve of the Conquest Lewes had thrown out suburbs east, south and west including a large maritime suburb at Cliffe on the banks of the Ouse. Its substantial seafaring trade is indicated by the render at the Conquest of twenty shillings annually for munitions of war whenever the Confessor's fleet put to sea (Brent 1985: 1).

In Surrey, Saxon urban development was more restricted. Eashing was dismantled as a *burh*, probably in the tenth century, and its successor, Guildford, was laid out as a town on the banks of the river Wey, although until the construction of its Norman castle it does not appear to have been very substantial. By contrast Southwark was already an important town at the Conquest with a minster of its own, a 'strande' and 'water street' bordering its tidal creek where ships were moored and business conducted, and a herring fishery. Important as were these Saxon towns the Norman Conquest was to add greatly to their growth and prestige.

The late-Saxon Weald

In contrast to the relatively intensive development of the Coastal Fringe and the Surrey fringes of London, much of the Interior South East in the eleventh century comprised the then largest remaining area of woodland and heath in England. Known to Romano-Britons as 'the great forest of the fort of Pevensey' (the Silva Anderida) and to invading Jutes and South Saxons as *Andredesleah*, it was still so extensive as late as 1018 for land at Ticehurst, Sussex to be described as 'lying in the famous forest of Andredesweald' (Barker 1948: 109–10; Ward 1936: 19–29). The existence of such a vast tract of relatively uncolonized terrain so late in the history of England contrasts with such areas on richer soils as Cambridgeshire and Leicestershire whose woods had largely vanished by the time of Domesday Book, or the thin soils of the downs of southern England from which the forest cover seems to have been cleared during prehistory. Broadly speaking, the survival of forest and heath on such a grand scale in Saxon England is to be explained by the mediocrity and intractability of the soils. As Everitt has remarked:

> the poverty of the Weald must not be exaggerated: so far as agricultural potential was concerned, it was not in the same category of poverty as that of the Pennine moorlands of Cumberland and Northumberland. Yet it needs to be borne in mind . . . (that) until well into the Saxon period both Kent and Sussex need to be thought

of as overwhelmingly regions of forest, and many centuries later their evolution was still largely shaped by this brooding presence of the *Wald* (Everitt 1976: 14).

For millennia the Weald functioned in the manner of the extensive areas of mountain, bog and forest in western and northern Europe as a great central resource of land for human communities on its more habitable fringes. In the pastoral stage of human occupation a system of transhumance prevailed in which the communities on the fringe of the Weald exploited it seasonally. As in similar areas of western Europe, the Weald initially formed summer pasture and its exploitation entailed the annual movement of livestock and the people tending them. From the very earliest Anglo-Saxon charters existing as copies whose authentication is not completely reliable, and probably much earlier in time, the headquarter villages and their subordinate settlements on the Wealden fringe came to have definite places within the Weald which they regarded as their own peculiar swine pasture.

The most remarkable legacy of transhumance to these prescribed outlying pastures is the survival of an extensive network of byways created by herdsmen in charge of animals travelling to and from the principal centres of the peripheral manors (or their preceding units) and the summer pastures. A small scale map, say on the scale of 1:250,000, will bring out clearly Witney's observation that because the Weald is roughly elliptical and drove roads normally took the shortest route into the deep Weald from the peripheral habitations, they change direction, crab-wise round the circumference of the Weald, tending south-west/north-east in the Surrey part of the western Weald, then roughly north-south in the east Surrey-West Kent area before turning on a south-west/north-east axis again in east Kent (Witney 1976: pp. 132–40). The transformation of the swine pastures, known in Kent and in the Hastings area as *denns*, in the central Sussex Weald as 'styes' and in West Surrey and Sussex as *folds*, tended to pass through a number of distinct stages of human occupation between that of sheds used as swinecotes and temporary huts of swineherders, to permanent farms, water-mills, churches and market towns.

It is possible to postulate a model based on a cycle of development of such an expanding frontier community, each stage being related to a certain type of rural settlement and a distinctive form of rural economy and society. In the earliest stage of exploitation of wealden *denns* their inhabitants were *drofmen*, drovers engaged in tending swine and cattle who would have divided their year between their 'winter house' in their parent village outside the Weald and their 'summer house' in the outlying, woodland pasture up to 20 miles distant. Relict features of this stage are the close network of former droveways and surviving fragments of the wood-commons such as the Mens and Ebernoe commons near Petworth. It has also left its mark on place-names. Several 'summer' names occur in the Surrey and Sussex Weald. Place-names also include the Old English element *(ge)sell*, meaning group of shelters for animals, herdsmen's huts, or both (the prefix *ge* having a collective function) as in the modern variants of this word in Breadsell in Battle, Bremzells in Herstmonceux, Boarzell in Ticehurst and Drigsell in Salehurst. In west Sussex place-names incorporating 'shot' or 'shott' are fairly common, being derived from *scydd*, shed. Names ending in –wick (*wic*) were also given to seasonally occupied swine-pastures, meaning a temporary abode dependent upon a larger settlement as were the 'styes' (*stig*) and the plentiful *folds* in the western Weald (Brandon 1978: 138–59).

The second stage is marked by villeins owing labour services to their lord, including reaping on the distant demesne at the manorial headquarters. It is through the efforts of these early pioneers that the parish churches and water-driven mills were erected. When documentary evidence becomes available towards the end of the thirteenth century we find them inhabiting not single isolated farmsteads but loosely-grouped clusters of small family farms on shared, named virgates of customary land. This was a territorial organization and economy superficially similar to Iron-age *clachans* (Jones, G. R. J. 1961; 1971; 1979). But mostly it can be shown to be the work of new and evolving communities quite distinct in time and origin (Brandon 1978: 155; Alcock 1962). Some of the churches have also subsequently founded subordinate chapels in this phase of colonization, e.g. Rotherfield had a dependent settlement at Frant with its own chapel before 1100. The High Weald churches are mostly on ridge-top sites and were probably almost isolated from the pioneer farms being established along the valley sides, as are the churches of Burstow, Worth and Itchingfield to this day. We have therefore the somewhat unusual circumstances in lowland England that many of the relatively outlying, peripheral settlements in wealden parishes are older than the central nucleated village, the reverse of the 'normal' development in England.

Despite these two earlier phases of human occupation the frontier of remaining wealden waste in 1100 still awaiting driving back by later colonizers was still so extensive as to have its own particular imprint stamped upon it during the subsequent medieval centuries.

The Norman Conquest

Even more than the rest of England, the South East was brought firmly under the iron hand of Norman rule. Elsewhere in England Saxon estates passed much as they had been to new Norman holders. In the South East, largely for defensive reasons, Saxon estates were broken up to give lords compact power bases (Searle 1980: 57). Almost as famous as the battle it commemorates is the Bayeux Tapestry, the spectacular southern-English masterpiece which provides a thrillingly detailed account of the battle itself (Backhouse *et al.* 1984: 195; Wilson 1985; Brooks and Walker 1978). On 27 September 1066 the duke embarked from St Valery-sur-Somme with a sufficient fleet and army to attack the pre-selected targets of Pevensey and Hastings in 'the heartland of the Godwinson patrimony'. This event has been called 'one of the most influential amphibious operations known to history' (Douglas 1969: 46; Bachrach 1985: 1–25). It demonstrated the technological superiority of the Normans in warfare. They could transport horses by sea and use them in battle whereas Saxons fought on foot. The Normans had also mastered quick and effective castle-building. An unopposed landing was made at Pevensey and a motte-and-bailey castle was hastily erected within the Roman fortress of Anderida. After some days William moved his invasion fleet to Hastings where the castle shown in the Bayeux Tapestry was raised. The Tapestry also records the ravaging of the countryside around Hastings where the scene of William's victory was accompanied by widespread desolation and destruction which is reflected in reduced Domesday values (Finn 1971: 19–23) (Fig. 2.1). Harold, King of England hurriedly marched south from his victorious battle in Yorkshire over Harald Hardrada, King of Norway, who had also made a bid for the English throne, assembled an army in London and accomplished a forced march across the Weald to the battlefield of Hastings where the decisive engagement was fought on 14 October. Harold gambled on crushing the Norman cavalry by a surprise attack (so repeating his successful tactics at Stamford Bridge) but the duke's scouts reported his approach seven miles away. The Norman army advanced from Hastings to impose on Harold's exhausted infantry a defensive action along a narrow ridge along which now stands the ruins of Battle Abbey and the High Street of the town of Battle, both abbey and town being founded after the battle. On Telham Hill to the south the Norman knights prepared for the successful offensive which was only concluded after a day-long battle of great ferocity (Brown 1985: 133–52; Loyn 1982: 315–30).

After the battle William made first to Dover where, too, he raised a motte in the Iron Age earthworks high on the cliff and thence turned inland towards Canterbury where the men of Kent came to make their submissions to him 'like flies settling on a wound' (Brown 1985: 154). Part of the invading army then defeated troops sent against them by the Londoners and burnt Southwark, but instead of assaulting the city directly the duke made a circuitous march around London through Guildford and Basingstoke to the capital city of Winchester, which submitted to him, before crossing the Thames at Wallingford in Berkshire and eventually intimidating London into submission and so making possible his coronation in Westminster Abbey on Christmas Day, 1066. This much we learn from contemporary chroniclers but they are silent on the immediate aftermath of the battle in Sussex and Surrey.

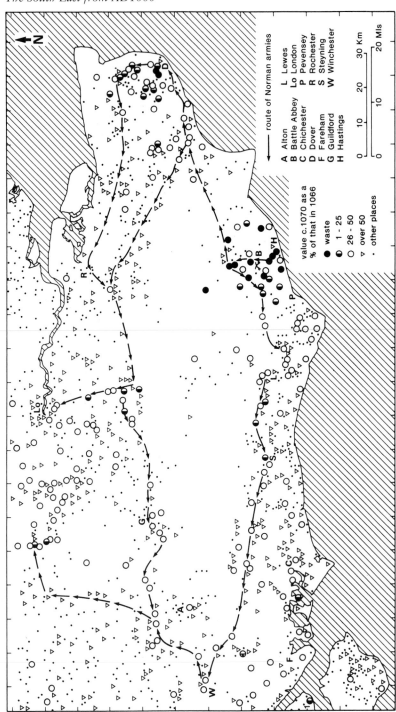

Figure 2.1 Domesday values 1086 and changes in value.

Fascinatingly, the marches of the Normans after Hastings can be traced in Domesday Book by the reduced values of manors after the Normans received them, brought about by the devastation. On this basis, the duke advanced via Westerham and Bletchingley to Lewisham and Camberwell to a camp at Battersea before apparently marching to Mortlake and Walton-on-Thames before striking south to Guildford and Farnham (Baring 1898: 17–25). In Sussex the same kind of evidence shows the desolating effect of the passage of another part of the duke's army along the westward route below the South Downs which seems to have joined the northern force before jointly making for Winchester (Finn 1971: 59; Douglas 1964:18).

The Conqueror's victory at Hastings was to prove but the first step in the harshest and most through-going reorganization of land in England in its history. This Norman land settlement was not the product of one sweeping change but of the passage of time and a number of afterthoughts. The Normans considered England as a colony to be exploited and the process began with the confiscation of the lands of King Harold and his family and supporters. The Conqueror committed the strategically important south-east shore of England to his own kinsmen and others of his closest and most privileged companions, persons of the highest rank whom the king regarded as particularly dependable and able – his half-brothers Odo, Bishop of Bayeux, tenant-in-chief of most of Kent, and Robert, Count of Mortain, the rape of Pevensey; Robert, Count of Eu, his father's cousin, the rape of Hastings and his more distant cousins William de Warenne and Roger of Montgomery, the rapes of Lewes and Arundel respectively. Inland, at the key castle of Tonbridge built to provide extra defence for the south-eastern approaches to London, his second cousin Richard Fitz Gilbert was placed. His huge Domesday estate was greater than any of the monasteries and of all the bishoprics except Canterbury and Winchester. Its key element was the lowy of Tonbridge, evidently a post-Conquest creation because the *denns* of Saxon manors outside the Weald were detached and granted to Fitz Gilbert to make a new tenurial geography. Such outstanding lesser men like the royal official Hugh de Montfort, lord of the district around Hythe, were also brought in to defend the coast and given a block of territory to enable them to do so. In Surrey the approach to London was secured by granting the larger part of the county to Bishop Odo and Richard of Tonbridge who held the lowy of that name (Mortimer 1981: 177–97).

The most radical changes were made in Sussex where the greatest concentration of Godwinson lands had been created. Saxon estates had straggled across the county ignoring the old administrative boundaries. Each tenant-in-chief now held Sussex lands only within his own rape. These lands were brought under a form of military occupation on the basis of compact *castellarie*. Castles were erected at Arundel, Bramber, Lewes, Pevensey and Hastings and each with its port became the administrative centre of an extensive district, the castle-holder in almost every case also holding all the non-ecclesiastical land in his respective district. These castleries were converted from Saxon divisions called rapes, analogues to the lathes of Kent, north–south Saxon corridors into England, but important modifications to their boundaries were made during the Norman reorganization, notably the insertion of the rape of Bramber which was a comparatively late formation cutting through the boundaries of the old Saxon hundredal divisions. This afterthought of *c*.1073 also entailed considerable re-allocation of land distributed by William earlier. A hundred was detached from de Warenne's rape of Lewes and put into the Count of Mortain's rape of Pevensey, and de Warenne lost a large strip of land on the west to de Braose's new rape of Bramber, for which he was compensated by the grant of manors in Norfolk described in Domesday Book as of 'the exchange of Lewes' (Salzman 1931: 25). The loss of land by Earl Roger to Bramber may have been compensated by the grant *c*.1072 of almost the whole of Shropshire on the Welsh Marches. The creation of Bramber castlery was probably brought about by the military requirements of defending the Adur estuary (Mason 1964).

Another fresh administrative division carved out by William was the so-called 'rape of Battle Abbey', a franchise taking the form of a leuga or lowy, a circular estate three miles in radius around the site of the abbey. The abbey was not solely founded to save the souls of penitential Norman conquerors. It also contributed an important bastion to the defence of the sparsely-inhabited, and hence weakly-guarded route into England that William had himself taken so successfully. Through the Abbey, settlers and resources swiftly flowed to plug the weak link in the defence of Norman England. This grant of land to Battle Abbey in the form of a lowy was evidently an afterthought, because Norman knights who were earlier enfeoffed there vainly resorted to litigation in defence of their rights (Searle 1980: 57). The critical importance of the 'Channel March' may also explain the king's particularly ruthless re-division of land in the district. In the remainder of the South East the old pattern of parent manor and wealden outlier was retained, except where new rapal boundaries necessitated a re-division, but in the Hastings district the Count of Eu's lands were based on compact, independent lordships carved out of broken-up Saxon estates.

The strategically important and fertile north-east Kent was also rich with dependable knights enfeoffed by Bishop Odo in 1070 and in the rape of Bramber the castle-holder William de Braose similarly planted knights such as Ralph de Bucy who came from his lord's same part of Normandy. In the relatively underdeveloped Weald the Count's *milites* tended to be planted on the outliers rather than in the older and more populous districts. The enfeoffment of knights preceding peasant settlement in thinly-inhabited woodlands of the eastern Weald gave a great impetus to colonization and economic development, complementing the similar work of Battle Abbey. These under-developed places were yielding soon after Domesday far more than ever under their new masters and produced descendants who were minor gentry and prosperous freeholders in the later Middle Ages (Searle 1980: 58).

The Norman land settlement in the South East was directly responsible for the creation of a number of new towns. Arundel is one of these. It did not exist in pre-Conquest times. The local Saxon *burh* lay within the massive earthwork across the river Arun at Burpham (Sutermeister 1976: 194–206), a site Earl Roger rejected when he raised his huge motte on the opposite bank, so attracting the first burgesses with their clustering houses. Another completely new borough was Bramber. When de Braose was granted Bramber rape *c.*1073 mention is made solely of his new castle. The town clustering around the castle is a 'new town' of Norman foundation. It appears to have been deliberately founded to curtail the trade of Steyning upstream, a manor held by the monks of Fécamp. The lord of Bramber built a causeway across the river Adur, so preventing ships reaching Steyning, built houses on reclaimed salterns and laid out a market place. His depredations against Steyning, were however, largely foiled and it may have been for this reason that he or his son Philip planted a second borough in this rape at New Shoreham on a better position at the mouth of the Adur (Hudson 1980: 11–29). New Shoreham, founded *c.*1096, reached the zenith of its importance as a gateway to the Norman lands overseas. Its ordered, rectilinear, street pattern suggests a planned town, the streets north of the High Street, being about a furlong in length, have been ingeniously conjectured to have been almost exactly duplicated in length on the south side of the High Street before coastal erosion destroyed half the town in the later Middle Ages (Cheal 1921: 30–1). The town is remarkable for one of the most striking Norman churches in England and a rare example of non-military Norman vernacular architecture, a stone-built customs house, now a museum.

Another 'new town' was Battle which grew rapidly in relation to its new abbey where no village had existed before the Conquest. At Domesday 21 bordars (small peasants) are shown as living in the then village of Battle. These were presumably settled by the Abbey because when it received its leuga from the Crown the devastation created by the English and Norman armies had rendered the neighbourhood virtually uninhabitable. By 1110, the date of the first Battle rental, a town of 109 householders had arisen on the present site of Battle. The large parish church was then in existence and a market place had been laid out on the edge of the town furthest from the abbey precincts. Of the householders, 78 gave English names, 19 Anglo–Norman and 12 have Norman names. The latter are clustered immediately around the new abbey and were presumably officials. The fact that the Anglo-Norman names are sprinkled amongst the English ones suggests that by this time inter-marriage was taking place between the two peoples (Searle 1974: 69–88; Clark 1980: 1–20).

The Domesday Survey: South-East England in 1086

Although the survey that King William ordered to be compiled in Domesday Book makes it the most famous English public record with no parallel in the history of Europe, the form in which it has survived makes it a very misleading guide to the extent and character of the rural settlements of south-east England, the size of the towns and their activities, or the utilization of resources in general (Sawyer 1976: 136). These deficiencies of Domesday Book arise both from its purpose and from manorial structure, possibly surviving from the Romano-British era (Jones, G. R. J., 1971; 1979). The eleventh-century region was a land of very large, complex, fragmented and composite manors variously called federal, discrete, or multiple estates by modern scholars. When these emerge into clearer light in the thirteenth century they are centred upon a head manor usually bearing the name of the whole estate, containing the principal church, the lord's hall and court, his demesne or 'home' farm and peasant cultivators. Numerous dependent settlements, probably hamlets initially but also including ones that had grown into nucleated villages, were dispersed over the estate, sometimes with chapels of their own, amidst still remaining reserves of wood pasture or downland grazings inter-commoned by peasants of the nearby settlements. The bond tenants in these subordinate places performed work services for, and paid dues to, the lord at the head manor and wherever else he may have possessed demesne land. Drove- and other highways criss-crossed between these various settlements, and in many cases still await reconstruction by field archaeologists (Fig. 2.2).

Such multiple estates were often huge in extent. The traveller could visit hamlet by hamlet for several miles along the winding lanes east and south of Farnham, for example, and still remain on the Bishop of Winchester's estate. As W. F. Maitland observed, 'the simple phrase in Domesday "the bishop holds Farnham" may dispose of 25000 acres of land' (Maitland 1897: 13). The archbishop's manor of South Malling which stretched across the Sussex Weald into Kent from the outskirts of Lewes, and bishop Odo's enormous aggregation of territory centred on Minster in Kent are but examples of estates which disposed of twice or more the acreage of Farnham. Unfortunately, Domesday was never intended to deal separately with settlements that were dependencies of estate headquarters and consequently the already fully articulated countryside of many parts of the South East does not appear in the Survey, nor do we have a ready way of separating this from the sparser and more primitive settlement of the backwoods. Thus Milton is credited with some 400 villeins and other peasants (representing a total population of perhaps 1500–2000 persons, 173 ploughs, 6 watermills, an unspecified number of churches and enough woodland to fatten some 2000 swine. Domesday is silent as to the distribution of these inhabitants and their various resources across the older settled, more populous parts of coastal Kent

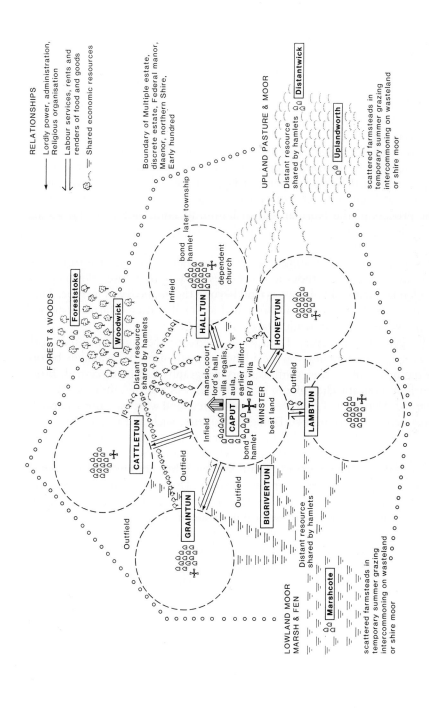

RELATIONSHIPS

→ Lordly power, administration, Religious organisation

⇒ Labour services, rents and renders of food and goods

≈ Shared economic resources

Boundary of Multiple estate, discrete estate, Federal manor, Maenor, northern Shire, Early hundred

FOREST & WOODS

Foreststoke

Woodwick

Distant resource shared by hamlets

CATTLETUN

Outfield

Outfield

Outfield

GRAINTUN

Infield

bond hamlet / later township

dependent church

HALLTUN

mansio, court, lord's hall, villa regalis, aula, earlier hillfort, R/B villa

CAPUT

MINSTER

Infield

bond hamlet

best land

Outfield

BIGRIVERTUN

Distant resource shared by hamlets

LOWLAND MOOR MARSH & FEN

Marshcote

scattered farmsteads in temporary summer grazing intercommoning on wasteland or shire moor

UPLAND PASTURE & MOOR

Distantwick

Distant resource shared by hamlets

Uplandworth

scattered farmsteads in temporary summer grazing intercommoning on wasteland or shire moor

HONEYTUN

Outfield

LAMBTUN

Figure 2.2 The discrete estate. (After Aston)

33

and in the less developed Weald. It is scarcely possible to make even a summary statement about the population of this, and similar composite manors, or of their agricultural development because we do not know from Domesday how far the various members of the manor had progressed beyond the woodland state and reached a stage of cultivation of whatever degree. Plotted on the basis of the headquarter settlement of the manors the Domesday data misleadingly gives a disproportionate importance to this place and correspondingly leaves blank spaces in districts of weald and marsh which, on other evidence, we know were not completely vacant.

Although as a rule Domesday does not provide individual entries to subordinate settlements within the large composite manors it does so exceptionally in the cases of parts of large estates which for one reason or another had been split off from their Saxon manor and added to another in the process of the Norman redistribution of land, and these entries are invaluable in allowing some cautious inference to be made about the state of development of neighbouring estates. By a fortunate circumstance some estates in the north of Hastings rape in Sussex had been detached from their former manors near Eastbourne and Lewes because of a strict Norman rule that a feudal manor should not extend beyond the boundary of its rape. They are separately distinguished and revealed as small scattered farms dispersed over the woodland and heath (Darby 1977: 412).

In general, however, Domesday needs to be supplemented with whatever sparse contemporary evidence of settlement is available before even the broad lines of eleventh-century geography can be discerned. From the earliest monastic chartularies of Sele and Lewes priories, for example, can be learned the names of churches and cultivated land which are not separately enumerated in the respective Domesday entries, such as those of Ardingly, Balcombe, Chiddingly, Cuckfield, East Grinstead, Shipley, Slaugham, West Hoathly and Wivelsfield, all of which existed before the end of the eleventh century in the wealden parts of central Sussex. When account is also taken of the Saxon church of Worth (but unrecorded in Domesday), and the Saxon or very early Norman architectural features of the existing churches of Horsted Keynes or Bolney, this part of heavily-wooded Sussex begins to take on a picture of a considerable and well-distributed population sustaining the parochial organization which had developed in places which on the basis of Domesday we might have considered vacant (Brandon 1969: 135–6). A similar use of cumulative evidence for other parts of wealden Sussex tends to support Lennard's salutary reminder that 'we must not be too ready to fill the Domesday map with imagined woodland and marsh' (Lennard 1959: 8).

From these various sources supplementing Domesday it seems that settlement was much less sporadic and localized than was formerly assumed. There is every reason to believe that the Saxons had been clearing the wealden woodland in earnest two centuries or more before Domesday so inadequately records their achievements. On the Low Weald plain of west Sussex late Saxon farmers had probably occupied all the better-drained soils of a lighter texture, commonly on raised lands containing the church and the oldest settlement. This would have brought into being islands of limited cultivation amidst a sea of remoter woodland awaiting clearance in post-Domesday times. In the more inaccessible and less rewarding Sussex High Weald population appears to have been sparser and confined to groups of small farms near natural highways running along the ridges.

Turning to Kent, three documents roughly coeval with Domesday furnish supplementary information to that record which greatly modifies and expands our knowledge of the eleventh-century geography. One known as the *Excerpta* is concerned chiefly with the lands of St Augustine's Canterbury in east Kent (Ballard 1920). The second, the *Domesday Monachorum* deals with the properties of the Archbishop of Canterbury and the Bishop of Rochester, amongst others. Its most important information in the present connection is a list of 104 churches in places unrecorded in Domesday making payment to Christ Church Canterbury which mainly lay in the eastern part of the Weald (Douglas 1944). The *Textus Roffensis* complements this with a further list of 48 other churches otherwise unrecorded in the bishopric of Rochester, mainly in the western part of the Kentish Weald (Hearne 1720). Omissions of settlements on this scale are one of the most striking demonstrations of the limitations of Domesday Book. Of particular interest is that 37 of the eleventh-century churches (and some of the others which have not been identified) lay in settlements in the Weald of Kent subordinate to great multiple estates centred outside the woodland. They are fairly evenly distributed over the Kent Weald and Romney Marsh across an area left blank on the Domesday map as seemingly uncolonized forest and marsh.

What should now be our revised estimate of the extent and origin of late-eleventh century settlement in the Weald? If we had similar lists of Sussex and Surrey churches they would certainly show that their wealds were far more thoroughly settled than Domesday Book suggests (Sawyer 1978: 137). In 1962 it was Darby's view that the old impression of the uncolonized Weald 'must be modified, but not fundamentally changed; even with the additional names, the Weald remains a relatively empty area' (Darby and Campbell 1962: 581). Since then there has been a revised emphasis on the continuity of Saxon with Romano-British settlement and the case has been made for an occupation of the Weald extending back to prehistoric times (Jones, G. R. J. 1979: 20–9) and with an ardour bordering on the reckless by Christopher Taylor (1983: 182). The outcome of the discussion remains controversial. The enormous extent of post-Norman woodland clearance must also be borne in mind. Darby's view is therefore still the correct one.

For all the limitations and difficulties latent in the interpretation of Domesday Book it provides useful information. As we have seen, it throws light on the Normans' devastations before and after the Battle of Hastings, and also on how quickly much of the land had been restored in value. Domesday also helps with its broad picture of population distribution. Darby's distribution maps of Domesday population reveal that the Coastal Fringe of Sussex and Kent were among the most populated of the English provinces with densities of 15 to 20 persons per square mile. The concentration of population on the west Sussex coastal plain is only matched by parts of East Anglia and contrasts sharply with the much sparser population of Wessex, Devon and Cornwall and the Midlands. Although some of the population allotted to the Coastal Fringe should be peppered across the Weald, as we have noted, Darby's figures do not include the urban population, which was substantial, and consequently the densities recorded on the maps underestimate the actual population on the fertile soils of the Coastal Fringe. Districts with low population densities are also notable, such as the then still frequently flooded lands of Romney Marsh, the intractable clays of the Weald, the thin hungry soils of the Bagshot Beds, and of the Lower Greensand formations in west Surrey.

The relative distribution of arable land is also broadly in line with that of population and the nature of the soil and terrain. The rich Brickearth soils of the coastal plain of Sussex and the corresponding part of north-east Kent figure prominently, but so also does the hinterland of Hastings where settlement had also been relatively dense and early. On the basis of the speculation that one plough team would plough 100 acres, the proportion under the plough in coastal Sussex and the area around Hythe in Kent was probably amongst the highest in England. The overall values of manors in Domesday have to be handled with great caution but they are worth scrutiny because they would reflect the non-arable activities of farmers which are not specifically covered by the Domesday Survey, such as pig-rearing, dairy-farming and especially sheep farming, together with any industrial enterprise. When these sources of revenue are taken into account Kent, which had a very strong pastoral economy in early times, is given an exceptionally high place in Domesday together with Dorset and Wiltshire (Witney 1988: 23–34; Everitt 1986: 32–4). To what degree this special economic importance of Kent is due to its pastoral activities or associated with its position on the main route to the continent, is unclear (Darby 1977: 225). Unfortunately, Domesday adds little to our knowledge of farming types and methods. For example, the only mention of shepherds is the ten recorded at Patcham near Brighton. The forest economy in the Weald is more clearly established in connection with the grand scale of woodland pig-fattening which produced renders paid by peasants of their respective lords implying tenants' herds of swine of more than 500 and exceptionally of as many as 1500–2000.

The Domesday information as to towns is so unsystematic and incomplete that it is usually impossible to form any clear view of the size of the town or the economic activities that sustained it (Darby 1977: 289). The number of places that seem to have been regarded as towns in 1086 was 112 of which 19 were in south-east England, making it one of the most urbanized parts of the country.

These solely comprised the pre-Conquest Saxon burhs because the new urban communities established adjacent to their castles by the leading lay holders of the late eleventh century, apart from Arundel, are unmentioned, presumably either because they were embryonic or non-existent, although in less than a generation they were to become important (Battle, Bramber, New Shoreham and Tonbridge). It is worth drawing attention to the striking way in which the towns had developed as ports along the older and more developed Coastal Fringe on radial roads south and east of London and especially at junctions with the north–south river valleys (Hill 1978: 174–89).

It is difficult to place the Domesday towns in any certain order of size but from the general picture available to us it would seem that Canterbury was a town of the very first rank, with a population of at least 2500 (larger than places such as Exeter and York), though smaller than the largest provincial cities of all, such as Norwich and Thetford. Sandwich and Lewes, according to Darby, might have had 2000 people. Chichester, Hastings, Hythe, Guildford and Kingston probably had populations of about 1000. The other Domesday towns were lesser places.

A salient feature of the information as to boroughs is the marked increase in wealth and population which the Conquest brought them, doubtless due partly to the growing traffic between England and Normandy and the settlement in their castles of Norman lords. At Pevensey, for example, the number of burgesses rose from 27 when Robert of Mortain received it to as many as 110 at Domesday, and Lewes was reckoned to have increased in value by nearly one-third. The Surrey Domesday folios contain many entries of dwellings in Southwark, the leading Surrey town first mentioned in the Burghal Hidage as *Suthringa geweorcke*, appurtenant to rural manors including distant ones such as Bletchingley, Banstead, Walton-on-Hill and Godstone (Walkinstead) which had presumably been charged with their share of the defence of the borough.

Other economic activities mentioned in Domesday Book should also be taken into account. The quarrying of stone in Sussex and Surrey; the thriving

Table 2.1 Towns recorded in Domesday Book

Kent	Sussex	Surrey
Canterbury	Arundel	Southwark
Dover	Chichester	Guildford
Fordwich	Hastings	Kingston
Hythe	Lewes	(unmentioned but
Rochester	Pevensey	certainly in existence)
Old Romney	Rye	
Seasalter	Steyning	
Sandwich	Winchelsea	
	(unmentioned but	
	probably in existence)	

herring fishery (Sandwich alone paid an annual rent of 40,000 herrings to Christ Church, implying a catch of almost half a million); the making of salt on estuaries near a supply of wood fuel; and the iron-working in the Weald, together completed a remarkably well-balanced economy (Witney 1988: 31).

The Early Medieval Church

With regard to the Church, William of Malmesbury, one of the greatest contemporary historians of the Anglo-Norman age, observed that:

> with their arrival the Normans breathed new life into religious standards which everywhere in England had been declining, so that you may see in every village, town and city churches and monasteries rising in a new style of architecture (Malmesbury 1887–9, ii: 306).

The prodigious outburst of building activity in the South East was intensified with the close military and trading connections with Normandy (Fig. 2.3). The continental influences were further strengthened by the habit of early Norman lords of creating priories and cells as dependencies of Norman and other European abbeys. The collegiate church of Steyning, one of the finest specimens of twelfth-century church architecture, was built under the supervision of monks from Fécamp and its nave has a strong resemblance to the Romanesque churches of northern France. There is also a striking similarity between Lessay Abbey in Normandy (founded 1056) and the churches of Old Shoreham, the intended collegiate church of New Shoreham and Boxgrove which was established as a cell of Lessay.

The regional role of the medieval church was also prominent on account of its enormous land holdings. At Domesday about 55 per cent of the arable land in Kent lay within ecclesiastical lordships, chiefly those of the archbishop, his community of Christ Church and St Augustine's Abbey, a higher proportion than anywhere in England (Witney 1988: 24). In coastal Sussex, and in Surrey closest to the Thames, church landlordship was also prominent. Consequently as observed in connection with Kent, the church has had a greater impact on the landscape and economy of the region than any other human agency (Everitt 1986: 181).

It was principally in the great buildings at Caen and Canterbury then under the rule of the famous Lanfranc that the Anglo-Norman High Romanesque emerged. Lanfranc adopted the style of his abbey church of St Stephen in Caen for the new metropolitan cathedral in Canterbury *c*.1070. Contemporaneously, the important abbey of St Augustine was being

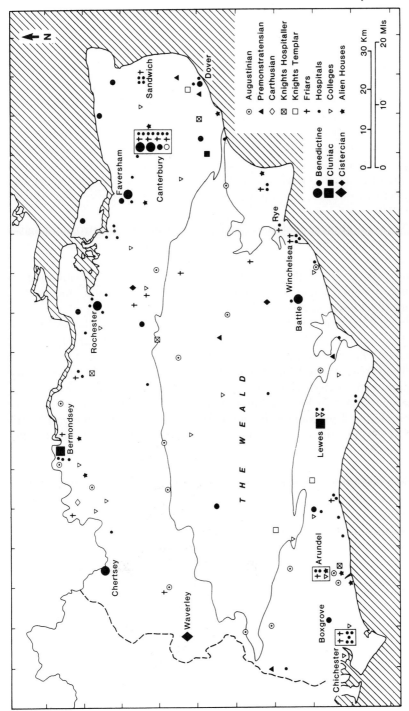

Figure 2.3 The religious foundations in the South East.

constructed in the same city, so making Canterbury the fountainhead of English Romanesque architecture. These two major churches, together with Caen, epitomize the great Norman eleventh-century church with the high altar and shrine set in an eastern apse, a long choir for the community of clergy celebrating the new liturgy, the lantern tower and flanking transepts and a long nave forming almost a distinct building at the western end of the church. Great cathedral churches in this style spread across southern England, notably to Chichester, whence the see of the bishop had been removed from Selsey *c*.1075, and to new towns such as New Shoreham where the magnificently grand church bears decorative evidence of Canterbury masons. Such enormous Romanesque buildings were among the largest and most daring in Europe and led directly towards the development of Gothic (Zarnecki 1951; 1978: 17–26; and 1984).

Normanization should not be thought of as abruptly destroying English culture. St Augustine's abbey at Canterbury under its abbot Aelthelsig was one of the centres of resistance to the Normans in Kent and it remained a centre of active Anglo-Saxondom down to 1089 while continuing to produce manuscripts in an Anglo-Saxon tradition well into the twelfth century (Backhouse *et al* 1984: 198).

In Kent the three largest and richest monastic houses were the Benedictine Christ Church Priory (Plate 2.2) and St Augustine's Abbey at Canterbury, and St Andrew's Priory at Rochester. At Christ Church under Anselm, the cathedral which had arisen on the Anglo-Saxon site was greatly expanded and new priory buildings were erected. The archbishop's new early-thirteenth-century hall is the second-largest in England after Westminster; and the frater range and other buildings were completely rebuilt. In his long priorate, Henry of Eastry (1285–1331) put the priory finances in order and did much to develop the landed estate. A start on the rebuilding of the nave occurred in 1379 and Prior Chillenden 'the greatest builder of a Prior that ever was in Christes Church', according to Leland, rebuilt the great cloister, chapter house, guest houses and other buildings. In the final phase of medieval building, the great central 'Bell Harry' tower was added. At the Dissolution Christ Church had a gross income of nearly £3,000 and was the third-richest ecclesiastical house in England after Westminster and Glastonbury. St Augustine's abbey developed into a huge new monastery in the Norman period, probably completed by Abbot Hugh (d. 1124). The middle and later years of the thirteenth century was another great period of rebuilding and expansion under Abbot Fyndon, culminating in the licence to crenellate the Great Gate in 1308. The very late fourteenth and early fifteenth centuries was also a period of active building, as at Christ Church. At St Andrew's, Gundulf, the first Norman bishop, rebuilt the cathedral and constructed all the necessary building for the monastery. In the early twelfth century the cloister and other buildings were removed eastwards beyond the Roman city wall.

Canterbury cathedral, rebuilt after a fire in 1174, had a decisive

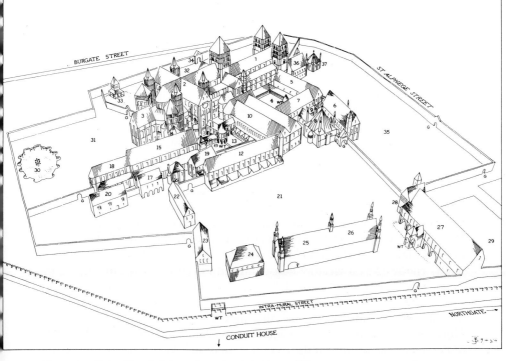

Plate 2.2 Christ Church Priory, Canterbury, in the twelfth century: a reconstruction.

Key

1.	Nave	21.	Outer(Green)Court
2.	Choir	22.	Bath-house and Camera
3.	Trinity Chapel	23.	Barn
4.	Great Chapel	24.	Granary
5.	Cellarer's Range	25.	Bakehouse
6.	Guest Hall	26.	Brewhouse
7.	Refectory	27.	North(New)Hall
8.	Kitchen	28.	Court Gate
9.	Locutory	29.	Almonry
10.	Great Dormitory	30.	Fish Pond
11.	Night Passage	31.	Monks' Cemetery
12.	Necessarium	32.	Lay Cemetery
13.	Herb Garden	33.	Bell Tower
14.	Vestry/Treasury	34.	Cemetery Gate
15.	Infirmary Hall	35.	Archbishop's Outer Court
16.	Infirmary Kitchen	36.	Archbishop's Great Hall
17.	Infirmary Necessarium	37.	Archbishop's Kitchen
18.	Infirmary Chapel	WT	Water Tower
19.	Prior's Old Camera	G	Gate
20.	Prior's New Camera		

(Tatton-Brown 1984: 174–5).

impact on the development of the Gothic style in England. The new style was closely related to contemporary practice in north-west France because the reconstructions were entrusted to William of Sens, who brought with him sculptors and glaziers from that district. In its pointed arches, delicate rib vaulting and detached shafts, its large aisle windows, rich capitals and the use of marble, the nearest counterparts were Notre-Dame in Paris, St Remi at Rheims and the cathedrals of Leon, Arras and Valenciennes. For the next 70 years most of the greater churches of England had their eastern ends rebuilt in Purbeck marble and lavish decoration. The spectacular shrine erected in 1220 to display the relics of the martyred Archbishop Thomas à Becket, which was the visual and liturgical focus of the church, was destroyed at the Reformation (Plate 2.3).

One of the most important of the new monasteries of Anglo-Norman England was Battle Abbey, a Benedictine institution 'born out of due place and time by the whim of military victory and the fiat of the king', and founded by a team of monks from the abbey of Marmoutier on the Loire. William I took personal interest in the founding of the monastery and from the beginning it was endowed as a wealthy house, fifteenth in order of wealth among the monasteries featuring in Domesday Book. The conventual buildings, originally unostentatious, were completed by Abbot Ralph (1107–24). The rounded apse, ambulatory and radiating chapels, then more common in the Loire Valley than Normandy, were to be repeated later at Canterbury and other cathedrals. The abbey's more active role in the colonization of the Weald and its flexible and enterprising estate management enabled it to rebuild almost all the monastic buildings on a grandiose scale during the thirteenth century. These buildings were themselves a massive achievement, reflecting considerable power and wealth. The rebuilding was achieved only with considerable difficulty, for the king's determination that the monastery should stand on the exact site of his victory imposed on the struggling monks the liability of a narrow hilltop. Therefore the new buildings had to expand in the form of cellars and crypts into the hillside and the creation of earthen platforms was necessary (Hare 1981). In the early fourteenth century the great gatehouse was added, signifying the threat of internal rebellion and of French assault. A large new abbot's hall was the main addition in the fifteenth century.

At Lewes William de Warenne and his wife Gundrada founded the monastery of St Pancras in 1077. The founders placed their monastery under the direct control of the Burgundian house of Cluny. This led the way to elaborate liturgy, chant and prestigious architecture. The church was larger and more richly ornamented than Chichester cathedral – for Cluny was then the fount of European art and learning and the centre for monastic reform. Further Cluniac abbeys were founded at Reading by Henry I and at Faversham by Stephen. Earlier, the Cluniac abbey of Bermondsey was founded and made subject to the house of St Mary's at Charité-sur-Loire. Bermondsey's location tended to draw it into the mainstream of national life and not suprisingly the house acquired vast landed possessions scattered over England.

These great monastic institutions of the 'Black' monks were soon followed by the first houses of the reformed order of Benedictines, called Cistercians from their head house of Cîteaux in Burgundy. Waverley Abbey near Farnham holds

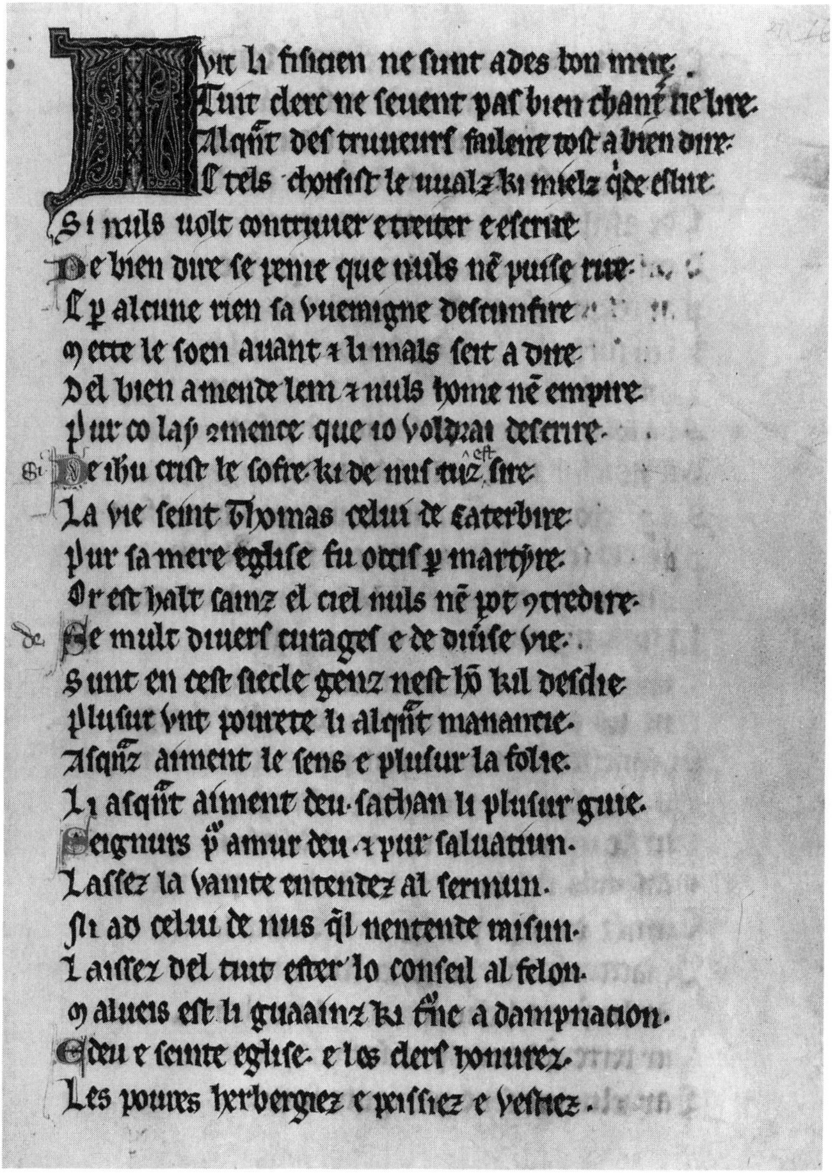

Tuit li fisicien ne sunt ades bon mire.
Tuit clerc ne seuent pas bien chanter ne lire.
Alquant des trouuerrs faillent tost a bien dire.
Et tels choisist le uualz ki mielz quide eslire.
Si nuls uolt contruuer e treiter e escrire.
De bien dire se peine que nuls nen puisse rire.
Et par alcune rien sa buesuigne destruire.
Mette le soen auant e li mals seit a dire.
Del bien amende lem e nuls home nen empire.
Pur co las comence que io uoldrai descrire.
De ihu crist le sofre ki de nus tuz est sire.
La vie seint Thomas celui de caterbire.
Pur sa mere eglise fu ocis par martyre.
Or est halt sainz el ciel nuls nen pot contredire.
De mult diuers curages e de diuise vie.
Sunt en cest siecle genz nest hom kil desdie.
Plusur unt pourete li alquant manantie.
Alquanz aiment le sens e plusur la folie.
Li alquant aiment deu sathan li plusur guie.
Seignurs pur amur deu e pur saluatiun.
Lassez la uanite entendez al sermun.
Si ad celui de nus qil nentende raisun.
Laissez del tut ester lo conseil al felon.
Maluais est li guaainz ki fine a dampnation.
E deu e seinte eglise e les clers honurez.
Les poures herbergiez e peissiez e vestiez.

Plate 2.3 Part of the Cathedral service commemorating the martyrdom of Thomas à Becket: thirteenth century. Thousands came annually from all over Western Europe to worship at the shrine of St Thomas à Becket and a special service was provided for them. Illustrated is part of the biography of St Thomas which was chanted in French by a priest to the congregation, and written about 1177 by Guernus de Pont-Sainte-Maxence in Picardy. Each stanza has 5 alexandrines, all ending with the same rhyme. The wording has been adapted for easy chanting. Deep hollows were created in the stone floor of the Cathedral by the kneeling pilgrims (British Museum Galba I: 4).

a position of great importance in church history as the first Cistercian house of England, founded in 1128 by William Giffard, Bishop of Winchester with monks from L'Aumône, Normandy. In 1187 mention is made of 120 lay brethren, seventy monks and around thirty plough teams at work on the estate. A new church was constructed in the early thirteenth century. Waverley became the principal source of the order's expansion in Southern England: within a decade it possessed four houses, expanding to ten by mid-century. The remains of the church have been excavated. The modest size, attenuated proportions and aisleless form of architecture contrasts vividly with the plan developed in the North of England, for example at Rievaulx. Waverley in fact reflects an older and short-lived tradition for Cistercian churches (Ferguson 1984: 25–7; 114–15; 140–1; 153–4).

Boxley in Kent was founded by William of Ypres, son of the Count of Flanders, in 1143. It became the second Cistercian abbey in England to be affiliated directly to Clairvaux. Partly on account of its site near the main London–Canterbury highway, its abbots played a prominent role in English political affairs in the late twelfth century. Alured de St Martin founded the Cistercian house of Robertsbridge with monks from Boxley. Originally founded at Salehurst, the abbey was removed because of floods. The only surviving fabric is the house known as 'the Abbey' at Robertsbridge, based upon the thirteenth-century abbot's house of the original monastery. It had a long crypt with high vaulted ceilings and grounds that include the ruins of the refectory and cloisters.

Other early religious foundations were Sele Priory, an institution founded by William de Braose I of Bramber Castle; the twelfth-century houses of the Premonstratensians at Bayham and Durford and of the Augustinians at Shulbrede and Michelham. In Surrey the Augustinians founded priories at Newark, Merton, Tandridge and Reigate. Carmelites settled at Aylesford in Kent. The Augustinian Priory of Michelham was founded in 1229 by Gilbert of Aquila, lord of the rape of Pevensey, on the edge of the extensive Dicker common. The conventual buildings occupied an area of about eight acres surrounded by a wide moat. By the last quarter of the fourteenth century the priory had run into debt through the damage caused to its buildings and lands by inundations of the sea, and grants of the churches of Alfriston and Fletching by the Bishop of Chichester in 1398 provided funds for repairs. Earlier the priory had been a target of the Peasants' Revolt in 1381, and the 1395 gate house tower gave greater protection. The frater, refectory and other parts of the south range of the priory were converted into a Tudor mansion.

As to parish churches, almost all these were rebuilt in the 'Norman' style in the decades following 1066. The basic style of the ordinary village church over the entire country consisted of a regular un-aisled nave and chancel. In Surrey a number of such little churches have survived with the minimum of change, such as Pyrford, Wisley and Farleigh; similar are many

Plate 2.4 Plaistow old church before destruction by fire in the early nineteenth century, depicted in watercolour by Henry Petrie in 1805. The church was demolished before 1851 by J. Butler of Chichester who replaced it with the present stone chapel. The first churches in the wealden forest clearings were often half-timbered buildings in the same vernacular tradition as farmhouses, barns and inns. The original Plaistow church was probably the last remaining church in Sussex in this primitive style. The roof was formerly thatched. Brick-nogging is apparent between widely-spaced studs. (Smith, V. 1979, number 260).

little West Sussex churches, notably Buncton, Chithurst, Hardham, Selham and Stoughton (Plate 2.4).

In thinly inhabited woodland districts of Surrey where good building stone was lacking, medieval constructions are notable for the amount of wood used in bell towers or turrets in the fourteenth and fifteenth centuries, as at Burstow, Horne, Horley, Leigh and Newdigate on the Weald Clay. Such timber towers are fine specimens of medieval carpentry, retaining massive beams and posts hewn from locally-grown oak. Surrey churches are also distinguished by their finely carved wooden screens: Compton church possesses the oldest such screen in England, and many other beautiful medieval screens survive as at Gatton, West Horsley, Leatherhead, Nutfield, Reigate and Shere, the finest of all being at Charlwood. Chaldon on the North Downs has a unique twelfth-century 'Doom' painting showing the monastic influence of the Greek Church.

On the downlands and heaths were numerous smaller and poorer churches which did not outgrow the simple nave and chancel constructed just before or soon after the Norman Conquest, for their populations, always small, expanded little after Domesday. Elstead church, Surrey, still possesses the single timber and plaster screen that served as a division between nave and chancel and Chelsham and Warlingham churches both had such a division. In the late eighteenth century Gilbert White wrote of the 'meanness' of 'Sussex houses of worship [with] little better appearance than dovecotes'. Coombes in the Adur valley, Chithurst near Rogate and Coates in the Rother valley are examples of these diminutive churches.

Conversely, all over the Weald are examples of the thirteenth-century rebuilding in the Early English style, reflecting rising immigrant populations and increasing prosperity. At Fletching, for example, the tower has traces of Saxo-Norman work but the present large structure is in the cruciform Early English style and was completed about 1230. The graceful shingled spire was added about 1340. Another church rebuilding symbolizing wealden prosperity is at Lindfield which was an important iron and cloth centre at least from the thirteenth century. Extensive building was also required for churches at Buxted, Heathfield, Rotherfield, Kirdford, and Waldron to accommodate the huge congregations that came to settle in these parishes during the last phase of woodland clearance. West Hoathly church records the progressive enlargement to keep pace with forest clearing particularly well. Originally a little rectangular Norman building, an aisle and chapel were added and the chancel, most unusually was extended to make it larger than the nave in the twelfth and thirteenth centuries.

The Medieval Castle

Castle building also began in earnest with the Norman conquest and continued throughout the early Middle Ages. The first Norman castles, constructed by William at Pevensey, Hastings and Dover are depicted on the Bayeux Tapestry as consisting of a mound (motte) with an attached fortified enclosure (bailey). Norman lords built such simple castles in hundreds in the century following the conquest and examples of surviving earthworks of this kind are at Abinger, Thunderfield, Walton-on-the-Hill and Cranleigh, Surrey; at Thurnham in Kent; and at Pulborough and Edburton, Sussex. Excavation of the Abinger site has revealed that it consisted of a timber tower within a palisade on top of an artificial mound, surrounded by a moat (Plate 2.5). Many such castles are now seen as 'burglar-proof houses' arising from security needed by the wealthy during the troubled period of Stephen's reign, and represent a transitional dwelling before both military sophistication and the demand for increased comfort created forts and country houses as functionally different.

These early defences were largely replaced by great stone castles at the power bases of the new rulers from c.1150. The most spectacular was constructed at Dover, where proximity to the European mainland and to

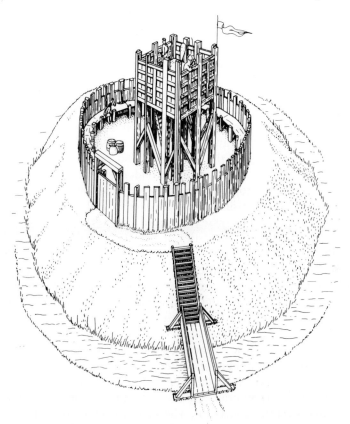

Plate 2.5 Abinger Castle: an early motte-and-bailey castle. A reconstruction of the early twelfth-century castle at Abinger, Surrey. Excavation has shown it to consist of a timber tower within a palisade on top of an artificial mound surrounded by a moat. Its form was very close to depictions in the Bayeux Tapestry (Longworth and Cherry 1986: 178).

London has always lent the site a special strategic importance, uniquely reflected in its continued use for military purposes from 1066 to the end of the Second World War. It was traditionally said that 'he who held the keys of Dover Castle held the keys of England'. Certainly to hold England required one of the most powerful fortresses in medieval Europe. The keep or *magna turris* of the early-medieval castle played an essentially passive role in resistance and remained the supreme expression of the idea that defence was a question of thick walls. Henry II's massive and dominating keep at Dover Castle, raised by the master mason, Maurice 'the engineer' in the 1180s, marks the high point of a development which began with William the Conqueror's tower keep in London. But the late twelfth- and early-thirteenth-century fortification at Dover also looked forward to new techniques of defence, notably in the Constable's Gate with its drum-shaped towers flanking the

47

entrance passage, in its curtain walls with regularly-spaced mural towers, and in its use of an inner and outer circuit of such walls, anticipating the concentric castles a century later. The fortified town which grew at the base of the castle was incomparable in England and as fine a species of permanently garrisoned town as any on the Continent. The castle stands above it on the Eastern Heights and as much as Canterbury Cathedral is a symbol of the entire South East of England.

Canterbury Castle, one of the first to be built after the conquest, was of flint bonded with Caen stone and some Roman material. Its ruins stand within the south-western corner of the City walls and protected the convergence of three routes from the coast towards London. This castle was repeatedly refortified by the archbishops. Most of the river-crossings were also defended with castles, such as the Bishop of Winchester's Farnham, the king's square keep at Guildford, and the Sussex group of Chichester, Arundel, Bramber, Lewes and Rye; and the Kent castles of Eynsford, Chilham and Rochester. The latter stood guard over the crossing of the Medway by Watling Street and its keep was the tallest in the country. It was begun by Bishop Gundulf in 1087 and although besieged several times during the struggle for power between the monarchy and the barons and being captured, with Canterbury Castle in 1381 by Wat Tyler's men during the Peasants' Revolt, it still towers over the town. At Lewes a formidable castle with a strong early-fourteenth-century barbican and a shell keep was placed on the south-western motte. A further motte, Brack Mount, probably of earlier construction, lies across the bailey to the north-east. The de Warennes, amongst the greatest of Anglo-Norman magnates, resided here in cramped and draughty quarters comprising four rooms around a central courtyard. The main living apartment was floored with glazed tiles. A kitchen range with a beehive bread oven lay adjacent. Fragments of glass indicate the site of a chapel, and sleeping rooms completed the suite (P. Drewett, Pers. Comm.).

The Clares built Tonbridge Castle, dominating the south-western approaches to London, and a smaller castle at Bletchingly, Surrey. No physical trace survives of the great royal fortification of Queenborough of Edward III, begun in 1361 as a completely new castle in the Isle of Sheppey for the defence of the Thames Estuary. Shortly afterwards the king began the building of the adjoining town, named Queenborough in honour of Queen Philippa. This became one of the foremost later-medieval castles and a favoured residence of the king. It was totally destroyed by the Parliamentary Commission after the Civil War but a surviving drawing by Hollar gives details of its remarkably early concentric symmetry (Brown 1976 edn: 93–5).

The Conquest of the Weald

The Weald (Old English *Wald*, forest) was the largest expanse of wild country cleared and settled for agriculture in England since Domesday. It therefore offers a classic example of the struggle between man and a continuously receding waste. The Weald is now generally thought of as the tract of country between the escarpments of the North and South Downs, joined together in their westerly extension between Petersfield and Alton. Historically the limits of the Weald were narrower, and broadly followed the line of natural division between the bordering Lower Greensand uplands and the Weald Clay, thus confining the Weald to the heavy-soiled and wooded districts of the Low and High Wealds. This boundary was that adopted between titheable and non-titheable woodland, which latter was a jealously guarded wealden custom and presumably a recognition that when the parish system was evolving into maturity in the twelfth century woodland in the Weald was awaiting clearance for agriculture and had no commercial value in its own right (Topley 1876: 243; Witney 1976: 5–11).

The Weald is one of the parts of England which was early imprinted on the national consciousness as a distinctive human region with an identifiable *genre de vie*. Thus archers, recruited by the king from the backwoods of Kent in the thirteenth century were described as 'wealdsmen' (*saggitariis de Walden*) and especially low valuations of land at the same period were acquiesced in by officials of the Exchequer with the explanation 'and [worth] no more because in the Weald'.

As so much of the Weald has only gradually succumbed to the axe and plough during the period of written records we can trace the evolution of its landscape and society in a unique degree of detail which imparts a sense of the wealden countryside in movement and subjected to a continuous alteration by slow degree over the course of centuries. The story falls into a sequence of fairly recognizably successive, but overlapping, stages. Most wealden settlement, both isolated farms as well as that of hamlets and villages, evolved from a stage of temporarily occupied huts and shelters associated with seasonal pastoral farming before they were permanently occupied by farmers who cultivated the land within ring-fenced fields. Thus most wealden place-names are much older than the farms, villages and towns that bear them. We have already considered the second state of this evolution, the fully-fledged farms which were evolving from summer pastures in the tenth and eleventh centuries. Early antiquaries concluded that the original wealden settlements were on the ridgeways and that the deep, densely-wooded valleys were cleared subsequently. Recent research suggests that the reverse is generally true. When farming partook of the character of pioneering it was the sheltered hollows with their denser woodland which had been used for grazing and pig-rooting which were most valued, and it was these sites that evolved first into fenced fields with the gradual removal of the woodland cover by grazing animals. The ridge-top settlements, including numerous compact villages, did not begin to cluster around once-isolated central churches until later stages of colonization.

The main task of wealden woodland clearance was accomplished by four or five generations of land-hungry backwoodsmen between the late twelfth and the early fourteenth centuries. It is then that a fast-moving frontier of settlement (using this term in the American sense as the edge of primitive settlement bounding yet un-won waste) emerges into the historical limelight. Drenched in this relatively clear light, we find back-country settlers in fast-growing communities hacking out their first fields in the High Weald (which had generally resisted earlier settlement) and also in the partially-tamed Low Weald, supplementing their land-winning with handicrafts such as making cloth, hammering iron, wood-turning and marketing produce at towns only a few years old. By the Black Death of 1348 even the most out-of-the-way corners of the Weald had been assimilated to frontier conditions and parts of the more accessible, or more favourable, former wildness, where the colonizing movement was already long past, were beginning to outgrow their 'colonial' character as mere adjuncts of the anciently developed Coastal Fringe.

This medieval clearing was to add two more stages to the evolution of the wealden rural society and landscape. The new wave of pioneers who entered the High Weald from *c.*1240 held small parcels of 'assart' land for a money rent. They brought into existence the familiar 'waste-edge' pattern of straggly rural settlement. It was these peasants who began to supplement their hard-won living by various kinds of by-employment, so initiating a long-standing characteristic of the Weald. This 'folk-flow' was followed slightly later by one overlapping with it, comprising tradesmen moving in to set up business and artisans building cottages when the supply of available 'frontier' land for agricultural colonization had run out. These migrants added cottages to the once isolated churches, so creating characteristic wealden hill villages, such as Mayfield, Wadhurst, Heathfield, Hawkhurst, etc., and they were also the first settlers of the newly built market towns serving the now-bustling Interior (see pp. 53–4).

Moore has thoroughly examined the chronology and scale of the woodland clearance in the manor of Laughton near Lewes. As late as *c.*1216 the frontier of colonization roughly corresponded with the southern fringe of the Weald Clay formation. The years *c.*1216 to 1240 witnessed the belated clearing of some 640 acres of the common waste on the claylands, after which date the search for new land led people to remoter parts of the manor on the fringes of the High Weald in the parishes of Chiddingly, East Hoathly and Waldron (Moore 1965). In the Low Weald of Surrey Saxon settlement had been considerable but extensive intervening wastes were still lacking in agricultural colonists in the early thirteenth century. Here peasants were taking up small parcels of customary land as woodland clearings ('breaches' or *rudings*).

Many of the occupants took as surnames the name of their smallholding: Henry de la Breche, Richard le Brechere, Walter atte Rud, etc. As early as the 1320s the little community at Ruckenham in the wildwood of Albury manor at Ockley had grown sufficiently in size to warrant two new water-mills. Nearby Oakwood, remote land in Wotton manor, was also developing at this time into a hamlet-community with expanding *ruds* (Evelyn Mss).

The clearance of the waste in the High Weald of Kent and Sussex was a long process of attrition. Before *c*.1240 it was still a region of forest clearings, as distinct from the more generally cleared forest on its edge. The lack of transport was probably the chief reason for this backwardness and an explanation for its settlers remaining backwoodsmen rather than farmers longer than any others in the South East. Beginning about 1240 a new wave of pioneers entered the region as assarters (Old French *essarter*, to grub up trees) holding land by money rents. The most dramatic gains of this vigourous colonizing effort were in the archbishop's manor of South Malling. In its beadlewicks of Mayfield (including Wadhurst) and Framfield alone (which constituted about half the land 'in the wood') more than 6000 acres were newly colonized between *c*.1240 and the onset of plagues in the fourteenth century. Of this clearing *c*.3600 acres is attributable to the final phase of this clearing after *c*.1273. Vigorous clearing is also striking in the neighbouring manor of Rotherfield. Between 1086 and 1346 the number of manorial tenants rose from the 24 recorded in Domesday to 294 individuals listed in the custumal of 1346, an increase partly attributable to the subdivision of existing holdings but mainly to the creation of new ones on freshly cleared ground. In terms of acreage some 1800 acres were cleared and settled as *riedlond* between 1086 and 1262 and another 1250 acres were taken into cultivation from the waste between 1262 and 1346. One of the indications of a mounting pressure on the dwindling land supply is the greater cultivation of marginal land in this period of late colonization. The late settlement of the 'stone rock' fields of Eridge and Rotherfield are examples of the colonization of this least workable of land. Many of these last settlements were new forms of rural woodland occupation, including the 'waste-edge' pattern of settlement which grew haphazardly around the major vestigial wastes, a formless scatter of assarting peasants' dwellings expanding here and there into shapeless hamlets on the fringes of greens and commons (Brandon 1969: 138–40).

Another indication of the rising pressure on land, in both the Low and High Wealds, is the sharply diminished size of land holdings. The customary holdings had a changing pattern of rural settlement based on persistent improvement of the farmland by successive generations of backbreaking human endeavour. The Rotherfield Custumal explains that each of the original peasant farmers had held a ferling of land, a division varying from 100 to 150 acres. This we may assume was the estimation of the approximate size of a pioneer family's farm when it was still largely in a wooded state in late Saxon or early Norman times. By 1346 each of these ferlings had been sufficiently improved to support several families each in their own dwellings, and some once single farmsteads had grown into hamlets, one being Hamsell. Another was *Gilderigge* (now represented only by Gillridge farm in Withyham) provided with a chapel in 1292 because the inhabitants successfully put the case that they were unable to reach their nearest church in Buxted during winter.

The same sub-division of former virgates is apparent at 'borghs within the wood' of South Malling manor. For example the virgate of Betesfeud in Wadhurst at the end of the thirteenth century was divided as follows:

Matthew le Freke	one twelfth share
Widow of Absolom and Frankelyen	one sixth share
John de Ecclesia	one eighth share
John Robyn	one eighth share
Richard de Betesfeud	one eighth share
William de Betesfeud	one eighth share
John de Betesfeud	one quarter share

total 185 acres

Source: Redwood and Wilson (1958)

Other divided virgates reveal various stages of division in their respective hamlets. In each a family takes its surname from the name of the virgate. Besides this group of relatives there are other persons, sometimes in groups bearing the same surnames. Some of these may have won their interest in the hamlet by purchase or inheritance. Collectively such evidence of split virgates is entirely consistent with the inference that the whole pattern of land-holding based on hamlets on the archbishop's manor represents the working of partible inheritance in a newly settled society and it may be a mode of the original settlement of much of England (Hallam 1981: 93). Taking a wider view, we can draw a similar conclusion from the sequence of settlement in the Kentish dens of which Gervase Markham observed:

> Albeit these Denns . . . be now broken into many several possessions so as the same one denn sufficeth twenty householders . . . yet it is very likely that each man at the first had his several denn wholly and unbroken whereof he and posterity beareth name until that the same was by a custom of gavelkind by sale or exchange divided and distributed amongst others into parts as we do now see them (Markham 1636: 4).

This explanation of the medieval origin of loosely-grouped clusters of small family farms on shared virgates in the expanding frontier community of the thirteenth-century Weald should be compared with Glanville Jones's hypothesis that many such settlements have their origins in the Romano-British period, or even earlier. Exceptionally, wealden hamlets may have come into existence in the distant past but the great majority appear to have arisen in the Great Clearing of late-Saxon and early-medieval times.

In some parts of the High Weald it is possible to trace an evolving rural community in some detail. Thus at Heathfield, Sussex in an outlier of the manor of Bishopstone near Seaford the earliest pioneers were probably no more than half-a-dozen families dispersed over half-cleared places within walking distance of their once solitary church. Shortly before 1257 this little colony of woodsmen was quickly expanded to include 32 new assart tenements on 310 acres of freshly cleared ground. By 1300 the number of assart tenements had doubled and in 1379 the tally of assarters was 72, of whom 47 had built cottages. The sharp falling off in numbers of assarters after *c.*1330 suggests that the axe was being laid up generally. As little hedge- and shaw-bound fields spread their lines up the freshly cultivated hillsides, tradesmen moved in and set up businesses. Their presence in such a remote place, cut off altogether by miry roads in winter, must have been necessitous. By 1257 a miller, a smith (*faber*), a baker (*pistor*) had taken up residence and three other tradesmen had opened up stalls (*selda*). Meanwhile the church was enlarged to accommodate the fast-growing congregation, a pest house was built and the Bishop of Chichester obtained for the new community the grant of a market and fair. This kind of evolution at roughly the same periods was probably the experience of the other wealden ridge-top villages in the Kent and Sussex Weald such as Hawkhurst, Mayfield and Rotherfield (Peckham 1925: 87–98).

Everitt has suggested that artisan-farmers were relatively recent phenomena in the sixteenth-century Weald (Everitt 1969: 22) but a similar examination in depth of surviving medieval rentals of manors 'within the wood' makes evident the apparent deep involvement of the medieval woodland economy in craft activities. The evidence rests largely upon tenants whose surnames are the names of their trade. By calling on this evidence, we can glimpse the daily work actually going on in the heart of the Weald towards the end of the thirteenth century. The scattered forest hamlets are found to be alive with business, very full of artisans supplementing their hard-won living from a relatively inhospitable land by various forms of by-employment, usually working a plot little more than a garden patch, in distinction to the holding of a fully-fledged farmer. A wide range of handicrafts quickly developed in each woodland community for many of the new colonists at once began grappling with the local raw materials of timber, clay, iron, water-power, wood and hides. The wood-crafts of coopering, turnering and tanning are well represented by occupation names. Numerous of the woodland clearers, for example at Ruckenham, were part-time farmer-artisans, including Godefrid le Verer (Glass-maker), Thomas and Robert Faber, possibly, as their name suggests, smiths or iron-makers, Walter le Chaboner (charcoal burner), and Thomas le Denere, a holder of 'pot-lands', i.e. places of pottery manufacture. At roughly this same period the monks of Sele priory had settled smallholders on their demesne at Crockhurst, south of Horsham, another place-name signifying a colony of potters. Similar evidence of another pottery-making community is the collection of tithes by the priory and convent of Selborne, Hampshire, from hand-dug plots on the edge of Alice Holt Forest including 'ye dykers croft, ye potteris crofts, ye Carpenters crofts' (Macray 1891 and 1894: 18; Jefferies 1975). Here again was another little swarm of part-time farmer-craftsmen. These various communities of wealden potters made both coarse pottery from the Weald Clay and superior quality pitchers from white clays in other strata, and were probably serving both a relatively thriving and expanding local market in the Weald and also the old-established market towns on the wealden periphery.

Also of interest is evidence of tenants in the woodland part of the manor of South Malling, and also in Rotherfield who bear names such as Weaver (texter), Dyer, Glover, etc., and at Uckfield and Wadhurst, where fulling mills were established, no less than eight tenants are designated *le fuller*. Each farming family probably spun its own wool and passed it on to cottage weavers in the locality who in turn brought it to local fullers and merchants. Another leading manufacture was that of iron. Its widespread nature is indicated by the twelve tenants of Framfield, Mayfield and Wadhurst bearing the name *Fabrica* (smith), others called *le Stel* and *le Colyer*, the latter doubtless making fuel used by the local smiths in their bloomeries and forges (Redwood and Wilson 1958: 30–83). Unfortunately, the kind of evidence examined throws little light on the scale and organization of this industrial activity. Much local craftsmanship probably catered purely for the growing neighbourhood but the textile and iron industries seem to have supplied larger markets.

Bearing in mind the various wealth-generating resources of different forms of pioneering, we can now consider whether the throng of peasants, apparently ill-provided with land, was a symptom of acute pressure on land resulting in over-population and all its attendant agrarian misery. We are still insufficiently informed on these matters to do more than speculate. One social characteristic of the thirteenth-century Weald, that of the migratory seasonal labourer, was a sign of poverty that was to bedevil the region for centuries to come. Such persons were presumably landless cottagers who could find no nearer agricultural work than the huge cereal farms in the Coastal Fringe (pp. 63–4). That the land itself was a hard task-master which could not fully sustain the small-holder seems to have been early recognized by the evidence of rural crafts. The large and varied company of peasants assessed to small taxes in the 1332 subsidy (108 persons in Mayfield and Wadhurst and 83 in Framfield and Uckfield), for example, indicates that most wealdsmen lived in hard social and economic circumstances and that rural life was tough. Certainly part of the wealden population must have been on the poverty line but the majority of the immigrant families may well have learned how to prosper in the enlivening and energizing episode that pioneering situations commonly were.

The first piecemeal clearances led to an irregular pattern of small fields and winding, minor lanes. As population expanded and new farms and assarted smallholdings were established away from the older centres, a dense network of sunken lanes developed which is one of the most characteristic features of the Weald. This pattern of by-ways remains essentially unchanged because unlike open-field areas of England it was little affected by subsequent enclosure, but a small proportion have become unused during the past two centuries and are now merely public paths or hollows across a field.

Wealden reclamation is often wrongly assumed to be always at the expense of trunks of trees. As early as the eleventh century the widespread intensive use of woodland for swine would then have had a deleterious impact on the tree cover, opening it out into semi-natural glades or 'laundes'. 'What pig snout had begun to clear peasant was avid to plough' (Searle 1974: 64). This man-induced change of vegetation on the Low Weald may explain its relatively early colonization. As for the High Weald, assarting does not appear to have been at the expense of prime woodland but of bracken and bramble with some beech, birch and a little ground oakwood. Hundreds of miles of surviving deer-leap fences suggest that the more extensive tracts of woodland existing in the twelfth and early thirteenth centuries had been appropriated for parks and forests.

Another of the most characteristic elements of the regional landscape in medieval times, was the wood common reserved as pasture for swine and cattle. The straggling concave outlines of surviving wood commons such as Ebernoe and Mens Wood near Petworth have been almost unchanged for centuries. Wood commons are of great significance in the present landscape as it is solely in such places that we can sense something of the old character of the wealden woods which have changed little in floristic composition over centuries, apart from a probable increase in elm and beech. The most distinctive of the former wood pastures were the lime woods of the small-leaved lime which were relicts of the wildwood of the late Mesolithic period when the lime was possibly the commonest tree. Lime trees are still abundant at places such as Lindfield, Sussex, which derives its place-name from OE *Linde*, a lime. Some of the woodland species are invaluable as 'indicator species' which can be used to determine ancient woodlands, in the absence of written documentation, by field study alone. These include the very slow colonizers such as Butchers's Broom, Wood Spurge, Sweet Woodruff, Yellow Archangel, etc. Some species of beetle and bugs associated with old trees are also indicators of ancient woodland that has been relatively undisturbed for centuries, but the most valuable 'indicator species' are epiphytic lichens (Rose, Pers. Comm.). Medieval woods are also identifiable visually by their shape. Characteristically they are very irregular, sinuous or zig-zag in outline and their boundary is normally a strong rounded bank and outer ditch.

The most distinctive of the wealden hedges are the strips of timber around fields called shaws. Speculation on their origin begins with William

Marshall who suggested that they were residual features from the period of the original woodland clearance by pioneer farmers. Fieldwork now being undertaken in various parts of the Weald makes it abundantly clear that Marshall's hypothesis that shaws are a faithful indication of medieval assarting is in need of drastic modification. Existing shaws are invariably located on the edges of lynchets or between a clearly defined earthen bank and ditch. Many shaws thus appear to represent the encroachment of trees and shrubs onto previously cultivated land and the development of shaws, far from being a relict feature of medieval pioneer farming, probably occurred in periods when the valuation placed on timber in its own right, or as an amenity, equalled or exceeded that of farmland, as during the peak of the charcoal iron industry in the late sixteenth and early seventeenth centuries and again during the heyday of the Victorian 'pleasure-farm' when park-like shaws were appreciated for ornament and game preservation (Marshall 1798, i: 48–50).

The Structure of Early Medieval Society and Land Management

Kent has been traditionally regarded as the ancient home of peasant freedom, giving its people a sense of identity and a conceit of themselves (Witney 1982: 230). But this needs qualification in certain respects. Kentish peasants in general enjoyed at least from the late twelfth century relative freedom of tenure in the custom of gavelkind which permitted a rather freer and more individualistic economy and society than in most parts of England. Gavelkinders, however, although personally free, owed various labour services to their lord as well as rents. By the mid-twelfth century, as conveyancing deeds belonging to Rochester cathedral attest, Kentish gavelkinders had successfully claimed the right to sell freely or to give their lands to whom they chose during their lifetime and after death their estates were equally divided among male heirs. Increasing activity in buying, selling and leasing land in the thirteenth and fourteenth centuries made Kentish society very different from what it might have been had anything at common law stopped this progressive partitioning. Its overall effect was to blur the old classification of customary tenants into the categories of freeman, gavelman, inlander (small-holder) and cotman (cottager) because by the thirteenth century the land market had put all the various tenures indiscriminately into men's hands. Thus freemen held of rich villeins and villeins held of villeins. The process of parcellation of lands did not go to ridiculous lengths because it was often more practical for one person to buy up shares of the co-heirs to keep an agricultural unit viable, thus enabling others to seek fortunes in other forms of activity.

The relative prosperity and freedom of the Kentish gavelkinder can be illustrated in respect of labour services. These were usually light in Kent, so as to bear almost no comparison to the regular week-work on the lord's demesne that was exacted in other parts of England. This meant that the Kentish husbandman could devote more attention to the care and improvement of his own land (Witney 1988: 30). A small amount of ploughing, sowing and harrowing was due for each yoke (virgate or yardland) but throughout Kent by the thirteenth century the contribution of this *gavelerth* to demesne cultivation was a minor one, it being normally commuted to a money payment. A money payment called *wodegavel* was also then generally paid for the remission of the obligation to fetch fuel for the lord. Reaping services were more onerous, for the Kentish corn crops were unusually bountiful and there was consequently a great need for seasonal labour, but this too was being commuted by the early thirteenth century for a money payment and casual labourers were being hired from the congested districts of the Weald. Any manorial obligations that still existed were discharged by the gavelkinders by a multitude of private money arrangements; few, if any, gavelkinders performed work services in person.

A full explanation for the relative freedom and individualism that prevailed amongst the Kentish peasantry is not yet forthcoming. It is commonly accepted that the ameliorative conditions obtaining from the mid-twelfth century represent a substantial advantage to the peasant on his former tenure which at this earlier time was not dissimilar to that elsewhere in southern England. Resistance of the peasantry to the more onerous obligations introduced by Norman feudalism is noteworthy. The probability exists that peasant tenure in Kent was earlier affected by the development of agricultural production for market than elsewhere in England. The position of Kent on the main route between London and the Continent must have stimulated the circulation of money and hence the mobility of society itself. As Du Boulay has suggested: 'it may be that what distinguished Kent from the parts of England where customary tenures developed into servile villeinage was that the rich Kentish peasant was strong enough to reject the exercise of lordships which pushed down their fellows elsewhere' (Du Boulay 1966: 143). However, on the great monastic estates the peasant was as heavily burdened as those of Sussex and Surrey, and everywhere in Kent the cottars' services were heavy (Mate 1985: 55–67).

The effect of the circulation of money and relative freedom of the richer Kent peasant was reflected in land management. The knightly estates enfeoffed by the archbishop in 1070 in north-east Kent (which in numerous cases became country seats of Elizabethan and later gentry) emerge into clearer light in the early thirteenth century as intensively farmed properties with little fallow, rich marsh pastures, meadows, orchards and large gardens and with a farm staff consisting almost entirely of hired labourers working under the supervision of a sergeant. This organization goes far to explain the high productivity of Kent agriculture in the thirteenth and fourteenth centuries (See pp. 66–9).

The effects on the peasants' lands was equally significant. In Kent the assessment of rents and services was by yokes, which in the thirteenth century by a process of partible inheritance and alienation, was often fiscally fragmented into small fractions. Yokes were physical units combined into borghs comprising scattered hamlets. The fields of the tenantry were invariably held in several cultivation in large open fields as at Gillingham (i.e. cultivation not in common but individually according to choice). In some cases a farm holding comprised dispersed hedged and fenced parcels as at Wrotham (Baker 1963: 393–401, 413). Demesne fields were normally fenced off as a compact block and farmed as a separate unit quite independent of the peasants' lands. On the downland of east Kent, however, the demesne arable was thrown open to tenants after harvest (the 'open-time') when tenants collectively grazed animals on the stubble, presumably because small farmers could not make a living off the poor land without the dung from a common sheep fold. The tenants' lands in east Kent were not regularly intermingled in strips as in Midland England but consisted of blocks of small fields and patches of crops within larger field units, the consequence of partible inheritance and the free land market. 'The whole sense and atmosphere is one of individualism and private enterprise' (Du Boulay 1966: 134). In effect, the process of continual land division with the growth of population in the twelfth and thirteenth centuries was counterbalanced by the freedom with which Kentish men engaged to buy, sell, and lease their portions so that consolidation could take place. The effect of this process on the rural landscape was to create a dispersed pattern of small settlements of dwelling-houses and farmsteads and barns in the fields and lanes rather than concentrated in some central nucleated village, as in the East Midlands. The reforming of closes and buildings within existing fields is thus a feature of Kentish life and economy since the thirteenth century.

In the Kentish Weald the earliest colonists who began the woodland clearance of the dens (probably contemporary with those of the Sussex Low Weald in the eleventh and twelfth centuries) took up lands assessed into yokes on the model of the anciently tilled lands of Kent, such as in the estates belonging to the archbishop's manors of Allington and Lyminge. When woodland clearances became vigorous, Kentish lords parted with their rights to the timber for an annual money payment. The later tenants filling up the remaining spaces in the dens such as those infiltrating into the 'wooded and desert part of the diocese' in the Cranbrook area after *c*.1260 were known as forelanders and held small plots for a money rent (Witney 1976: 193).

Although there was a clear difference between Kent and Sussex with regard to peasant status, in that Sussex knew no gavelkind and villein servility on manorialized estates was general, Sussex was nevertheless a county with numbers of free tenants. These mostly existed as small men as a result of the assarting of woodland or the reclamation of marsh in the thirteenth and fourteenth centuries. These new holdings held in free tenure represented measures taken by landowners to attract new settlers to difficult areas, a practice commonplace in medieval western Europe. Consequently, free tenures multiplied in the extensive wooded and heathy areas which survived into the last great period of land settlement, notably in the Sussex High Weald. This has left its own individual mark on the landscape in the chequer-board of minute, irregular fields bounded by strips of wood (shaws) or thick hedges and dispersed farmsteads interconnected with a myriad of minor lanes.

By contrast, hereditary servile status with onerous obligations was the lot of the bulk of the Sussex peasantry, especially in the districts of central and west Sussex dominated by large landed estates. There was a recognizable division in the thirteenth century between peasants with holdings of twelve to fifteen acres (half yardlanders) or more and those with smaller holdings. The former corresponded to the continental *laboureur* and without necessarily being affluent their holdings could support a family. The smallholding cottars had to reinforce their incomes with work for wages on the lord's demesne or on land of the bigger peasant holdings. On the Fitzalan estates of the thirteenth century by far the heaviest labour services were at Bourne on the West Sussex Coastal Plain where cottars worked 'from Michaelmas to Lammas . . . every second day except Saturday and feast days and the three festival weeks . . . and from Lammas to Michaelmas, so long as harvest lasts, every day except Saturdays and feast days' (Clough 1969: xxi). The custom whereby tenants ploughed, hoed and harvested a given acreage was also general and tenants were required to give so many days' work at harvest and haymaking. Villeins were also required to travel frequently on the lord's business. At Prinsted they had to expect to travel a day's journey in any direction; Donhurst tenants went frequently to London, but were paid expenses beyond Guildford. At West Dean tenants used packhorses on the lord's business but at North Stoke near Arundel bondmen carted food to Arundel castle and fetched seed corn by cart as far away as East Dean. By the thirteenth century commutation of many of these heavily burdened dues and services was being made for cash. Heavy labour services were also performed on the great ecclesiastical and lay estates on the Coastal Plain near Chichester, such as the archbishop's manor of Pagham, the Bishop of Chichester's estate of Selsey and the royal manor of Bosham. Such large estates on fertile land were not so much open-field communities on the Midland model as federated grain factories with relatively few virgaters (and hence no large nucleated settlements or open-field systems) and an unusually large proportion of cottagers, dispersed in hamlets, who were dependent labourers. The assured existence of plots of land cultivated, rather like allotments by families in their own fashion seems to have made peasants more willing to contribute to the running of these big estates.

In Surrey, too, hereditary servile status was normal. An interesting feature of early Surrey society is the large number of slaves (*servi*) recorded in Domesday Book. It is possible to envisage a process by which slaves were being placed on outlying woodland swine pastures for the task of clearing woodland

and cultivating demesnes before the practice of encouraging freeholders to do the same work began. On this reckoning a large number of those who were ultimately absorbed into the general body of the Surrey unfree tenants must have been descendants of Anglo-Saxon slaves. Although these villeins holding land of virgates cleared from the forest at an early date, as also in Sussex, were tenurially disadvantaged in comparison with Kent, landlords rapidly relinquished the active cultivation of wealden demesnes in the later thirteenth century so that local peasants could take up leases of parcels of demesne land in addition to that of their own holdings. Overall, the tenurial conditions in Surrey were very variable and represent a picture of free tenure due to assarting alongside the heavy villein services of more ancient origin on highly organized estates. That these two sets of conditions could exist within a few miles of each other, resulting from the juxtaposition of tenants of very different juridical status and economic position, added considerably to the tensions of the countryside in the later Middle Ages and contributed to the early enclosure of common fields.

These variations and anomalies in peasant status in Sussex and Surrey prepare us for variants of open-field agriculture which are unorthodox in terms of the 'Midland model' prevailing, say, in Northamptonshire or Leicestershire. Gray in 1915 found evidence of open-field farming confined to the peripheral areas of south-east England, on the Coastal Plain, downland and scarp-foot zone of Sussex and along the corresponding edges of the North Downs in Surrey. In the wealden portions of the two counties he concluded that fields had been in severalty from the first ploughing. Subsequent enquiry has shown that open-fields were ubiquitous in the inner Weald on the Lower Greensand outcrops of Surrey and Sussex, though these tended to be small and enclosed in the fifteenth and sixteenth centuries. Nor was the Weald Clay area proper entirely without open-fields, for in the Adur Basin, on mid- or late-Saxon colonized woodland, similarly early enclosed open-field systems existed at Shermanbury and Twineham, and possibly at Cuckfield and Wivelsfield (Brandon 1974: 122–3). Common fields extended onto the down crest at Harting and other examples are known at Upper Beeding and Saddlescombe, but in general in Sussex the downland sheep pastures had an overriding importance. For this reason prominent flights of medieval lynchets cut into the scarps are not typically representative of the South East, as for example they are of 'Chalk' Wiltshire.

The most important feature of the downland settlement was the numerous hamlets, as many as four or more to a parish, each with their own self-contained systems of open-fields divided among several manors and surrounding a 'head' settlement, or nucleated village. In the case of the parish of Ringmer near Lewes, four separately differentiated open-field systems existed at each of its anciently settled hamlets of Ashton, Middleham, Norlington and Wellingham, though not at Ringmer itself, a 'head' settlement which thus appears to have had a later origin than its dependent hamlets. Somewhat similarly, the parish of West

Firle comprised three sets of open fields in hamlets at Charleston, Compton and Heighton St Clair, now reduced to single farms; while many villagers in Firle itself, the sole nucleated settlement, had strips of land in the adjoining hamlet systems. Many further examples of this type of organization could be quoted from the Sussex downland. It is difficult to resist the conclusion that the multiplicity of field systems functioning as self-contained local units interspersed between large nucleated villages represents the bones of an agrarian structure which combines the smaller settlements of the Romano-Britons with those of infiltrating South Saxons.

A man's holding, termed a virgate or yardland in west Sussex was called a wist in the eastern part of the county. Its size was a great deal less than in many other parts of England, suggestive both of a relatively dense population, the relative fertility of the soil and of the importance of sheep grazing, and also the feasibility of more intensive cropping than that of the standard three-course rotation. At Alciston, East Blatchington and some other manors in east Sussex the wist was as small as ten customary acres or even less, the average being about 12–14 statute acres. The west Sussex virgate was no larger. Each virgate was dispersed in strips over a considerable number of furlongs grouped together for the purpose of cultivation into three 'seasons' and divided by markstakes or sarsen stones. The turn-wrest plough laid land flat on dry soils in east Sussex but heavier soils of the Coastal Plain and the scarp-foot 'maam' were ploughed in ridge and furrow. At Tangmere and Eartham the standard size of a strip was about half a tenantry acre, called a *hilf*, a variant of half. This *hilf* was usually ploughed in at least two ridges called stitches with a water furrow dividing. Scraps of common field persisted on the maam soils into the eighteenth century or even later and such stitches and water-furrows are still imprinted on the landscape, as at Plumpton in east Sussex and at Steyning.

The anatomy of Sussex and Surrey open-fields can best be studied by means of a case-study, that of Alciston in east Sussex for which an almost unbroken sequence of bailiff's accounts and detailed surveys enable an unusually complete reconstruction of their organization and layout. In addition to Alciston the subsidiary hamlet of Tilton had separate open-field systems. The land in villeinage at Alciston lay entirely in dispersed strips in open-field and was grouped for cultivation purposes into three 'seasons' and subdivided into 32 furlongs and over 400 separate parcels. For each wist of land 30 sheep could be kept on the tenantry down and 3 cattle on the common. The Battle Abbey demesne lay in severalty (except for a small portion of former common-field land which could not be let after the Black Death), on the rich and tractable maam soil and constituted a compact block considerably larger than the combined area of the peasants' fields. This was managed as an intensively worked 'grain factory' with fallow reduced in favour of the nitrifying properties of legume husbandry. A group of intermittently cultivated fields on the northern part of the manor lay on the Gault and

Upper Greensand formations where fields were generally under pasture but periodically broken up and sown to improve the sward. It is clear that Gray's categorization of Alciston as a 'three-field' manor based on its cropping acres is highly misleading for such a flexible and complex farming system which became even more unorthodox during the late Middle Ages (Fig. 3.1, p. 105) (Brandon 1962: 60–72).

Agricultural Techniques and Productivity

Until recently medieval farmers were scarcely thought of as profit maximizers or even as rational decision makers. Agriculture within feudalism was seen as technologically stagnant and constraints on economic growth determined by Malthusian demographic forces. There was little room in this view for the liberalizing effects of the market, the cash nexus and its effect on the adoption of crop rotations, on regional specialization and the disappearance of serfdom in the most advanced areas of agrarian development. More or less uniform systems of husbandry were assumed to exist over fourteenth-century England so that the Hampshire estates of the bishops of Winchester could be deemed representative of the whole of English farming (Postan 1972; Titow 1972).

There is now a more flexible view of medieval society and an increased awareness of its local and regional complexity and achievements. Studies emphasizing the regional diversity of fourteenth-century English economic life have begun to identify urban-agrarian complexes loosening feudal bonds similar to those in the progressive parts of continental Europe. Such advanced and dynamic regions had higher population densities than most other parts of England and above average urbanization ratios. Land was used more intensively than in other parts but with yields equal, if not higher, to those of less populous areas. Hampshire is not England, just as England is not the world (Hallam 1981: 11).

By the end of the thirteenth century the Coastal Fringe of the South East affords clear evidence of advanced farming techniques which we were accustomed to associate only with profit-minded improvers of the sixteenth and later centuries, such as convertible husbandry, and a market-orientated agriculture flexibly treating land as arable or grass according to market demand and other factors such as seasonal or secular changes in weather. Another early innovation was the suppression of fallow in favour of rotations involving pulses used mainly for fodder four centuries and more before their adoption in the Norfolk Four Course (Brandon 1971d: 113–34).

Yet such is the diversity of soil quality in the South East that agricultural productivity ranged from the exceptionally high to the exceptionally low. Ever since man took over the forested Weald for agriculture few parts of Europe have been less rewarding to the farmer than its most tenacious clays. The soil's intractability, its deficiencies in plant nutrients, the badness of the roads for much of the year and the long distance farmers were obliged to go to market made fields expensive to prepare for corn and other crops. So severely limited were farming possibilities in the Weald and on the hungry sands of the Lower Greensand that general arable husbandry failed to reach the modest levels of the low-productivity agriculture that the bishops of Winchester administered. By the end of the thirteenth century we see unmistakeable signs that the wealden peasant and his lord were using minimum inputs on semi-derelict land and achieving a subsistence income and lifestyle not tolerated elsewhere, and supportable only with income supplements from forestry or off the land, e.g. in handicrafts, which with the exception of brief interludes of artificially high corn and meat prices, has been characteristic of the wealden economy ever since.

'We may feel certain', wrote Thirsk, 'that in some regions the conditions of life at the beginning of the sixteenth century were an ancient story'. The South East is one such region. We can read its regional specializations far back into the past, so pursuing the problems of farming regions to more distant origins than is normally possible elsewhere in England. We can also trace an agricultural technology that far from being static in the thirteenth and fourteenth centuries was undergoing advancement in the form of expanding legume husbandry, more livestock (hence more dung for the fields), flexible crop rotations and thicker sowings to raise a surplus for sale. Yet it is an illusion to think that we can describe the economy of the fourteenth-century South East when so much of the necessary evidence of peasant farming is not at our disposal. It should be noted, however, that with the high stocking level of the common sheep fold, the standard device by which the peasants collectively sustained the fertility of their lands on the chalk soils, we should not automatically expect the villagers' grain output per acre to be much lower than that of a well-managed demesne worked by wage labour.

Hitherto it has been thought that English agriculture lagged behind that of the Low Countries until the so-called Agrarian Revolution of the seventeenth and eighteenth centuries. It is now clear that in certain restricted localities of south-east England, East Anglia and elsewhere, agricultural methods were well abreast of the best continental practice. The differences in soil patterns and qualities within the South East had as early as the thirteenth century given rise to regional and local comparative cost advantages leading to some degree of specialization. In much of medieval England the potential regional advantages remained comparatively unexploited since the costs of transportation over land, particularly the transport of grain in bulk, were generally too high to permit specialization in agricultural production. The key to the precocious development of the 'advanced' districts of the South East was accessibility to waterway and sea as much as to the soil and climatic advantages. The role of

Kent in the development of the London food market in medieval times has still to be investigated. But the close connection between Faversham and London in the seaborne grain trade from as early as the thirteenth century suggests that it was a London market in embryo which even then so effectively offered scope for early regional specialization in north-east Kent, which in the sixteenth century was described as 'a vast granary for the city's service' (Fisher 1934: 46–54). Coastal Sussex, another 'early developer' probably also greatly gained from accessibility to the sea.

Conversely in the Weald, fields were extremely susceptible to the effects of weather. Lenten crops such as legumes were vulnerable to spring droughts and unseasonable cold on the clays. A wet summer prevented the indispensable ploughing and marling of the fallow and two successive wet seasons were extremely deleterious, putting the land 'out of season' for several years following. Clearly, agricultural possibilities were severely limited. On the poorer clays around Newdigate, Rusper and Nuthurst on the Surrey–Sussex border, on the East Sussex Low Weald between Wivelsfield and Lewes and on similar land in the Kent Weald the mode of husbandry was basically unvaried for centuries as it did not admit of improvements associated with the introduction of new crops and more flexible rotations on the lighter and more fertile soils.

Gervase Markham aptly observed in 1625 of the Weald that 'It is throughout (except in very few places adjoining to brooks or rivers) of a very barren nature and unapt for either pasture or tillage until that it be holpen by some manner of comfort, as dung, marl, fresh earth, fodder, ashes or such other refreshings' (Markham 1636: 2; 1638: 31–5). This was as true of medieval times as in the seventeenth century, the principal form of soil improvement being the application of marl. Marl, a calcareous clay, was dug from bell-pits in suitable horizons in the Weald, winched up in buckets and transported to fields to be liberally spread and ploughed in to enrich the soil, one application being regarded as effective for 15 to 20 years. Almost every field in the Weald is dimpled by marlpits around its edge.

In the late thirteenth and early fourteenth centuries extensive applications of marl were made in the Weald. Some thirteenth-century landlords aimed to marl their entire demesnes regularly. Thus all 50 acres of the Sapperton arable near Heathfield were assessed as marled land and 80 acres of the 120 had been treated at Buckhurst on poor land bordering Ashdown Forest by 1271. At Chalvington, near Lewes, where the entire arable was also regularly dressed on a rotational basis (dry summer weather permitting) 11½ acres were dressed in 1347 by seven men and six boys, mainly hired labourers from the High Weald, work which lasted eight weeks and cost 7s per acre. By this date, however, there are indications that landlords were finding the direct exploitation of their wealden demesnes unprofitable by comparison with the leasing of parcels in life tenancies to land-hungry peasants of modest means, a further suggestion of increasing population. The Earl of Arundel was leasing out parts of his demesne at Cuckfield and Keymer in the Low Weald in 1343–4. Again the transactions centred upon the indispensable marling of land. Here leases were generally for twelve years and relate to small parcels of a few acres each lying within the larger field units of the former demesne. In many cases the lessee was required to hedge his parcel, which draws attention to the fact that residual small fields do not necessarily imply the enclosure of common fields. Those who took up land as *permarliaverit* were to receive an additional parcel of land by way of recompense for the cost of marling; others took up land on the basis of 'half marling' (*pro medietate marliando*) in which case the earl presumably paid the remaining expenses (H. Warne, Pers. Comm.).

The normal method of cultivation in the medieval Weald was by some form of convertible husbandry. This was devised for soils which have never been valued very highly and except on specially treated fields the cultivated ground quickly becomes foul and exhausted and requires periods of rest. The classic account of convertible husbandry is Bishop's study of crop rotation at the Abbey of Westminster's Kentish manor of Westerham between 1297 and 1350 (Bishop, T.A.M. 1938). This gives a fascinating view of farming activities over a cleared area expanding from rather more than five hundred acres *c.*1300 to more than seven hundred acres by the middle of the fourteenth century, partly at the expense of Westerham park. Bishop's most important conclusion was that certain fields after some years of continuous cultivation were wholly abandoned for long periods and recorded as *frisc* (uncultivated) in the grange accounts. Thus there was no distinction between arable and grassland, and agriculture at Westerham was revealed 'as a system of convertible husbandry under which a relatively small, and fluctuating and on the whole declining area of cultivation shifted within the limits of a relatively large and expanding cleared area'. This Bishop designated the *infield* in distinction to the more sporadically cultivated *outfield* (expanding from some 400 to 600 acres). Although infield land was mostly fallowed every third year this was not inflexible since a number of cases of 'inhoking' – partially sowing fallow with spring crops – occurred. On outfields cropping was irregular but they were not 'the scheme of a merely extensive and perfunctory cultivation but formed with their restorative periods under grass an integral part of a general scheme of Westerham agriculture'. Significantly, legume cultivation steadily grew in importance at this time as was characteristic of most southern manors in the fourteenth century.

Convertible husbandry of the Westerham type with its irregular and heterogeneous rotations and tendency for nearly every field to revert at frequent intervals and for varying periods to grass was part of the agricultural routine of most southern manors on wealden clays and sands. It was also normal on all other soils which were particularly susceptible to weather, such as the marshlands and Weald as well as the Gault Clay formation in the scarp-foot zone. Its basic principle was to take the plough around the fields in turn, the frequency and regularity depending upon physical factors such as weather and soil quality and also on access to markets and general economic conditions. Thus standard medieval farming techniques at Westerham and at places such as Barnhorne in the Pevensey Levels (Brandon 1971d: 69–93) anticipate by more than three centuries the principles enumerated by Gervase Markham and other seventeenth-century writers for the Weald of Kent.

If the norm of medieval agricultural efficiency was a two-course rotation of crops, leaving half of the farmland fallow in any given year, it is significant that the Weald failed to reach even this modest degree of agricultural development. For example, on the lean sandy soils at Wotton near Dorking, only 80 arable acres were cultivated out of 200 in 1280, and only 40 in 1300. Many similar examples of low intensity arable cultivation exist. Even allowing for fraudulent understatement in *inquisitiones post mortem* most of medieval Surrey appears to have been significantly under-used land.

The primary basis of the prosperity of the Coastal Fringe was its sheep-and-corn farming. The soils are diverse but they nevertheless shared common properties advantageous for arable husbandry in an era when farming was critically dependent on weather conditions. Moreover cereal crops in the Isle of Thanet and in the Manhood peninsula ripened earlier than any in England. Although coastal north-east Kent and coastal south-west Sussex comprised the two most important large-scale cereal-growing districts the labour supply of the two parts had dissimilarities. In Sussex thirteenth-century cereal farming was largely dependent upon the classical manor of Vinogradoff and Seebohm with its huge demesne farm (held in severalty) and large body of servile cultivators, especially near-landless cottars, who were exceptionally important in the big estates of the Chichester district. Thus Apuldram, a Benedictine estate of Battle Abbey in 1300 had 500 statute acres of demesne, worked largely by the services of nine 'major' cottars (holding four acres each), six minor cottars and ten virgate holders (with 8–24 customary acres). At the huge arable manor of Westbourne no less than 90 cottars, in addition to 192 customaries contributed to the running of the estate. In the fourteenth century commutation of work services became general and a regular staff of wage labourers was engaged. But on Kent estates tenants' services were light and wage labourers had made an appearance before the mid-thirteenth century. Sheep-and-corn-farming, developed to a high degree, was exceptionally labour intensive and in both districts the need for large numbers of seasonal harvesters was met by hiring migratory labourers from the High Weald. In east Sussex manors near Eastbourne, for example, reapers from the overcrowded assarted districts ten to fifteen miles away were normally employed for about five weeks. At Alciston and Lullington alone, Battle Abbey gave seasonal employment to 50–60 hired labourers from Framfield, Heathfield, Waldron and Warbleton (Brandon 1971b: 118).

Both north Kent and coastal Sussex were among the leading legume producers of medieval England. From the earliest extant ministers' accounts of 1270–80 they emerge as major producers to the extent of 25–30 per cent of the total sowings. Legumes were normally sown at the expense of fallow. This 'bean husbandry' was an early development in parts of Italy and is traceable in Flanders in the fourteenth century. It is likely to have been general in east Kent from at least the end of the thirteenth century, and probably earlier, and its ancient persistence in coastal Sussex has already been noted (p.22). The virtual elimination of fallowing in medieval England was first recognized in 1915 when attention was drawn to the evidence of continuous cultivation on the demesnes of Giles de Badlesmere in north-east Kent recorded on the extents attached to the *inquisitiones post mortem* of 1338 (Gray 1915: 301–2). These specifically state that all the acres in the demesne could be sown yearly – *possunt seminari quolibet anno* – and the high valuation of 12d per acre was general. Such annual tillage of the entire demesne has since proven not to be exceptional in east Kent. In each case the intensive cultivation is associated with exceptionally high valuations per acre. Similar evidence exists for the Sussex Coastal Plain (Fig. 2.4) (Brandon 1971d: 126).

Campbell's major study of medieval arable productivity now makes it more possible to place these 'islands' of intensive arable in a national context. In 1915 Gray was of the opinion that annual tillage was seldom to be met with outside Kent. Campbell has demonstrated, however, that in eastern Norfolk medieval demesne agriculture was as advanced as that of the most progressive Kentish estates, if not more so, by the last quarter of the thirteenth century (Campbell, B.M.S. 1983(a), 1983(b), 1988).

In Kent the flexibility of cropping created local and even regional differences in production. Smith, using account rolls of Canterbury Cathedral Priory for 1291 demonstrated the specialized production of barley (presumably for malting) in the Coastal Fringe of north-east Kent, a development which paralleled that in medieval Norfolk (Smith 1963: 147–60). Fertility was maintained from the use of nitrogenous legumes, by marling, but especially via the sheepfold. This latter provided a means of consolidating the light chalk soils which would not otherwise have been suitable for intensive tillage, and as a method of dunging it was unsurpassed for its cheapness and efficiency. The adaptability of the device must have contributed to the early development of flexible rotations on ephemeral parcels of land. The sheepfold was properly regarded as the very basis of successful corn-growing and manorial customals testify to its importance by specifying the regulations to be observed in its operation.

A high level of productivity by medieval standards was reached. Until recently this has been obscured by concentration on ratios of seed to grain harvested which did not give due importance to the thicker sowing rates adopted. In terms of net yields per acre the crops were bountiful, exceeding the 11 bushels of wheat per acre which the anonymous author of *Hosebondrie* deemed a proper return and which so few demenses of the bishops of Winchester attained. The same superiority was reached in barley and oats (Brandon 1972: 414–19).

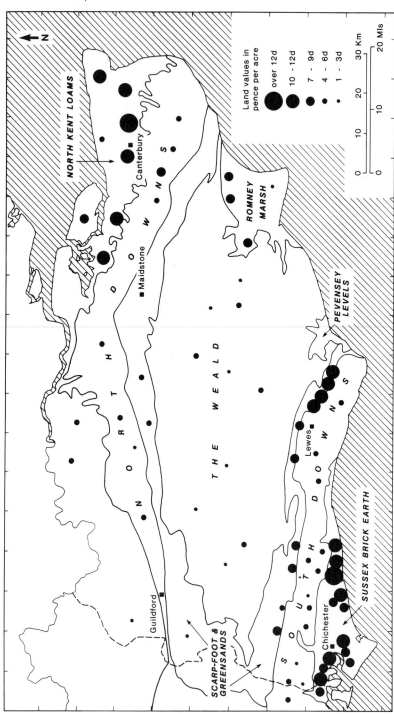

Figure 2.4 Land valuations: the evidence from the inquisitiones post mortem.

A lively debate on medieval productivity is now developing. Theoretically, nitrogen is the principal governing factor in soil fertility and the implications are that in broad terms the higher productivity of Kent and Sussex estates accrued from superior nutrient supplies derived from legume husbandry. The physical condition of the soil was also improved by the addition of nitrogen and care in weeding. It is probable too, that organic matter in the topsoil increased with more intensive husbandry. There is also the possibility that the comparative incidence of cereal disease was lower under legume husbandry than under the normal fallow system; for long-continued experiments at Rothamsted have shown that fallow is less effective than break-crops like legumes in the reduction of disease transmitted by cereals. Further improvement of physical soil properties would have resulted from the heavy marling (a practice largely absent on the Bishop of Winchester's estates) which quite apart from its effect in counteracting acidity would have had a beneficial effect on tilth. If these advantages of legume husbandry are broadly correct one can postulate a cycle of more fodder (legumes) leading to more livestock which in turn produced more manure and hence higher yields. The significance of this improvement of crop husbandry on the arable productivity of medieval England has barely yet been recognized.

The Benedictine institutions of Battle Abbey, Christ Church Priory, and St Augustine's Priory became prominent as arable farmers par excellence. On such church estates in the thirteenth and early fourteenth centuries can be traced the hallmarks of High Farming – rising production, big capital investment, technical improvement, flexible rotations. Among the most famous of high farming churchmen was Prior Eastry of Christ Church who acquired rented property, made improvements to farm buildings, and invested heavily in water- and windmills, land drainage, marsh reclamation and soil improvement (Smith 1943). With their continuity of administration over so long a period, the leading Church institutions were a permanent element in the medieval countryside. In the present landscape some of the buildings erected to store the expanding produce still exist, notably in north-east Kent, where huge aisled barns reflect the exceptional productivity of landed estates in that district such as the barn of 210 feet long at Frindsbury on a demesne of St Andrews, Rochester, with its thirteen bays and construction details suggesting a building of *c.*1300. Littlebourne (172 feet) and Godmersham Court Lodge barn on a demesne of Christ Church Priory are also magnificent. Until recently gigantic barns existed at Chislet Court and Lenham on former demesnes of St Augustine's (Rigold 1966: 1–30). In Sussex a surviving barn, 170 feet long and of striking beauty, is on a former demesne of Battle Abbey at Alciston. Here the remarkably complete complex of medieval buildings, including the fourteenth-century manor house with its unique stone arches, is a fitting record of the entrepreneurial efficiency and foresight which established a farming regime unmatched generally in England until 400 years later (Mason 1978a: 59–62).

Deer Parks, Forests and Chases

Few parts of medieval Europe reveal a greater reverence of woodland for hunting than that bestowed on the great tract of the Weald and its wooded borders. Appropriately, the oldest English book on hunting, *The Master of Game*, was translated from Gaston de Foix's *La Chasse*, by the second Duke of York *c.*1403–4 at Pevensey. Hunting as practised by the nobility and gentry had then become an elaborately organized affair which had little connection with modern equitation or the jumping and fast galloping now associated with fox hunting. While hunters ate a hearty breakfast and arrayed themselves in the richest apparel, grooms prepared their mounts. Meanwhile the *valet de limiers*, the kennel man, led out his *limiers* on a leash and silently tracked down the deer, by which time the beasts had settled after their night's roaming. On his return the chase began to the accompaniment of a succession of different airs on horns, recording each episode of the hunt, such as 'hounds cast', 'several deer sighted', 'hounds running well', 'hunted stag', 'he has crossed the stream', right up to the climax of the kill when the horns sounded *les honneurs*, and the three long notes for the withdrawal (Bise 1978).

Parks of some kind had existed before the Norman Conquest but essentially parks owe their origin to Norman deer husbandry to provide the luxury of venison at table. Their number increased rapidly with the late twelfth-century introduction of fallow deer from the continent. This species was easier to keep within a park pale than the wilder native red and roe deer (Robinson 1987: 292). After the legal disafforestation of King John the possession of parks became a status symbol and their ownership moved downwards in society from the king and the great magnates, both lay and ecclesiastical, to the knights and other lesser gentry. A pre-requisite for enclosing deer or park enlargement was a licence from the Crown. The granting of such licences rose to a peak in the late thirteenth century but continued as a trickle into the late Middle Ages and even into the first half of the sixteenth century, when the general trend was for disparking for agricultural use (Cantor 1982: 77–8). On the basis of the actual park records and that of licences (not all of which may have been executed) the number of parks in early fourteenth-century Kent, Surrey and Sussex was approximately 380. The leading laity and ecclesiastics then each possessed a number of parks. The Earl of Arundel possessed twelve parks in Sussex alone and owned a number in Surrey. The Archbishop of Canterbury possessed eighteen parks in Kent and Sussex and each of his principal residences in Sussex – Mayfield, South Malling and Slindon – had their local parks. The Bishop of Chichester, by no means the wealthiest of medieval prelates, nevertheless had seven parks. Indeed, not to possess a park was a visible sign that one was not a gentleman and thus even the poorer of the knightly families each possessed a small park.

Medieval imparkment was nominally of 'waste' which was not under cultivation. We must not, however, fall into the error of assuming that all imparked land was protected from the plough. During the period of intense pressure of population on land in the half century before the Black Death, some parkland had to be brought under cultivation, notably by the monks of Westminster at Westerham, and park enlargement invariably brought semi-derelict farmland within the perimeter of the park. Nevertheless, many medieval parks, or substantial parts of them, have survived as relatively unmodified plant habitats for several hundreds of years during which time human interference has successively re-shaped the landscape outside. For this reason a number of medieval parks contain mixed woodland and plant species which are prime examples of relict woodland and their associated lichen flora is the richest in the region. Outstanding fragments of this old woodland ecology are to be found in Eridge Old Park near Tunbridge Wells, in Heathfield and Ashburnham parks and also in Forests such as St Leonard's, Balcombe and Dallington (Rose, Pers. Comm.).

Formidable fences were necessary around parks to retain deer. The typical fence took the form of a wide ditch dug inside a bank raised with the soil from the ditch and surmounted by a hedge or a paling fence. These earthworks have commonly survived. The optimum shape of a deer park was circular giving the maximum internal area for the minimum length of fence. Most medieval parks did have a roughly circular or oval outline and consequently such a space devoid of old farm buildings and other settlement can often be regarded as *prima facie* evidence of the possible site of a medieval deer park. The size of parks varied substantially. Areas as small as 25 acres would have housed up to 40 fallow deer. The average-sized park was about 100–150 acres. Parks were impaled in Sussex in part by customary tenants who owed regular week work. To fence his two miles of boundary fence around Aldingbourne Park, the Bishop of Chichester drew on customary tenants living up to twenty miles away, though probably the most distant of them commuted their obligation for a money payment (Peckham 1925: 39–41). The archbishop not only made his tenants 'in the wood' enclose his parks but required them to assist with the hunting for 6–12 days annually. He so valued sparrow-hawks' nests (valued at 40s each, about twenty times a labourer's weekly wage) that tenants were expected to guard them from theft and damage at ½d per season (Redwood and Wilson 1958: 36).

Deer were the most important livestock in parks. As they are primarily woodland animals the most successful deer enclosures were well wooded but as they are also grass feeders many parks comprised 'wood pastures' in Oliver Rackham's phrase, consisting of trees and pasture intermixed. Others were 'compartmental parks' where glades or 'laundes' bordered coppices enclosed against deer when the shoots were young. Domestic animals were consistently agisted in parks during summer, though never in the 'fence' period, i.e. usually the period of one month at midsummer following the fawning season. Sheep and goats were commonly excluded from parks (and from forests and chases) because their grazing habits interfered with the keeping of deer. The ancient common right of pannage for swine continued in parks, notably in Kent, where the parks occupied all other parts of former dens. Rabbits, introduced from the continent in the early thirteenth century were also denizens of parks. These were encouraged to breed in artificial warrens (*coningerths*) in which pillow-shaped mounds were erected within a fenced-off enclosure. At Petworth 'mending palings around la conyghere' and the repair of the gates into the warren were regular fourteenth-century payments and young trees in the park were coated with tar to prevent them being nibbled by rabbits (Robinson 1987: 192). Fishponds were commonly constructed in parks, many of which became landscaped lakes. Building timber, bracken (for litter) and wood fuel were important secondary products of the deer park. Timber production has had a major effect on tree shapes for the trees were commonly standing trees pollarded successively for ship's timber and bearing great spreading crowns for purposes of shape and pannage (Bise 1978).

Hunting grounds comprised chases and forests. A chase was thickly-wooded and well-hedged countryside over which a magnate had freedom to hunt beasts of the chase normally reserved for the king. Some of the finest hunting ground in the region was afforded by the scantily populated Vale of Holmesdale and the adjoining North Downs between the rivers Mole and Medway, where *c*.1200 the game comprised such wood-loving creatures as fox, hare, partridge, pheasant and the woodland cat (*felix sylvestris*), as well as native deer (Brandon 1978: 13). The Bishop of Chichester's deer chase extended over the holdings of his tenants in Henfield, Cowfold, Warninglid, Albourne and Wyndham (Peckham, 1925: 124). Further east on the Weald Clay, were extensive areas of commons and clearings which were highly prized chases, including those of Freckbergh, Shortfrith and Cleres (Brandon 1974: 166) and which must have militated against tenants' farming. Forests lay on the exposed high wealden ridges and comprised in the early thirteenth century some 50,000 acres, about one-tenth of the whole area of the Weald. When this huge acreage, equivalent to about 250 deer parks is added to land imparked it answers Rackham's question as to why the Weald had only a little above the average density of parks (Rackham 1986: 123). St Leonard's amounted to 7,000 acres in 1326, excluding some 9,000 acres in the parks of Bewbush and Sedgwick. In the adjoining rape of Pevensey were other forests, the largest being Ashdown, which may have extended over 20,000 acres; Waterdown, including Rotherfield (Eridge) Park, and the Forest of Walderne, each about 4,000 acres. In the rape of Hastings, Dallington included about 2,000 acres of which half had been assarted by 1334 and the smaller Worth Forest in Brightling. In Kent were the forests of Tonbridge and Frith (Fig. 2.5).

The core of Ashdown Forest was the area specifically reserved for harbouring deer, described as *in defenso*. Into this part centred on the lodges, the king took agistment cattle and had the right to the first lay of mast, the residue being available to commoners after Martinmas (November 1). The

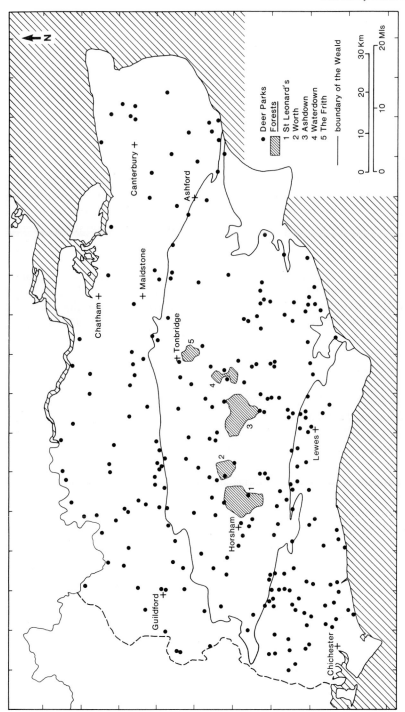

Figure 2.5 Deer parks and forests.

73

commonable part of the forest, mostly within the pale of the forest lay on ridges surrounding the central core. Commoners grazed swine except during the fence period, when the forest was reserved for deer; and were entitled to fern, heath and broom for fuel. The pasture could be improved by burning provided that no damage was done to trees. Considering the poor pasture afforded by Ashdown Forest it was well stocked in the thirteenth century. Apart from more than 100 head of deer, about 2,000 agistment cattle were depastured annually. Additionally, peasants fattened some 2,000–3,000 swine. This relatively heavy depasturing, together with the practice of burning the herbage to improve the quality of the grass, had a deleterious effect on vegetation. The virtual extinction of a cover of oak wood is suggested by the cessation of *pannage ad glandes* (corn mast) by the late fifteenth century. At this time the forest was described as barren heath with beech trees and some covert and very little underwood. A further practice severely limiting the regeneration of trees was the custom of letting part of the forest as rabbit warren. A similar transition from open woodland to heath was also an occurrence on the high ridges to the east. The deforestation of the Forest Ridge of the High Weald thus appears to have been largely completed before the heedless cutting-down for the iron industry in the sixteenth century utterly impoverished the commonlands (Brandon 1969: 147, 150; 1974: 156).

The Medieval Coastline

Early thirteenth-century ships' captains sailing along the south coast passed by a long shoreline which bore little or no resemblance to its present configuration, so dramatic were the changes of the later Middle Ages. Instead of the existing shoreline smoothed and worn back by the actions of tides, waves and winds into a long shallow inward curve and with river estuaries deflected eastwards by shingle bars, the medieval sailor steered between a succession of far-out headlands, wide embayments and open estuaries, some being shelters against adverse winds rather than harbours proper. Longshore drifting and the reclamation of marshes has been responsible for the withdrawal of the sea from the old ports of New Romney, Lympne, Hythe, Sandwich and Northeye. Coastal erosion has virtually extinguished numerous once major seaports and naval bases, including Old Winchelsea, Seaford, Shoreham and the port of St Richard (an outport of Chichester), familiar enough to twelfth-century mariners to be depicted on a map of the British Isles commissioned of Arab cartographers by the Norman king of Sicily. For all its inaccuracies, this map vividly shows the intricate and deeply-embayed shoreline before the medieval agriculturist and engineer, and natural causes, were to re-shape the sea bays and bare marshes into richly diversified farmland and domestic building (Plate 2.6) (Cunliffe 1980: 37–55; Brookfield 1952: 153–63). To round off this picture of great change, Waghenaer's sea chart of 1586 gives a good impression of the configuration of the Channel coast after the devastating late medieval storm floods had taken their toll of ports and low-lying marshland (Plate 2.7).

The South East can thus be considered to have several coastlines: a present-day one, and those of the past. The thirteenth-century coastline bordering Romney Marsh is traceable inland by the old cliffline bordering an upland plateau, whereas the existing coastline is fortified for the greater part of its length by a massive sea-wall. Westwards, the thirteenth-century shoreline of the Adur estuary is marked by a wave-cut edge of raised beaches marking still earlier shorelines, as at the Sussex Pad Inn, North Lancing. Even on the coastal plain of Sussex the old harbours, creeks and estuaries and their connecting causeways are still visible on the ground by their low, sinuous, banks of sand and shingle. Something of the early character of the eleventh-century shoreline is also evident from the mention of salterns in Domesday. These are clearly associated with areas of coastal alluvium which must have then been flooded (Darby and Campbell 1962: 456).

An important factor in the evolution of the coastline has been the relative level of land to sea. The general course of this fluctuating relationship is not in doubt. The Romano-Saxon land surface in the North Sea basin and the English Channel is estimated to be 5.06 ft above the then high spring tide mark. Throughout the Saxon period the land surface was gradually subsiding. Between AD 900 and 1000 the high spring tides started to overflow the lower parts of the land surface but natural conditions were still favourable to the reclamation of marshland until the early thirteenth century when the overflow of high tides had reached such a frequency and extent that the first sea and river embankments were erected to exclude it. The marsh margin has subsequently shifted in historical times according to changes in sea-level, climate, and the success or failure of man's attempts at drainage. The fall in the relative level of the sea, particularly marked between the mid-thirteenth and the sixteenth centuries, combined with the increased storminess in this period, led to the overwhelming of most of the embankments erected earlier and the long-continued submergence of former agricultural land on an extensive scale (Salzman 1910: 32–60).

Accelerating such natural processes has been the reclamation by man of the tidal marshes in estuaries, an activity known as 'inning', which inevitably reduced the width of the tidal compartment of the river, so reducing the power of the tide to scour the bed and maintain a direct entrance to the open sea. This does not appear, however, to have been the crucial factor in the obstruction of these estuaries, since the mouth of the Ouse was deflected eastwards to the farthest possible point under Seaford Head in the eleventh century, before reclamation of the marsh within the tidal estuary had made much headway. Brookfield has argued that similarly an unobstructed

Adur estuary postulated by Cheal as late as the fourteenth century is unlikely with the powerful effect of longshore drift along that stretch of the coastline (Brookfield 1952: 153–63).

The Coastal Plain of west Sussex, although relatively crowded with large estates and their closely-spaced peasant communities in the eleventh century still retained extensive areas of water, salt-marsh and estuarine pasture, solitary shingle beaches, wide inlets, estuaries, inaccessible islands and peninsulas which must have combined to make stretches of its coastline some of the most remote parts of England. The appearance of the Coastal Plain in the Dark Ages resembled the original home of the South Saxons in coastal Friesland and Saxony with settlement on low rises separated by strips of alluvium giving rich grazings but periodically inundated (Yates 1975: 118). Six and seven centuries later this description was still partially valid and this presumably helps to explain a more modest medieval prosperity in the lay subsidy return of the fourteenth century than its modern fertility and drainage would lead one to expect. Before the rivers were restricted by the gradual innings and embankments, medieval salt-making in the Adur valley was an important activity near Bramber. Its massive stone bridge of four arches and great cutwaters spanned the river, not to cross the present tiny stream but the strong tidal ebb and flow in the then wide tidal compartment. This is now buried in alluvium resulting from the late medieval submergence (Holden and Hudson 1981: 118). As the reclamations proceeded in the Adur estuary the loss of water flowing off the salt marshes on the ebb tide would have been a major cause in the failure of the river to keep its channel clear at the port of Shoreham. In so doing the tidal channel would have been deflected to the east, 'bringing the whole of its still considerable erosive power against the land and the town of Shoreham, particularly during periods of storminess when it can be envisaged that the offshore shingle bar, driven onshore very rapidly, would be frequently breached and overtopped by storm waves' (Brookfield 1952: 153–63). This is a very plausible sequence of events and it probably had numerous parallels along the Channel coast.

The evolution of Romney Marsh, both in physical terms and through the interference of man, is one of the outstanding examples of changes in coastline (Cunliffe 1980: 37–55). This is still being debated, in outline, for the necessary scientific analyses and the reassessment of the rich documentary evidence have only recently begun. The view from the old cliff edge at Stutfall Castle at Lympne is of a singular landscape, quite unlike the remainder of Kent in some ways and with a strong sense of solitariness and strangeness

---

Plate 2.6 A fourteenth-century map of southern Britain. This early map (*Bodleian Ashmole 1352*) names the ports of Dover, Romney and St Richard's (near Chichester), as well as Beachy Head.

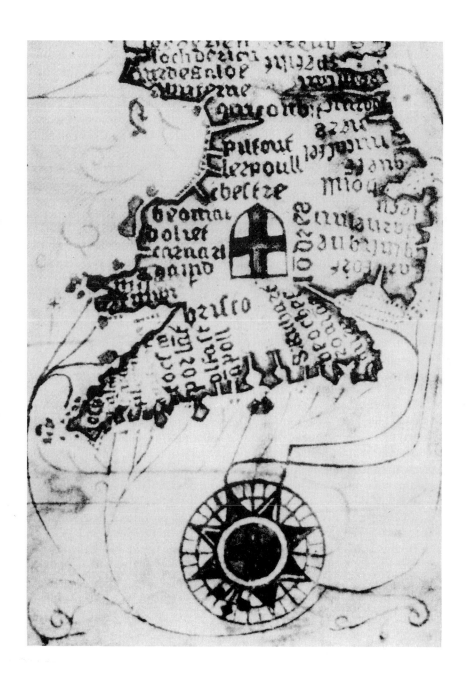

which must have been shared in the remote past by the Sussex Coastal Plain. In palaeolithic times the existing Romney Marsh was a broad shallow bay open to the sea and confined to cliffs which rim the marsh today in a wide semi-circle of low hills (Fig. 2.6). As sea level rose in later prehistoric times detritus deposited from erosion by the rivers Rother, Brede and Tillingham formed a newer, not submerged, sea cliff, the line of which is now represented approximately by the 10 fathom contour. On the seaward edge of this former coastline a sand bar, represented by the Midley Sand, was formed. A marine transgression stratigraphically related to the Buttery Clay of the Fenland in the late third and early second millennia was followed by an extensive layer of peat which overwhelmed former dry land covered with oak forest, the stumps of which are exposed as 'moorlag' below low tide marks. In time the peat was covered by a layer of fine alluvium attributable to another marine transgression during the first millennium BC. Romano-British settlements were created on low ridges between a complex system of creeks opening north-eastwards and behind extensive spreads of shingles which were forming the Dungeness foreland, corrugated by storm beaches cast up earlier on which much of the later history of Romney Marsh is dependent. The late Saxon period is well documented by a series of land charters. A number of these relate to the colonization of land on the banks of the northern branch of the river Limen, a channel of the river Rother, now defunct, but identified as the Sedbrook Sewer just south of Ruckinge and followed in part by later roads. This old creek served as the boundary of seven parishes which implies that this reclamation of marsh in Romney Marsh proper was carried out between the mid-eighth and the mid-eleventh century (Brooks 1981; Eddison 1983: 56–7).

The medieval reclamations mainly occurred in Walland, Guldeford and Denge marshes to the south of Romney Marsh proper and in the sector protected by the shingle beds of the accumulating Dungeness foreland called 'the most remarkable shingle promontory in the world'. Here shingle is heaped up in low rounded ridges or 'fulls', alternating with shallow hollows. Each 'full' was at one time a sea beach and its direction, position and height provided a chronology of the storms that shaped the cuspate headland and relation to wind directions and strengths which throw light on previous climatic regimes. Behind these great spreads of shingle the marsh is hollowed and brackish water became capable of reclamation to dry land. Lewis and Balchin have suggested that the highest of the shingle fulls on Dungeness should be equated to the storm of 1287 (Lewis 1932: 309–24; Balchin 1940: 258–85). The lines marked as past shorelines in Fig. 2.6 show the extent to which the headland

---

Plate 2.7 A sixteenth-century sea chart of the English Channel. This sea chart by the Dutch cartographer, Waghenaer, was much used by sixteenth- and seventeenth-century navigators. He gives prominence to all landmarks useful for sitings through the Channel, such as Fairlight church near Hastings, and numerous windmills on the South Downs. The estuaries are also prominently distinguished but the omission of the Adur probably indicates that it was then virtually closed to vessels by a shifting shingle spit and bar (Maritime Museum, Greenwich).

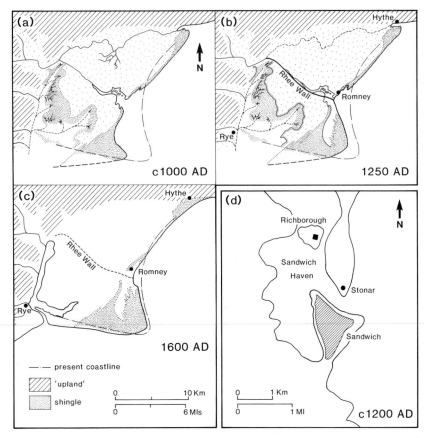

Figure 2.6 The changing shoreline of Romney Marsh and the Wantsum Channel (after Cunliffe 1980).

must have advanced in its rapid growth caused by the exceptional storms of the previous decades.

There was a great contrast between the continuously humanized lands east and west of the Rhee Wall which is the westerly boundary of the Romney Marsh proper and which reflects the quite different settlement history of the two halves of the marsh. To the east the marsh parishes are roughly circular in shape with the parish church in a central position (Burmarsh, Newchurch, Hope, Snave, etc.), but West of the Rhee Wall the parishes are narrow and elongated, with straight boundaries following the edges of medieval 'innings' (Brooks 1981: 78).

Another important distinction can be made between historically ancient parts of Romney Marsh and more modern areas of reclamation. The 'calcareous' soils of new marshland have been subjected to inundation by the sea within historic times and the 'decalcified' old marshland has had its calcium largely leached away after centuries of natural drainage (Fig. 2.6) (Green 1968).

An interesting feature of parish boundaries on Romney Marsh is their relationship to the various river courses of the river Rother or Limen. The parish boundaries are unrelated to the Rhee Wall, indicating that it was not of Roman origin as formerly believed. The boundaries are also independent of the Romney branch of the Limen which preceded the Rhee Wall. This suggests that the parish boundaries are older than the river-course that cuts through them just as they are older than the artificial Rhee Wall. By contrast the northern branch of the Limen coincides with parish boundaries and is suggestive of reclamations of the early Middle Ages (Ward 1934: 129–32).

Much of the medieval reclamation centred upon Walland Marsh where the sea defences and water-courses bear the names of medieval archbishops of Canterbury who held office from 1161 to 1292. Until recently it has been assumed that the respective 'innings' of the marsh were due to the initiatives of the archbishops but the construction of the sea-walls and drainage channels is probably to be assigned on other proof to the twelfth century and earlier. The connection of the archbishops with this part of the marsh may relate to a re-organization of the defences and water-courses in connection with the conversion of the original pasture land for arable in the late twelfth and thirteenth centuries (Eddison 1983: 56–7).

The Rhee Wall cuts across parish boundaries, for this massive artificial water-channel was constructed in the mid-thirteenth century in a vain attempt to save the port of Romney which suffered from the silting of Old Romney creek and the advance of a shingle headland which encroached upon the port with the loss of tidal scour in the estuary. A little later, in 1250, exceptionally high tides destroyed much of Old Winchelsea which was totally destroyed in the great storm of 1287. This storm also destroyed Broomhill and flooded all the marshes south of the Rhee Wall, consequently devastating Romney which was virtually destroyed. To this day one has to descend five steps from the present street level to the floor of the nave of New Romney church. The old river Rother broke away from its bed and pursued a new course through the choking sand and shingle into Rye Bay. This part of Romney Marsh had to be reclaimed again in the sixteenth and seventeenth centuries (Cunliffe 1980: 50).

The Cinque Ports

The permanent confederation of the Cinque Ports was a successful experiment in local administration which conferred fiscal concessions and a high degree of local autonomy in return for the provisioning of ships for the king's navy. It evolved from a looser organization originating before 1066 into a stronger one providing for the better defence of England and the enhancement of common interests of the ports themselves. The significance of the ports lay in their strategic location. Their important harbours commanding the cross-channel passage gave them complete control of the narrowest part of the English Channel. The early thirteenth century marked the culmination of the naval importance of these guardian ports and their political influence on the internal affairs of England. From 1337, for reasons which are not entirely clear, their control of the Channel was broken down by the French. Technical changes in naval warfare also combined with the decay of their harbours to make them less vital to the Crown. Paradoxically, although the special conditions which had brought the confederation into being had ceased to exist by the mid-fifteenth century, and had been on the wane for one hundred years previously, the constitution of the Cinque Ports became ever more elaborate during that period when it existed largely for the 'purpose of maintaining the obsolete privileges of an otherwise purposeless association' (Murray 1935: 228; Hull 1966: xi). Through the haze of romance their constitution and role have been greatly exaggerated. Their privileges were not dissimilar to those of medieval boroughs and they are not comparable in influence and wealth with that of the league of Hanse towns.

The original Cinque Ports were Romney, Hythe, Hastings, Dover and Sandwich. During the Middle Ages more than thirty other places in Kent and Sussex, and one in Essex (Brightlingsea), were affiliated to the head ports and collectively discharged an annual service of ships to the crown. Chief among the affiliated members were the towns of Rye and Winchelsea, attached to Hastings before 1190 and later given the special status of 'Ancient Towns', together with a standing as head ports in view of their new prominence. Each town member received the right to share in the privileges of head ports in return for a share in the burden of ship service. In cases where this was confirmed by royal charter such towns were known as Corporate Members. Such were Pevensey and Seaford, members of Hastings; Tenterden, member of Rye; Lydd of Romney; Folkestone and Faversham of Dover; and Fordwich attached to Sandwich. Lesser ports, called 'limbs' were also affiliated. Thus by the mid-thirteenth century the confederation stretched right around the coast of Kent and Sussex from Grange, near Chatham, to Pevensey (Fig. 2.7). Every creek and haven between London and the Continent fell into the hands of the portsmen.

This achievement marks the vigour and astuteness of the Cinque Port confederation in its prime. In the later Middle Ages the corporate body continued to offer additional affiliations, but it was then a sign of weakness rather than strength. Thus Rye incorporated Tenterden in 1449 because the town had 'come to such waste and poverty by the tides and burnings committed by . . . enemies', while the incorporation of Seaford by Hastings in 1544 meant

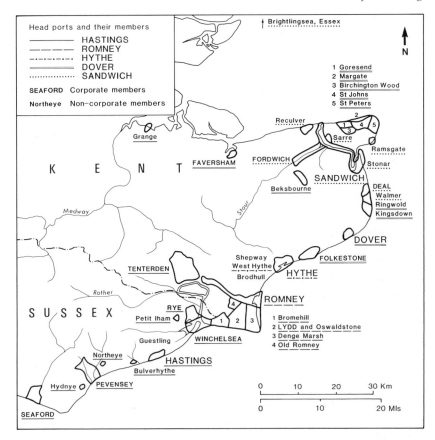

Head ports and their members
——————— HASTINGS
— — — — ROMNEY
—·—·—·—·· HYTHE
════════ DOVER
················ SANDWICH

SEAFORD Corporate members

Northeye Non-corporate members

† Brightlingsea, Essex

N

1 Goresend
2 Margate
3 Birchington Wood
4 St Johns
5 St Peters

Reculver
Grange
Sarre
Ramsgate
FAVERSHAM FORDWICH Stonar
K E N T
SANDWICH
Beksbourne DEAL
Walmer
Medway Ringwold
Stour Kingsdown

DOVER
Shepway FOLKESTONE
West Hythe
TENTERDEN Brodhull HYTHE

Rother ROMNEY
RYE 1 Bromehill
Petit Iham 4 2 LYDD and Oswaldstone
S U S S E X 1 2 3 3 Denge Marsh
Guestling WINCHELSEA 4 Old Romney
Northeye
HASTINGS
Bulverhythe
Hydnye PEVENSEY

SEAFORD

0   10   20   30 Km

0   10   20 Mls

Figure 2.7 The Cinque Ports (after Murray 1935).

---

that the two decayed harbours were being administered together. By this time the head ports had so greatly decayed that they could not perform their naval service and the limbs, which were often more flourishing than their erstwhile rivals, now sought higher shipping assessments in order to claim greater tax exemption.

The portsmen themselves were fishermen rather than traders. At Sandwich, for example, a major commercial port and a wool staple in 1377, trade was largely in the hands of aliens. The primary source of legalized wealth was the herring fishery of the North Sea in which the confederation won the privilege of landing at Yarmouth and holding the herring fair there. In the herring season, which finished with fishing off Scarborough, virtually every male decamped: courts closed, regulations became inoperative, and the harbours were deserted of ships (Hull 1966: xxiii–v; Murray 1935: 146–54). The most profitable activity of the portsmen up to the mid-fourteenth century was piracy. Barely discriminating between the king's friends and enemies they marauded as far afield as Hull and Bayonne, fighting without scruple against Jew and Gentile alike for their money and goods, and slaughtering French crews 'quicker than it takes to eat a biscuit'. This aspect of the portsmen's character made them invaluable defenders of the thirteenth-century Channel and their naval service for Edward I was a major factor in the subsequent reduction of Wales and the king's Scottish campaigns. It was to prove less of an asset in the fifteenth century when formal naval engagements, regular patrol work and the more disciplined use of royal ships and impressed merchant vessels became standard practice.

The reign of Edward I, in fact, marks the summit of the political power of the Cinque Ports. The strategic importance of the Channel awakened portsmen to a sense of their common interests and in the king the necessity for their control. The result was an elaboration of the confederation from a casual connection into a close confederation. A Lord Warden, answerable to the Crown, discharged the duties of sheriff and convened the Court of Shepway at Dover, primarily concerned with the king's interest. This office still survives. At their own initiative the portsmen established the general court of the *Brodhull* (named after the original place of meeting near Dymchurch) which dealt with matters of local government and increasingly with the organization of the Yarmouth fishery. A further court of the Guestling was held infrequently to deal with special matters. In retrospect, it was the very decline of the ports which brought them more closely together.

The fourteenth century marks the beginning of their decline in both naval importance and as a national institution. In part this was due to successive French harryings and burnings, which had destroyed all shipping in Hythe and Romney by 1341 and desolated Seaford by 1356. In 1380 and 1385 both Rye and Sandwich petitioned for help in walling their towns, sites of constant battle, now that they were too poor to accomplish it themselves owing to frequent attack. Plagues added to their distress and further diminished their populations. Once well-inhabited, New Winchelsea, 'being burned by the King's enemies and much more by the withdrawal of burgesses' was in 1384 'so desolate and almost destroyed that the proprietorship of vacant plots and tenements can scarcely be known'.

Another factor was the decay of the havens. As early as 1230 the harbour of Hythe was silting. Northeye, a limb of Hastings, was destroyed by the sea in the late thirteenth century, as was Old Winchelsea. Reculver and Stonar were destroyed by coastal erosion in the early fourteenth century. Folkestone suffered the same relapse from prosperity to decay, and for the same reasons. John Leland, the early-sixteenth century topographer, found much to satisfy his predilection for ruinous places contrasting their decay with their ancient fame. Hythe was 'a very great town in length and contained four parishes that now be clean destroyed'; Romney had once been a 'metely good' haven but the sea was then two miles distant, 'and so thereby decayed that where there were three great parishes and churches sometime is not scant one well maintained'. As for Stonar, 'sometime a pretty town', nothing was left but the ruin of its church. The haven of once-famous Sandwich (Fig. 2.6d), formerly a 'metely walled' town, was then stopped up by a 'great arising of the sandes and shelves'.

The decline of the Cinque Ports cannot however be attributed entirely to geographical and fortuitous causes. A further factor was the changing technique of warfare. The requirement that the Cinque Ports were to furnish 57 ships for 15 days' service a year at the rate of 21 men and a boy per ship was suited to early-medieval conditions when vessels rarely exceeded 30–60 tons. By 1347 crews of at least 65 men were normal, manning ships of 100 tons. Although it became the practice to ask for half service in ships but double the equipment this meant that the proportion of the royal fleet supplied by the Cinque Ports became less. Purpose-built royal ships from Southampton and impressed merchant ships from the West Country filled the gap. Perhaps nothing demonstrates the total eclipse of the confederation of the Cinque Ports more than the little contingent of five ships and one pinnace sent to the great fleet that opposed the Armada. But on behalf of Rye, it could still be said in the sixteenth century that it was 'such a scourge to France as the like is not in this realm' (Murray 1935; Hull 1966).

Early Medieval City and Town

Medieval urbanism evolved like so many other cultural patterns within the contrasting framework of the 'old' Kent, Sussex and Surrey on the peripheral areas of primary settlement and arable cultivation on the one hand and that of the Weald with its retarded development and once sparse population on the other. The Domesday boroughs were exclusively in the old-settled Coastal Fringe, and in point of size Canterbury and Lewes were among the leading towns of England in the eleventh and twelfth centuries. The first 'new towns' founded by the Normans in the early Middle Ages were also confined to the precociously developed border zones. It was not until the early thirteenth century that towns became notable in the developing Weald, and none of these grew beyond the scale of modest local markets until the fifteenth century, when the development of such towns as Cranbrook, Tenterden and Wonersh helped to undermine the prosperity of old-established urban centres, such as Canterbury, Godalming and Guildford.

The largest medieval town was Canterbury, despite disastrous conflagrations which wiped out almost the whole city in 1161 and caused serious loss of buildings in 1198 and 1224. Lesser fires are also reported in 1067 and 1247. Another in 1174 carried sparks to the roof of the choir from the burning thatch of cottages in Burgate Street, destroying the east end of the cathedral, less than four years after Becket's martyrdom. The Canterbury monk and chronicler, Gervase, was an eye-witness: 'The house of God, hitherto delightful as a paradise of pleasures, was now made a despicable heap of ashes, reduced to a dreary wilderness, and laid open to all the injuries of the weather'. Through this accident of fire the great Gothic cathedral was built. It also resulted in exchanges of land by the monks of Christ Church to create on demolished property an *enceinte* around the cathedral to lessen the fire risk. It is probable that many other towns were periodically swept by fire in the early Middle Ages, for their municipal records have not survived with anything like the completeness of Canterbury's (Cantuarensis 1932 edn).

As was to be expected of the ecclesiastical capital of England, the stake of the Church in medieval Canterbury was immense – two vast Benedictine abbeys, priory, nunnery, three friaries, five ancient almshouses and a score of parish churches. The extant rentals of Christ Church are remarkably complete and give precise definitions of some four hundred holdings in the city from *c*.1200. Between 1198–9 and 1223–4 an apparently rapid expansion of Canterbury caused a remarkable increase in the income from houses and shops let, and further steep rises in rents occurred throughout the thirteenth century:

Table 2.2 Christ Church Priory – income from rents in Canterbury

1198–9	£24 11 10d
1223–4	over £60
1230s	average £70
1281–2	more than £100
1300	more than £110

(Source: Urry 1967: 23–39)

This almost five-fold increase in rents during the thirteenth century reflects the rapid growth of the town. By the early thirteenth century it had about 200 shops and numerous markets. Domesday mentions two gilds in Canterbury, one of clerks and one of burgesses. A merchant gild was founded in the late eleventh or early twelfth century and craft gilds emerged in the early thirteenth century. Cloth-making, leather, victualling and building trades, goldsmiths and moneyers, priests, shopkeepers, Jews and aliens all contributed to Canterbury's regional importance. The mint was the only one to survive outside London after the centralization of 1218. The ground plan of medieval Canterbury has survived largely unaltered to this day, and also in many cases has the ground plot of the citizen of 750 years ago (Fig. 2.8) (Urry 1967: 191).

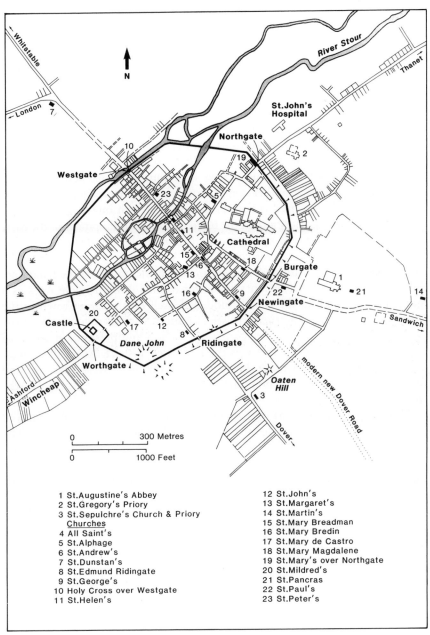

Figure 2.8 Medieval Canterbury (after Urry 1967).

1 St.Augustine's Abbey
2 St.Gregory's Priory
3 St.Sepulchre's Church & Priory

Churches
4 All Saint's
5 St.Alphage
6 St.Andrew's
7 St.Dunstan's
8 St.Edmund Ridingate
9 St.George's
10 Holy Cross over Westgate
11 St.Helen's

12 St.John's
13 St.Margaret's
14 St.Martin's
15 St.Mary Breadman
16 St.Mary Bredin
17 St.Mary de Castro
18 St.Mary Magdalene
19 St.Mary's over Northgate
20 St.Mildred's
21 St.Pancras
22 St.Paul's
23 St.Peter's

In Sussex the small walled city of Chichester presented the richest medieval urban scene. The encircling wall defining the town's jurisdiction is on Roman foundations and still largely intact. The street plan is an equally striking legacy of the Roman period. The most important decision in the early Middle Ages that still affects the present townscape was the removal of the South Saxon see from Selsey to Chichester about 1075. This resulted in the building of the cathedral at the turn of the eleventh century in the south-west quadrant of the town. The ecclesiastical quarter south of the cathedral contains several medieval buildings, notably the fourteenth-century gateway of the Bishop's Palace and the fifteenth-century houses in Vicar's Close. In the spacious walled gardens and narrow lanes of this quarter something of the medieval scene still permeates the present. Another conspicuous medieval characteristic that has not completely disappeared is the abruptness by which building ends at the city walls on the west and south of the town. Another development of the early Middle Ages which has left a permanent effect on the layout of Chicester is the separate jurisdiction which was vested in the Archbishop of Canterbury in the south-east quadrant. Much of this sector lay in the archbishop's palatinate (hence the local name of Pallant) which functioned in the Middle Ages as a miniature town within the city. It modelled itself on the larger town to the extent of having its own cruciform street pattern with its own market-cross at its centre. The north-east sector had a function and presumably outward appearance of its own for this was the burgesses' district. At its south-west corner stood the market place. Fields took up the north-west quadrant and the sites of former friaries, now large gardens, existed on the fringes of the city (Plate 2.8).

Guildford emerged as the main town of west Surrey and enjoyed prosperity as an important royal residence of Henry III and Edward I. The shell of the square keep is still well preserved on its partly artificial mound. The street topography suggests a planned late-Saxon or early-Norman town. The early medieval town was a parallelogram less than a quarter mile from east to west and about a furlong in depth. Surrounding it was the 'king's ditch', first mentioned in 1274 but doubtless much older. This was intersected at regular intervals by narrow ways called gates, several of which still exist. By the early fourteenth century Guildford was a prosperous little town with a cloth industry and a fair granted in 1308 on St Catherine's Hill. The presence of royalty and state business attracted money-lending Jews, including one Joceum, known as the 'Jew of Guildford', who was murdered and robbed by thieves. Preaching friars worked among the poor from their friary on the outskirts of the town

---

Plate 2.8   Chichester *c.*1200: a reconstruction. The city wall is shown, with the South Gate in the foreground. South Street, with its market stalls, runs from the gate into the city. To the right of the Cathedral, seen in its eleventh-century styling, is the Vicar's Hall. The Bishop's Palace and his chapel lies on the other side of the Cathedral. In front of the Cathedral is a chantry (Chichester Cathedral Publication 1988).

and a charitable hospital dedicated to St Thomas the Martyr was established to support the sick and elderly.

Lewes is one of many towns in medieval England that rose to prominence as an adjunct to its castle and priory. Petworth, Arundel, Midhurst, Reigate and Chilham can also appropriately be called 'feudal' towns since their layout was strongly influenced by the residence of a family descended from the holder at Domesday. Petworth's urban status, for example, originated with the rise of the Percy family and the narrow, tortuous streets of the urban core grew up contiguous to a medieval manor house, fortified in 1309.

The replacement of Old Winchelsea, totally destroyed in late-thirteenth century Channel storms, occupies a special place in the history of English medieval towns. New Winchelsea was founded by Edward I in 1288 and was the most ambitious of the planned towns he created on the model of the bastides of Gascony. The king set up a commission 'to plan and give directions for the necessary streets and lanes, for places suitable for a market and two churches'. As Tout observed, 'in these minute directions we have the most detailed evidence of conscious town-planning by royal authority that the age was to witness'. The new town was laid out on a hill-top promontory at Iham above the river Brede. A chequer-board of five long north–south streets intersected at right-angles by eight other streets divided the town into thirty-nine *insulae* (rectangular-shaped plots). New Winchelsea was meant to be no ordinary town. Its large size (about 150 acres), the scale and magnificence of its church (although incomplete), its fine public buildings and the excellent craftsmanship of the surviving dwellings clearly show that it was meant to be an English town worthy of its function expressed in a contemporary document as a 'key, refuge and guard of these parts against the tempestuousness of the sea and the insults of our enemies'. The ambitious undertaking was, however, never completed. Impoverishment by plagues and French raids, together with the silting of its harbour, brought about abject decline. The rent roll of 1292 shows tenements held by as many as 700 persons (Tout 1917: 26; Homans 1949: 22–41).

Not a little of the waxing and waning of towns was due to the competition and hostility of rival lordships. The conflict between the great monastic houses of Christ Church Priory and the Abbey of St Augustine had its effects on the daily lives of citizens in the port-towns of Sandwich and Stonar on opposite sides of the western entrance of the Wantsum Channel (Fig. 2.6). The Wantsum was originally open sea, into which discharged the waters of the Great and Little Stour. For centuries it was a sheltered shipping lane on the main route between England and the Continent. It had been guarded at both entrances by the Roman forts of Reculver and Richborough and the Jutish landfall traditionally placed at 449 was made at Ebbsfleet at the western entrance. Along its route a chain of ports, part of the Cinque Ports federation, emerged to serve the highly productive farming region of north-east Kent. Fierce competition between the two monasteries had broken out before 1023 when King Cnut restored all profits of the sea-entrance to Christ Church. In 1127, however, the priory complained that the abbey had 'begun to build small houses on the opposite side of the haven at a place called Stonore where ships went in fine weather so that they might stop there and toll and customs taken . . . which should have been collected by the officers of Sandwich'. In the twelfth and thirteenth centuries Stonar grew into a rival port. The abbot took advantage of changing natural conditions by inning the silty waters of the Wantsum. The earlier arm of the Wantsum was reclaimed in the middle of the thirteenth century and protected by the Sarre wall against floods. This in turn adversely affected the tidal scour at the western entrance and both ports suffered in consequence. Further inning by the abbot led to the closure of the Ebbsfleet Channel, the main seaway into Sandwich. In retaliation the men of Sandwich repeatedly damaged the abbot's sea embankment, some eight miles long protecting his lands at Minster, which also seriously reduced the tidal scour at Sandwich Haven. Among other obstructions were fish weirs (kiddles) owing rent to the abbot. By 1280 Stonar had seriously declined in importance but the port held on until almost destroyed by severe floods in 1359 and 1365–6. An attack by the French in 1385 seems finally to have extinguished the town. Sandwich enjoyed growth in the first half of the thirteenth century, followed by persistent decline, the Old Haven of the port being deflected in a great loop northwards into Pegwell Bay. Apart from Sandwich which maintained close ties with London, Faversham also stood in intimate relation with the capital, its cellars and wharves loaded with east Kent grain and wool bound for London markets (Butcher 1974: 19).

The wealden market towns which arose in the early Middle Ages as the culmination of piecemeal woodland clearance constituted a new form of urban development. Horsham was granted corporate right of a borough *c.*1210 when 52 burgage plots, mostly around the market place, paid rent to the de Braoses of Bramber. The grant of a yearly fair followed in 1253 and a large new church was erected *c.*1250. From 1306 assizes and a coroner's court were held in the town. By the later Middle Ages a number of burgesses were living in cross-winged houses, an indication that they were men of substance (Mason 1969; Hughes 1988).

Robertsbridge, as its name implies, grew up *c.*1180 at a river crossing formerly used by cattle, when it was founded by the abbot of Robertsbridge Abbey. A rental of *c.*1225 records 56 tenants, most of whom appear to be craftsmen, including cloth-workers, fullers, dyers, coopers and smiths. The nucleus of a town was probably the long, narrow burgage plots to the west of High Street. Expansion before the Black Death resulted in the building-up along the north side of East Street and the east side of High Street (Martin 1974a: 21). The origin of Battle has already been mentioned (pp 30–31). While Battle Abbey flourished, the town prospered. In the 1367 rental about 110 dwellings are identifiable, suggesting a minimum population of about 1,000 persons, a large town by the standards of the time and certainly an under-estimate of the importance of the town as sub-tenancies are only occasionally and incidentally mentioned. Its influence was comparable to that of Chichester, supporting a community of specialized and luxury-goods craftsmen which gave its market a real advantage over its local rivals. Sevenoaks also successfully emerged as a little market town around its church in the late twelfth century. The great scale of the church rebuilding in the thirteenth century is positive evidence of considerable new wealth. Sevenoaks was still prospering early in the fifteenth century. New rents were being taken up for shops and houses fronting the market place. This activity may be related to the acquisition of property in the area by wealthy Londoners (Du Boulay 1966: 245–6; Clarke and Stoyel 1975: 96).

The chief Surrey town was Southwark which was of the first importance in its own right by the thirteenth century, having grown out of its origin as a Roman and Saxon bridge-head settlement. Its particular character arose because of its peculiar connection with the City of London. Although the only part of the south bank of the Thames to be effectively linked to London, by virtue of London Bridge, it lay outside the jurisdiction of the sheriff and coroner of London and of the city gilds. Many of its residents lived in Southwark because of its comparative lawlessness: felons on the run; craftsmen who did not wish, or who were not allowed to join a city gild; prostitutes driven out of London congregating in brothels licensed by the Hospital for Unmarried Mothers; and cut-throats and pickpockets. The greater laxity of Southwark's government was also an ideal atmosphere for the coarser forms of London entertainment: bawdy-houses, doubtful taverns, bear gardens, bull rings, cock pits and fighting booths. Here also gathered the more obnoxious industries using Newcastle 'sea-coal', such as leather-tanning, soap-making, and lime-burning. In addition Southwark shared the rise of London as an industrial city in the fourteenth and fifteenth centuries, becoming full of workshops and forges, many operated by aliens who led a precarious life making and selling goods in the town. Among much squalor and poverty amidst its four prisons including the Clink on the river bank, were the sumptuous town houses of great churchmen, established before these social and industrial changes, such as those of the abbots of Hyde Abbey at Winchester, Battle (with its great garden, later to be called the Maze), St Augustine and those of the prior of Lewes and the bishops of Winchester and Rochester. These adjoined the numerous taverns, including Chaucer's 'Tabard' in the Borough, demonstrating how convenient Southwark was as a place of assembly for all parts of the South East and Wessex (Myers 1972).

Chapter 3

The Later Middle Ages

Demography and the Agrarian Economy

The fundamental cause of the agricultural malaise following the Black Death in 1348 was demographic. The tremendous fall in population resulted in severe dislocation of the regional economy. The severe mortality was followed by further cut-backs in the population from the plagues that followed in 1361–2, 1387 and 1396 and for most of the fifteenth century the demographic picture seems to be one of falling population or at best stagnation. The effects of the Black Death cannot be assessed solely by the state of the agrarian economy even as late as the 1380s: long-term effects have to be taken into account which did not surface prominently until after the 1390s. Consequently, agriculture in the fifteenth century was a far more risky venture than fifty and more years earlier. With falling prices and rising costs lords were 'very unsure of what path to take and switched back and forth between farming out their manors and keeping them in hand, before finally moving over to wholesale leasing in the 1390s' (Mate 1983: 352). Thereafter the general policy of lords was to shore up increases by settling for low, fixed rents. Moreover, in addition to the serious drop in income and mounting debts resulting directly from the Black Death and later pestilences, estates suffered from other setbacks damaging their economy, such as runs of bad harvests and disease in sheep and cattle, which appear at least in part to be due to a deterioration in weather.

Yet the immediate effects of the Black Death were not disastrous to lords. With continuous high prices after 1348, demesne agriculture recovered remarkably quickly, helped by flexible estate management, remaining buoyant for the next three decades. But cutting back on labour to reduce expenses made tillage less clean, with a consequent fall in cereal yields and a greater susceptibility of crops to mildew and other fungoid diseases (Mate 1984: 347).

Despite the serious problems created by the Black Death Bridbury has suggested that it was 'more purgative than toxic' (Bridbury 1973:

341). Certainly from the standpoint of the peasant the fall in population in the fourteenth century without notable recovery in the fifteenth was on the whole favourable. As demesnes shrank in size, the work of customary tenants was commuted for money payments. The peasants' standard of living improved as relatively higher real wages could be earned than formerly, so that the peasant could afford more meat and dairy products, which earlier had been regarded as luxuries. Peasants on marshland manors of St Augustine's and Battle Abbey, who had previously eaten oaten bread, insisted on being paid in barley, though this had to be brought in from upland manors elsewhere. A later generation of peasant labourers was able to do better still in terms of diet. In times of low wheat prices as in 1463 and 1464, seasonal labourers on manors of Battle Abbey were powerful enough to withhold their labour until they were given generous board 'at the lord's table' (Brandon 1971d: 118). In other respects the peasant was better off after the Black Death than before. More money could be spent on houses, their furnishings and utensils, and the leasing of land after the 1390s for low, fixed rents was the most crucial event of all. Many of the more able or fortunate among them became substantial tenants, with considerable freedom of action, thereby driving a great wedge into one of the last bastions of feudalism, a dependent peasantry.

Social Mobility and Civil Unrest in the Later Middle Ages

As Du Boulay has noted of the archbishop's estates in Kent and Sussex:

> the contraction of the total area under cultivation did not itself mean poverty for any section of the community as such, but it was accompanied by a natural willingness on the part of the lord to let land, and by estate building in a substantial way by a proportion of tenants, who were free to select their property on the market and deal with them as the moment dictated . . . (Du Boulay 1966: 41).

This circumstance greatly added to the complexities of fifteenth-century landownership and leasing. There was a steady drift of peasant families, perhaps not moving far from their original homes. Men left their villages in search of higher wages in agriculture and industry and moved from one holding to another. Successful yeomen and gentlemen amassed little complexes of private property by shrewd business methods. In Kent this was a process already possible and familiar in the thirteenth century, if not earlier, but it was now intensified through the new opportunities for enrichment. In Sussex the more feudalized lifestyle did not prevent a rapid breaking-up of holdings and their re-consolidation. Lords themselves actually facilitated the process in their own interest of improving property for sale or lease by conniving at tenants devising land by the making of entails and the sale of remainders and reversions. The manorial administration actually helped them to do so (for a price) and provided copies of the court roll entries as evidence (Clough 1969: xxx)

For a period of forty years or so after the Black Death, however, these trends were hindered by many manorial administrations who pressed hard on tenants the matter of labour services in connection with the intensive exploitation of demesnes. On estates of the Cathedral Priory of Canterbury, for example, labour services which were re-introduced after the famine of 1314–17 and the drought of 1325–6 were still being strictly exacted between 1340 and 1390, despite increasing resistance (Mate 1985: 55–68; 1984: 341–54). The archbishops also took a stringent attitude towards their tenants and this produced much friction and resentment. Archbishop Courtenay punished tenants of Wingham for their unwilling performance of carting services, although these were light, by the imposition of ecclesiastical penance in 1390. Earlier Archbishop Islip had found services difficult to exact in Otford in the 1350s, a 'troublespot where the tenants refused the service of reaping and mowing in 1381 and where they often refused rents in the fifteenth century'. Refusal of service was in fact widespread in the South East during the later fourteenth and fifteenth centuries and increasingly labour dues were being redeemed for money, although not without strong rearguard attacks on the part of the lords. In Sussex the conflict between lords and peasants took on a more serious note, for status as well as obligations were at issue. As an example, Archbishop Islip upheld the institution of villeinage on the manor of South Malling in 1359 by forcing villeins who had removed themselves from his lordship and power to admit his case and to place themselves in his grace for their rebellion (Du Boulay 1966: 189). In Sussex freedom had to be hardly won, and it was not until the early fifteenth century that a steady drift of peasant families moving around is discernible. A study of the physical mobility of the rural population of the downland manor of Alciston has revealed a large turnover of tenants between 1433 and 1489, only a fifth of the tenant families surviving a fifty-year period (Brent 1968: 101).

From the 1390s lords acknowledged the changing conditions and began as a general rule to lease part or all the manorial demesne on profitable terms. The earliest of the lessees in the late fourteenth century were small men who had equipment on their own account which made the 'good' farmers in the eyes of landlords from whom they leased parcels of demesne and borrowed livestock. The later lessees remain a shadowy group for they preserved no systematic records and there are no south-eastern counterparts of the famous collections of correspondence for the Paston, Stonor and Plumpton families. Numerically, they constituted a large and important group of people. The See of Canterbury's tenants, for example, were from the mid-fifteenth century in complete and continuous possession of the archbishop's forty or so demesnes and this picture could be repeated across the South East. Broadly, the phases of leasing in the South East conform to regional patterns observed elsewhere. Thus when the See was in difficulties over leasing in the 1450s and 1460s and was sometimes forced to let demesne piecemeal on short leases, the same trend is found in contemporary Norfolk where farmers were similarly trying to offer less rent or demanding longer terms and other advantages such as that the lord should do all repairs (Du Boulay 1959: 62).

All social classes were engaged in leasing demesnes: gentlemen, thrifty yeoman and husbandmen (a term which appears to be synonymous with yeoman in the late fifteenth century) and upwardly-mobile yeomen freely succeeded gentry and vice versa so that the farmer might be the social superior of his lord. The largest and longest leases were usually held by wealthy yeomen or gentry such as the Knatchbulls (who eventually entered the nobility) who paid £168 annual rent for a large estate at Penshurst, and the Morleys of Glynde who leased Ranscombe in Sussex. A husbandman, Miles Hodgson, leased 300 acres of the archbishop's demesne at Tarring for £18 and occupied one hall house, some cottages, shops and fields in several neighbouring parishes. Parks were generally rented by persons of superior social position.

Certain areas of the South East became lands of the yeoman farmer, *par excellence*. Thanet is a prime example. Lords continued to be concerned with the maintenance of soil fertility and the care of pasture and controlled these by inserting covenants into leases prescribing specific rotations, soil nutrition and other beneficial practices which had become locally traditional. This is observable in leases which yeomen were taking up of farm tenancies of Merton College demesne in Surrey in 1485 for terms of between twelve and twenty years. The leased demesnes of Malden and Farleigh near Croydon included the plough animals, the dairy herd, some farm equipment and basic furniture in the farmhouse. Strictly applied conditions were prescribed for the proper maintenance of soil fertility. On taking up the lease, fallow had already been manured by the sheepfold and by compost of wheat straw and the contravention of these practices incurred a fine. Sown crops, or seed corn, were also reckoned in the valuations. Lessees bound themselves to keep the houses, barns, walls and fences in good repair and to protect the coppices from cattle. The leasing of demesne woodlands is notable for the careful provision for all mature oaks and also adequate provision of younger oaks, 'stathelles' (standards) 'for storrs and standers of the best and likely to be tymbre', a forestry practice later to be accepted as a national standard by the legislation of Henry VIII. When the contract was terminated the stock was handed back and the land was required to be sown and left fallow in the same condition as at the begining of the lease. The lessor made all manner of personal arrangements in these leases. Thus the manor of Catteshall (Cateshill) near Godalming was leased in 1439 except for one part of the manor house, 'my great room upon the hye dees' with the dovecot, a meadow and its fishery which the owner wanted to retain for his vacations. Similarly John Strode and his wife in 1424 leased his share of the manor of Loseley to a local husbandman for four years but retained the rabbit warren and a coppice for their own sport (Christ Church Mss). It is not yet clear whether families who throve to yeomanry were still successful some generations later. Farming of demesnes saddled lessees with heavy expenses and it was not always 'the high road to prosperity which it sometimes appears to have been'. Hard times for landlords are not always good times for tenants.

The bitter struggle between peasants and their lords erupted twice into revolution in the South East, in the Peasants' Revolt (1381) and Cade's Rising (1451). Although seigneurial services in Kent were light generally the great ecclesiastical estates imposed more arduous obligations and exacted various dues with unmitigating tenacity. Men of Kent had acquired a reputation for obstinacy and individualism, and in the new circumstances prevailing after the Black Death considered the idea of servility as shaming and an affront (Du Boulay 1966:186). Tenants of the great estates in Kent and Sussex had earlier been content to work their land-holding in the general protection of their lord. Men rising socially with new opportunities in crafts and trade now began to question the role of manorial officials who were representative not only of wealth, but of their subjection.

The Weald became the main theatre of conflict. It had become a by-word for lawlessness and discontent quite as much as for the poverty of its soil. Here communications were notoriously difficult and social control traditionally weak. Dense woodlands offered refuge for insurgents (as well as criminals) and the maintenance of law and order was well-nigh impossible on account of the largeness of parishes (Goring 1978a: 2). Officialdom seldom moved away from the coast and towns. A criminal underworld, with its terrorist activities was constantly fed by unbiddable, underemployed peasants who paid off old scores on each other when opportunity offered for a rampage. No medieval government appears ever to have effectively controlled the remoter parts of the Weald after the Black Death, the only recognized authorities being the retainers and officials of the big estates and what we would now call the Mafia. With the virtual collapse of Henry VI's corrupt government in the second quarter of the fifteenth century, murders, rapes and robberies pervaded the Sussex Weald (Clarke and Stoyel 1975: 93). The legitimate grievances of law-abiding wealdsmen at the time of Cade's rising unfortunately also attracted a ruffianism which was damaging to the insurgents' cause. The spirit of disobedience was strongest among the now socially-rising cloth workers of Cranbrook and Tenterden, and the unruly craftsmen of the Sussex High Weald, in whose radicalism and anti-clericalism is traceable the mainspring of dissent which was to surface repeatedly in the regional history of the South East.

The uprising of the Peasants' Revolt started in Kent and was led by a priest, John Ball, together with Jack Straw and Wat Tyler. As the insurgents advanced on London they pillaged manor houses and opened gaols as they went. Joined by rebels from Sussex and Surrey, they sacked the Palace of the

Savoy, home of John of Gaunt, who was very unpopular in the High Weald. They then pillaged Southwark and killed the Treasurer and the Archbishop of Canterbury, then Lord Chancellor and responsible for the Poll Tax. King Richard II issued letters of pardon and briefly rode out to meet the rebel forces at Smithfield. When Straw and Tyler approached the king, the lord mayor of London, Sir William Walworth, struck off Tyler's head. With the mob leaderless the king rode among them saying 'Sirs, will you shoot your own king? I will be your captain.' Ball still remained in London and a wave of murder and arson spread over the city. Foreigners, particularly Flemings, were ruthlessly hunted down and murdered, 35 victims being beheaded on a single block at the church of St Martin in the Vintry (Webber 1980: 111). Ball was eventually hanged, drawn and quartered and his remains were put on show around the country. His egalitarian philosophy is summed up in the little rhyme of which he was the author:

> When Adam delved and Eve span
> Who was then the gentleman?

which could hardly have been more relevant to the increasing domination of the rich in the High Weald.

The Kentish rising of 1450, usually described as Jack Cade's rebellion, was in fact a series of disturbances under the leadership of men such as Parmenter, Wilkins and Hesildene. Numerous gentlemen and yeomen also joined Cade's army, including Bartholemew Bolney, chief steward to the Abbey of Battle, and the abbot of Battle and the prior of Lewes were also implicated. The rebels' grievances largely arose over the extortion of money by manorial officials, great and small, working in their own interests. Many of these held places in the archbishop's administration. The climax of disorder broke out when extortions were connived at by the king's minister, the Earl of Suffolk. Cade's well-organized host from Kent and east Sussex occupied London but were thrown out by citizens alienated by their indiscipline. The record of a government commission established to investigate the discontent identified over 100 gentlemen, a large number of town tradesmen and craftsmen, many yeomen and numerous cloth workers, many from the Sevenoaks, Wrotham and Penshurst districts, where lived the king's Treasurer, Lord Saye and Sele, lord of the sub-manor of Knole. Cade, who had connections with Heathfield, fled to his native woods but was apprehended and died on the journey to London. Cade's rebellion had some striking responses in London. Sir John Fastog, an important merchant, for example, fortified and garrisoned his house on the south bank of the Thames (Clarke and Stoyel 1975: 92–7; Du Boulay 1966: 189–92).

An interesting example of how these social changes were affecting the use of buildings is revealed by a detailed survey of the parsonage at Hawkshurst, Kent, in 1556. The parsonage was arranged around an impressive 'Great Court' entered under a gatehouse built adjacent to a

corn granary. On the south of the Court an old house of three bays was
in use as a brewhouse. Another old house of two bays had been converted
into a 'millhouse'. A stable, two barns, a 'kyllhouse' (slaughter-house) and a
dovecot completed the farm buildings. On the west side of the house was
a half-timbered dwelling of three bays which appears to have been ruinous.
The mansion house was in the occupancy of three families who each lived in
self-contained rooms, the tenant-farmer of the demesne, the parson and the
curate. The parson occupied most of the house. His hall of two bays at the
south end still had a hearth in the middle and was presumably still open to
the roof. A pantry and buttery lay to the south side of the hall and an entry
led to a large kitchen provided with a 'large chimney' and over these rooms
was a 'fair chamber' but with no chimney or 'house or office'. At the north
end of the hall was the main living room with glazed windows, an external
chimney and a fine chamber above. Another chamber in this wing had glazed
windows and there were rooms for servants in the attic. The farmer, his wife,
children and maids, occupied two 'very small' rooms without a chimney on the
upper floor, a separate access being provided to their quarters. By their hall
was a little room used as a larder. The curate's four rooms, including a room
lined with wainscot and provided with a chimney, lay on the ground floor at
the north end of the hall. He had use of a part of the cellar and had entry to
a little 'court garden', wood ground, orchard and well which bordered upon
the main gardens reserved for the exclusive use of the parson (Christ Church
Mss).

The migrant seeking to improve his condition was probably the most
consistent element in fifteenth-century migration. The extent and pattern of
rural—urban migration and its effects on the social composition of a town
can be illustrated by a case study of Romney in Kent. Compared with Dover,
Sandwich and Canterbury, the scale of fifteenth-century Romney's activities
was small and declining yet its hinterland was approximately thirty miles
and trade connected the town to London and with east- and south-coast
ports and the continent. Between 1453 and 1523 almost 400 freemen were
enrolled who came to Romney along lines of communication established by
the town's trading activity. Approximately one-quarter of the total number
of migrants came from within five miles of the port (within the hinterland of
its busy market). A further one-quarter of the migrants came from between 6
and 30 miles. From between 30 and 50 miles came only a single migrant but
a further quarter of the total came from the rest of England, East Anglian
ports and towns providing the greatest numbers, together with many from
Sussex. Butcher has demonstrated that the poorer migrant could, and did,
rise through the ranks of urban society, the entry fine for freemen being
relatively low. The degree of mobility was also very high, judging from
a comparison of the early-fifteenth century population with the Poll Tax
return of 1377. The migration was not simply rural–urban in direction
because those who could afford it moved back to their native village or

town on retirement. Among Romney's migrants were considerable numbers of aliens, Dutch preponderating. Not only freemen gathered there but others such as apprentices and labourers taking the opportunity for taking up work with craftsmen, tradesmen and merchants (Butcher 1974: 16–27).

One of the more pronounced effects of this increasing physical and social mobility was the gravitation of population towards London. Du Boulay has remarked of the archbishop's estates that the geography of the landed rents was changing in the fifteenth century with the apparent shift of rent-paying tenants from the remoter parts of Kent and Sussex towards London and at last the concentration of taxable tenantry in the Surrey and Middlesex manors was even challenging the rich and prosperous lands of north Kent which since the tallage of 1168, the earliest detailed break-down of manorial income, had held the highest position in rental value (Du Boulay 1966: 246). Brown has also noted how places within easy access of London were gaining favour, so extending the metropolitan influence over the district of north-west Kent and the nearer parts of Surrey. Sevenoaks was one of the most prestigious of the new residential areas, and Knole the supreme example of a luxurious residential estate gathered together by lay and ecclesiastical magnates (Du Boulay 1974: 1–10; Brown 1977: 145–56).

It would appear that rich gentry who had business and political interests in London have always been relatively widespread in these areas, at least from the late fourteenth century. The changing social conditions of the fourteenth and fifteenth centuries enlarged this group still further, encouraging those who principally lived and worked in the capital to escape from its pressures and the recurrent dangers of plague by retiring to country houses. Such persons are buried in country churches of the South East, and commemorative brasses testify that they were rich benefactors of churches and local charities. The 1436 Lay Subsidy roll for London discloses that of 358 men with assessments of over £5, 37 are also specified as holding land in Kent, 33 in Essex, 35 in Middlesex and 17 and 15 respectively in Surrey and Hertfordshire. Kent was the most popular choice, partly because land was held in gavelkind tenure and could be alienated at will and so freely negotiable on the land market. Country residence was doubtless stimulated by the cheapening of land since the Black Death, making it an ideal investment. A significant sign of the reciprocal relations between London and its countryside was the practice by Kentish yeomen of sending sons to be apprenticed in the city.

The process whereby the London merchant infiltrated into Kent can be clearly discerned as far back as the early fourteenth century when John Pulteney, draper and four times mayor of London, acquired the whole manor of Penshurst and in 1340 constructed its magnificent beamed domestic hall. Another of the new social geographies discernible towards the end of the Middle Ages is the growing delight of the well-to-do to escape periodically in summer from unpleasant but necessary London into the countryside of north-west Kent, especially to Greenwich, and also into the pure air of London's western fringes. Chaucer himself celebrates this ecstasy for London's countryside during his busy working life by day in the Custom House at London Dock, and at nightfall in his chamber over the archway of Aldgate:

> When Comen is the May
> That in my bed ther draweth me no day
> That I nam up and walkyng in the mede . . .

This social change altered attitudes to the environment. As early as 1510 the archbishop's surveyor at Bexley was as concerned as much with the amenity of woodland as with its commercial value (Du Boulay 1966: 218).

Rural Dereliction

The Weald

The effect of the population decline on the age-old wealden colonization and on the appearance of the countryside was dramatic. Evidence supplied by detailed rent rolls and custumals and by the enumeration of rents (including uncollected rents) in manorial *compoti* applied to the Weald makes it clear that its persistent deforestation over several preceding centuries ebbed away after the Black Death and had virtually ceased by the early fifteenth century. This is true, for example, of the manor of Rotherfield, the Bishop of Chichester's outlying wealden estate at Heathfield and the archbishop's manor of South Malling, all of which still had extensive colonizable reserves but which now lacked men to clear them. Broadly speaking, assarting continued on a very substantially reduced scale in the second half of the fourteenth century compared with the previous one hundred years and gradually fell away altogether in the early fifteenth century when only tiny plots of roadside waste were being taken up, suggestive of the use of the land for the erection of a house, shop or smithy by those who worked in small-scale industry or trade, rather than in agriculture (Brandon 1969: 143).

The manorial *compoti* also reveal wealden tenements which fell vacant through lack of a tenant. With regard to this aspect of rural dereliction, the number and acreage of land holdings that were vacant for lengthy periods at any time in the later Middle Ages would appear to have been small. Locally, however, the *decasus*, the list of uncollected rents, does imply a considerable reversion of formerly cultivated land to woodland and scrub. The poor exposed ridges of the High Weald were most susceptible to dereliction, especially the high-lying districts adjacent to forests and chases. In these districts lands appear to have been dropping out of cultivation because they were physically and economically marginal, as for example, on the margins of Ashdown Forest and on Waterdown Forest in Kent. In some places land never recovered for decades from the effects of the Black Death and the later pestilences. Wrotham in Kent, for example, was severely damaged by the catastrophe of the plague and its effects were so long lasting that the archbishop's demesne was unoccupied between 1463 and 1486 (Du Boulay 1966: 187). Similarly lands in Marden on the North Downs appear to have fallen derelict for years on end. Another category of land that lacked tenants for long periods was that with particularly unfavourable tenure. The derelict state of many of the Battle Abbey tenancies in the *leuga* of Battle should be seen in this light (Searle 1974: 368).

However, we should not visualize the encroachment of woodland and scrub on a scale extensive enough to overwhelm groups of farms and farm buildings as happened in parts of Germany and central Europe during the fifteenth century. There seems little doubt, though this has yet to be put to the proof, that peasants from the strongly feudalized Coastal Fringe were taking up land in the Weald as an opportunity to free themselves from irksome labour dues. Assart land, held for a money rent, was probably attractive to villeins who were elsewhere liable for carrying and other services. It should also be borne in mind that the fifteenth-century Weald offered expanding opportunities in various handicrafts and land could well have been taken up in conjunction with supplementary employment.

Despite this relative buoyancy of the wealden land market in the fifteenth century, the documentary evidence is generally of falling rents, a lack of competition for holdings in the mid-fifteenth century, sharply falling levels of soil improvement in the form of marling and in other ways (until the 1480s when the economy went into the upturn), reductions in livestock and the increasing disrepair of farmhouses, barns and other buildings. With the lowered pressure of population following the Black Death there appears to have been a sharp decrease in arable land in the Weald and a corresponding increase in lightly grazed poor pasture. As we have noted, wealden agriculture being based on the principle of convertible husbandry, was especially adaptable to fluctuations in the economic climate. In economic depressions the plough simply went less frequently and regularly round the farm.

The implications of this reduced ploughing would be a sward of ever-deteriorating pasture colonized by docks, thistle, bramble, broom and furze followed, in extreme neglect, by scrub and woodland where men had formerly harvested corn. We can presumably imagine fields far from supplies of manure degenerating into underused rough pasture, the squalid appearance of hedges growing wider and thickening into strips of wood (shaws), ditches silting up and causing bad drainage, walls and fences breaking down, buildings in want of repair. Much woodland would have become unkempt though lack of care.

Detailed surveys of the mid- and late-sixteenth century suggest a reversion of land to poor pasture at least equal to and probably greater than that of the years between the two World Wars this century. Large areas of the High Weald do not seem to have been ploughed for decades, all the holdings being kept mainly as permanent pasture and on the Low Weald the arable had shrunk within itself to fields near the barns. With bitter effort the work of field reclamation had to begin over again to mark another stage in the repeated short-lived triumphs of reclamation which have ever characterized the history of wealden farming (ESRO Danny Mss).

The Downland

On the coastal plain and downland, the downward movement of population led to the abandonment of once-thriving rural settlements. The origins of village decay go back to the period before the Black Death to the reports of poverty and adverse weather in the *Nonae* Rolls of 1341 (Baker 1966: 1–5). This source needs to be interpreted with great caution as the evidence of decline was gathered during the 'harvest' year 1340 which was notorious for its appalling winter and summer weather and severe flooding. Consequently not all the loss of land from cultivation may have been permanent. The Black Death, however, was a turning point in the history of many villages and hamlets and thereafter most settlements appear to have progressively declined in population which in extreme cases, resulted in 'shrunken' or deserted habitations.

The agencies responsible for this destruction are plentiful. The losses of rural settlements on account of coastal erosion are themselves numerous. The loss of a whole line of little ports, as well as villages and farms along the margin of the Sussex Coastal Plain is clearly indicated by the present smoothed coastline (Brandon 1974: 117). Further east other ports and harbours lost to the sea include Aldrington, Broomhill, Bulverhythe, Hydneye, Iham, Northeye and *Pende* near Shoreham. The probable effect of the Black Death on a number of downland villages is suggested by the sharp drop in taxpayers between the lay subsidy of 1327 and the Poll Tax of 1377–8. Hangleton near Hove is an example. In 1377–8 only 18 persons over the age of 14 years paid Poll Tax compared with 25 contributors to the Subsidy of 1327 (presumably all householders) and only two householders are recorded there in 1428 (Holden 1963: 59–71). In Kent the recession of rural settlement in the later Middle Ages still remains largely unexplored but a widespread retreat is indicated by the numerous dependent downland churches and chapels that failed to survive the demographic decline (Everitt 1986: 2, 157, 222).

In most cases the precise causes of depopulation are not apparent and it is also frequently impossible to identify the precise period of the most severe decline. Yet there is evidence that for many settlements surviving the Black Death and other pestilences, the mid-fifteenth century was a period of marked depopulation. The degree of immunity and vulnerability to depopulation varied partly with the nature of the soil. The areas best fitted for arable production, the coastal plain of Sussex and north-east Kent appear to have been least affected by population decline whereas areas more marginal for arable cultivation, notably those of the South Downs, were more seriously affected. From the evidence given to the Commissions of Inquiry in 1517 and 1518 the downlands of the south of England do not seem to have been seriously affected by the depopulation in connection with the transfer of arable to pasture which was a serious problem in the Midlands at that time. The depopulation of the downs occurred earlier and is more likely to have been caused by a movement away from more marginal land as a result of the wider choices that had become available with the contraction of population. There was a steady drift of tenants away from the South Downs during the fifteenth century: whether this was to the Weald or to towns is not clear.

A further major factor behind the downland depopulation was probably the enclosure of the open fields which was making great headway during the fifteenth and early sixteenth centuries. Gentry and wealthier yeomen were engrossing holdings and consolidating open field strips into hedged enclosures and expanding their sheep flocks at the expense of smaller tenants. This process can be illustrated by reference to the Alciston village community near Lewes. Although still a large nucleated village with 31 households in 1433, the number of tenants had declined considerably since the Black Death, for the common fields of Tilton, a neighbouring hamlet, had been engrossed into a single holding and some fifty acres of the demesne were interspersed amongst tenants' lands (Fig.3.1). At Wiston one of the tenants was granted leave to enclose eight acres in the village fields as early as 1428. By 1466 common grazing over the remainder of the arable was greatly reduced to take into account considerable piecemeal enclosure by agreement. Similarly at Apuldram in 1430 tenants' holdings comprised both dispersed parcels and individually-held arable fields, suggestive of the partial consolidation of former scattered strips. At West Firle Bartholomew Bolney was exchanging arable strips and buying others to achieve the same result in the mid-fifteenth century. Such instances of the supersession of the old communal system of agriculture greatly multiply during the later fifteenth and early sixteenth centuries (Brandon 1974: 145–6).

Deserted or 'shrunken' villages were a widespread phenomenon. Both Sutton and Chington have long been represented in the landscape by single farms but they formerly constituted a populous parish with its own church. The 1296 Subsidy Roll bears 56 names drawn from both townships, Seaford being assessed separately. To re-create the medieval past at Sutton, the site of which is now occupied by modern buildings, we have to imagine a scene of peasant cottages and little farmhouses with their attendant hedged gardens,

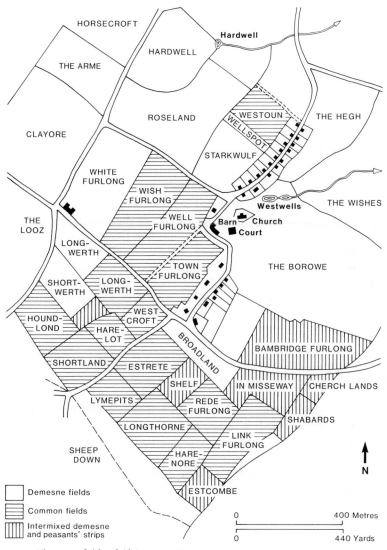

Figure 3.1 The open fields of Alciston *c.*1430.

tofts and crofts, set about a small green. In 1340 Sutton was one of the many Sussex parishes reporting substantial acreages of untilled land, said to be due to the poverty of the tenants and the adversity of the weather. Unfortunately, the Poll Tax assessment of Sutton does not appear to have survived but in the 1428 return of parishes with less than ten householders, Sutton, with West Blatchington, is one of the two Sussex parishes with no recorded inhabitant. In the early fifteenth century the church is reported as being in a very bad state of repair and in 1509 the parish was united with that of Seaford because 'the church is utterly destroyed and [there are] no parishioners, save for a few neat-herds . . .'. West Blatchington has a similar story. The settlement seems never to have been large, since tax assessment was combined with either Brighton or Patcham in 1332 and earlier. In 1340 it had lands untilled and it mustered only sixteen persons assessed to the Poll Tax of 1377–8. In 1428 the parish was devoid of any inhabitant and in 1596 the church was reported unused and there was only one dwelling in the parish. Evidently the medieval village had become co-extensive with a single sheep farm. Although the engrossing of tenants' lands for sheep ranches is not a major cause of downland depopulation as in the east Midlands it often explains dwindled settlements. Old Erringham near Shoreham is a good example. In Saxon and early medieval times it comprised a small hamlet with a chapel subordinate to Old Shoreham. By 1525 the tenants had disappeared completely and the 'village' was in the hands of a single occupier. Apart from major villages there is a host of former downland hamlets which formerly had separate open-fields systems and villeins and cottars to work them, but which had shrunk to single sheep farms during the late fourteenth or early fifteenth centuries (Burleigh 1973: 45–83; 1976: 61–8; Brandon 1974: 162–4).

The Drowning of the Marshes

The Saxo-Norman marine regression which had facilitated the colonization of the marshes of the North Sea basin and of the English Channel was followed by a fall in the relative level of land to sea in the thirteenth century which was associated with a worsening climate characterized by increasing storminess and more frequent and longer spells of dreaded wet 'foule wedere'. Along the Channel coast early 'forerunner' floods such as the 'great flood' which damaged Apuldram in 1275 were manifestations of this submergence which led to the destruction of Old Winchelsea in 1287 and caused widespread flooding. Major flooding is reported on a number of occasions in the early fourteenth century, notably in 1331–2 and land devastated from this cause between 1291 and 1340 and recorded in the *Nonae* Rolls was considerable (Baker 1966: 1–5). The marshland on the Hooe Level, a part of the Pevensey Levels, was however, put into working order again in the 1380s and not again abandoned until the 1420s, years which mark the culmination of flooding on the Channel coast. On the basis of monastic account rolls there is an important distinction between the sea floods of 1340–60 which although numerous were not of 'disaster' proportions such as those of 1369, 1374–5, 1378–9 and 1386 which were followed by the worst floods of all, those of 1401, 1402 and 1409, and the devastating floods of the 1420s including the outstanding disaster of 1421 (the 'St Elizabeth flood') which also wrought much havoc and loss of life in the Netherlands (Brandon 1971a: 1–17).

With these early fifteenth-century floods, the initiative in matters of sea defence in Kent and Sussex, previously held securely by the great landlords, was temporarily lost. Walland Marsh in Romney Marsh was abandoned as was Denge Marsh and large areas around the port of Old Romney. Considerable areas of the north Kent marshes also suffered severely. In Sussex repeated attempts to save the Pevensey Levels proved abortive and a similar fate overtook the 'brookland' in the estuaries of the eastern Rother, Ouse, Adur and Arun. Former low-lying medieval moated sites such as Stretham manor, Henfield, were engulfed and reports of 'great rewyn' are ubiquitous (Brandon 1971d: 69–93; 1971c: 94–106).

The severe incidence of sea floods was accompanied by a number of short cycles of exceptionally wet and erratic weather generally which appear to be due to vigorous atmospheric activity. Something of the history of weather changes in south-east England can be ascertained from the accounts rendered annually for audit by officials of the larger manors and because these documents also supply data enabling the yield ratios to be calculated it is possible to establish certain correlations between weather and the quality of the harvest. Summarizing the weather experienced in the South East during the one hundred years from 1340, patterns of alternating good and bad harvests are detectable together with some evidence of a deterioration in the weather towards the end of the period. The short runs of particularly good grain yields fall into the years of the 1370s, with particularly bountiful harvests in 1372 and 1376–9 (corresponding to favourable weather all over Europe) and the period 1285–6, except low-lying areas which suffered flood damage during those years. After 1388, outstanding harvests are confined to single years such as 1393, 1400 and 1406. The bad runs of harvests suffering from spells of inclement weather are, with the exception of the 1360s, confined to the latter half of the period under review, viz. 1400–4, the 1420s and 1435–9. These spells of wet weather were severe enough to cause hardship and even starvation and death. They would have been particularly severe on the Weald clay (Brandon 1971a: 1–17).

The overall effect of these inclement spells in combination with increased storminess and the related submergences proved the *coup de grâce* for many marshland communities. In the Lewes and Laughton Levels, for example, winter floods were common in the fourteenth century and frequently the flood waters remained throughout the summer on the lower meadows and occasionally submerged crops on the bordering flanks. In 1422 a Commission of Sewers was appointed to restore the banks and drainage between Fletching and the coast. That the deterioration continued into the mid-fifteenth century is indicated by the changing condition of some 400 acres of the archbishop's meadow at Southerham which were converted into a permanent fishery known as the Brodewater. The virtual collapse of the drainage of more than 6,000 acres of the Levels continued into the first half of the sixteenth century for in 1537 it was reported that 'all the Level upwards (of Seaford) lay in a marsh all the summer long' and that 'When abundance of water cometh by rain and other floods of the sea it is yearly drowned and overflowed with water' (Brandon 1971c: 97).

The abandonment of the Pevensey Levels resulted in the loss of some acres of farmland, most of it rich pasture and arable land. The persistent sea attack in the period 1352–88 had left repeated references to crops lost through serious flooding, though these were not serious enough to galvanize officials into drainage and embanking. Major works at the Pevensey Haven outlet in 1396 and 1402 also helped to stave off damage. These improvements permitted substantial acreages to be regularly under the plough until the early fifteenth century. A gradual abandonment of the Levels was necessitated from 1402. In the winter of 1408–9 floods put the entire marsh out of action for the season and during the following summer gales and inclement weather added to the difficulties. The bailiff of the manor of Barnhorne responded to this calamity with vigour: extra workmen were hired to scour the sluices and water channels, to repair the walls and to replace the gates and bridge washed away by the floods with new ones strengthened with iron. This permitted sowing on a substantially reduced scale. By the 1410s it is clear that drainage expenses were rising steeply and that cropping the marshland had become extremely hazardous. The final catastrophe came with the St Elizabeth flood of 1421 and a series of lesser floods in the later 1420s, which effectively terminated the old farming economy of the Levels. The early fifteenth century marks the transition from an essentially arable economy to that of a cattle ranch. The increasingly pastoral bias can also be detected in the gradual abandonment of crops: dredge corn was not sown at Barnhorne after 1346; winter oats not after 1353; vetch not regularly sown after 1369 when the crop was lost to floods; the last extant record of rye is in 1388 when it was submerged by the sea; peas were an exceptional and minor crop after the great flood of 1402 (Brandon 1971d: 69–93).

Late-Medieval Domestic and Castle Building

The South East contains many thousands of late-medieval medium-sized houses, including manor houses and smaller farmhouses, whereas the flimsy cottages of the poor have rarely survived. These were built mainly of local materials by local craftsmen and are invaluable for casting light on the economic background of the area and the living conditions of the better-off inhabitants. The diverse geology of the region has influenced the wide variety of building materials used and the ease of importation through Channel ports meant that building materials could readily be brought over long distances, such as roofing tiles from Devon (Holden 1965: 67–78; 1989). Although stone such as Reigate Stone and Kentish Ragstone from the Hythe Beds and sandstone from the Hastings Beds was available, it was normally used in the Middle Ages only for churches, public buildings and larger houses. In a forested area like the Weald timber was undoubtedly cheaper than stone and it was normally the first choice for manor and smaller houses in the Middle Ages (Melling 1965: 1).

The vernacular tradition of domestic building in the South East is thus not of stone as in the Cotswolds or cob which is traditional to Devon but timber-framed houses with exposed timbers and an infilling either wholly of lath and plaster or of part brick, part plaster. In Kent, always the least feudal and most individualistic because one of the most intensively cultivated and industrialized of counties in the later Middle Ages, freeholding yeomen were able to build a larger and more luxurious and solidly constructed version of the common medieval family house and in greater numbers and somewhat earlier than elsewhere.

Among the finest examples of Kentish timber-framed architecture are the fifteenth-century hall houses built by the Flemish and other clothiers whom Edward III's and subsequent governments encouraged to produce finished cloth in England rather than export wool to Bruges and Ghent. The basic type of dwelling comprised an open-roofed hall with central hearth in which cooking was done as well as meals taken, smoke finding its own way out through the unglazed windows set as high as possible in the walls. The master's end of the hall communicated with the parlour, above which was the principal bedroom, used also by womenfolk during the day. At the other end was a cross passage with doors at either end with side doors opening into a pantry and storeroom. There was often some access to sleeping rooms above them. Timber, which was then abundant, was the normal material of construction, with thatch for the roof, although tiles were introduced earlier than in most districts. As the timber-hall of the house was enlarged, with a higher and wider hall, a construction problem arose of how to carry the increased weight of the hall's roof or its loftier walls without buttresses. The problem was to prevent the rafters thrusting the walls outwards. The earliest type of roof had been propped up by internal posts arranged in arcades as in larger houses and churches. The fourteenth-century solution in the South East was found in a combination of the tie-beam and the use of the flanking units as buttresses for the hall roof. This produced the apparent recessing of the hall front between the wings of the houses. Actually, the front is not set back but the first storey of the wings is jettied outwards so as to carry a continuous plate-beam supporting the hall rafters of the hall-front which were relieved of thrust. The overall effect has always been considered very pleasing, being designed to impress the high-quality features on passers-by or

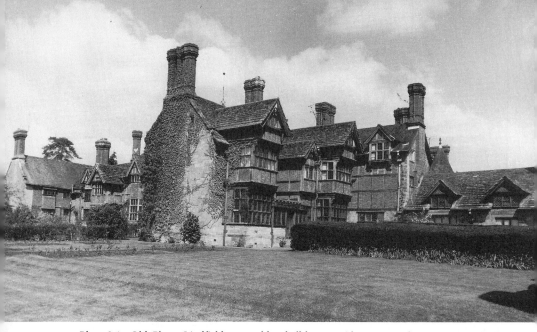

Plate 3.1 Old Place, Lindfield: a wealden hall-house with seventeenth-century stone-built dwelling. Charles Eamer Kempe, the Victorian glass designer, added a spectacular south wing in keeping with the older portion.

visitors (Plates 3.1 and 3.2). Although the tie beam, unnecessarily massive, is the main structural element in the roof, a traditional supporting post called the 'king post', often finely carved, was inserted so as to appear to be supporting the collar-beams, although it served no structural purpose. This lavish and lovely use of timber, more particularly in the roof of the halls, adds greatly to the charm of these clothiers' and yeomen's houses (Mason 1969;1975: 1–6; Wood 1965: 218).

Such wealden hall houses extend from their heartland in the Maidstone and Cranbrook districts into the bordering areas of Surrey and Sussex and they are also found relatively plentifully in the Surrey and Sussex clothing districts such as around Guildford, Godalming, Petworth and Lodsworth. Martin has found an interesting correlation between the proportions of the hallhouses and the sizes of the holdings that maintained them. On the whole a substantially built house with a ground floor of between 70 and 150 sq. yds would be supported by a freehold or copy hold tenement of some 50–125 acres (excluding woodland) while larger holdings were capable of maintaining proportionally larger buildings. It is uncertain whether agricultural profits alone accounted for these houses. It is likely, in the main, that builders were supplementing their agricultural incomes with cloth or other craft activities. Few medieval houses survive for holdings with less than 50 acres, which suggests that they were of inferior construction and have been replaced. The still flimsier cottages of the poor have similarly not survived (D. Martin, Pers. Comm.).

Apart from rural settlements, a high proportion of medieval town houses have survived in Burwash, Robertsbridge, Sedlescombe, Steyning and Ticehurst dating to *c*.1500 or earlier, most of which are comparable in size to rural dwellings. Robertsbridge was a 'new town' in the early thirteenth century, beginning with long burgages and having avoided severe contraction or expansion, these have survived into recent times as 50 medieval houses. Steyning was a pre-Conquest borough, long stabilized with about 125 houses, of which more than half of the surviving older houses are medieval. From an analysis of the size and other features of these houses it appears that many occupants of the small wealden market towns had attained a high standard of living by the later Middle Ages 'almost certainly considerably better than that enjoyed by the majority of the rural population', as Martin has noted. Very few instances of economies in building design have been found. Money was not conserved by structural economies as in the homes of the poor, but costs were reduced by close vertical studding being used for aesthetic effect only on front and sides, the rear walls being constructed with large daub panes.

The simplest wealden houses and their sparse furnishings are only glimpsed in some fifteenth-century records. At Hooe and Barnhorne, for

---

Plate 3.2 Bayleaf farmhouse interior. The diagram shows the fifteenth-century jetty in its simplest form, unglazed mullion windows, simple crown-post roof, and recessed hall, all carrying connotations of a high social status (Barley 1986).

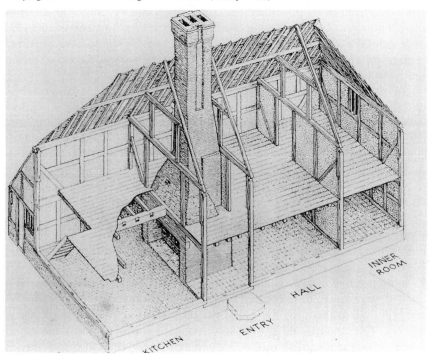

111

example, little homesteads comprising only three rooms, hall, bedroom and kitchen were apparently single-storeyed houses with a service room at either end of the hall. Bell's Farm in Slaugham and Hashland Farm in Horsham are two similar surviving farmsteads. William Creche's homestead in Hooe was sparsely furnished with only the barest necessities - a table, two benches, a form and a chair. His kitchen housed the cooking equipment brought back and forth from the hall fire and in the bedroom were two plainly furnished beds, a bench and 'two coffins in readiness' (Brandon 1974: 142–3).

A different building tradition prevailed in the downland. At Hangleton, the only major medieval deserted village to be fully excavated, timber-framed houses were replaced about the middle of the thirteenth century by new ones incorporating flint walls which in turn gave way to fifteenth-century farmhouses oriented on a fresh axis. The spade has thus revealed a complicated story of organic growth and decay which gives the lie to the still widely-held assumption of the age-long stability of the medieval village. Cottagers lived in humble buildings comprising only two rooms, a living room with a partition at one end for the bedroom. The early medieval farmsteads had affinities with longhouses of upland Britain, being long in relation to breadth and having two living rooms and a cross passage which separated a third room used for some farming purpose, though at present it is uncertain whether animals were housed in this part as no central drain has yet been discovered (Holden 1963: 106; Hurst and Hurst 1964: 94–142). The relative size of the later farmsteads lived in by downland peasant farmers can be gauged at Alciston where a number of still-surviving dwellings are recorded in a survey of 1433. These comprise substantial rooms on two floors which would have provided ample space and relative comfort for everyday living purposes and for storing seed corn and other goods (Brandon 1974: 131–2).

In the medieval seaports well-constructed vernacular architecture is sparse, doubtless because of their impoverishment in the later Middle Ages. At Hastings, for example, Martin has noted some very low-quality fifteenth-century buildings skimped in almost every particular and at Shoreham, a major port in the thirteenth century, but sadly decayed in the fifteenth, only three or four medieval houses survived the great storm of 1703 and these have nothing like the lavish construction of the Weald (D. Martin, Pers. Comm.).

With the aid of medieval surveys and inventories we can ascertain something of the nature of fourteenth-century manor houses. Old Woking in Surrey was a grand complex on the banks of the river Wey with a great hall in 1327, a private chapel for the lord and his family and another for the household, two large chambers with a pantry and buttery adjoining, a kitchen, bakehouse, brewhouse, fulling house and laundry. Under another roof were apartments for the lord's treasurer and for visiting knights and esquires. The orchard and garden were enclosed within an inner moat and on the outside of a second moat were the guard house and other apartments, and the farm buildings, ox stalls, the barton (the main barn), two granges, rickyards, stables, cartsheds, cowshed and dovecote (Brandon 1977: 47).

A prominent feature of the south-eastern landscape was the moated homestead but this is too inadequately recorded and excavated as yet for its social and economic significance to be fully understood. A provisional list of Surrey moats (Turner 1977: 89–94) suggests that the county was not so moat-bearing as Essex with its more expansive clays. Kent has 93 known moats and Sussex 190 (Aberg 1978:2) but neither of these figures is based on systematic research. A characteristic moated homestead site of the eastern Weald is a relatively humble and somewhat elongated moat surrounded by a single ditch, as represented by Batchelor's farm, Edenbridge, which contains an ordinary 'wealden' house with room for a cattle byre within the moat. This type may characterize the many homesteads cleared from the woodland on larger farms by freemen (franklins) in the twelfth and thirteenth centuries, but the period of moating is inconclusive at present. The existing houses on moated sites are unlikely to be original: at Rivington, Kent, the late hall house replaced earlier houses in similar positions going back to the late thirteenth century (Rigold 1978).

Towards the top of the social scale was the moated site of Eltham Palace, perhaps the grandest single moated site in the South East, complete with huge forecourt outside the moat and structures at base dating from an episcopal phase *c.*1300 and with bridges of brick masonry of the fifteenth century. Occupying an intermediate social status was the classic moated site of Ightham Mote, a place of unrivalled beauty, on a new assart of the late twelfth or early thirteenth century. Bridges cross the moat to an imposing gatehouse, part Tudor, part medieval. The stone-built Great Hall dates to the 1340s and several of the forecourt buildings are of the same period. From the sixteenth century these medieval buildings were engulfed in a romantic resemblance of a façade-castle (Rigold 1978). Many of the largest moated sites were the headquarters of important seignorial manors, lay or ecclesiastical, and typically comprise a spacious platform with various domestic, ecclesiastic and farm buildings and with often two or more moated enclosures, one occupied by the manor house itself, others being various buildings and gardens. Old Woking is an example of this type (Brandon 1977: 47). In the Arun valley is a string of large moated enclosures, mainly manorial or sub-manorial, where barns and other farm buildings lay within the moated enclosure, still leaving extensive room for livestock at night. Such moats were probably built as a protection from wolves and marauders before the establishment of surrounding villages but whether the moat was primarily defensive or to some extent a status symbol is one of the many aspects of moats in the South East yet to be elucidated (Taylor 1972: 237–49). From about 1500 increasing political stability and rising standards of comfort brought the abandonment of large numbers of moated homesteads.

As for the homes of the nobility, Bodiam castle is one of the most perfect examples of the new style of castle-building which began in late fourteenth-century England, primarily for purposes of defence but not without convenience and comfort. It was built *c.*1386 on the banks of the river Rother commanding the marshes stretching to the sea at Rye and Winchelsea by Sir Edward Dalyngrydge, a veteran of Crecy and Poitiers, as a defence against the French who had earlier twice sacked the locality. The needs of defence were met by the width of the moat surrounding the island on which the castle was erected and the thickness and height of the walls. The smallness of the few windows and the innovative castellated architecture, eight lofty drum towers, the curtain walls, machicolated entrance and the elaborate fortifications of the approaches made it impregnable. The stone keep of the old-style castle was omitted. Entering the castle involved crossing three drawbridges leading to the principal gate tower and a multiplication of other defences. This gave access to the offices of the guards, the chapel and sacristy, the private apartments, the banqueting hall and other state rooms. These were liberally provided with fireplaces, windows and latrines. The buttery, cellar and great kitchen lay near the south-west tower, which protected the Great Well. The western side of the castle was the servants' quarters and finally in the north-west angle were the garrison, stables and workshops. Vessels of considerable size could then reach Bodiam by every tide. The spectacular stronghold was bought with money acquired by years of successful marauding in France and was probably designed on the basis of castles that Dalyngrydge had encountered in France. It gives a vivid idea of what a castle of a well-to-do English knight was like at the close of the fourteenth century. As Lord Curzon, a former owner has said: 'Whether for sport or dalliance or more serious affairs, whether for a life of pleasure or hazard of war, Bodiam castle was equally well planned' (Curzon 1926).

Other fortified rural residences built primarily for defence in the reign of Richard II include Westenhanger in Kent, now a ruin, and Scotney castle on the borders of Kent and Sussex, since incorporated into a picturesque landscape. Amberley castle, built by William Rede, Bishop of Chichester, in 1379 was most similar in shape and dimensions to Bodiam. This grand residence similarly grew from a modest manor house of *c.*1200 with a first-floor hall with a great chamber over the service end and a chapel. Bishop Rede increased the size of his residence more than ten-fold by means of a courtyard castle and corner towers, Great Hall, comfortable private apartments and extensive timber-framed lodgings over stables (Barley 1986:

Plate 3.3 Herstmonceux Castle: an aerial view. Although the castle appears formidable, it was built as a stylish country house containing every luxury known to the mid-fifteenth century. By 1776, the building had been allowed to deteriorate to such an extent that the then owner demolished the interior. During the nineteenth century the castle was totally abandoned. The major reconstruction, begun by Col. Claude Lowther, was completed by Sir Paul Latham in the 1930s. In 1946 the Admiralty bought the house and grounds to provide a better site for the Royal Observatory, but in 1988 the castle was sold.

88). Amberley castle recalls the large retinues of a medieval bishop, his constant travel on affairs of state and diocesan administration and is indicative of the growing wealth and prestige of the Church. In 1382 Archbishop Courtenay similarly began to refurbish the twelfth-century Saltwood castle as his principal residence.

The magnificent moated castle of Herstmonceux built *c*.1440 on an impressive scale by Sir Roger de Fiennes has an outstanding place in English architecture as the earliest of the great brick houses south of the Thames (Plate 3.3). All the numerous lodgings and offices of a major castle were incorporated into a single block so that the whole castle could be viewed four-square and in the round (Binney 1988). It is the chief of a group of fifteenth-century houses in the novel material of brick constructed by wealthy nobles who had become high officials at Court after campaigning in France. The stupendous gateway is as much a *tour de force* as that at Warwick castle. The actual site lies very low. As Walpole observed: 'The building for the convenience of water to the moat sees nothing at all!' (Walpole 1906 edn, ii: 299). Not yet did the great magnates build a mansion to command a broad prospect. After nearly 150 years as a ruin it was restored as a country house in the first half of this century. Both as a precursor of the Renaissance house and as a source of inspiration to the Gothic revivalists of the eighteenth century, it is an artistic achievement of the first order.

It was not until the sixteenth century that castles were constructed exclusively for military use. In this final stage of castle-building, Henry VIII undertook when faced with the threat of a French invasion in 1538–9 'the one system of comprehensive coastal defence ever attempted in England before modern times'. These fortresses were designed for the mounting of cannon and had an elaborate concentric structure including a circular keep rising above six attached bastions within an outer ring of six larger bastions surrounded by a deep moat. The parapets were curved to deflect gunshot. The most powerful of Henrician castles and also the most complete surviving example is Deal castle (Plate 3.4). Camber castle was constructed in three phases between 1512 and 1543. It began as a central tower; four bastions were added later and finally an immensely strong fortress with four massive semi-circular bastions was added on the perimeter. Other castles of this type were Walmer, a similar but smaller castle of the Deal type, the official residence of the Warden of the Cinque Ports, and Sandown. Fortifications necessary for the defence of the Thames estuary include Tilbury Fort erected by Henry VIII and Upnor Castle begun in 1559 to guard the developing Tudor dockyard of Chatham.

Plate 3.4 Deal Castle: an aerial view. The Tudor coastal forts of Deal, Walmer, Camber and the rest were exclusively military defences belonging to the Crown, to protect the anchorage within the Goodwin Sands. As such, they mark the demise of the castle, which had also possessed a residential function. Deal rose in the shadow of its castle as a victualling base on the busy shipping lane of the English Channel.

The Lifestyle of Late-Medieval Nobility

'Nobility' is used here in the broadest sense to include the lesser ranks of what became commonly referred to as 'the gentry' in the fifteenth century. Although this segment of medieval society comprised vast differences in wealth, and hence in social status and political influence, its lifestyle was based on lordship which, as we have noted, bore more heavily on the peasants of Sussex and Surrey than those of Kent. It has been observed of lordship that it:

> Achieved what it was designed to do: to transfer wealth into the
> pockets of lords and to place in their hands effective machinery for
> control of the mass of the population . . . Lordship in the Middle
> Ages was much more than landlordship. The yield of the soils and
> the labour of the peasant combined with the skill and enterprise of
> the artisan or merchant . . . provided the noble with the means to
> sustain his lifestyle. They built his castle, equipped him for war,
> funded his travels, paid for his leisure and his hospitality, salaried
> his servants and underwrote his largesse . . . (Given-Wilson 1987:
> 25).

Closest to the centre of political power in the fourteenth century and
among the half-dozen or so richest men in England was Richard Fitzalan II,
Earl of Arundel (d. 1376). Restored to his father's earldom by the young King
Edward III, he served him assiduously as royal counsellor and courtier until
his death. His son, Richard III (d. 1397) was also one of the greatest feudal
lords of the fourteenth century, who led bands of adventure-hungry knights
on expeditions into France and the Low Countries. Much of the Fitzalans'
wealth now arose from money-lending to the Crown, other nobles and religious
institutions, but the basis of their power was their landed estate. The Fitzalans
were originally Marcher lords but in 1243 the Honor of Arundel was acquired
through marriage and in 1347 the Honors of Reigate and Lewes were added
from the de Warenne inheritance. Additionally, Earl Richard II consolidated his
Sussex estate, focused on Arundel, by the purchase of more than twenty manors
and smaller estates. By his death his Sussex estate was colossal, comprising 64
manors, twelve forests, thirteen deer parks, 13,000 arable acres in demesne and
10,000 acres of woodland. Arundel itself became the earl's chief seat and then
his administrative headquarters. The earl, however, was frequently resident at
the castles of Reigate and Lewes, as well as at other places on his estate such as
Stansted, favoured for hunting. His presence at court made a London house
also a necessity. A major difference in estate administration is noticeable
between the Honors of Arundel and Lewes. The former was under a strong
lordship and the earls of Arundel were looked to by local community leaders
to provide for their own advancement and aspirations. In the more recently
acquired Lewes Honor the Fitzalans did not always fulfil what was expected
of them. Earl Richard III for example, was unpopular with the citizens of Lewes
because he declined to defend the castle for them unless they paid for the cost
of the 400 men needed to man it. This may explain why insurgents during the
Peasants' Revolt of 1381 broke into the castle and damaged it. The Fitzalans'
management of the Lewes Honor was also much looser than that of Arundel.
Manors such as Ditchling and Rodmell were early farmed out to tenants,
who were themselves invariably absentees. This allowed the emergence of
gentry families enhancing their own social positions and also encouraging the
conversion of customary and other unfree tenancies into freeholds, so offering
a social ladder for the lower echelons of rural society. The will of Fitzalan III,
made in 1393, gives glimpses of the splendour of Arundel, with its magnificent

armoury, great stores of domestic furniture, richly-embroidered tapestries and silken hangings, and the immense hoard of money in the castle keep (Salzman 1953: 32–52; Clough 1969: xxv–xxxv).

Fourteenth-century knightly society can be glimpsed through three families of knightly rank who lived in east Sussex - the Etchinghams, the Sackvilles and the Waleys (Saul 1986). The Etchinghams were one of the oldest and most distinguished of the Sussex gentry, being descended from Reinbert, the first Norman steward of the Count of Eu's rape of Hastings. They held land in the High Weald and also the valuable corn-and-sheep manor of Beddingham near Lewes. The Sackvilles claimed descent from Herbrand, a Norman knight who accompanied the Conqueror. A junior branch of the family was established at Buckhurst, adjoining Ashdown Forest from c.1200. They also held the manor of Chalvington and much property outside the South East. The Waleys were lords of Glynde near Lewes and were probably descended from Godfrey of Malling who was holding land in Glynde of the Archbishop of Canterbury c.1090.

Each of these knightly families owed most of their wealth to landed estates. Thirteenth-century families directly farmed their own wealden properties as well as the more fertile ones in the scarpfoot zone of the Chalk. They were giving up direct exploitation of the wealden ones by the end of the thirteenth century when they resorted to leasing. They held their other estates in hand until the 1380s and 1390s after which they opted for the administratively easier and cheaper policy of leasing these when wages rose and land values fell. The Waleys of Glynde, in common with neighbouring estates, produced so much corn that they employed seasonal migratory harvesters from the Weald. The Etchinghams' Beddingham manor was also a great producer of wool but its productivity in corn did not match that of the Battle Abbey manors of Lullington and Alciston which had greater inputs of labour and capital. All three families probably experienced a downturn in income from land during the fifteenth century but unfortunately it is not clear from surviving documents whether they were obliged to make economies in their lifestyle.

Although well-connected and wealthy country gentlemen, the three knightly families did not have a residence of their own in the capital. When drawn there on business they either had to stay with friends or to find a room at an inn. This suggests that even the landed gentry found it difficult to break out of local patterns of life in which the peasant was deeply embedded. The Etchinghams' rootedness in their Sussex homeland is symbolized by the rebuilding of Etchingham parish church in the 1360s by Sir William de Etchingham. After the fashion of his time he chose to make the parish church rather than a monastery (Robertsbridge) the focus of the religious and social aspirations of his family. A striking characteristic of the church interior is the heraldic decoration of the stained glass windows. In the east window of the chancel Sir William placed the coats of arms of the king and members of the royal family and in the windows flanking them, those of earls. The arms of his knightly neighbours he placed in the nave. As Saul has suggested 'the fabric and decoration of the new building were conceived by the patron to bear visual witness to his family's place in the pecking order of local society . . . with a sense of delight in the use of heraldry for heraldry's sake' (Saul 1986: 148–9).

Another vivid insight into the living conditions of the time is found in the inventory of the contents of Sir Andrew Sackville's wardrobe drawn up in 1370 which included his bed with canopy and hanging curtains, several coverlets, a pair of velvet-lined plates of armour and several furred robes with cuffs of miniver (the pale winter belly of the red squirrel), a high grade fur, and also of ermine to which he was not entitled by rank but which had perhaps been a gift. Sir Andrew had a busy career in the military service of the Earl of Arundel which took him on active service in Scotland and the Low Countries. Judging from the amount of bread and ale consumed in the 1380s, the Waleys may have had a household of between 15 and 20 persons. Sir William de Etchingham's predecessor paid for the schooling of two boys at Lewes, doubtless by way of preparation for service with him.

The dwellings in which these families lived are homes no longer. The sites of Hawkesden and Glottenham, moated dwellings of Etchinghams, have been excavated, however. That Robert de Etchingham, the occupier of Glottenham, had higher standards of living than earlier occupiers is attested by the archaeological evidence of cinder-paving in the form of a court-yard in front of the buildings and outside the rear doorway of the hall. He buried rubbish tidily in pits and used high quality polychrome jugs imported from Saintonge. Yet the construction of the house with a minimum of masonry suggests that Robert was not a man of unlimited financial means.

Another insight into the regional gentry is provided by their role as stewards of Battle Abbey, many of whom after 1330 were young men from well-connected local gentry families beginning their careers in law and administration. Most of them had a legal education. Robert Belknap was an ambitious man who served the abbey for a quarter of a century and rose to become a powerful man as Chief Justice of Common Pleas. Another steward of Battle Abbey was Robert Oxenbridge, a man on the make, who gave less priority to the abbot of Battle than to Sir John Pelham of Laughton, a rising star at court (Saul 1986: 70–1). The man who served Battle Abbey longer than anyone else was Bartholomew Bolney, appointed in the 1420s in the office of steward and who held the appointment for fifty years almost until his death in 1477. Bolney is a prime example of a man of legal training who combined estate management with private and public service to build up a modest fortune and social advancement. He retired to West Firle, where monumental brasses commemorate him and his wife, and married his daughter into the wealthy family of the Gages, who were to acquire Battle Abbey property at the Reformation (Plate 3.5). What makes Bolney particularly significant is his *The Book of Bartholomew Bolne*, a unique record of the building-up of

Plate 3.5 in text below:

Bartholomew Bolne and Eleanor, his Wife.
West Firle Church. Sussex.

Plate 3.5 The Bartholomew Bolney Brass, West Firle: a drawing by W. T. Quartermain in 1865. By using the law as a step-ladder to social success, Bolney epitomises the social mobility of the fifteenth century. His little estate at West Firle, which he amassed, involved the consolidation and exchange of formerly interspersed common field strips of arable land.

his little country estate piece by piece 'as an up-and-coming member of the administrative middle class' (Clough 1964: xxviii).

The Late-Medieval City and Town

In the early sixteenth century only two of the forty leading English towns were located within the South East (Phythian-Adams 1979: 27). In the upper reaches of the urban hierarchy was Canterbury which in the late medieval period, as in Roman times, was the most populous town, although then in the process of long-term decline. Formerly a rival for such provincial towns as Bristol, York, Salisbury or Exeter, it had only 766 taxpayers in 1525, indicating a population of some 3–4,000 and a market circuit of thirty to forty miles (although with a social influence much wider) and was fairly typical of the second tier of English towns in later-medieval England. Chichester was a scaled-down version of medieval Canterbury in size and function. Contrastingly, East Anglia could boast at the end of the fifteenth century eleven of the largest towns in England, including Norwich, the leading provincial city of the time and south-west England contained ten such towns. If the somewhat risky business of allocating population on the basis of recorded taxed population in the Lay Subsidies is allowed for, this comparative lack of larger towns is a clear sign of the inhibiting metropolitan influence of London to which towns in the South East had yielded, and which was already beginning to mould the regional economy of the region in the late Middle Ages. This process was greatly aided by the comparatively good river and sea communications with the metropolis. The relative lack of large towns also reflects the fact that the prosperity of the South East was at that time primarily based on the agricultural produce of its estates and farms. Consequently, the South East was a region of shire towns and markets.

There were also internal reasons why the urban particularism of the South East lacked the diversity of more self-contained regions of England by the end of the fifteenth century. Haven decay had long relegated the Cinque Ports and other seafaring towns along the Channel coast to vulnerability. Furthermore, industrial concentration at older-established urban centres such as Canterbury, Maidstone, Sandwich and Guildford was being undermined by places with claims to an urban status in the Weald, such as Wonersh, Surrey and Cranbrook and Tenterden in Kent, from whence Wat Tyler and Jack Cade had drawn support that made London tremble. By reason of their lower labour costs, absence of gild restrictions and costly civic overheads these were gaining at the expense of the older towns. Although the South East had a multitude of towns, they were essentially markets servicing rural hinterlands of varying sizes. Some, like Kingston, Croydon, Guildford, Lewes, Faversham, Dover, New Romney and Rochester were bustling places with an economic hinterland of some fifteen miles and populations of between 1,000 and 1,500. These were also administrative and sometimes ecclesiastical foci for sub-regional hinterlands of greater extent. Towards the bottom of the urban hierarchy were 'simple' market towns with populations very much smaller which were not genuine urban centres at all but had only rudimentary economic activity over a hinterland of eight miles or so. The wealden market towns founded in the thirteenth-century woodland clearance generally remained small, impoverished places. East Grinstead, founded *c*.1250, still possessed only 48 burgages and 47 burgage plots four centuries later when High Street was the only built-up street. Four of the oldest burgage tenements date to the first half of the fourteenth century when it is inferred that the street frontages had been finally taken up, at which date cottages and shops in Middle Row, a line of buildings in the centre of High Street, also probably existed, on the site of the former town market. Its single street is a vivid reminder of the poverty of the wealden environment centred upon Ashdown Forest. Uckfield, another very late starter, glimpsed in embryonic form in *c*. 1273, still remained in 1500 a place of unremarkable growth and prosperity (Cornwall 1976: 1–26). Smaller, mostly non-corporate market towns abounded in Kent. The townsmen were mostly retailers, many of whom were in addition craftsmen or processors, farmers, graziers, or fishermen in the case of coastal towns. Absent from such places were the purveyors of luxuries and more specialized craftsmen such as grocers, mercers, goldsmiths, scriveners and notaries, found only in the larger towns (Dulley 1966).

The lack of surviving court rolls for towns in the South East has meant that few contributions to the current debate about urban development have emanated from within the region. Nevertheless, on the basis of rents there is convincing evidence of growth during the later fourteenth-century, and equally good evidence of persistent contraction in most towns between 1420 and 1524, when the Lay Subsidy was taken. The years between 1352 and 1407 seem to be the only period of economic growth, a period coinciding with urban growth outside the region, e.g. at Colchester. Due in large measure to the paucity of relevant sources, the study of local markets and domestic trade in the economy of the South East is relatively unexplored. This is regrettable because the vital domestic trade, whether local or regional, occupied a critical position in the medieval economy, notably in terms of employment, expansion of trade and the growth of towns.

The clearest expression of urban decay is at Canterbury. Here the ownership of property and rent income was concentrated in the last quarter of the fourteenth century into perhaps only 5 per cent of the total population, and eighteen of Canterbury's citizens had cornered most of the urban property market. The majority of townsmen earned a modest living in trade and crafts. Their fortunes during the later Middle Ages in a period of high mortality and falling demand with its concomitant conditions of urban decline can be investigated in broad terms through levels of rent income. Canterbury Cathedral Priory owned 156 messuages and tenements, 123 shops and five inns spread across all wards of the town. In the early fourteenth century the prior's income from Canterbury rents was about £145 per annum. In the 1370s and 1380s this was bettered, with annual figures as high as £181. From the early fifteenth century the picture alters adversely. Records between 1407 and 1521 reveal a sustained and profound fall in income from urban rents due to unpaid income on urban property, and downward adjustments to rents in general, notably in house and shop rents. Early sixteenth-century Canterbury accounts record properties in ruin, or prolonged vacancies and lapsed rent payments on a large scale. The prior's properties in the commercial heart of the town, where property values tended to be highest, had suffered severely. In general there appears to have been a significant fall in the demand for property between 1409 and 1432 and no rebuilding went on. There was little alleviation in the 1450s and 1460s and the most severe reductions in rents occurred in the first two decades of the sixteenth century, in commercial parts of the city and in other parishes alike. The overall picture of general economic decline in Canterbury is clear but it was not the making of the fourteenth century. Its turning point of decay, giving it an air of dereliction, was the 1420s and 1430s and its nadir was between 1475 and 1525. The fluctuating fortunes of Canterbury citizens, in so far as they can be assessed by levels of rent, must have reflected in large degree the relative economic depression of its supporting rural hinterland.

On this basis, the town's resilience in the 1370s and 1380s, when despite high rates of mortality, the town gained from rapid immigration and changed patterns of consumption, is perfectly consistent with the marked revival based on demesne agriculture (p.95). Conversely, the persistent decline from the second quarter of the fifteenth century, and its nadir fifty or more years later coincides with the trough of agricultural depression in Kent. Further case studies of urban rents would probably throw much needed light not only on the urban elite and urban society as a whole, but would also reveal in their peaks and troughs much-needed evidence for local comparisons of the fortunes of their supporting lords and peasants in their respective hinterlands, which by their very different soil patterns and rural societies may not have responded to economic changes to the same degree or at the same time (Butcher 1979).

The possibility, however, is that a close symbiosis between urban and rural development did not always exist. This needs to be borne in mind when considering the fortunes of Battle. Whilst Battle Abbey flourished, the town of Battle prospered. In the 1367 rental of Battle about 210 dwellings are identifiable, suggesting a minimum population of about 1,000 people, a large town by the standards of the time, and this is certainly an under-estimate of the houses as sub-tenancies are only occasionally and incidentally mentioned. At this time Battle's population was comparable to that of Chichester, supporting a community of specialized and luxury-goods craftsmen which gave its market a real advantage over its local rivals. After the early 1330s, however, there is evidence of population decline. It was already a shrunken town that was devastated by the Black Death and by the 1370s depopulation is very evident in the town's records. Messuages were then being taken at reduced rents and entry fines for new tenants were lowered. Tenements also lay in hand and were absorbed into adjoining messuages. Former house sites were now merely gardens or crofts. Some survivors of the plagues were now accumulating, enlarging and making their houses more comfortable. Decay is not necessarily implied by the abandonment of the ancient market hall and market place at the end of the fifteenth century, because burgesses may have preferred to sell their wares in High Street shops or at home. Burgess craftsmen now needed storage, work-space and display areas, another sign of improved living conditions and social change. This is also suggested by the thorough restoration of the parish church and the building of houses in stone, or with new stone fronts which came to replace lath and plaster cottages. 'There is evidence of a solid prosperity, rather more generally shared than before 1350' (Searle 1974: 351–67).

Upwards of twenty market towns in Sussex can be identified in the Subsidy Rolls for 1524–5 but few were of any size and none was large. In Sussex not a single town exceeded a population of 2,000. Chichester and Lewes each had a population of upwards of 1,500, that is no more than their populations in 1086. Rye was possibly larger; certainly it was the fastest growing (Dulley 1969). Hastings might have had about 1250 people. Petworth, Midhurst and Winchelsea were at about the 500 mark. Other market towns such as West Tarring, Storrington and Hailsham, and Elham, Chilham and Smarden were probably rather smaller. 'What does emerge is that however viewed Sussex towns were a long way from being centres of wealth and were not relatively more prosperous than many villages, (Cornwall 1976: 15).

The later Middle Ages were also a period of fluctuating urban fortunes. The rise of Horsham, Battle and Cuckfield reflect the burgeoning of the Weald, as does that of Petworth which owed its prosperity to the cloth trade and was able to afford an efficient public water supply utilizing wooden pipes from a water-driven pump at a spring a mile away. 'Everything indeed points towards a few favoured towns, well spaced out, coming to dominate districts of some size, while others, established in an earlier age and in very different circumstances, were fading into obscurity' (Cornwall 1976: 17).

Forming a special category of urban decay were the Channel ports which all suffered from silting, coastal erosion and war. The earlier prosperity of Shoreham is reflected in the great size and dignity of its parish church. This was followed by a long decline and abject decay caused by devastating sea floods and coastal erosion between c.1375 and 1425 when the river was increasingly deflected eastwards by a sand and shingle bar blocking the port and driving the river on to the southern half of the town, which seems to have been destroyed. Only a series of short 'stumps' of former streets now exist. Only the stone-built building known as Marlipins appears to have survived the sea attacks of the later Middle Ages. Once a customs house, this was turned into a private residence of the prior of Lewes when trade declined (Cheal 1921: 18).

Newhaven originated in the 1530s when an artificial channel was cut through the shingle bar blocking the mouth of the Ouse, so providing a new harbour in succession to that of Seaford and also serving to mitigate the flooding of the Lewes and Laughton Levels and to facilitate inland navigation. That it was the first 'new town' to be created in the South East for more than one hundred years is itself a sign of the severity of the urban crisis of the late Middle Ages (Brandon 1971c: 94–106).

The Cinque Ports, apart from Rye, were in a parlous position by the early fifteenth century. Leland's notes of his itinerary in south-east England in the late sixteenth century include his observation that Folkestone was, 'marvellously sore wasted with the violence of the sea'; Hythe, 'a very great town in length and contained four parishes but now be clean destroyed'; Romney 'hath been a metely good haven [but] the sea is now two miles from the town, so sore therby decayed that where there were three great parishes and churches sometime is now scant one well maintained'. Sandwich, once 'metely walled' was then decayed by a great sand bank encumbering the harbour; Stonar in Thanet, 'sometime a pretty town', had nothing left but the ruin of its church. Lympne 'sometime a famous haven' was no more.

It was the expanding walled city of medieval London that had the greatest concentration of wealth, talent and population in England. London was surrounded by spreading suburbs such as Southwark, a town in itself, and Westminster, dominated by the royal palace and abbey. In the thirteenth and fourteenth centuries London developed as the administrative and economic capital of England. In part this is connected with the substantial withdrawal of the Crown from Winchester which declined from its pre-eminence as the national capital in the twelfth century to merely one of a number of smaller provincial towns. Correspondingly, London rose to be the nation's capital and the centre of a region embracing some 50 to 75 miles, including much of south-east England. After the pestilences foreign trade still prospered and the city retained and even increased its economic dominance over other English ports, despite a reduction in its population by up to one-third. In the South East London's maritime role increased at the expense of the regional ports because they had suffered so generally from coastal erosion, silting and war. Consequently, the network of London's trade began to spread over the entire South East. Gentry households sent to London for spices, sugar, salt fish and other imported goods, all to the detriment of the region's own markets. The economic dominance of London over the region also coincided with the burgeoning of crafts in fourteenth-century London, such as the book trade, the working in wrought silver, tin or white lead. The rise of London was not wholly to the disadvantage of the South East. Towns near the city, such as Kingston and Croydon had unusually good opportunities to market agricultural produce in London. Under this influence manors moved towards a higher economic specialization and concentration of property. Fatstock and dairy produce became components in Surrey's agricultural development on the fringes of London (Veale 1969: 133–54; Thrupp 1969: 251–74; Stow 1603 edn).

The rise of Southampton as a major distribution centre for southern England in the fifteenth century also usurped much of the former trade of the west Sussex port-towns and markets. Carriers operating by sea as far east as Brighton, made frequent sailings to Southampton with small consignments of grain and fish, collecting for the return trip salt, alum, tar, iron, fruit, wine and spices (Bettey 1986: 117–19; Coleman 1960–1: Stevens and Oldig 1985).

The Changing Distribution of Regional Wealth and Population, 1086–1520

The quickening of the national and regional economy in the early sixteenth century makes the end of the Middle Ages an appropriate point in time at which to survey changes in the distribution of regional wealth and population in the preceding centuries. In so far as this can be measured from the evidence of taxation, three cross sections in time are available: the Domesday Survey of 1086, the 1334 Lay Subsidy return (particularly valuable as it enables us to see the situation on the eve of the Black Death), and that of 1524–5. Despite the limitations of each and the differences arising from direct comparison of one source with another, they each provide a broad guide to the changing regional significance of each part of the South East during the medieval period and since each of these returns covered England as a whole, the region's performance can be compared with the rest of the country at these dates.

As we have seen, the map of the Domesday South East recorded an epoch when men and action had made a limited impact on the heavy clays of the Weald, in contrast to the relatively dense settlement on the highly-productive rich alluvium and loamy wolds and downs, and the well-weathered soils in the Thames Basin. It was the achievement of generation after generation of medieval farmers and craft-workers to transform the relatively poor and backward community of the Weald into one of the wealthier districts of England by 1500. It was also a medieval accomplishment to produce on the best cereal-growing lands on the Coastal Fringe some of the highest yields and largest sheep flocks recorded in England. Both these developments are discernible in the taxation returns.

The contrasting challenges and potentialities of the region are fascinatingly illustrated by the Lay Subsidy rolls of 1334 (Fig.3.2). The association of backwardness with the Weald and development with the coastal belt still held good in several respects. The most striking feature of the 1334 map is the comparative poverty of the Weald and Romney Marsh relative to north-east Kent and coastal Sussex (which would have been a still greater disparity had the Cinque Ports not been exempt from taxation). Glasscock has written: 'Clearly

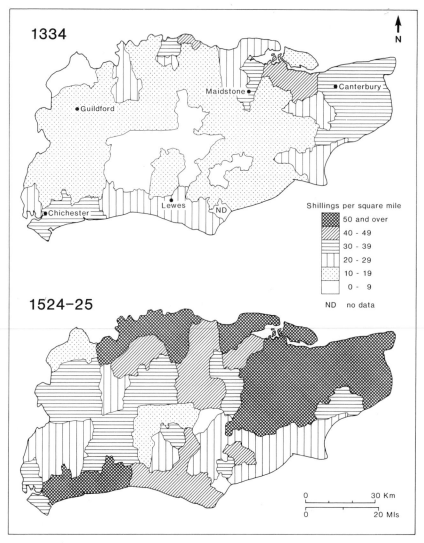

Figure 3.2 Changes in regional land values 1334–1525 (after Glasscock 1965 and Sheail 1972).

the Weald was an area of subsistence rather than of commercial agriculture and as such we are unlikely to find many people producing much surplus to be taxed as moveable wealth' (Glasscock 1965: 61–8). While the prosperity of north-east Kent and the coastal belt of Sussex can be partly explained by soil fertility and efficient agricultural practice and organization, the low tax assessments of the Weald probably under-record the economic activity of this district, for many taxpayers drawing upon its resources of wealth were taxed at the places of 'most resort' outside the Weald and Romney Marsh. A notable omission in the 1334 return of the Weald are the big taxpayers of the coastal zone who were important merchants, wealthy farmers and graziers, many of whom were exploiting the Weald. This 'colonial' character of the Weald in 1334 must therefore be allowed for. The lowest values in the Weald are on the Weald Clay and on the poor ridge soils of the central Weald. The north Surrey, Kentish and West Sussex assessments are rather higher. This situation probably had its origin in the nature of the soils themselves and it still is imprinted on the landscape. All the forests shared common characteristics. They were primitive areas possessed of soil too poor to have attracted reclamation on a great scale but with some mineral wealth in the form of iron ore. Hence in these places the Weald was still a 'waste' supporting a subsistence way of life to a greater degree than anywhere else in the South East. The survival of such a primitive agricultural society was probably one of the chief obstructions to its economic and social advancement and over the centuries this became clearer for as other places advanced their economies they left the poorest parts of the Weald more and more behind.

The highest assessments reflect the rapid growth of Southwark and its vicinity as a suburb of London and the highly efficient agriculture developed on the coastal zones. North-east Kent on account of its position, fertility and agricultural organization was the largest continuous area assessed at over 20s per square mile, one of the highest figures in the country and comparable to much of Norfolk, central Cambridgeshire and Oxfordshire, all very rich agricultural areas. In conclusion it seems that Glasscock's remark that the 'prosperity of the coastal fringe of south-east England, outside the Weald, was due not only to its fertility but also to its nearness to markets at home and on the Continent, and the sea transport whereby to carry the produce' goes a long way to explain the high tax assessments of the periphery. It is not likely to be a coincidence that the most highly rated part of Kent between the Medway and the Swale estuaries emerges in the thirteenth and fourteenth centuries as one of the leading exporters of grain to the London food market.[*]

The 1524–5 tax subsidy not only reveals the continued wealth of the coastal belt, where farmers, especially in north-east Kent, looked to London as the hub of their economic activity, but also the spread of prosperity into the Weald and the Thames valley. The Kent Weald in particular, is revealed with high tax assessments as are parts of Surrey nearest London and even many places of formerly moderately assessed wealth show considerable development. North-west Kent in particular was an area of the well-to-do. 'The nearer to London, the greater was the commercial value of woodland and the more marked the dominance of the rich' (Du Boulay 1966: 214). Regarding the Weald, the tax returns are indicating forms of wealth supplementary to the yield of the land which were being derived from the cloth and iron-making and glass industries. Tanning, too, was an important and lucrative industry with its own similar wealth-releasing effects. The highest taxed districts were those closely identified with the production, preparation and marketing of cloth and iron, notably the Cranbrook district of the Weald of Kent, such towns as Godalming and Guildford, and the Petworth and Midhurst district of west Sussex. In all these areas considerable numbers of aliens were present. More intensive forms of farming may also have influenced tax assessments in the Kent Weald where cattle rearing and fattening, associated with an expanding arable, was developing early in the sixteenth century, although the wealth that was to pour into the Weald from hops, cherries and other orchard fruits had not yet begun.

As we have seen in connection with the Weald, it was the development of handicrafts such as the cloth trade in the thirteenth century that led to the emergence of villages and market towns and also to the enlargement or rebuilding of the parish churches. Yeomen farmers supplying wood and other products to these growing industrial districts also greatly increased their prosperity. For more than two hundred years from the end of the fourteenth century the Weald was an energetic, active area, with plenty of work for craftsmen and opportunities for farmers and clothiers to make fortunes. The headwaters of the Medway and its tributaries the Teise and Beult, are lined with the sites of water-mills, relict features of the time when the district's villages were full of cloth workers and water-power was used for fulling cloth.

The impact of London is also evident, though clearer in the case of Surrey than for Kent because of the better surviving documentation. As Sheail has noted the densely settled area of north-east Surrey, including the adjacent part of the North Downs reflects 'places of most resort' of many wealthy persons who belonged economically to London. This is especially true of the many surtaxed payers. The comparative poverty of the Bagshot Sands is clear whereas the higher level of return from the heavy clays of the vale of Holmesdale suggests that the scarpfoot lands were under more intensive agriculture. The low assessments for Romney Marsh are notable. This probably reflects the adverse effects of late-medieval flooding which altered the economic and social basis of the whole marsh. A contemporary observed the 'Romney Marsh where corn and cattle were plentiful has fallen into decay. Many great farms and holdings are held by persons who neither reside on them nor till nor breed cattle but use them for grazing with Welsh cattle' (in Sheail 1972: 126).

The outstanding prosperity of Kent with its almost uniform spread of high tax assessments is a striking feature of the geography of wealth in the South East. As Sheail has written: 'The basis of wealth in Kent was the same as elsewhere – the excellence of the croplands, the woodland and the waterways but in Kent there is such an abundance of these advantages. The county simply had richer husbandmen and craftsmen. The richness of land and the nearness of alternative employment raised the level of wages'.

In 1524–5 the region's total taxable wealth placed it among the foremost parts of England, only East Anglia and parts of the West Country matching it in the wealth-releasing power of its resources. Although the pattern of wealth still shows a very clear relationship to topography and soils, other factors such as the pull of London and the rise of industry were at last beginning to modify the traditional patterns of the past (Cornwall 1956).

Chapter 4

The South East in Transition, 1520–1660

In 1520 the South East had still retained much broken-down, later-medieval feudalism. But in the next 140 years many surviving values came under close scrutiny as religious landownership gave way to that of the Crown and secular power; as patterns of worship and spiritual thought were transformed into a Church of England, centred on Kent; as rural economies were radically changed by industrial production which boomed and slumped, and by agricultural innovations which picked their way selectively among the differing ecologies of the region. And while political and religious issues were debated either on its London doorstep or actually within the region, the main devastation of the civil war touched the South East hardly at all. Life in towns became more accepted as they grew, evolved new corporations, and fostered urban oligarchies of their own.

The period was therefore fundamentally important in transforming the region's economy, and locking it into national and international markets. Such change was never uniform and there were increasingly important social and spatial cleavages within the region. Town differed from country, and Interior differed from Coastal Fringe in the speed of change and its intermeshing with past practices. The influence of London was also paramount and growing, although once again there were regional variations.

It should also be noted that the quantity, quality and variety of information is immeasurably improved for this period. Topographers, artists and travellers; surveyors and clerks; central, county and parochial officials; all left accounts of the region, and statistical information on population, agriculture and employment can be gleaned from many sources ranging from tax returns to visitations, parish registers and probate inventories. We can therefore discern some statistical changes: Kent moved upwards in terms of tax assessment from rank number 13 in 1502 to 5th by 1672, and Surrey even more dramatically from 22nd to 3rd. Sussex fell back from 24th to 27th (Buckatzsch 1950; Schofield 1965), underlining the barrier of distance from the capital, the decline of iron-working and the lower incidence of up-and-coming gentry.

132

It is clear that during this formative period the South East was pulling further away from regions to the north of London in terms of wealth and political influence. The region was now seen not only as a continental bridgehead of vital strategic importance, but a touchstone and barometer of governmental control.

The Reformation in South-East England

The South East was at the very centre of the storms over religion and state in both the sixteenth and seventeenth centuries, and much of the debate and action which was to be of such far-reaching importance, was played out on its stage. The interaction between national or even international events and the South Eastern region was paramount. Many men in Henry VIII's Privy Chamber, for example, had their bases in the South East, and for the Tudors this region was in many respects the key to control the entire kingdom. Henry VIII ostentatiously developed his palaces: Sheen, following a fire in 1501, was renamed Richmond; Hampton Court was a 'gift' from Wolsey in 1525; and Oatlands was also acquired somewhat dubiously. Nonsuch was built on land acquired in 1539. The Crown also had eight large parks in Surrey, on either the Bagshot Sands or good agricultural soils. Certainly the Tudors effectively controlled the region, and only Wyatt's rebellion, involving religious factions during Mary Tudor's reign, disturbed the peace here. This was very different from the preceding periods when the Peasants' Revolt (1381), Cade's rebellion (1450), Clarence's rising (1469), and Buckingham's rebellion (1483) had all rocked the region.

Nevertheless, religious change, enforced centrally but interpreted locally, did not proceed uniformly. The acknowledgement of royal supremacy, changes in doctrine and worship, and the monastic dissolution and redistribution of Church lands all met with degrees of local resistance. Many people were apathetic on religious issues, or else highly conservative. However, several trends were emerging here as elsewhere, and pushing towards change. From within the Weald came a repeated call for radical reform, associated with the heretical Lollard movement. There were also demands for reform of monastic life from within the Church itself, highlighted by the findings of the 1511 Commission. It was now quite clear that these remaining centres of semi-feudalism had slipped far below the standards of dedication to God formerly expected. And finally there were capitalist entrepreneurs and landowners in the South East, who allied themselves with a growing anticlericalism and who saw the redistribution of wealth from spiritual to lay hands as long overdue. Therefore from inside and outside both the Church and the region, change was pressing.

Strong demands for reform had come from the Lollards, mostly located in the eastern Weald, where cloth workers enjoyed some freedom of movement, where Flemish artisans had been settled by Edward III in 1331, and where Cranbrook, Tenterden and Benenden in particular had become noted centres of heresy. The mobility of the middlemen, the high population density, the low degree of manorialization, and isolation within large wealden parishes, all favoured heterodox beliefs. In 1428 William Whyte of Tenterden, a Lollard chaplain, had fled to Norfolk with his disciples, many of them clothworkers, to escape enquiry. But in 1438 five Tenterden men had been executed for heresy and the movement went underground. By 1511 Archbishop Warham's enquiries uncovered 46 cases from the same area and clearly some form of organization had either survived or lain dormant among the merchants and woollen manufacturers, linking up with clothing centres in East Anglia, Yorkshire and London. Literate, independent and well-travelled craftsmen and traders provided a circulation network for ideas and books within the South East and on the Continent. The Medway Valley was another route, and in 1505 John Morress, a Rochester weaver, 'attacked Christ's passion and the person of the Virgin'. Extreme anticlerical views remained a feature of wealden Lollardy in the early sixteenth century. In the 1520s north Kent was also affected with isolated pockets of heresy at Gravesend or Rochester, with attacks on ceremonies, fast days, pilgrimages and sacraments. In 1528 even the precentor of Rochester Cathedral was charged with possessing the Bible in English (Davis 1966: 191–201; and 1983).

Late in 1528, Cardinal Campeggio, already embroiled in the first steps of Henry's divorce campaign, arrived in Canterbury. But on the day of his arrival Archbishop Warham was informing Wolsey of the early activities of Elizabeth Barton, the Nun of Kent. Certainly her religious trances attracted the full attention of Cranmer and the authorities, and after her denunciation of Anne Boleyn's coronation, she was executed at Tyburn in 1534. The following year John Fisher, Bishop of Rochester, was executed on Tower Hill for refusing to recognize the King as head of the Church. Similar resistance was offered by the Grey Friars, the Friars Observant, at Greenwich, Richmond and Canterbury and several members of the order were exiled, imprisoned or executed; and the houses of all Friars Observant were suppressed. Obviously 'the quality of the response' was locally important. Strong anticlerical feelings in Sandwich were fully vented at this time and in Canterbury the teaching of Cranmer was combined with anticlericalism and robust factional in-fighting (Clark 1977: 38).

Rye was particularly turbulent. With a population of about 2,500 this chartered borough and Cinque Port returned two Members of Parliament. Close to traditional Lollard areas, and having continental fishing and trading contacts, Rye was a convenient channel through which to import heretical ideas. By 1538 Rye Protestants were enlisting the aid of Thomas Cromwell to rid themselves of their traditionalist priest, and the ensuing Edwardian period marked a thorough transformation to Protestantism. In 1548 church plate was sold to buy new service books, to paint the inside of the church, especially where the rood loft had been, to provide a communion table, and for 'clensying ye chaunsell from poperye'. Rye's fortunes, political ambitions and rivalries as at Canterbury or Sandwich, mirrored those of England as a whole, but provided local contexts with which national decisions came to mix (Mayhew 1982: 152–6; and 1987).

Kent was the first English county to be entered into the *Valor ecclesiasticus*, and the first to receive a visitation as a preliminary to the Dissolution. The dismantling of the smaller religious houses had begun in earnest in 1536, although Higham Abbey had been suppressed in 1522; Lesnes (Erith) and Tonbridge in 1525; together with the small Sussex Austin priories of Calcetto and Hardham. The 1525 suppression at Bayham brought out local men 'with painted faces and visurs', armed with long-bows, crossbows, arrows, swords and clubs to reinstate the evicted canons and to hold the house for about a week. The people were reckoned to be 'as ungovernable as the terrain' but the rioters were probably those who stood to lose by its closure – tradesmen, tenants and labourers. Taxation by Wolsey had also borne heavily on this area in the preceding five years, and there were possibly also more distant but very powerful backers to the riots, perhaps the Catholic George Neville from Eridge, third baron Abergavenny and steward to Warham, and Alexander Culpeper, principal landowner in Goudhurst (Goring 1978a).

The main suppression began with the Cistercian abbey of Waverley, which surrendered in 1536, and Chertsey in 1537. St Augustine's, Battle and Faversham Abbeys; and Dover and Lewes Priories followed in 1538; Canterbury and Rochester in 1540. Also from 1536 there were accessions to the king's demands for property. Cranmer handed over Otford and Knole to the king; and Wimbledon, Mortlake and Burstow to Cromwell, and by 1546 a large amount of Canterbury diocesan property was transferred out of Church hands, exchanged for ex-monastic property, mainly in east and south-east Kent.

The overall result was a decline in diocesan fortunes. Over 160 religious foundations in the South East (Fig. 2.3) were dealt with, ranging from Cathedral churches to alien houses. Land transferred to the Crown was alienated to other magnates both during Henry's last years and throughout Edward VI's reign. The small Priory of Combwell (Goudhurst) for example, was granted to Thomas Culpeper in 1537, but passed after his attainder to Sir John Gage in 1542 (*VCH, Kent*, II: 113,161). The Priory of Sheen surrendered early in 1539 and became the property of Edward, Earl of Hertford (afterwards Duke of Somerset) in 1540, and in 1552 the residence of the Duke of Suffolk. The live and dead stock of the Austin Priory of St Mary at Merton was offered to Cromwell for his own household, while the fabric was demolished and re-used in the building of Nonsuch Palace (*VCH Sy*,II;101). Lewes Priory was also handed over to Cromwell. In Surrey the suppression of the six largest religious houses alone entailed the transfer of £3,800 per annum from ecclesiastical (and hence at least partly for charitable and educational purposes) to lay hands. Nationally about 2.5 per cent of the 'spoil' was granted away to magnates such as the Duke of Norfolk, while the rest was sold almost at once or leased, with a peak occurring in 1544–5. More than two-thirds of the land had been alienated by 1547. Local squires, groups of London speculators buying for quick resale, and established landowners took the bulk. But above all, it was the gentry, lawyers, government officials and merchants who gained. In east Kent the redistribution favoured the smaller gentry, while in west Kent it was the larger holdings that were acquired. Wealthy Londoners such as the mercer, Robert Palmer, obtained Parham at the dissolution of the monastery of Westminster (Plate 4.1). Waverley Abbey was granted to the Earl of Southampton in 1537 and in the ensuing 225 years there were no fewer than 19 owners (eight different families). Merton Priory had 18 owners in 200 years (Hoskins 1976: 147; *VCH* Sy, I, 372). In the highly mobile south-eastern land market there were few landowners by the eighteenth century who did not owe a substantial part of their estates to the augmentation by their ancestors at this time. More advowsons too, came into lay hands, increasing gentry power over the parish clergy, while alienated tithes were also frequently in lay hands. The Earl of Southampton held 17 impropriations in Sussex alone, which were passed on to his half-brother Lord Montague, who also obtained another six from his father, Sir Anthony Browne. In Sussex, Browne was granted the 22 manors of Battle Abbey together with its lands, and also acquired Waverley, Easebourne and Bayham. The Bakers, Fitzalans and Sackvilles fared similarly well.

Some foundations, such as Michelham, became manor houses. Others, such as Robertsbridge disappeared almost completely. Of 69 monastic establishments in Sussex, 41 have virtually disappeared, although those churches which also served the parish have survived, as at Easebourne or Boxgrove. But in Surrey Cuddington church was demolished, while chapels such as that at Brookwood near Chobham were allowed to decay. The monks and nuns were pensioned off or obtained benefices elsewhere. The Prior of Horton in Kent, Dr Richard Brisley *alias* Gloucester, became Archdeacon of Lewes in 1551; John Sennock, leaving Lewes Priory in 1537, became vicar of Kemsing from 1542–48, while his colleague David Mitchell became rector of Horsted Keynes in 1548. The Abbot of Battle, John Hammond, continued to live in Battle until his death and most of the monks and nuns fared reasonably well.

Following the visitations and surrenders, Deans and Chapters were appointed to Canterbury and Rochester cathedrals in 1541, and the destruction of the shrines began here with the shrine of St Thomas. At Boxley Abbey the celebrated Rood of Grace, an image with supposed powers of movement and speech and an object of pilgrimage, was found to be a fraud when dismantled. In the 1540s the suppression of the charities, hospitals, chantries and colleges added to the number of foundations which were transferred via the Court of Augmentations in this great upheaval in English landholding. The feudal power of the Church was now lost, and here perhaps was the real finale to the Middle Ages in the South East, with the ending of pilgrimages, fundamental changes in

Plate 4.1 The Elizabethan Great Hall of Parham House. Medieval Parham was a grange of Westminster Abbey. At the dissolution the manor was acquired by Robert Palmer, a wealthy London mercer, who built a grand new house in 1577 on the newly-fashionable E-plan. The original mullioned windows gave an unusual amount of light to the Great Hall, which is still entered via the original passage and screen. The ceiling was restored and modified in 1832.

devotional practice, the destruction of monastic communities and the break-up of Church estates. During the early 1550s many extremists removed altars, rood screens and images; whitened walls and purchased the new Bible and communion tables (*VCH* Kent,II: 78). Many in government were very worried about such extremism, and indeed, the radical Joan Boucher, 'Joan of Kent', was accused of heresy and burned at the stake in 1550.

As with the Reformation, so too with the short-lived English Counter-Reformation, the South East was an important setting. In the reign of Catholic Mary Tudor the execution of Archbishop Cranmer and his replacement by Cardinal Pole signalled a reversal of the changes. Many clergy were deprived, frequently because they had previously taken the opportunity to marry. In London, Kent and Sussex there were more executions than elsewhere in the country. At Southwark, Canterbury and Lewes, Protestant martyrs were burnt in the 1555–8 period, building up resentment rather than affection for the old faith. Of the 25 Sussex martyrs whose address is known, 15 came from the Weald, including five from East Grinstead alone; while others from Tenterden, Rolvenden and Smarden, their testimonies containing strong undertones of Lollardy, were burned at Canterbury.

Already the rebellion led by Sir Thomas Wyatt and about thirty of the Kentish gentry in 1554 had nearly succeeded in toppling the queen. Gathering an army from the Medway and Bromley areas as they moved slowly towards London, the rebels were held at Southwark Bridge and then turned back as they marched on London via Kingston and Ludgate. Although the causes of the rebellion are still disputed, the intended Spanish marriage and fear of Catholicism were very important. The leaders included those with kinship links such as the Fanes and Culpepers, and substantial gentlemen and clergy from south-west Kent were also supportive. Once again wealden Lollardy re-emerged. Maidstone in particular was a strong centre of Protestantism and here Wyatt provided a focus for many clothiers who remained discontented after some years of depression in the trade.

The Protestant religion was re-established and confirmed with the accession of Elizabeth. Aided firstly by the able Matthew Parker until his death in 1575 and later by Whitgift, the Protestant faith was nurtured, and grew from Kent. The Spanish ambassador noted that 'all the young men and most of the old are attacked with heresy', and that 'London, Kent and the sea-ports are very heretical'. Although many had now become somewhat

---

Plate 4.2 Sir John Gage, West Firle church. His tomb, one of the great masterpieces of the 16th century, shows him in knightly dress with his feet on a ram, signifying the Gage family crest; his wife, a member of the Guldeford family from the edges of Romney Marsh, has a flaming tree trunk, her family emblem, at her feet. Sir John (d.1557), having enriched himself by the acquisition of the extensive properties of Battle Abbey near Lewes, had been Chancellor of the Duchy of Lancaster in Henry VIII's reign, and Catholic Chamberlain to Queen Mary. His brother, Edward, is perhaps best remembered for his role in the arrest and persecution of the Marian martyrs, burnt outside the Star Inn, Lewes.

indifferent except in their support of the government of the day, by the end of 1559 the English service was already in use, while in the Sussex Weald, Hailsham Church was desecrated by Protestant rioters in 1559.

The Elizabethan period began with almost 40 per cent of Sussex parishes lacking clergy, and with half the cathedral clergy having departed. Bishop Barlow removed about 25 per cent of all incumbents fairly swiftly, but their places were manifestly difficult to fill. At large churches such as Winchelsea, New Shoreham or Boxgrove there was no incumbent. There was scarcely a priest to be found in the great block of land between West Grinstead and Tunbridge Wells. Partly this was the result of the influenza epidemic of 1557–9, but there were many in the region who were as anticlerical as anywhere in the country. Problems of extremism, pluralism or non-residence stirred such feelings, although there were also more conservative views. Except for east Kent, the downland remained fairly conservative in religion, with gentry such as the Gages of West Firle having taken an active role in the Marian persecutions (Plate 4.2). Canterbury diocese Thanet and Romney Marsh were the most conservative areas, but the eastern Weald continued with the ports to be overtly and radically Protestant, with Rye, Winchelsea, Hastings, and Sandwich having been exposed to Continental reformist influences over a long period.

The Reformed Church and its Socio-Political Connections

This regional pattern was also a social one however, for the strength of Protestantism depended on the more educated and well-travelled, on merchants and substantial townspeople or on yeomen farmers. The role of the 'middling classes' was fundamental here. However, there were many humbler Elizabethans as well as the nobility who still clung to the old religion.

During Elizabeth's reign there were six noble families in Sussex, and at the beginning of her reign all were Catholic – as Bishop Curtyes noted 'more than one shire can well bear. Specially if ill affected or doubted and agreeing all together and having often meetings' (in Manning 1969: 221). These were the Earl of Arundel, the Earl of Northumberland at Petworth, Viscount Montague at Cowdray, Baron Lumley at Stanstead, Baron de la Warr at Offington and Baron Buckhurst at Withyham. The most troublesome was the conservative Earl of Arundel, Henry Fitzalan, from a pre-Tudor peerage. As Lord Steward of the Royal Household, privy councillor and Lord Lieutenant of Sussex 1559–69, he exercised considerable influence, before becoming involved in the Ridolfi plot to re-establish Catholicism and to marry his son-in-law, Thomas Duke of Norfolk, to Mary Queen of Scots. With his name linked to that of the seventh Earl of Northumberland, he was confined to his Nonsuch home until after the execution of his son-in-law and the Earl of Northumberland in 1572. Another son-in-law, Lord Lumley, was similarly involved in plotting, and remained steadfastly Catholic until the end. 'Almost all places in our part of the World are full of Papists and Popishness' wrote the Chancellor of Chichester to Sir William Cecil in 1568 (Manning 1969: 129). Deep in political intrigue, Henry Percy, eighth Earl of Northumberland took full advantage of his location on the far side of the Weald. When Walsingham proposed a visit by the queen in June 1583 he wrote back that there were many obstacles to such a visit:

> Up the hill and down the hill, so as she shall not be able to use ether coche or litter with ease, and those ways also so full of louse stones, as it is carefull and painfull riding for any body, nether can ther be in this cuntrey any wayes devysed to avoyd those ould wayes (Mousley 1955: 193–4).

Two years later he died in the tower for his part in the Throgmorton conspiracy.

Islands of Catholic recusancy survived around such noblemen, at places such as Battle, Findon, Clapham, Patching or West Firle. Many of the important Catholic families were in West Sussex with the Montagues pre-eminent in the entire South East, but with the Carylls, Shelleys and Kemps all forming nodes of resistance. The Montagues were also very moderate and loyal to Elizabeth, and this attitude undoubtedly set the tone for the lesser Catholic gentry, contributing to a general lack of crown persecutions. In Surrey by 1581 there were 65 propertied recusants paying a regular composition, such as the Copleys of Gatton and Leigh, the Sanders of Charlwood and Ewell, the Furnivalls of Egham or the Westons of Sutton Place.

Many withdrew from parish affairs to become 'seignorial Catholics', receiving communion at home, and choosing priests from a distance. Missionary priests were received and channelled through to safe houses in London, and priest holes were common, as at the Darrells' Scotney Castle or at the homes of the Sussex Carylls. In Kent the Darrells, the Ropers at Linstead and Eltham, and the Loves at Mereworth kept up the old religion, while many old dynasties such as the Finches, Guldefords and Culpepers also contained recusants. The Dowager Lady Roper was still a focus for Catholics at Sittingbourne as late as 1637 when Archbishop Laud noted their stronger prevalence here than elsewhere in his diocese. There were also Catholic sympathizers, such as Sir John Baker, Chancellor of the Exchequer, and father-in-law of Sir Thomas Sackville, whose will nevertheless included the injunction to obey the Crown above all things. Outward conformity was the rule (Clark 1977: 153). However, the queen's excommunication in the 1570 bull, the establishment of Catholic colleges on the Continent and the 1579 papal expedition to Ireland increased the activities of the south-eastern Catholic gentry. By August 1580 leading Catholics were imprisoned, stiffer fines were now imposed and lands confiscated following the 1581 Recusancy Act. The net further tightened with executions following the war years and the Armada scare. By the 1580s there were no Catholic commissioners of the peace or members of the lieutenancy. Thus after 1586 the moderate Lord

Buckhurst shared the Sussex/Surrey lieutenancy with Howard of Effingham, rather than with his old colleague Lord Montague. However, some Catholic gentry appear to have weathered the storm and even to have prospered, as did the Shelleys, Gages, Carylls, or Ashburnhams. But social and economic isolation from Protestant neighbours increased the importance of kinship links and intermarriage. Few south-eastern gentry families were without Catholic members, but the need for the administrative support of these families precluded action. Thus the office of sheriff, although not as powerful as before the Tudor changes in officialdom, was held in Sussex by Catholics eleven times between 1558 and 1603. Nevertheless, by the latter date Protestantism was confirmed as the cornerstone of national social and political stability.

The most successful and pragmatic south-eastern landowner in the Elizabethan period was Sir Thomas Sackville, created Lord Buckhurst in 1567 and first Earl of Dorset in 1604 (Plate 4.3). His father, Chancellor of the Court of Augmentations in 1548, first cousin to Anne Boleyn and known as 'Sackfill' or 'Fill-sack', had gained property, impropriations and advowsons, and became governor of Kent in the 1560s. Sir Thomas was thus already wealthy when he married Emily, daughter of Sir Richard Baker; but as a privy councillor, he lived infrequently at Buckhurst. Cousin to the queen, he was probably a Catholic sympathizer and may have been converted on his deathbed. His daughter Jane married the heir of Lord Montague, while his daughter-in-law was the sister of the Earl of Arundel. Nevertheless, he was fully committed to the Tudors, enforced recusancy laws and discharged his various offices efficiently. His scattered south-eastern possessions included Buckhurst itself; Knole, which he had rebuilt in 1603; and property in Lewes and London. In 1561 he was proclaimed Master Forester of Ashdown for life; in 1576 he purchased the barony of Lewes for £4,000, and in 1599 succeeded Burleigh as Lord Treasurer.

Religious Stress and Political Breakdown: the Growth of Puritanism in the South East

Marian exiles returned to the South East from Germany and Switzerland with strong Calvinist leanings and by the 1560s they probably held about ten per cent of the parish livings in Kent (Clark 1977: 150). Their influence was bolstered by the advent of 'Stranger congregations', exiled Huguenots

Plate 4.3 Sir Thomas Sackville. Born at Buckhurst, Withyham, in the reign of Henry VIII, he typified the rising Protestant elite under Elizabethan patronage. Created Baron Buckhurst in 1567 and Earl of Dorset in 1603–4, he became Lord High Treasurer before his death in 1608. His preferred residence became Knole.

and foreign Protestants in Sandwich, Maidstone and Canterbury. The English publication of Foxe's *Acts and monuments* in English also added the memory of the Marian martyrs to the movement, and all these factors, allied to the local influence of the radical Protestant gentry, ensured an early development of Elizabethan Puritanism in Kent. Thence it spread throughout the rest of the South East.

Many with strong Puritan leanings prospered from the later sixteenth century. The Medway valley and wealden landowner and MP, Sir Thomas Scott rebuilt Scots' Hall, Ashford at this time, enjoying favour with the Earl of Leicester and kinship ties with the Sackvilles, Dudleys and Bakers. Other Kentish Protestants included Edward Boys, Sir James Hales, Edward Dering, Thomas Wotton and the Sidneys (Clark 1977: 129–37, 151–2). In Sussex the Coverts of Slaugham exercised great influence in the 1580s and were signatories of the Puritan petition to King James I from the Sussex gentry in March 1604. The Pelhams, Bowyers, Morleys and Mays families likewise progressed. The Pelhams in particular came to hold high county offices, and Pelham's uncle had been a supporter of Wyatt. There were also strong family ties with the Carews and Sackvilles. Both Pelham and Morley had been Marian exiles, and their names were also on the Puritan petition. The nominal leader of the Puritan movement in the South East was Sir Thomas West, third Baron de la Warr from 1602, governor of Virginia, whose name was given to the State of Delaware, and whose signature headed the 1603 Puritan petition to James I. Such men were typical of those gaining power in a secular movement linked to Puritanism.

From the 1570s, much through the influence of Richard Curtyes, the zealous Bishop of Chichester, Puritanism came to spearhead the Reformation in the South East. A 'tradition of parochial radicalism' developed, with well-educated visiting preachers giving additional support to ministers, themselves often sponsored by Puritan landowners (Clark 1977: 166). Changes in religious practice rested with improvements in standards of scholarship and preaching, and Rye corporation acted early to appoint an adequate preacher from the 1570s. By about 1570 Feregod Edwardes was baptized in Sussex, an early example of the Puritan style of baptismal name which was to become so common in the Weald during the next decade. Here the large parishes had always proven difficult for the established Church to administer.

In the wealden hinterlands of radical Rye and Lewes, far from the bishop's seat, such free-thinking could take root, and Rye received a large number of Huguenots after the Massacre of St Bartholomew's. In 1584 the Puritan Richard Rogers was appointed Dean of Canterbury, and gradually the radical Puritan grip strengthened. By the 1620s and 1630s many communities possessed licensed preachers, and lectureships at Rye, Lewes, Horsham and Midhurst extended preaching to the towns with the full support of the local gentry (Fletcher 1975: 71–2). Thereafter Sabbatarianism gained ground with its suppression of games and disorder, thereby linking itself with respectable governing circles. Separatism too began to grow, again in east Kent (and Sandwich in particular) and in the Weald.

However, the first twenty years of the seventeenth century saw few problems among the clergy, despite the continuing ceremony of the established Church. The significance of the appointment of William Laud to two Kentish livings was not apparent until the 1620s. Indeed, Puritan JPs were probably as active as ministers at this time, and local feeling could run high, as in 1611 when Herbert Pelham from Catsfield was alleged by a churchwarden to have declared that 'Hee had as leefe see a sowe weare a saddell as see a minister weare a surplice' (Fletcher 1975: 73–4).

Religious, political and economic problems appeared again in the 1620s. Harvest gluts (1618–20) were followed by dearth (1622, 1624, 1630); foreign wars; Channel privateering; and the continuing decline of rural industry. Any religious *rapprochment* between conservative Protestant and Puritan was now sundered. Puritan radicals pushed for change, becoming increasingly dismayed at James's Spanish sentiments and the French marriage of Charles. When Charles came to the throne in 1625 his adviser immediately became William Laud, and the Catholic Ropers of Teynham returned to the Kentish commission of the peace. Clearly, religious polarization was increasing. Separatist conventicles flourished and wealden sects such as the Brownists began to multiply. Respectable farmers, small tradesmen and craftsmen made up these groups, and Laud reported to Charles in 1635 that there were 'very many refractory persons to the government of the Church of England about Maidstone and Ashford . . .' (Chalklin 1965: 225).

Laud's enforcement of Arminianism through his bishops was blatantly divisive. At Chichester Bishop Montagu from 1628 to 1638 propounded extreme views against Puritanism and stressed ritual in very much the same way that Laud was attempting to do. Canterbury cathedral was tidied up, but standards of care for churches and churchyards were now to be exacted from churchwardens who were normally hard put to carry out their obligations. At North Mundham the churchwardens, resentful of the new order, declared that they knew of 'no offence done by swyne to the graves', while the parish clerk could not 'medle above his office' since he could neither read nor write! (Fletcher 1975: 83). Laud's theological niceties were lost on most clergy and laity and remained unfulfilled, especially in the eastern Weald, by 1641.

By the 1630s hard opposition to Arminianism, king and court emerged from south-eastern gentry. Few supported the revocation of the royal grants of privilege to the 'Stranger churches' carried out by Laud in 1635, forcing congregations to disperse from their meetings in Canterbury, Maidstone or Sandwich and to attend their parish churches henceforth. There were 900 Walloons at Canterbury at this time, 500 Dutch at Sandwich, and 50 Dutch at Maidstone – more than 25 per cent of the total national membership of foreign churches in England. They soon drifted back to their own churches however, and there was no more state interference after 1640 (Chalklin 1965: 225). Chairman of the Sussex Michaelmas Quarter sessions, Anthony Stapley of Patcham, was persuaded by Puritans to deliver a harangue against the bishops in 1639. Tension grew and in February 1641 Stapley and Sir Thomas Pelham presented a root and branch petition to parliament from Sussex (Fletcher 1975: 93.)

Opposition grew, especially among Kentish moderates, to the king, Laud and Buckingham. The many and various taxes were unpopular, including ship-money which after 1634 was extended to inland areas behind the ports. The county refused to pay this unprecedented demand, and also the forced loan demand which followed, and increasingly looked to parliament for redress. Opposition came from mid- and west-Kent and from urban areas in particular (Clifford 1982). The sheriff of Kent, Sir George Sondes, took no action against those refusing to pay. Purveyance, knighthood fines, tonnage and poundage, wardships, fines for enclosing (which hit Sir Anthony Roper in Kent), patents and monopolies, such as John Browne's iron-making monopoly, were all highly unpopular.

Elections showed the increased importance of urban and religious radicalism. In 1624 Puritans had won Canterbury and Hythe elections, and now wealden radicals, Sandwich Puritans, clothiers and lawyers began to vote together, forming the beginnings of the committed radical party of the 1640s. The 1628 elections returned anti-court candidates to the parliament which Charles dissolved in 1629 (Clark 1977: 335–60), and in 1639–40 Kentish military preparations to march against the Scots were halted by the disenchanted deputy-lieutenants. Latent anti-Catholicism also resurfaced, and although Sussex in particular contained as high a proportion of recusant households as many of the northern counties, few Catholic gentry openly supported the king. Among the aristocrats, only the Earl of Dorset and Lord Abergavenny stayed with him. 'County Communities' had now arrived, united against the policies of the Crown.

The Civil War and Commonwealth, 1640–1660

Overall, the South East, including London, was firmly committed to the parliamentarian cause. But compared with some other regions, there was little fighting, although 'malignity', chaos and fear existed here, as elsewhere.

The period is a difficult one to analyse regionally. There are few pointers to any regional affinities within the South East for king or parliament, since neighbour argued with neighbour and kin with kin. Without undertaking an examination of the surviving but admittedly imperfect muster rolls, pension lists or lists of suspected royalists collected by the major-generals in 1655–6, we do not have this information for the South East in the way that Underdown has revealed it for parts of Wessex (Underdown 1985).

However, within Sussex there were contrasts in gentry attitudes between a more strongly Puritan east and a more royalist west, although there were as many neutrals as there were either royalist or parliamentarian. And superficially at least, the old radical Protestant areas: the wealden, Surrey and Medway clothing and iron-making districts; towns such as Rye, Lewes, Sandwich, Canterbury or Ashford were more firmly committed to the Puritan and parliamentary cause. These areas, also faced with economic decline, support the contention that 'regional culture was a crucial variable in the determination of allegiance' (Underdown 1985: 204). Here was a distinct culture which now drew on its own traditions: generations of dissent related to the process of underdevelopment. By contrast, interspersed throughout the South East and centred on traditional family seats, were the royalists – with tenants, servants and others in receipt of patronage conscripted to support the king. To some extent the downland displayed a royalist (or at least more 'localist') sympathy. However, the lack of enthusiasm on the part of farmers and husbandmen, and their willingness to change sides if necessary, renders further regional analysis of politico-religious affinity somewhat dubious.

The elections to the Short Parliament of 1640, in which moderate Puritans generally triumphed, were fought on local issues interlaced with national affairs. Ship Money was an obvious grievance at Hastings, for example, but the state of the harbour was the main concern at Rye. Sir John Culpeper was a candidate here, and he wrote to the Mayor and Jurats that he had 'bin an actor in head and purse to lay open 1500 acres of salts for the benefit of your harbour, but never inned any' and furthermore 'have often declared my opinion that the inning of salts hath produced (as a necessary consequence) the decay of your outfall' (Fletcher 1975: 246–51). Local men were clearly finding favour, and this was even more apparent in the 1642 elections for the Long Parliament, when the members returned were still more radical. Culpeper was now returned for the county of Kent, together with Sir Edward Dering, and the assertive Sussex group was led by Pelham and Stapley, with strong wealden support. In west Sussex, MPs, such as Sir Thomas Bowyer now came under local pressure since he alone of the active Sussex MPs took the king's side when war broke out. In Kent there were tensions between moderate and radical views. Sir Roger Twysden and Dering moderated their opinions as a county petition denounced extremists on all sides, calling for a reformed episcopacy under the leadership of a national synod. But Dering was expelled from the Commons and the organizers of the petition were arrested. A radical petition presented by Sir Edward Scott was more sympathetically received, and Dering's seat was taken by the arch anti-royalist Augustine Skinner. The Earl of Northumberland, now a committed parliamentarian, arranged for general musters at the end of May, and a force was sent under Colonel Sandys to confirm the allegiance of Kent, precipitating the gentry into choosing between parliament and king. The majority of moderates went to parliament's side (Clark 1977: 388).

Between July and November 1642 the fighting began amid great enthusiasm in the eastern Weald. Royalist gentry who declared themselves early included the king's companion John Ashburnham, but there were many who were too fearful for their estates to come out openly in support. Ashburnham was groom of the bedchamber to Charles from 1628, but was discharged from his parliamentary seat for Hastings in February 1643, and his estate was sequestered. During the war he acted as the king's treasurer, staying with him for much of the rest of his life. Also with him were men from old Kentish families such as the Nevilles, Diggeses and Bakers, with Sir John Boys of Goodnestone, and Sir Anthony St Leger of Boughton Monchelsea.

In the western Weald and west Sussex generally, the response was more equivocal. Chichester was split between a mercantile parliamentarian and a royalist gentry faction, with Sir Christopher Lewkenor, Edward Ford and Sir Henry Compton opting early for Charles. But many remained inert until jolted by Ford's plan to take control of Sussex for the king. He certainly took control of Chichester in November 1642, but in marching eastwards was met by Morley's parliamentarian force, and he did not reach his target of Lewes. In December Chichester was recaptured and garrisoned by Morley and Sir William Waller; parliamentarian troops pillaged the cathedral and its library, and Stapley was appointed governor. Ford was captured but released through his influence with his brother-in-law, General Ireton. Others captured and fined included Bowyer and Lewkenor, recently expelled from his parliamentary seat for Chichester. The newly-consecrated Bishop of Chichester, Henry King, was forced into retirement until the Restoration (Hobbs 1987: 139; Thomas-Stanford 1910: 55–6).

The parliamentarians were perhaps fortunate that the king never had the troops to spare or the opportunity to exploit rifts and royalist sentiments within the South East. However, they had to contend in December 1643 with a renewed attempt by Ford to take Sussex by a surprise attack across the Adur, advancing eastwards on the frost which made the muddy roads briefly passable. Arundel fell but the advance was halted at Bramber Bridge. However, the attack precipitated the concept of a south-eastern association for defence to match those in the East, East Midlands and South Wales, allowing Waller to muster 10,000 men as well as forces from Surrey, Hampshire and trained bands from the City of London. On 1 January 1644 Waller was appointed major-general of the associated counties of Hampshire, Surrey, Sussex and Kent. Arundel was recaptured on 6 January, changing hands for the third time within the war. This effectively ended the first civil war in the South East; royalist pressure on London was relieved, and the wealden ironworks secured for parliament.

South-eastern landowners, if proven 'delinquent', were liable to have their estates sequestered for the use of parliament. There were 76 Surrey (many institutional e.g. Peckham's Merton College) and 81 Sussex landowners, for example, who compounded for 'delinquency', although Thomas, Earl of

Arundel allowed his estate to be sold rather than acknowledge the authority of parliament. John Ashburnham was fined £1,270, half the value of his estate, but most escaped with a fine amounting to about one-sixth value. Lord Montague, the Carylls and the Gages all suffered. The Earl of Thanet was fined £9,000 in October 1644, on the basis that his estate was worth £10,000 per annum and that he had sent plate and money to the king. This was on top of having already paid £2,000 to avoid sequestration; having lost plate, horses and sheep worth £20,000; having had parks and deer destroyed; and having had household items removed from his houses in Windsor, Heathfield and London. Nevertheless, the County Committee complained bitterly that he should not have been allowed to discharge his 'delinquency' since he had been one of the chief 'malignants' (Thomas-Stanford 1910: 124).

The County Committees were initiated during 1643 to raise money, defend the counties, and administer parliament's wishes. In eastern Sussex there were plenty of men waiting to undertake these jobs, but in western Sussex it was more difficult, and 'rising men' and merchants filled places that went to gentry in the east. In Kent, the size of the county necessitated 'a numerous offspring' of sub-committees to undertake the enormous array of tasks. The ruthless Sir Anthony Weldon of Swanscombe co-ordinated the Kentish committees with a rod of iron, being described as a man whose 'desire of rule brought hym to run with ye forwardest' (Everitt 1957: 23). As with other administrative spheres, so too in the Kentish County Committee from 1643 to 1660 there was a social change from baronets and knights in the 1640s to esquires and gentlemen by 1660. The proportion of indigenous men also fell and soon included the detested regicide Sir Michael Livesey, at odds with superiors and inferiors alike. Here, moderation clashed with radicalism; and county affinity with the need to draw together with other south-eastern counties, and ultimately with parliament for defence.

The atrocious roads, the large number of 'neuters', and the generally recalcitrant nature of the impressed soldiery had made any extended campaigning difficult in the wealden area. Waller was often frustrated by refusals to comply with regional requirements for military assistance, and many of the moderate Kentish committee-men cared more for their localities than for the regional or national good. Many captured troops changed sides, having little commitment to either, as indecisive confrontations continued; and provisioning and quartering of troops were resented. In western Surrey such free-quartering was held to have had a particularly deleterious effect on the payment of taxes, and south-easterners were now clearly discontented with the campaigns. In November 1643 Waller wrote asking parliament for money to pay the citizens of Godalming and Midhurst for the coarse cloth, linen, shoes, boots and stockings he had commandeered, feeling that assurances of payment would be best both for his soldiers and for the country (Thomas-Stanford 1910:68). Not all commanders were as generous.

However, isolated civilian resistance in 1644 became more concerted protest in 1645. Spreading through the southern counties, protection from army plunder was organized, which soon spread into open revolt as the Clubmen movement. Comprising smaller west Sussex and wealden farmers, the movement was easily dispersed but it highlighted once again the lack of national interest and the intense rural parochialism. And during the next three years such resentment arose again.

In August 1647 large numbers of New Model Army troops had been billeted in Surrey and Kent as Fairfax prepared to advance on London. In May 1648 a Surrey petition requested a treaty with the king but on its presentation to the House a riot ensued, ending with several dead and about 100 wounded (Thomas-Stanford 1910: 196). In June a similar petition was delivered more peaceably from the less radical 'knights, gentlemen, clergy and commonalty' of Sussex, but the Kentish petition was followed by open war with the battle cry 'For God, King Charles and Kent'. Wealden Horsham now provided the focus for a semi-royalist and popular uprising against the County Committee, refusing to pay taxes to non-local people whose rule was now mistrusted. Fearful of disorder, the committee had agreed to the dissolution of the Chichester garrison, easing local financial burdens. But south-eastern fears of extremism had been vindicated. In Kent the radical-moderate coalition against the king of the early 1640s collapsed with gentry resenting the increasing dominance of parliament in their local affairs. The radicals themselves splintered into Presbyterians, sectarian groups, army supporters and others, and there were fears of an extremist coup within Kent. The Levellers had appeared from London in some force in several west Kent towns and with heavy taxation and military levies the county was also faced with epidemics in 1645–6; poor harvests in 1647–8 and an economic depression. There were Fifth Monarchists at Canterbury and Sandwich; and Diggers near Boxley, mid-Kent.

In December 1647 rioting began in Canterbury. Long-standing issues were mixed with local and immediate causes, related to the Puritan suppression of Christmas festivities and the ever-unpopular taxation. Early in 1648 the country gentry then became involved in disputes over the trials of the rioters, and frightened at the prospect of social upheaval as evidenced in Leveller or Clubmen activities, decided to take local control and call for a swift end to the hostilities between king and parliament. Sandown, Deal and Walmer castles were 'deteyned for the King', and coastal trade disrupted as their cause was joined by royalists and naval mutineers. A force was assembled to oppose Fairfax's advance at the end of May 1648, comprising cavaliers, London apprentices, seamen and local countrymen, but was decisively beaten at Maidstone. Although many of the gentry had drawn back from the final conflict, and although the battle had been taken over by outside royalist groups, the gentry were thereafter purged from county offices. Livesey arrived at Horsham in July 1648, driving the rebels there out. Composition fines were now exacted, and most, like Sir Roger Twysden, thereafter withdrew to their estates until the Restoration.

In Pride's Purge in December 1648, even those radicals who had stood aside from the conflict were tainted. MP John Boys, who had succeeded Culpeper in 1645 was excluded, together with half of the county members. Men of more radical persuasions and of generally lower social standing were now brought forward, both in the local magistracies and in parliament. Lawyers, army officers and lesser gentry now filled the county offices, and by December 1648 their petition for the king's execution was supported predictably from the more radical wealden centres and from Canterbury, Ashford and Sandwich (Clark 1977: 388–93). The nine south-eastern regicides helped see the execution realized. Downes, from Sussex, broke down, but Stapley, Cawley, Temple and Norton (Sussex), Mounson (Surrey), Dixwell, Garland and Livesey (Kent) saw it through (Underdown 1971: 366–90; Gurney forthcoming). In Sussex and Kent, minor gentry and townsmen now filled the places vacated by Pelham and other alienated moderates: 'Upstarts were feathering their nests' (Fletcher 1975: 293–6).

During 1650 obedience was sworn to the new Commonwealth. Military presence now became overwhelming in an insecure period but no resurgence of royalist activity materialized initially beyond the smuggling of Charles II by boat from Brighton. For the maritime South East, the presence of royalist privateers, and French and Dutch threats were more important, and merited parliamentary protection. Gradually the magnates, traditional moderates and county communities, led by Morley and Sir Richard Onslow, strengthened their local grip, often in opposition to Cromwell's army and appointed major-generals. With Oliver Cromwell's death, the many Kentish factions threatened to break down the structure of Kentish government and society completely, and once again, as in 1648, the moderate gentry seized control. This time a moderate parliament was restored and finally, in May 1660 Charles II was readmitted to his kingdom, with an enthusiastic welcome from the gentry of the South East who now prepared to take up the reins once more.

Meanwhile the livings of the region had been filled with Puritan ministers. Many former incumbents had been ejected, although many former 'lecturers' or preachers taking up country livings would eventually accommodate themselves to moderate religious persuasions. But everywhere notions were affected by the rising radicalism and freedom of religious practice (except for Catholics) at this time. In February 1655 two northern Quakers toured nonconformist Kentish centres canvassing support, leaving behind converts at Dover, Lydd, New Romney, Cranbrook and other wealden centres (Clark 1977: 394). In Sussex three Quakers 'declared the truth' first in the market at Horsham in February 1655, and the spread of the new ideas was promoted by a visit from George Fox during that year. Their advent was certainly a divisive issue but the strength of Sussex Puritanism at least can be judged by the fact that at the Restoration, about one-quarter of all the clergy were ejected from or resigned from their livings, rather than accept the Act of Uniformity in 1662 (*VCH* Sx, II: 38–9).

The Early-Modern Town

Population growth, rural to urban migration, urban growth, especially of London, the emergence of new towns and the quality of urban life were all factors of considerable importance to the region between 1520 and 1660. Stifled by the proximity of London, a city whose size astounded contemporaries, the region's towns had little power to expand. But the old centres remained, fulfilling local and regional roles and emerging from a period of difficulty with some vigour. There was a large number of medium-sized towns. Canterbury had a population of about 3,000 in the 1520s; Faversham, Dover, Maidstone and Rochester had between 1,000 and 2,000 people. By the seventeenth century Canterbury had reached about 6,000; Rochester, Maidstone and Dover about 3,000; and there were about a dozen with between 1,000 and 2,500, including Dartford, Ashford and Sandwich; together with the smaller towns such as Tonbridge with between 500 and 800 people (Chalklin 1961).

Although much of the South East shared the national population increase in the sixteenth and early seventeenth century, smooth population growth was probably exceptional. Uncertain food supplies, malnutrition and disease brought 'dismal peaks' of mortality, ensuring that any overall urban population growth was dependent upon heavy in-migration from the countryside.

London south of the Thames

Above all, London began to throw out its suburbs on the Kent and Surrey side of the Thames. With 70,000 people in 1550, London was a world metropolis – the seventh or eighth largest town in Europe, and second in 1650 (behind Paris). Growth was rapid in the second half of the sixteenth century, at more than three times the national rate. By 1600 population totalled about 200,000, rising to 400,000 by 1650 and perhaps 575,000 by 1700. Its markets, society, political intrigues and fashion generally permeated every part of the South East (Finlay and Shearer 1986: 37–59; Boulton 1987a: 107).

A confusion of manors, liberties, ecclesiastical palaces and religious houses typified Southwark at this time as population and local government units proliferated. There were four parishes within Southwark proper: St Saviour's, St Olave's, St Thomas's, and St George the Martyr. St Saviour's was in turn divided into three districts: the Clink, Paris Garden and the

Boroughside. There were also three manors with jurisdiction, but they were not coterminous with the parishes. The Guildable Manor had belonged to the City for a long time, and King's manor and Great Liberty manors were purchased by the City in 1557. From this date the three manors were referred to as Bridge Ward Without, and were administered from the City, while those parts of Southwark not included in the three manors, such as the Clink and Paris Garden liberties, were still part of Surrey. Confusion arose as to the precise legal, military and political powers of the City and the County of Surrey over taxation, control over trades, and the organization of musters.

Before the dissolution there were also the lands of Bermondsey Priory, and the land of the Archbishop of Canterbury and of the Bishop of Winchester (Corporation of London 1878: 57, 232, 473–4; Boulton 1987b: 9–12). Possibly the dissolution affected Southwark more than most parts of the South East. Much employment had been afforded by the large houses and grounds of Bermondsey, St Mary Overie, and the town houses of the abbots of Battle, Lewes and Beaulieu; together with Lambert and Winchester House (*VCH*, Sy IV: 428–9). Occupations were variable. There were three major prisons (including the original 'Clink'), St Thomas's hospital (also purchased by the City in the 1550s), theatres, and numerous inns and trading places along the Borough High Street, whence came carriers from the rest of south-east England. Watermen and leather dressers dominated the Clink and Paris Garden, where water and windmills also worked. Textiles, especially feltmaking, were more important in St Olave's, and there were numerous breweries, a large soaphouse and a dyehouse. Many livings were marginal and supplemented by poor relief or pawning belongings to wealthier neighbours. Many dispossessed families made their way here, and residential mobility was very high, although much was very short-range to nearby houses or streets. Southwark was part of what has been termed a 'third London' of suburban manufacturing (Beier 1986: 156), complementing the seventeenth-century growth of the City on the one hand and a West End geared to conspicuous consumption on the other. By 1680 this extra-mural element formed over 60 per cent of London's population. Lower rents and greater space for tenter grounds, etc., together with lesser civic and gild control over dubious or polluting trades outside the City limits, all help to explain this change. By 1547 the population of Southwark was between 8,055 and 9,238, rising to 25,718 by 1631 and 31,711 by 1678; although alternative calculations give a 1680 figure of around 50,000 (Finlay and Shearer 1986: 43–4; Boulton 1987b: 19). Because of the poorly drained Thames-side location, building was not possible throughout the district, and eastern population densities were extremely high among the subdivided properties in the alleys and yards of Boroughside.

These large population figures certainly correct earlier ideas that there had been little growth on the South Bank before the eighteenth century. By 1600 Southwark in fact contained 10 per cent of the entire population of the City of London, and it was the second-largest urban area in England after

London itself. However, annual burials regularly outnumbered baptisms and immigration was fundamentally important in fuelling growth, especially in the face of deaths associated with plague or smallpox, occurring in Southwark in 1543, 1563, 1593, 1603, 1625, 1636 and, of course, 1665. Plague mortality was probably higher than in the wealthier central areas of the City, and the marshy conditions contributed to 'Borough ague'. Overcrowding was reported from the 1590s onwards, as families began to occupy single rooms, and as cellars were used for living accommodation. Such conditions were exacerbated after the Dissolution by yet further subdivision of former Church property. The house of the Abbot of St Augustine's, for example, passed to the St Leger family from Ulcombe, but by 1600 this was divided into small tenements; and the same fate awaited the properties of the bishops of Rochester. Montague House was converted into tenements in 1612. Adjoining areas, such as Newington Butts, were also becoming overcrowded (*VCH* Sy, IV: 75).

A long-standing reputation for disrepute was gained. Described in 1583 as a site for 'unchaste interludes and bargains of incontinence', it was on tidewater, close to London but with a weaker local government, and with medieval rights of sanctuary enjoyed in the liberties of Paris Gardens and the Clink, the site of notorious stews. Numerous inns, some with galleries which were the forerunners of Elizabethan theatre, lined the street leading to London Bridge, although many were later destroyed in fires of 1676 and 1689. Bear gardens, bull-baiting rings and bowling alleys alternated with theatres in the Clink and Paris Garden (Fig. 4.1) after the actors had effectively been expelled from the Puritan-controlled City in 1575. Queen Elizabeth attended bear and bull-baiting here, as did Pepys in 1666 after the 'sport' had been restored alongside the monarch (Corporation of London 1878: 17n.1, 478; Stow 1603, ii: 54). In 1580 a theatre was opened at Newington Butts together with others including the Rose Theatre *c.*1587, the 1588 Paris Garden Theatre, the Swan, and the Globe in 1599. Into these dubious surroundings came Shakespeare, Beaumont and Fletcher, with Shakespeare having a house at the Boar's Head opposite St Mary Overie. By 1639 Paris Garden was described as having many attractions: 'there have you the shouting men, the barking of dogs, the growling of the bears, and the bellowing of the bulls, mixed in a wild and natural harmony' (*VCH* Sy, I: 396–7; IV: 126–41).

City merchants owned land in Southwark on some scale by the sixteenth century. The liberty of Paris Gardens, 'dark and much shadowed with trees', and with aits shrouded in willows close by, was conveyed in 1580 to Thomas Cure, the Queen's saddler, who conveyed the freehold part of the property to Francis Langley, citizen and draper of London. In 1602 this was alienated to a member of the Inner Temple, Hugh Browker and thereafter to his son Thomas. In 1655 the estate passed jointly to a city haberdasher and a grocer, and thereafter part went to a Lombard Street woollen draper in 1667. The parcellation, sub-letting and development of the properties was thus facilitated (*VCH* Sy IV: 150–51). Paris Gardens was swampy and originally subdivided

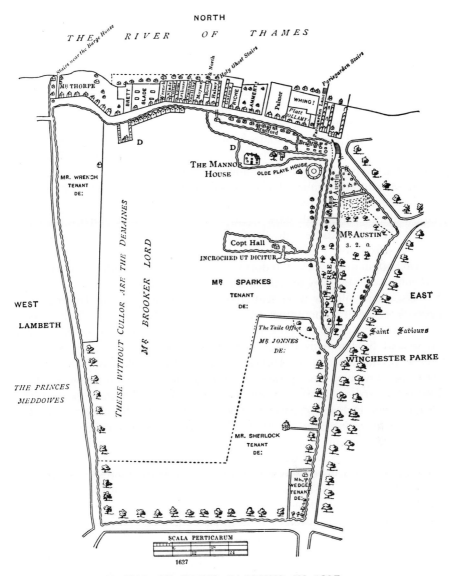

MANOR OF PARIS GARDENS IN 1627.

Figure 4.1 The Manor of Paris Gardens, Southwark in 1627 (Source: Norman 1901). The conjunction of Thamesside building and backing meadows and fields, gradually being encroached upon, is shown here. Note the 'Olde Playe House' and the land of the Bishop of Winchester to the east. By 1745 the central area was not yet built upon, but Blackfriars Bridge had replaced the Holy Ghost Stairs and building had spread along both east and west fringing streets. Blackfriars Road ultimately ran north-south through the centre of the manor.

by open drains or ditches, but by 1671 there were over 600 families living there (Norman 1901: 60).

Southwark, looking northwards to London and southwards into the South East, derived great importance from its Thames bridging function. Socially, it was fairly self-contained and although it always had a large contingent of itinerant families, there was also a solid core of kinship within such areas as Boroughside. However, marriage links were more with London than with Surrey and Kent. By about 1660 Southwark probably accounted for two-thirds of London's south bank population. At Bermondsey, where the river was controlled by banks and dikes, the Cluniac Abbey had dominated everything, but all grandeur was lost with the Dissolution, and by the seventeenth century the riverside population was largely occupied in the flourishing leather industry. The Thames supplied water for power and industrial use, while oak bark could still be obtained regionally, or from further afield. The Rotherhithe (Redrith) waterside developed as an important landing place below London Bridge, and this merged with Deptford, where a growing population worked in docks, boat-building yards on reclaimed land, and gunpowder mills by the end of the sixteenth century.

Elsewhere villages were scattered alongside or near the Thames, in a network of small communities becoming socially and economically drawn into London's sphere of influence. To the west, fashionable Lambeth was dominated by Lambeth Palace with its extensive garden and park. The houses of the bishops of Rochester and Carlisle, dukes of Norfolk and other wealthy men gave prestige to the district, although hemmed in by Lambeth marshes. Further south, Camberwell and Peckham were small villages, and Dulwich consisted of little more than the college, founded in the early seventeenth century by the former Southwark owner of the Rose theatre. At rural Merton the abbey formed the centrepiece before its dissolution. The Crown retained the site and in 1600 granted it in trust for Lord Howard in recognition of his services at the time of the Armada. Putney, birthplace of Thomas Cromwell, was another village surrounded by open fields, where the beginnings of civic pride are perhaps discernible in a petition to Oliver Cromwell in 1656 to pave the long and broad high street. This followed the use of the village as a headquarters by the Parliamentarian army in 1647, and in the following year the Surrey petitioners to Parliament met on Putney Heath before marching to Westminster. Barnes and Putney also shared the grazing rights over the swampy Barnes Common. Sir Francis Walsingham lived at Barn Elms, the manor house at Barnes, where the Earl of Essex also came to live until his death in 1601. At Battersea, the hamlets of Roydon and Wassingham were the only sizeable settlements, although several large houses were scattered throughout the parish by the seventeenth century. Much was marshy or common, with market gardens appearing in the open fields. Streatham comprised a 'small scattering village about a mile in length' by the end of the seventeenth century, and had become a popular residential area, enhanced by the 1660 discovery of the Spa Well. Wandsworth was a small village on the banks of the Wandle. A bridge was built to replace the ford in 1602, but this had not to interfere with the milling and carrying trades along the Wandle; nor with the brass manufactures, begun by Dutch refugees in the sixteenth century. Hat-making, calico-printing and bleaching were also introduced by foreigners at a later stage, and all provided much employment. Ironplate mills are noted in the Parliamentary Survey of Wimbledon Manor in 1649, through which the Wandle also flowed (*VCH* Sy, IV: 3–162).

London was both a catalyst and a consumer in its relations with the rest of the South East. The demographic, economic, cultural and political influences of London on the kingdom have been examined elsewhere (Chartres 1986: 168–96), but innovations in commercial organization, in fashion or culture emanating from the capital, together with substantial wage differentials and purchasing power between London and the rest of southern England help to explain the sustained volume of in-migration. Consumption levels were very high, both in luxury imported goods such as tobacco or brandy, and in English provincial products. Market gardening became a feature of Thames-side at this time, as did the provisioning of milk, calves and pigs.

Large areas of north Kent and Surrey and southern Sussex were oriented towards the production of corn, fruit and hops for London's population (pp. 179–80). In 1649–50, for example, London received 989 shipments of corn from throughout England, of which 527 came from Kent. Wheat was exported coastwise from Faversham or Milton Regis; malt and barley from east Kent and Thanet. Sussex supplied the capital less regularly at this time, but large amounts of malt, meal and grain also went overland through Kingston or Croydon, together with barley to east Kent for malting and re-shipping to London. In 1624 Kent ports shipped 27,957 qrs of grain to London, compared with just 5,722 from Sussex (McGrath 1948: 145).

There were few areas which did not supply livestock to London at least occasionally. Romney Marsh and its immediate wealden hinterland was the chief area of supply for cattle, with sheep and lambs also going to Boulogne and the garrison at Calais. By the Civil War there were close metropolitan supply linkages in wealden fat cattle and sheep to London butchers. Large farmers hired drovers or sent their own men with herds to the capital. Smaller farmers relied on the round of fairs, or on local butchers to send their stock onwards. The Coastal Fringe was, of course, fully enmeshed within London's radius. Chichester was on the edge of that area supplying London with corn by sea, while mid-Kentish and north Kent cherries and fruit were supplied via the Medway and Swale. In the area around Teynham, several London fruiterers purchased the season's crop or leased their own orchards, often being related to the fruit farmers here. Thanet farmers in the early seventeenth century frequently sent malt to London factors who were their own kinsmen (Everitt 1967: 510–3).

The supplying of London was undoubtedly a lucrative business for most people concerned, although terms of trade were not equal. Londoners tended to extract middlemen's profits via hoymen or drovers away from the south-eastern rural producers, in a form similar to that proposed for the relationship between Coastal Fringe and Interior as a whole. There were few regions in the country where market town and countryside came together in such a sophisticated agrarian capitalism as within the southern hinterland of London. In return, this demand for foodstuffs helped support increased acreages and stimulate farming techniques and structural change as in no other region of the kingdom. From the most remote producers, a network of trackways and rivers brought supplies to the market towns which were intimately linked with the capital. However, such trends were not always positive. Grain riots in Kent, Sussex and the Thames Valley were sparked off by the fear that London was siphoning off local foodstuffs, and in dearth years local disorder was a more negative consequence of London's proximity. There were riots in many towns in the 1590s, as at Canterbury in 1596; or in 1630 at Faversham, Sittingbourne, Herne, Whitstable, Canterbury, Woodchurch and Cranbrook – cutting across the spectrum of settlement size and location (Walter and Wrightson 1984: 113–19). Carriers and middlemen were the immediate targets as elsewhere in England at this time, and at Canterbury in 1596 it was these men who were restrained, whereas no corn was actually touched.

There were also compensating beneficial counter-flows. It has been calculated, for example, that over 40 per cent of all Kent's charitable funds in the Stuart period were from London benefactions – by far the largest for any county in England. The London benefactors comprised only 4.35 per cent of all Kentish benefactors, so the amounts they gave were very large indeed, with the average sufficient to found a modest grammar school. Indeed, most of the money was for education or the poor, and it was particularly focused on north-west Kent, and more especially in the Hundred of Blackheath where an'economic and cultural inundation' by Londoners had taken place by 1600, 'as it were from a certaine riche and wealthy seed plot' (Jordan 1961: 133–8, citing Lambarde).

Sixteenth and seventeenth-century new towns

The main urban developments also owed much to the capital: Chatham grew as a dockyard town with the expansion of overseas trade and the need to safeguard its passage, while Tunbridge Wells relied on fashion and culture as London's social elite came to drink the waters on the wealden commonland. Other seventeenth-century developments included Epsom, Deal and Sheerness. Strictly speaking, much development also came after 1660, but it will be convenient to treat it here.

The south-eastern naval towns, located near London as well as near continental strategic need, had formerly been Deptford from 1513, Woolwich, and to a lesser extent, Greenwich. Tudor and Stuart expansionism engendered further growth, but the older dockyards nearer to London were overtaken in the early seventeenth century by Chatham. First used as an anchorage in 1550, and with the first reference to shipbuilding there in 1586, Chatham became the leading government dockyard by the Civil War. Equipped with dry docks, forts and all necessary shipbuilding facilities, the royal dockyard was extended in the early 1620s, with more developments in the 1650s and 1660s. By the 1660s Deptford's population had reached 4–5,000 and Chatham's had increased from under 1,000 in 1600 to about 3,000 by 1670, despite the loss of about 900 people in the plague years of 1665–6. It had risen to over 5,000 by 1700, with many paupers migrating from London for work. Chatham was frequently requesting help from the county JPs, but by the end of the seventeenth century the Kentish ship-building yards were employing several thousand men, who in turn provided the livings for local craftsmen, etc. Cordage, timber, workmen and ordnance could be obtained from within Chatham's hinterland and extensive network of suppliers and contractors. Demand for wealden timber, ordnance and ironwork; North Kent bricks and tiles; marshland reeds; Maidstone gunpowder and a host of minor products ensured that Chatham's success had wider ramifications, stimulating the local economies of north Kent and the Weald in particular. Even shipping at Ramsgate was involved in importing Baltic softwood to Chatham. Men such as Sir John Banks prospered in victualling the Chatham dockyards from their own and their neighbours' estates, and sending hops, cereals, beef and wood from mid-Kent (Coleman 1963). But as the seventeenth century progressed the increasing size of naval vessels brought difficulties. First Harwich and then Sheerness were sought as deeper-water bases, with Sheerness being developed during the Dutch wars when dry docks and cleaning facilities were installed. From 1666 all large ships were ordered to Sheerness for cleaning as Harwich declined (Harris 1985).

These new towns were not planned layouts, and Chatham has been described as a 'shapeless agglomeration of dwellings, most of them shabby' at this time (Clark and Slack 1976: 36–43). This is perhaps unfair to Chatham – for at least next to the church a development of artisan and dockyard worker dwellings was laid out in the later seventeenth century as leasehold from the Chapter of Rochester Cathedral (Chalklin 1965: 26). However, there were few urban institutions, no charter, and Chatham looked to nearby Rochester for schools, services and a market before the Restoration. Specialized naval supplying was the *leitmotif*. Thus the one early hospital in Chatham was the 'Hospital for Decayed Mariners and Shipwrights', founded by Sir John Hawkins in 1592. Services and administrative control were late arrivals, although an active sectarian religious fervour developed here, as elsewhere in the Lower Medway. Such growth was unparalleled in the South East, and was perhaps the nearest thing outside South London to the industrial developments in northern England in the nineteenth century.

Tudor expansionism was also responsible in part for the growth of

Deal. Fishermen and pilots passing through the Downs had long used the shore and Henry VIII had three castles built here in 1539–40. Nevertheless there were still probably only about 40 houses here in the 1620s, but the town grew steadily in an unplanned fashion during the later seventeenth century as victualling and general trading increased. In 1699 a charter of incorporation was granted with the right to hold a market, and Deal ceased now to be dependent on Sandwich in this respect, a dependence which had echoed the relationship between Chatham and Rochester (Chalklin 1974: 232–3).

The contrast between Chatham and the other major south-eastern new town of this period, Tunbridge Wells, could not be more absolute. The former owed its expansion to war and colonial trade, Tunbridge Wells to elite society. The former was plebeian, artisan or military, the latter a genteel resort; with a vogue for inland spas and social freedom away from the court, both Epsom and Tunbridge Wells provided south-eastern equivalents to Bath or Buxton. About 1606 the Tunbridge Wells springs were 'discovered' by Lord North, a somewhat dissolute youth, who took the waters for his health and subsequently lived to a great age. Their popularity was almost immediate, although development was initially slow. Queen Henrietta Maria was a visitor here in 1629 and by the 1630s families were coming to lodge with local farmers and tradesmen. Dr Rowzee of Ashford publicized the medicinal properties of the springs in *The Queen's wells: that is a treatise on the nature and virtues of Tunbridge water* (1632), and the original Walks (Pantiles) were laid out in the later 1630s. Most of the visitors stayed initially at Southborough or Rusthall, with the former becoming a centre for royalist sympathizers in contrast to the latter's more parliamentarian leanings.

The great development of such a resort, of course, had to await the Restoration and in the 1660s visits from Charles II's court confirmed its importance. A market catered specifically for visitors and from the 1680s development began in earnest along the Southborough Road and on the north side of the common, although the freeholders who controlled the common near the well initially refused to allow building. There were four principal landowners here at this time and one result was a multi-centred development around the common which only coalesced much later. At the junction of three pre-existing parishes (Tonbridge, Speldhurst and Frant), Tunbridge Wells had no church of its own until the 1680s when wealthy visitors contributed to its erection, and when the Walks was also developed with shops, taverns and a walkway. Building for lodging houses began at nearby Mount Sion, and local tradesmen and gentry were joined by London speculators as the town grew onto what later became Mount Ephraim. By the end of the century there were specialist professions here, indicating the dependence of the local tradesmen on the visitors. By about 1700 the Walks had a watchmaker, two confectioners, an upholsterer, an 'indian gown man' and a milliner. Celia Fiennes noted the shops 'full of all sorts of toys, silver and china' and also 'two large coffee houses for tea, chocolate etc and two rooms for the lottery and hazard board' (Chalklin 1965: 258–9; 1974:234; Barton 1937).

Epsom, about 15 miles from Westminster Bridge, developed at much the same time with the discovery of the medicinal wells in 1618. In 1629 one East India Company traveller described it as 'on the rise of a very large heath, where one always finds somebody who serves the visitor with glasses and otherwise'. Epsom Salts (sulphate of magnesia) were famous by the 1630s, and fetched high prices, although not patented until the 1690s. Development again awaited the Restoration and London capital. William Schellinck's engraving of *Epsom Common and Wells* (1662), just to the west of Epsom village, shows little more than one small building housing the wells, and with horse-riding and talking seemingly the main diversions. The social centre was Epsom itself, where one early eighteenth-century commentator suggested that 'you would fancy yourself on the Exchange at St. James, or in an East India factory, or with the army in Flanders' (in Brandon 1977: 69–70). Box Hill was also an attraction, where it was easy for 'gentlemen and ladies insensibly to lose their company in these pretty labyrinths of box-wood and divert themselves unperceived', so that 'it may justly be called the Palace of Venus' (in Clark and Slack 1976: 35). Nevertheless the developments here were slower than at Tunbridge Wells, and the zenith of Epsom's fortunes came in the eighteenth century as a centre of popular amusement and horse-racing (Clark 1960; Lehmann 1973).

Markets, country towns and ports

Country towns formed the base of the urban hierarchy. Many, such as Sevenoaks, had no charter and several were far from secure as trade ebbed and flowed. Thus, by the sixteenth century the markets at Bletchingley, Haslemere and Leatherhead were in decline, and by the following century Shalford's sheep fair (the setting for Bunyan's 'Vanity Fair') was merely a social and no longer an economic event. Even at more substantial Lewes, the church of St Martin was lost before 1545, while St Nicholas was converted into tenements by 1592 (Reed 1986: 181). Many with market or even borough status were very small, such as Elham in the Kentish downland, or Haslemere and Smarden at opposite ends of the Weald, and many were dormant. Bletchingly, a medieval borough and the smallest of the Surrey towns, had its two MPs elected by just 46 voters by 1640. The borough of Reigate, a market town since the thirteenth century, declined so that it contained just 90 tenements by 1622 (O'Connell 1977: 7, 45; Gulley 1960: 213). Ewell's market was 'so inconsiderable that it does not deserve the name'; Leatherhead's was decayed by 1650, when that of St Mary Cray was 'very inconsiderable' (Everitt 1967: 472; Cowley 1964: 228–9; Ashworth 1967: 108–12).

Official market days or fairs were held throughout the South East (Fig. 4.2) but with notably few markets within the Interior, although even in the Coastal Fringe there were areas such as the Blean, Isle of Thanet or

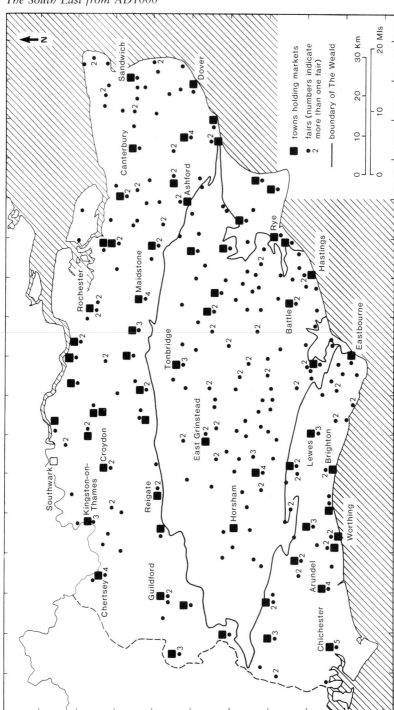

Figure 4.2 Markets and fairs in the early-modern South East.

Stour Levels where markets were absent. Fairs were frequently held outside towns, with over half those of Kent held in rural locations. Many had only semi-official status, and their numbers fluctuated. By 1756 the South East had the highest density of fairs in the kingdom (Chartres 1985: 430–9). Some towns had specialist fairs. Maidstone, Ashford and Lenham had well-known cattle fairs for northern and Welsh cattle. Hops were also traded at fairs, and from Maidstone, Canterbury and Farnham, via the Medway, Stour and Wey respectively large quantities went to Stourbridge Fair (Clark and Slack 1976: 19; Everitt 1967: 498–543).

In the South East as a whole the number of markets increased from 43 in 1588 to 51 in 1611, 54 in 1656, and 58 in 1673 (Dyer 1979: 123–34). New markets were often inland and closer to London rather than coastal. Godalming was a sixteenth-century clothing town rather than a market centre but in 1575 it was granted borough status and permission to hold a market and fair, yielding prosperity which has left its mark in sixteenth-century buildings in the High Street and Church Street. Chertsey and St Mary Cray were also Elizabethan foundations; Bromley is first recorded as a market in 1635 and Northfleet and Westerham in 1659. The 1649 survey of the manor of Dorking mentions the town with a weekly market on Thursdays, an annual fair on Ascension Day, and 'almost every day furnished with all sorts of sea-fish' (Sy RO 196/2/1). Woolwich appears by 1673 and Woking soon after. Others were re-creations, such as Westerham where the 1337 grant had long fallen into disuse, as had the markets at other Holmesdale centres such as Kemsing, Shoreham, Seal and Otford. Local tradesmen persuaded Sir Thomas Gresham, lord of the manor, to lease a site to them, and a market was founded by 1620. Westerham consequently developed into a prosperous cattle centre.

Further away from London there were also new markets, for example at Wye (1588), Folkestone (1659), Storrington (1673), and Haslemere by 1690.

Table 4.1 Market town specialization in the South East in the sixteenth and seventeenth centuries

1. *Corn markets* Canterbury, Chichester, Croydon, Dartford, Dorking, Farnham, Faversham, Guildford, Horsham, Lewes, Reigate, Sandwich	4. *Cattle markets* Ashford, Chichester, Lenham, Maidstone, Rye
2. *Malt markets* Dartford, Dorking	5. *Poultry and wildfowl* Chichester, Dorking, Horsham, Malden
3. *Fruit and hop markets* Canterbury, Maidstone	6. *Cloth market* Canterbury, Godalming

(Source: After Everitt 1967: 589–92)

Cuckfield, 'seated in the dirty part of the country' (Blome 1673: 226), was in 1611 a 'discontynued markett towne' as was Ditchling (Cockburn 1975: 55). However, most were caught up in the surge of entrepreneurial activity in the second half of the seventeenth century. Cattle markets in particular multiplied with London's demands. Only Northfleet, Sittingbourne and Leatherhead (and Godalming temporarily in the 1670s) died out as market centres near London, although the Sussex situation was more complex, with decaying markets being replaced by new ones. By 1673 Shoreham, Eastbourne, Ditchling, Hailsham and Winchelsea briefly disappear, as had Pevensey, Bramber, Broadwater and Robertsbridge (all of which had gone by the 1630s). On the other hand Horsham, the most significant of the central wealden markets, 'hath a great market on Saturdays for corn, and all sorts of provisions, especially fowl, which is bought up by the London haglers' (Blome 1673: 225). In 1611 Horsham had 'one fayer yearlie kep in the month of Julye called St Thomas's Fayer and there is within the said Borroughe a markett kept uppon the Satturdaye everie weeke' (Albery 1947: 55).

Substantial markets also multiplied at the older centres. Although only about one town market in every four in the South East was specialist, such markets grew, as at Canterbury where the fifteenth-century Old Poultry Cross was joined from the mid-seventeenth century by a 'handsome market place, with several rooms over it for public use, part of which was used as a repository for corn, against time of dearth' (Hasted, in Everitt 1967: 481–501). Specialist sheep, cattle and poultry markets existed, and the Oxindens or Twysdens knew that the best hop market was in Canterbury, that fruit did best at Maidstone, and cattle at Ashford. The prosperity of the period is reflected in the Elizabethan gildhalls of Sandwich and Faversham, or the shops and shambles at Sevenoaks, Petworth and Westerham (Table 4.1).

Croydon was growing by the early sixteenth century, with an Old and a New Town mentioned, and shops beginning to cluster around the market place. As the management centre for the Archbishop of Canterbury's estates in Surrey, Middlesex and Hertfordshire, the town was important. The archbishop's house was primarily a summer residence although the great banqueting hall and other amenities, together with proximity to London, made it a royal retreat on occasion. A market house was built in 1566 and a profusion of coaching inns arose along the main London highway. Whitgift founded a considerable hospital here in 1596 (*VCH* Sy,IV: 205–28). Guildford was a clothing centre as well as the location for a royal palace by the early sixteenth century, but situated on the main road from London to Winchester and Portsmouth, the coaching and market trade became increasingly important. More housing and

---

Plate 4.4 Abbot's Hospital, Guildford. This survives as one of the finest examples of Jacobean architecture. It was endowed by Archbishop Abbot, a native of the town, as an attempt to mitigate the widespread poverty that had arisen by the 1620s from the decline of the local cloth trade.

a grammar school arrived during the sixteenth century, reflecting in-migration of cloth-workers from the surrounding countryside, perhaps due to the enforcement of the 1557–8 Act which attempted to forbid manufacture of cloth outside an established cloth town. The decay of the clothing industry affected the town's prosperity, although there were schemes to revive it, such as that of George Abbot, who projected a change from manufacturing kersies to broadcloth in 1614. Nothing came of this, nor of his 1627 proposal when he later became Archbishop of Canterbury for a change to the manufacture of linen. By the late seventeenth century the trade had gone completely (Chamberlin 1970: 68–82). Abbot did, however, found the hospital in Guildford, along the lines of his predecessor's at Croydon (Plate 4.4), while the gildhall has a seventeenth-century Renaissance frontage.

Trade depended upon access. Movement by road was not always easy, and the volume of trade told on miry clay subsoils, especially in the Weald where market produce jostled with iron products and timber. Legislation was constant and ironworks were correctly singled out for their effects on the deteriorating routeways. Acts of 1585, 1597 and 1623 all attempted to remedy this problem, while local JPs attempted to keep roads and bridges passable and free from encroachment or digging.

The easier movement for bulky material was by water, and several improvements were attempted at this time to make such passage feasible. The Earl of Arundel extended the Arun navigation northwards in the later sixteenth century, and similar attempts were made to link the Interior more efficiently with the main corn-supplying towns for London which ranged around the south-eastern peninsula at Kingston-upon-Thames, Faversham, Maidstone (via the Medway), Sandwich, Chichester, Arundel, Shoreham and Newhaven. However, these schemes caused bitter local political rivalry. Rivers such as the Rother, Medway or Stour had riparian owners with weirs and mills which blocked boats; while Rye's trading prosperity was constantly threatened by the inning of the adjacent marshland – hence the popularity of Culpeper's appeal to the Rye electorate in the 1620s (p. 147). The Medway navigation was a hotbed of intrigue (Hood 1979; 1981). By the early seventeenth century Maidstone was the head of navigation for most craft, serving as the regional collecting and distribution point for fruit, hops and timber. Extension of the navigation upstream towards Tonbridge would have facilitated exports of wealden timber and iron, but successive attempts to improve the upstream navigation foundered until the 1664 Medway bill was successful, backed by ten former royalist promoters from upstream of Maidstone. In 1651 the Wey Navigation from Weybridge to Guildford, thanks to the enthusiasm of the royalist Richard Weston of Sutton Place, similarly opened up timber, flour and paper exports from south-west Surrey to London.

In 1559 the first sluice was built to help scour Faversham Creek, and Tudor Faversham thereafter was a major corn-exporting port to London, as well as an importing venue for London merchandise. It acquired the second-largest parish church in Kent, a major gun-powder manufacturing works, granaries, warehouses, inns and officials' offices, a paved town centre by 1549, a grammar school, market house and gildhall, and a mercers' company. In 1580 Faversham's population had reached about 1,400 and there were as many as 70 officials administering the entrepôt. However, in time Londoners themselves began to engage in direct marketing relations (as noted above with reference to fruit) and the number of local merchants trading with London declined as the seventeenth century progressed. While the volume of trade remained high overall, Londoners had taken over Faversham's former mediating role (Clark and Slack 1972: 13).

The ports were vital to regional prosperity. These varied in size and importance from London itself down to the many creeks and inland harbours up the rivers, in the silting estuaries and along the mud flats of north Kent. Patterns of trade fluctuated considerably as commerce shifted from older ports which were silting up at Rye, Pevensey, Sandwich, Canterbury and New Romney. The latter, suffering from shingle accumulation, had no ships by 1587. Trade from Rye and Hastings continued with East Anglia, the West Country and the Continent, but in a muted fashion, while the port at Winchelsea was defunct by 1600 (Gulley 1960: 212–25).

Some seafaring towns had no harbour. Brighton's boats were hauled onto a sheltered beach protected by a western offshore bar located towards the Adur estuary. By 1570 Brighton's population was about 1,200 and this tripled over the next 80 years, mainly due to its fishing fleets which prospered by their local fishing, as well as by their work off the North Foreland and in the North Sea. By the mid-seventeenth century Brighton was sending more boats to the Yarmouth area than any other south coast town: 45–50 boats compared with Rye's 4, Hastings' 23, Hythe's 2, and about 18 in all from the combined towns of Dover, Folkestone, Broadstairs and Margate. But Brighton's foreshore was becoming eroded, and in the later seventeenth century the Yarmouth fisheries became less attractive, and coastal carrying, especially of coal, became more dominant. One such coal-carrying vessel, *The Surprise*, provided the means of escape for King Charles II to France after the Battle of Worcester in 1651. Decline in the fisheries was not unique to Brighton. The south-eastern fishing fleets rarely took part in long-distance expeditions, as did those of the West Country. Only Broadstairs could boast an Icelandic fishing industry. With underused facilities, relatively static populations and underemployment, the development of resorts was to come as a saviour to these towns (Farrant 1985: 59–76).

Urban society and economy

There was considerable variation at this time in urban economic and social structure; the balance between the size, functions, power and attitudes of the ruling elites; and the numbers of middling classes and poor. Patronage and wealth were increasingly channelled through cliques or 'civic oligarchies', as at Maidstone, Hastings or Sandwich (Clark and Slack 1972: 21). Many towns, such as Canterbury or Rye, still looked for regulatory powers to the medieval gilds; and craftsmen, tradesmen and professionals, often with kinship links, ruled through a magistracy which was often very harsh and conservative in religious terms: Canterbury was ruled by Catholic cliques through to the early 1570s (Urry 1988: xix–xxii, 1–5). However, for reasons still not fully explicable, but in part related to the intensity of religious schism and the exclusion of many from power-sharing, many towns veered strongly towards Puritanism in the 1580s. Ashford, Cranbrook and Sandwich became closely identified with nonconformity or separatism, and by 1600 Catholicism was a minority rural, rather than urban, religion.

Wealth and social status were rarely polarized since most towns contained numbers of middling craftsmen and small tradesmen. In early seventeenth-century Petworth, for example, there were about 50 different trades and occupations. But the distribution of wealth and power was very uneven. About one-quarter of all the working population of Canterbury were too poor to be taxed by the 1520s, while two-thirds of those who were taxed were assessed at the lowest possible rate. Just 3.8 per cent were assessed at more than £40 (Clark 1977: 8). The clothing industry had collapsed here and the Reformation would reduce Canterbury's ceremonial importance. Rural poor had flocked to the suburbs but they met dearth, poverty and plague by the mid-sixteenth century. Households were small, being mostly labouring families, with poor widows frequently heads of household (Clark, P. and Clark, J. 1983: 65–86).

Lured by hopes of employment, amusement or charitable relief, large numbers of poor migrants threatened south-eastern urban society. Three different types of migration at this time have been discussed (Clark 1972: 117–63). Planned *betterment* migration involved the movement of tradesmen or apprentices in search of improvement. Personal knowledge and kinship links were important here, and typically apprentices would come from within an 11-miles radius of towns such as Canterbury, Maidstone or Faversham. Village links were often retained, with return for harvesting a frequent phenomenon.

On the other hand poorer or displaced vagrants tramped in *subsistence* migration, pushed from their rural homes by bad harvests or changes in agrarian organization. Longer distances and more frequent moves characterized these migrants in their search for work, and the suburbs provided them some shelter. By 1600 Canterbury was operating more than twenty relief funds (Clark 1972: 145). The problem of the vagrants vexed south-eastern town councils. Many attempted to prevent settlement, thereby keeping their poor rates at reasonable levels. In 1594–5 the Lord Mayor of London issued orders against vagrants, bemoaned the state of property in Southwark and attempted to prohibit the building of small tenements to prevent urban toe-holds for migrants. The young without work and the Irish were of particular concern to Southwark by the early seventeenth century, and in times of stress London Bridge might be guarded to prevent access by mobs into the City (Corporation of London 1878: 357–8).

In 1572 Canterbury appointed beadles to arrest beggars, and at Sandwich in 1578 the council prohibited the subdividing of tenements, in moves commonly repeated all over the region. As early as 1528 Faversham had issued decrees 'against unwanted incomers', while Brighton, complaining that the town 'is more burdened and charged with poore than heretofore it hath beene', attempted to regulate the letting of accommodation to newcomers, although this probably failed in the absence of resident gentry or an established oligarchy. Between 1580 and 1640 about 60 per cent of Brighton's male deponents in archdeaconry courts had been born elsewhere (Farrant 1985: 63). Only after the slowdown in population growth in the mid-seventeenth century and the establishment and enforcement of the Act of Settlement in 1662 did migration lessen.

The final category of migrants were the *foreigners*, very important to towns such as Canterbury, Sandwich or Maidstone, bringing skills and capital. Although they might incur local jealousy at times of stress, and threaten entrenched cliques, such people often became prominent citizens. Also desirable were the ex-Londoners who endowed local schools or charities. Canterbury elected a prominent London lawyer, John Hales, as MP in 1514; and received an annual bequest from Chief Justice Fineux towards a new market house in the 1520s. New families also moved into Sevenoaks at this time, including lawyers from London's court circles (Dunlop 1964: 100–25).

Despite the loss of ceremonial functions during the Elizabethan period, the economic position of the towns had improved. London now fuelled south-eastern trade as never before, and this was linked with a growing agrarian capitalism (pp. 170–184) which found its outlets through the towns for the most part. Apart from economic and social stress in the 1590s, the growth of overall prosperity continued into the Jacobean period, with the 1604 peace with Spain opening up North European trading links once more. By the 1620s, of course, religious and political factionalism was in evidence again. The elections of the 1620s brought out the full force of urban radicalism, allied with religious fervour. Additionally there was economic stress as the clothing trade slumped, as estuarine silting continued unabated, as privateering increased, and as London buyers of country produce purchased directly rather than through the towns. The levying of Ship-money thus came as a considerable burden to many ports. In 1635 25 per cent of Kent's tax was levied on the towns, strengthening the cause of radical anti-court factions there, and stimulating the 'resort to the plantacions' in America of many quite substantial clothiers from the Weald, Sandwich and Canterbury as noted by Dering (Bodl Ms, Topog Kent, a 1 f. 26). Smouldering resentment and open radicalism combined with the hardships of civil war to make the towns centres of faction and warfare in the 1640s. Chichester and Arundel were fought over repeatedly, Canterbury was the scene of rioting which sparked off the second civil war in 1648, and it was small wonder that such centres were thereafter controlled as Puritanism and revolution were expunged.

With internal peace also at hand, towns could look forward to a period of consolidation and Georgian growth. And growth was all the more possible with the final extinction of the 'closed civic commonwealths'. Pressures brought during this period by external and internal economic, social, cultural and political transformation, and by the sheer bulk of immigration, broke down the powerful cliques and opened the way to a much greater late-seventeenth century receptiveness to change. Increasingly the towns became stages for county society, or else they aped London's manners and styles as they looked outwards for economic and social contact.

The Changing Countryside

Between 1520 and 1660 changes in the south-eastern countryside reflected those within the dominant social and economic relations, which were now firmly capitalist. Farming patterns incorporated new crops and a more specialized, market-orientated outlook, while the structure and social relations of farming were reshaped by the Dissolution and by the emerging triad of landowner–tenant–labourer over much, though not all, of the South East. Population shifts continued, with a greater emphasis now on growth in the rural Interior and in the region's towns.

In part this spatial shift reflected industrial growth. The establishment of the first English blast furnace at Newbridge on the northern slopes of the Ashdown Forest in 1496 was followed by an innovative wave outwards rendering the High Weald the workshop of the Tudor armaments industry. There was also wealden and Surrey cloth-making, and glass-making in west Sussex and Surrey, giving the Interior a high proto-industrial profile. Such an emphasis was counterbalanced by the highly capitalized farming of the Coastal Fringe. Together these twin emphases – industrial Interior and agricultural Coastal Fringe – produced a region of great prosperity and significance in this 'Age of exuberance'.

The south-eastern farming regions are described more fully in Chapter 5. Here an account will be given of the early-modern farming systems and the changes within them. The regions are those depicted in Fig. 5.1 (p. 206).

The Wealden Interior

By 1520 patterns of dispersed settlement and amorphous enclosed fields were long established. The combination of gavelkind partible inheritance, the presence of iron, glass and cloth working, and a buoyant land market acted in concert to keep holdings small and the number of large estates and manors limited. Holding sizes in the eastern Weald between 1502 and 1639 have been estimated at 41 per cent under 5 acres; 38 per cent between 5 and 50 acres; and with very few over 300 acres. Old demesnes were now leased but there were also large numbers of freeholders, especially in Kent, together with those who held by copy and by assart tenure. A bewildering kaleidoscope of tenures could not easily be amalgamated into larger holdings and this served to delay the worst excesses of engrossment. Conversely, partible inheritance could have dramatic effects, and actual fields were subdivided at Southborough Common and Chevening by the early seventeenth century. Partible descent was altered by the enforcement of disgavelling statutes between 1539 and 1624 although the free alienation aspects of gavelkind continued strongly. Robertsbridge manor extended into 14 parishes and Allington into 22, covering 6,000 acres by 1608, but manors were more usually small or fragmented. The parish of Hailsham, for example, included land held of 14 different manors (Gulley 1960: 154; Baker 1963: 321; Brent 1973: 210–20).

In the later-sixteenth century Kentish Weald the most extensive estate was that of the Baker family, stretching into about twenty parishes around Sissinghurst. In Sussex, the Buckhurst estate, beautifully mapped for the Duke of Dorset in 1597–8, reached 16,000 acres. Most gentry estates were far more limited, although many eastern landowners also held land in Romney Marsh. Walter Roberts of Cranbrook (d. 1580) held 1,500 acres in three adjacent parishes and 60 acres in the Marsh. Freeholds (the oldest type of tenure) tended to be the most fragmented, followed by copyholds, and with leaseholds (the newest form), the least fragmented. In the Kentish Weald many landowners were also clothiers, and many smallholders had secondary sources of income to supplement family-based food production. Tradesmen and craftsmen might also keep livestock and grow crops; while ironmasters, glassmakers or woodbrokers were also farmers, employing part-year industrial workmen. A diversified proto-industrial economy emerged strongly at this time, attracting still more marginalized families to the area.

During the later sixteenth century no new arable crops appeared in this largely self-subsistent economy. Instead, about half the sown area was under poor wheat or winter grains, half in spring-sown oats, while peas, tares and fallow were also still very significant. Although there was probably more arable in the Weald by the seventeenth century than at any previous period, there was still little artificial grassland and no root crops to be found. However fruit and hops were innovations at this time: apples, pears and plums were grown for local consumption or drunk as cider and perry in the north-eastern High Weald. Hops, their cultivation first described in 1573, were already localized in the same area, and especially in the mid-Kent Lower Greensand. In 1581 a stranger 'using ye trade of making hopp gardens' was buried at Mayfield, and by 1640 hops were being cultivated as far west as Cuckfield, by which time they were the subject of a thriving export trade to London.

Cattle rearing and fattening, using stalls as well as grassland, was of paramount importance. Leonard Mascall of Plumpton described the local breed as a red stock, valuable for its working and beef qualities, in his *First book of cattell* (1596), but much stock came from the North or Wales. Oxen were invariably used for haulage and ploughing. Most holdings had a few house cows to give a little poor milk, cheese and butter; and most kept sheep, especially in the slightly drier High Weald, for domestic supplies of mutton and wool, but they were kept neither commercially nor for folding.

Wealden soils were fertilized by heavy applications of downland chalk or lime, and by marl. In 1626 an East Grinstead leaseholder agreed to put '160 wads of marle' on every acre of pasture or woodland which he ploughed up for corn. This was in the year following the publication of Markham's *Inrichment of the Weald of Kent*, advocating the re-introduction of marling, although the practice seems to have persisted through the inflationary years of the late sixteenth century, stimulated no doubt by the rising prices of foodstuffs. In the 1630s Thomas Pelham at Laughton illustrated how poor land might also be improved by 'devonshiring' (often corrupted to denchering or denshiring). Rough turf, pared off with a breast plough, was burnt and the ashes scattered and ploughed in, often with applications of lime and/or marl. In the 1640s the account book of one progressive Plaistow yeoman, Richard Bax, contained references to denshiring as well as to the sale of peas, oats, wheat and hops. Crops were also improved by the wider adoption of convertible husbandry, and later by clover, advocated by Markham as 'most fatning and profitable, both for sheepe and bullocks'. But such improvements were by no means universally adopted. Richard Weston experimented with sainfoin in the 1640s at a time when Dutch White, perennial Red and broad clover were being grown more widely in the wealden clay vale. But Dutch clover was still being imported to Herstmonceux, so presumably there was no extensive local trade as yet.

By 1520 woodland and waste proliferated more in the Sussex and Surrey component than in the Kentish and north-eastern Weald. However, perhaps as much as half of the large parish of Tonbridge was still wood and parkland awaiting reclamation; while the area of common was still sufficient for the parish of Lamberhurst to allow rights of common in 1568 to all animals without stint. But by 1664 three-quarters of the 5,000-acre Southfrith in Tonbridge was converted to farmland. Typically up to 50 per cent of the area of sixteenth-century wealden estates was reserved for woodland used commercially for coaling. Sir John Pelham in 1580 commanded that after felling, an area was to be 'incopsed, for the preservation of the spring of that wood for the better continuance of the wood there' (Brent 1976: 39; Thirsk 1967: 59; Baker 1963: 246).

Nevertheless, many field names appear for the first time during this century as testimony to a new phase of wealden clearance, while many internal field boundaries were removed to give larger, more manageable fields. Much of the remaining waste was enclosed and the Ashdown Forest margins and Forest Ridges were actively colonized, often for cottage and garden plots on roadside waste. Sometimes the lord of the manor was requested to grant waste to 'honest poor', as in the case of John Alexander who had a large family, and on whose behalf the tenants of Chiddingly requested the grant of a piece of land at the Dicker. But illegal encroachments could create ill-feeling, and after 1589 local magistrates enforced the statute forbidding the building of cottages without at least four acres of appurtenant land (31 Eliz I C7). Agitation by villagers over the enclosure of commons was frequent, as at Petworth after enclosures by the Earl of Northumberland in the 1590s, at Chailey in 1624, and intermittently on Ashdown. Disputes could also arise between larger landowners, such as that between Sidney and Pelham in 1602 over an enclosure on Brightling Down (Gulley 1960: 108–10).

Disparking among the 50 parks of the Weald, covering perhaps 10 per cent of the area, brought still more farmland into operation. The 690-acre Great Park at Petworth and the 1,700 acres of Shillinglee (Kirdford), were both disparked in the early seventeenth century, and parks at Cuckfield, Horsham, Hurstpierpoint and elsewhere underwent similar transformations. St Leonard's Forest was disparked in 1608 but the various schemes to bring the 14,000 acres of Ashdown into farmland during the seventeenth century proved abortive. Many parks now in fact combined their traditional deer, cony, fish and timber production with cattle grazing, swine pannage and even arable cropping (Gulley 1960: 68).

The Scarpfoot Zone

Surrounding the High and Low Weald was the 'antechamber' of the Scarpfoot, Lower Greensand or Holmesdale Zone (Fig. 5.1). This was a highly diverse area which is only conflated here for the sake of brevity. The zone included the Petworth and Western Rother Valley below the Greensand lowland heaths; the heavy Gault Clay and low Sussex Greensand hills; the Surrey Greensand heath of the Hindhead area, stretching eastwards to Mid-Kent where the lower altitudes and warmer mid-Kent soils formed the basis for one of the most prosperous agricultural districts in the South East. Thereafter, the Vale of Ashford, together with the Vale of Holmesdale between Maidstone and Farnham diversified the zone still further. Such an area was not self-contained and as well as the growing contacts with London and other urban markets, there were older functioning units to consider. The old manorial units, the parishes and the larger farms partook not only of the soils described in this section, but also of chalk downland and of Weald clay, thereby imparting great flexibility to the rural economy.

By 1600 the lighter soils of the sandstone ridges were farmed in a more truly mixed system than anywhere else in the South East. There was more corn than in the Weald, but less livestock, although there were also excellent fattening pastures. Barley now emerged alongside wheat and oats; and with peas, beans and tares constituted the arable. Soils were judiciously improved with manure and lime, the latter easily obtainable from downland lime-burners. On the heavy 'cold, weeping clays' in the Vale of Ashford a description of 'up-and-down' husbandry was given to the Georgical Committee in the 1660s. The land was 'not fitt to bee continued in tillage, but we lay it down for pasture and meadow for ten or twelve yeares, then we convert it to tillage' (Georgical Committee, no. 28).

The mid-Kent 'red hills' area was one of England's leading fruit-producing localities by 1600. Orchard land was worth at least twice the value of farmland, and hops were firmly established here during the late sixteenth century, well before their spread to north Kent. Gentry in these Chartlands were encouraged to grow hops by the increasing accumulation of expertise by growers, labourers and factors; a sophisticated marketing system; the proximity of Southwark market; and by the specialist provision of pole plantations. At Chart Sutton by 1604 George Franklyn, gentleman, had ordered the planting, dunging and dressing of five hop gardens totalling 16 acres for the last 16 years. Picking was undertaken by 50–60 people, including many 'soe extreame poor that they did lyve uppon the almes of the parishes and poore mens boxe where they were resident' (Chalklin 1965: 94). In 1598–9 he was dispatching his hops to London via Rochester and presumably obtaining good prices, since the hops were stated to be virtually the sole support of his family.

In the Ragstone hills, on the Lower Chalk bench and in the Vales of Holmesdale, Ashford and Western Rother, farming was prosperous and progressive. Former open-field strips were enclosed, or in process of enclosure, by the mid-sixteenth century and consolidation and increasing farm size provided a good basis for investment. The former scattered demesne parcels at Chalvington, east of Lewes, were consolidated by 1559 (Brandon 1963: 218). At Petworth the 1606 Treswell map shows a series of long, narrow closes suggestive of a transitional stage during which enclosure was proceeding. Around the scarpfoot villages and on the Greensand, enclosure progressed especially on the former demesne lands in the half-century after the Dissolution, as at Alciston, Folkington, West Firle, Amberley or Sutton, although scraps of open field persisted through into the early nineteenth century, as at Plumpton, for example. Sixteenth-century Woolavington demonstrates the slow change. Part of the common fields had already been enclosed to form small crofts before 1520. In 1549 three Woolavington copyholders were licensed to exchange their lands in the common fields and to enclose them with hedges and ditches. By 1574 most of the common arable was enclosed, but in 1579 several tenants were presented for tearing down hedges dividing a neighbour's land (Brandon 1963: 307). In the Kentish scarpfoot the process of enclosure was probably easier, for no evidence has yet emerged for *common* as opposed to *open and subdivided* fields being used there. At Wrotham in Holmesdale most of the demesne was enclosed by 1520, although the 'common field' was subdivided, presumably because of gavelkind partitioning, into 17 unenclosed parcels, shared among three people in severalty. By 1658 this area was held by one man (Baker 1963: 127–35). The pace of change here was similarly quick before 1600 with consolidation, enclosure and purchase proceeding without the need for parliamentary act or chancery decree. In Wrotham, and by implication in most of Holmesdale, the sixteenth century witnessed a growing inequality in holding sizes as consolidated former demesnes were leased out.

Elsewhere in the Scarpfoot Zone the sterile Lower Greensand was used as heath, wood, rough grazings or severalty farmland. The heaths, which put Defoe in mind of 'Arabia deserta', constituted a huge reservoir of commonland, as at Blackheath or Woolmer Forest, or among the smaller commons at Brabourne Lees or Chart Sutton. The heaths yielded bracken, sand, marl, turf and peat, while the Kentish 'Petts' (quarries) supplied excellent ragstone for building. The 'drye and heathye ground' at Witley and Thursley totalled more than 5,000 acres and provided heath for burning limekilns here after about 1600, while underwood might come from the scanty woodlands, as about Frensham. Thin corn crops were produced with the aid of 'heathcropper' sheep which were intercommoned, as at Linchmere or Godalming. In 1635 'all manner of cattell' could be intercommoned at Langley Heath, Kent at a time when small-scale enclosure was being undertaken (Baker 1963: 238–44; Ashworth 1967: 161–2).

The Downland

The downland tops were largely relegated to sheepwalk and common pasture in east Sussex and east Kent, or to timber in west Sussex, west Kent and east Surrey. Much of the Clay-with-flints, even in densely-settled east Kent, was virtually useless. Hasted described Paddlesworth as 'barren, with a great deal of heath or common throughout it, a wretched and miserable country'. At Swingfield Minnis in 1632, 37 people were reckoned to have rights of pasturing sheep, horses or cattle, while in west Sussex swine were sent from Arundel to the 'hogg commons' at Singleton and East Dean (Brandon 1963: 136; Everitt 1977).

By contrast the lower dipslopes were completely cultivated in fields which, apart from Romney Marsh, were the largest in the South East. At Gillingham there is evidence for the subdivision of former large fields by the early seventeenth century; the extension of orchards, especially for cherries; and the consolidation of holdings. The number of lessees of the enclosed demesne at Gillingham fell from 5 in 1608 to just one by 1649. Enclosure from the downland proceeded apace at this time as high profits from the London grain trade brought a search for new land. At Barton farm, Dover an 11-acre field was described as 'new close' in 1640, 'taken out of the down'. There were also still many unenclosed but subdivided fields at Eastry,

Deal or the Hoo Peninsula. Wheat was dominant and accounted for 43 per cent of the cropped area in early seventeenth-century inventories compared with 25 per cent for barley and 17 per cent for oats. Farms were large and increasing in size throughout north and east Kent as the competitive land market now over-rode the divisive effects of gavelkind partitioning. Engrossing and consolidation seem to have been general on the east Kent downland throughout this period, as at post-Dissolution Eastry (O'Grady 1987). However it is also in this area that the open fields of Kent survived, at parishes such as Broomfield, Sturry, Shepherdswell and Wingham. Hasted observed at the end of the eighteenth century that Ripple was 'much inclined to Chalk, tho' there is a great deal of fertile land in it. The country is mostly open and the lands unenclosed; it has no wood in it'. But neighbouring Great Mongeham was different, 'more flat, even and more enclosed with trees and hedgerows of elm, the soil is more fertile, having less chalk and much loam, and deep earth throughout it' (Hasted 1797–1801, IV: 134, 138). A correlation between open fields and Upper Chalk has been argued by Baker, and we are reminded again of the enormous variations in local conditions within the downland.

Mixed teams of oxen and horses pulled heavy turnwest ploughs. There was little 'up-and-down' husbandry here, but sheep flocks were very important for wool, mutton and folding; although the latter quality was nowhere as highly prized in Kent as on the South Downs. In east Kent and Thanet a sheep/corn husbandry flourished, with peas and beans important as fodder and with large amounts of cereals going to London via Sandwich or Faversham. Hartlib in 1651 also noted the growing of sainfoin on the chalk at Cobham Park, Gravesend where on 'dry barren land' it yielded good cattle fodder. The high land values generally militated against hedges, as did bleak winds and dry Upper Chalk soils. Livestock were controlled instead by temporary fences or by tethering.

By 1640 12 of the 42 Sussex downland parishes were fully enclosed, mostly to the west and many within the previous one hundred years; and nearly all the demesnes were now enclosed, consolidated and block-leased. Farms frequently surpassed 500 acres, as at Alciston or Rottingdean, and might include areas of open field. By 1574 one of the three laines at Falmer was enclosed, but much of the rest of the area lay 'in divers laines and parcels plain without hedge or such enclosure'. The open arable on the Lower Chalk slopes was composed of strips (paul-pieces) separated by markstakes, with well over 1,000 such paul-pieces around Brighton at this time. In some parishes, such as Northease and Rodmell, larger farming units were appearing, and there is evidence for continued increases in demesne size, in the purchase of copyholds and the conflation of tenant holdings (Brent 1976: 35–6 and 1973: 197). At Stanmer John Michelbourne turned the manor into a large-scale farm by the early 1630s, as did the neighbouring Dobells at Streat, and as was also happening at Falmer, Coombes and Monkton (West Dean). Complaints against engrossing were made, as against Richard Elderton in Preston and Patcham in 1545, but exports of corn to London and wool to the Kentish clothiers brought huge profits.

The sheep common or tenantry down of east Sussex was the most extensive on the downland, despite enclosure by 1520, extending to over 2,000 acres in Patcham and at Falmer. However, reclamation for cereals reduced stints, and the most generous stints remained those in the manors sharing the west Sussex downland such as Charlton and Bury. The latter's sheep common was in Mens Wood, also used for swine pannage. On these wooded or long-grass, more acidic and wetter downs the long-legged, taller horned Dorset or Hampshire sheep were preferred to the fine-wooled, shorter polled sheep of the east. Small copyholders contributed to a communal flock guarded by one shepherd who folded them at high densities, each tenant bringing his own wattles for the fold. In this way the small copyholder survived, as did the medieval framework of open fields and communal agriculture into the seventeenth century, at which time all were undermined by the sale, leasing and amalgamation of copyholds.

Wheat and barley were most important on the highly-cultivated east Sussex downland, with more rye in the west. Farming was labour-extensive, with harvest gangs being imported where necessary, and while depopulating enclosures were rare in the South East, other activities outside farming were minimal, and there was an overall lack of employment. By 1637 there were only two households left in Hangleton and the 1664–5 Hearth Tax returned just three households in Aldrington and Ovingdean. On the Surrey downland a string of open fields persisted at Ashtead, Fetcham, the Bookhams and the Clandons on the calcareous loams of the dipslope/tertiary interface. At Headley a 1612 Court Roll map shows the original townfield to have been supplemented by four further fields in the sixteenth century. Ashtead's strips were of arable and also meadow, with the latter divided into strips of just 2 perches by 1656. In these parishes communal grazing rights over the arable continued, although they lacked any clear pattern of communal open-field organization. A system of stinted tethering and folding operated at Ashtead by 1575 and tenants here were reminded in 1603 that sheep should not be allowed near the fields until 'ten days after the fielde is void of corne'. Multiple open fields were the rule for extra-wealden Surrey, as in Kent; and the buoyant land market and extant inheritance procedures probably exaggerated this tendency (Bailey and Galbraith 1973: 73–87; Ashworth 1967: 91–5; Parton 1967: 25–6).

The Sussex Coastal Plain

Downland productivity was quite overshadowed by that of the adjacent tertiary and brickearth deposits on the Sussex Coastal Plain and in north Kent. The former was the wealthiest part of Sussex, according to the Subsidy Returns for 1524–5, although such wealth was highly concentrated (Cornwall

1976: 1–26). Arable fields were interspersed with commons – heaths such as the Manhood of 1,000 acres divided between several manors – common brookland and salt marsh, and common woodland on the gravels of the poorer 'shravey' at the downland foot. During this time much of the heath was enclosed and some of the marshland reclaimed. The bishops of Chichester in particular, the largest landowners on the Coastal Plain, were very active in enclosing their lands. In 1634 160 acres of Norton Common, Aldingbourne were enclosed, with part divided among the tenants and the rest leased (Brandon 1963: 213). The Earl of Arundel had enclosed Lyminster Common and part of the marsh at Mundham by 1568. At the mouth of the Adur about 66 acres of salt-marsh at South Lancing were inned by 1612 and at Old Shoreham the tenants were similarly reclaiming and dividing the marshland between themselves.

The small amount of Coastal Plain common field was also transformed. One of Climping's three fields was enclosed in 1542; those of Ford, Aldingbourne and Middleton were probably enclosed in the late sixteenth century, as was most of the remaining open demesne arable. At Southwick in 1584 the Lewkenors, the main landowners, were busily exchanging strips as a preliminary to enclosure (Brandon 1963: 373–4; Cornwall 1953: 193). By 1600 piecemeal exchange and enclosure had extinguished the open fields at Ford, Merston, Portslade and Sidlesham, and the early seventeenth century saw the process speeding up and spreading over much of the remaining area. At Middleton and Funtington enclosure occurred in the first decade of the seventeenth century, and by 1640 it had reached Burton, Walberton and Climping. There were also many small hedged common fields to be found at Tangmere or Westbourne in the early seventeenth century, together with small fields known as muse plots or 'holy-breads' which resulted from earlier enclosures of common fields. But even on the open field strips there were signs of progress. During the sixteenth century leys were introduced, and thus in 1560 at Worthing the tenants were sowing their wheat, barley and tares at the same time 'so as one of them shall not hurt another by reason of their land lying lay', and by 1597 leys were being sown in the common fields at Selsey (Brandon 1963: 266, 291–2). One result of this innovation may have been the subdivision of three fields into four, as at Selsey and Worthing in the early seventeenth century; or the part-enclosure and re-allotment of strips as at Climping (1541) or Goring (1638). Hints of the complexity and versatility of these open fields are given in the glebe terrier for Climping in the 1630s.

> There are divers garden plots commonly known and called by ye name of holy breads wch hitherto alwaies have and at this present do pay tithe to ye vicar of Clymping, whether they be sowed with wheat, barlie, oats, pease, tares, hempe or flax or sett with beans or lett lie lay wch though they are well knowne as being usually a long time tythed to ye vicar, yett cannot possibly be bounded in writing, manie of them lying intermixt in larger fields and nothing to distinguish them by but a furrow, a bush or a lands end and ier [eye] knowledge (BL Dunkin Coll.,CXLII, Ad ms 39, 467).

Heavy crops of wheat, barley, peas, beans and tares were grown. Legumes had long been part of farming operations, mangolds for bullock fattening were introduced in the seventeenth century, and clover was recorded in use at Selsey by the 1690s. Through part or full enclosure of the open fields, reclamation of heath, wood and marsh, and by the introduction of new crops and rotations, the Coastal Plan underwent a more significant transformation in farming than anywhere in the South East at this time. Less than 6,000 acres of open field remained to be enclosed by parliamentary act in the nineteenth century, and all this was fuelled by an internal system of rural indebtedness, and access by sea to London.

Pressures to farm more intensively did invoke local hostility over engrossing and eviction. Star Chamber cases were heard for Ecclesden (West Angmering) and Heene (Worthing). At Ecclesden John Palmer evicted tenants in 1540 and five years later the 'solid and respectable' tenants were seeking to enlarge their holdings at the landlord's expense (Cornwall 1960: 127–8; 1975: 7–15). Heene had common fields in 1535 but about 1600 the joint lords of the manor:

> being lords of all or a great part of the town, the inhabitants being customary tenants by copy of court roll, for their own private gain and lucre, in the six years past have taken the said houses (which numbered 60) into their own hands, turned out the inhabitants by great fines . . . the orchards are dug up, the town is depopulated and there remains no sign of the houses (Brandon 1963: 380).

North Kent

North Kent remained the key supply area for London's grain. Prosperous in consequence, much still belonged to the Church in the early sixteenth century. Rochester Chapter held much land in the lower Darenth and Medway valleys, although with the upheavals of the sixteenth century the Tufton family came to own a 1,800-acre estate near Gillingham by the end of the sixteenth century and Oxford and Cambridge colleges were also endowed from here. St John's college, Cambridge owned the 900-acre demesne at Higham, together with about 550 acres held by 30–40 manorial tenants, and also land at Staple and Ospringe in north Kent (Howard 1935).

In the seventeenth century London's demand for grain tripled (see pp. 157–8), stimulating coastal reclamation and enclosure. At Iwade much of the former marshland was ploughed up for grain; and small areas of open field were left scattered among more numerous enclosed parcels, such as at Chalk, Cliffe and Northfleet by 1608.

Wheat and barley reigned supreme throughout north Kent, supplemented by peas, beans and oats. Sheep were kept for their manure, wool or meat. Convertible husbandry became widespread during the seventeenth century although as much as two-thirds of the farmland was arable – the highest proportion anywhere in the South East. New crops, grasses and roots were introduced, together with the specialized cash cropping of fruit and vegetables. Metropolitan fruiterers began to ply the 'cherrie gardein and apple orchard of Kent' between Rainham and the Blean, making Kent the leading English fruit-growing county. Richard Harris, the king's fruiterer, was credited by Mascall with the initial planting of apple and cherry orchards in the 1530s, which apparently became a source of supply for the whole area (Hartlib 1651: 21–2). Hops did not reach north Kent until the end of the seventeenth century, probably owing to their high initial costs, the risky nature of the enterprise, and the profits already being made from existing farming operations in the area.

From 1561 Walloons had settled in Deal, Sandwich and Dover following the victories of Alva in the Netherlands, and they brought intensive vegetable production and advanced market gardening techniques with them. In 1623 Aquila Jekin died at Canterbury leaving tools such as spades, rakes and axes, together with 'pease, beans and other seedes planted in one yard and a half of grounde in his son Danniell's garden' (KAO PRC 10/53). The Sandwich borough records include the 'Forren book for the Strangers' which includes names and occupations of Huguenots who actually comprised over half the total population of this decaying port by the 1570s. Among many others, Crystien Lamott, Jacobbe Collend and Charles Hengibert are recorded as 'gardyners'. And in Sandwich probate inventories of the 1620s and 1630s there are abundant references to such items as 'karret seedes', 'thezells', onions, flax and canary seed which were mostly exported by sea to London seedsmen and wholesalers.

Everitt has warned that London's commercial importance should not be overemphasized since metropolitan influences varied greatly between neighbouring *pays*, and while accepting this general caveat, it would still be difficult to overstate the importance of London to this particular part of the South East (Everitt 1976). North Kent's rural economy was quite simply the most diverse and prosperous in the South East.

The Marshlands

Coastal reclamation continued unabated. In the Romney Marsh, the East Guldeford Level had been inned by 1500; between 1537 and 1562 730 acres were inned to the south-west of Winchelsea; and by 1604 230 acres were reclaimed along the River Tillingham north of Rye. The creeks draining into the Camber harbour south of Rye were inned in the 1530s and 1540s and draining continued here throughout the rest of the century. At decayed Pevensey by 1595 the former harbour was a common marsh and a thriving cattle fair had come to reflect the changed priorities of the surrounding area. During the seventeenth century drainage and care were bestowed on the small river and ditch complexes draining the Pevensey and Romney Marshes, but

Blome reminded his readers in 1673 that the area was 'Wealthy but not healthy, as lying low and moist in the marshes, and by consequence very aguish' (Blome 1673: 122)

On Romney Marsh specialization was acute. Absentee graziers ran huge sheep flocks, incurring few expenses and no personal health hazards, but with corresponding decreases in cultivation and mixed farming. Between 1570 and 1670 the population may have declined by at least one-third, since 'lookers' or bailiffs brought with them no crafts, nor any demand for labour. This transition was far advanced by 1610 when Rye corporation noted that the immediate marshland around the town was entirely in the hands of graziers. There were no commons here, and any diversification relied upon the few residents who grew a little corn in severalty closes, improved with 'sleeching' (spreading ditch mud) every three or four years.

Undoubtedly the sevenfold increase in cattle and sheep prices between *c.*1450 and *c.*1650 stimulated interest in livestock here. By 1600 herd sizes were greater than on the downland or north Kent. Breeding and fattening cattle were kept, for example, by Nicholas Toke of Godinton who rented marshland for his Great Chart estate from Sir Norton Knatchbull. He fattened Welsh, northern, Scottish and local cattle on the Marsh, thereby demonstrating the full inter-regional integration in breeding, rearing and marketing of livestock which was coming to characterize even this remote corner of the South East. The main interest, though, was the breeding and fattening of sheep and the production of wool. At the beginning of the seventeenth century the flock sizes here were more than triple those of the rest of Kent, and this disparity increased throughout the century. Some wintered their sheep in the surrounding 'uplands', whereas others, including Toke, overwintered their flocks in the Marsh. Huge weights of wool made Kent one of the leading wool-exporting counties of England. During the seventeenth century the fleeces became coarser and longer, and with sheep stocked on the Marsh at three per acre, the profits could be large. Toke sold mostly through Rye to London, a common trend especially after the collapse of the local clothing industry in the early seventeenth century (Chalklin 1965: 101–3).

In Pevensey too, there had been changes since the fourteenth century. In 1340 the corn value of the Pevensey parishes was among the highest in Sussex, yet by the early eighteenth century it was 'full of feeding grounds . . . where an infinite number of large sheep are fed every year . . . and an abundance of large bullocks'. In 1547 on the site of the old settlement at Horseye, by then deserted, James Burton of Eastbourne was depasturing cows, bulls, oxen, steers and young beasts, ewes and wethers. Burton was typical of those from both Weald and downland who used the high-value Pevensey pastures; and men holding land in the Levels by 1649 included farmers from as far away as Chiddingstone, Maidstone and even Sidlesham. Grazing rights were often limited: one farmer holding fives acres at deserted Northeye (formerly a Cinque Ports limb) in 1656 could graze just 2 cows, 2 calves, 10 sheep, 10 lambs and other animals between 8 September and 11 November. The export of 'mares and jades' to Dieppe was also conducted from the marshland, some horses being bloodstock but most destined for the knacker's yard (Gulley 1960: 91; Brent 1976: 43–7).

The London Basin

In the southern London Basin, villages and commons mixed with woodland and parks, all changing under metropolitan influences by the sixteenth century. Commons abounded on the cold, sour London Clay on the lower downland slopes at Ashtead, Epsom or Clandon; capping the hills at Beckenham or Bromley where rich Tudor merchants lived just ten miles from London Bridge; and at Esher, Oxshott or Wimbledon. In the east the Oldhaven Pebble Beds also yielded commons at Blackheath, Hayes and Dartford. At Bromley footpads robbed Evelyn in 1652. At Esher, and west of the River Wey to the Cobham Ridges were the barren Bagshot sands; Marshall's 'broad, blank margin of Surrey'. Wretched farmsteads and squatters' cottages pushed at the edges of this area and livings were cobbled together from heathland resources such as peat and conies. By the 1650s Chobham produced 'meane corn' on 'furzie and barren ground' together with conies and 'heathcropper' sheep. 'the sweet but little mutton [which] hereabouts is taken note of by travellers' (Aubrey 1718–19, II: 213; PRO E134 Sy 13/14 Chas 2 Hil 7). On the overlying gravels and brickearth, as at Mitcham Common, along Thames-side and on the aits, much of the soil was also manured and intensively cultivated as market gardens. At Chiswick osiers were harvested for basket-making for the market gardeners.

Along Thames-side there was also a complex landscape of common field remnants, fossilized severalty strips, lammas lands and common meadows. Wheat was sold; madder was grown; and hay was provided for cowkeepers, calf rearers and house lamb specialists. At Esher and Cobham calf-merchants imported animals from the Aylesbury area for fattening and dispatch to London, while poor chalkland sheep were fattened on drained marshland at Deptford, Charlton or Battersea for the 'cutting butchers' (Brayley 1850, I: 236). Birds, for whom canary seed was imported from Sandwich and east Kent, fish ponds and pigsties added to the mixture.

Many open fields were enclosed during the sixteenth century although demesnes had been enclosed long before. The shotts (furlongs) were the real farming units together with the minutely subdivided Thames-side meadows. At Putney and Mortlake about 40 per cent of the fields were enclosed by 1617 and by 1610 Wimbledon was enclosed by agreement. Copyhold land was frequently held by London merchants. The Twygges, who enclosed part of Putney Lower Common in the late fifteenth century, were mercers and haberdashers, and connected with the Staple at Calais (Bailey and Galbraith 1973: 81–2). Exchanges of strips heralded enclosure at Putney, where one landholder secured the whole of an open field by purchase and exchange from four others, and by 1636 rectangular fields up to 12 acres in size replaced the shotts. At Roehampton enclosure between 1580 and 1600 allowed an increase in grassland to meet the demand for animal produce from London. However, the otherwise large numbers of smallholdings in the London Basin probably militated against a speedy enclosure overall, and strips still awaited enclosure by 1800. As well as on the Chalk/London Clay boundary, they persisted also at Chobham, Egham, Thorpe and Petersham. Enclosure of a different kind occurred at Richmond in about 1612 where 40 acres of the open Lowfield was taken into Richmond Old Park upon the park's enlargement, although such losses were partly offset by cultivation inside other parks, as at Henley by 1607 (PRO E134 Sy 32 Chas 2 East 3; Kerridge 1967: 175).

Market gardening was a successful innovation in this period. Importing London's 'dunge and noysommes', gardeners worked rented plots by the mid-sixteenth century. A seventeenth-century membership list of the Gardeners Company recorded over 50 gardening localities, with Battersea, Westminster, Greenwich and Lambeth the most favoured. Many growers were not Company members but were actually husbandmen growing parsnips, turnips and carrots in open-field strips. Certainly by the early seventeenth century carrots were being used in rotations on the Surrey downland dipslopes; at Chertsey and Weybridge heathland was reclaimed for carrot cultivation; while Croydon's common fields were also worked by farmer-gardeners for vegetables. By the end of the seventeenth century such crops were also joined in farming, as opposed to gardening operations, by the potato, which had been introduced to Thames-side gardeners one hundred years earlier. Flemish gardeners also moved in from Sandwich during the seventeenth century and at Wandsworth, Battersea and Streatham market gardens became intermixed not only with farms and paddocks but with the large, spacious houses of wealthy Londoners. At Wandsworth was the Putney nursery, an early plant centre. Hartlib cited 'old men of Surrey' who remembered the first gardeners bringing Dutch or Flemish varieties of cabbages, cauliflowers, turnips, carrots and parsnips with them. Access to markets, cheap London labour, and pumped Thames water reinforced locations along the southern edge of the capital (Webber 1968: 58; McGrath 1948: 195–207; Ashworth 1967: 99; Thick 1985: 507; Harvey 1973: 135–42).

Many of the more remote villages had their own preoccupations. Norwood and Brixton's cowkeepers sold unedifying milk; and both Bromley and Croydon were noted for their charcoal production and trade with London, although the associated pollution was noted in a 1622 verse from Patrick Hannay's, *The Nightingale, Sherentine and Mariana* relating to the North Wood (Norwood):

> In the midst of these stands Croydon, cloth'd in blacke,
> In a low bottome sinke of all these hills,
> And is receipt of all the durtie wracke,
> Which from their tops still in abundance trills,

Plate 4.5 Richmond Park: an aerial view. The present character of the park is largely the work of Romantic landscapes commissioned by George II and Queen Caroline. It had been unpopular locally since Charles I had taken land from six parishes to form his 'New Park', one of his wilful and controversial acts which accounts for his unpopularity. By the early eighteenth century it was seen by Horace Walpole as a 'bog, and a harbour for deer-stealers and vagabonds', with disputes rumbling on over common rights to firewood, turf and gravel (Dunbar 1966: 122–5; Thompson, E. P., 1975: 181–2).

The unpav'd lane with muddier mire it fills,
If one shower falles; or, if that blessing stay,
You may well smell, but never see your way

By contrast, Epsom's development as an inland resort had a positive impact on the surrounding rural economy (see p. 161):

you would think yourself in some enchanted camp, to see the peasants ride to every house with the choicest fruits, herbs, roots, and flowers; with all sorts of tame wild fowl, with the rarest fish and venison, and with every kind of butcher's meat, among which *Banstead-Down* mutton is the relishing dainty (Aubrey 1718–19, II: 207–8).

Agricultural Change

The development of fruit, market gardening, vegetables and hops diversified and boosted rural economies. Fruit and hops penetrated the Interior, in advance of artificial grasses and roots, which were slower to make any impact there. Piecemeal enclosure was perhaps the most fundamental reorganization, at least in the Coastal Fringe, where the extinction of common rights was hastened if not obliterated. Common waste was attacked also, legally and illegally and by rich and poor alike, and this horizontal expansion and quest for *new* land complemented the more productive use of existing lands. New fields might be won from woodlands, from Interior commons, from roadside waste, from the coastal marshes, or from disparking.

It would indeed be strange if south-eastern farmers had not responded to the great currents of the sixteenth and seventeenth centuries: to the great redistribution of lands, to inflation and population increases, to the growth of a World city on their doorsteps, and to the innovations in land management and cultivation which were beginning to flourish.

Wealden industries

Until superseded by new techniques elsewhere, continental technology and the skills of immigrants raised the sixteenth-century Weald to a pre-eminence among the industrial regions of England. A firm basis had already been laid during the Middle Ages, since for generations the need to offset poor agricultural returns had bred resourcefulness in many domestic handicrafts. Cloth-making beyond the needs of a local market had become established in the late thirteenth century and was boosted when Edward III in 1341 invited John Kempe, a Flemish clothier, to come to England. Successive waves of Flemish immigrants settled mainly at Cranbrook, where they expanded fulling and introduced variously coloured broadcloths. Coarse bottle-glass manufacture was established by French and Flemish workers in the western Weald where sand lenses in the clay and ample wood fuel supplied the necessary raw materials for what was then a luxury item. Families such as those of Alemayne and Schurterre joined the Peytowes and the Strudwicks of Chiddingfold and Kirdford as early glassmakers. The surnames *Vitrearius* or *le Verir* occurring in the fourteenth-century tax subsidies also probably record glass manufacturers. The wealden iron industry had also expanded during the later Middle Ages, an important development being the early fifteenth-century introduction of the water-powered bloomery forge from the continent (Cleere and Crossley 1985: 87–110; Kenyon 1967; Awty 1978, 1981; Winbolt 1933).

During the sixteenth century these industries rapidly expanded until the whole Weald became a rural workshop supplying the Crown and the growing markets of London and the South East. Building on its medieval precedents, clothworking became concentrated in the Kentish Weald, although it was of wide-ranging significance, especially in the Guildford–Godalming area. Glass became concentrated around Chiddingfold, Alfold and Kirdford in the western Weald Clay, while iron-making developed among the High-wealden headwaters of the eastern Rother, Cuckmere, Ouse and Medway (Crossley 1981).

The Kentish cloth industry was based on domestic carding, spinning and weaving put out to cottagers scattered across the wood/pasture environment of the eastern Weald. Clothiers controlled the dyeing and finishing processes, and supplied capital for equipment, wool, vats, etc., and organized sales outside the Weald. Population growth and wealth could result. John Leland observed of the market town of Petworth *c.*1540 that it was 'right well encreasid syns the yerles of Northumbreland used little to ly there. For now the men there make good cloth'. New wealth from the cloth trade was to be found also in towns and villages such as Lodsworth, Steyning and Midhurst and at Ash, Farnham, Haslemere, Wonersh, Guildford and Shere. This trade was controlled by the cloth merchants of Godalming who organized the flow of materials, controlled quality and fixed prices. The principal products were blue kerseys for the Canaries market sold through London agents. Guildford was the most important Surrey finishing centre, on the fast-flowing Wey with its tumbling tributaries (Brandon 1977: 55–7).

The fluctuating fortunes of wealden iron can be outlined (Table 4.2). The principal sources of iron ore were nodules in the Wadhurst Clay of the High Weald but supplies interbedded in the Weald Clay and Lower Greensand were also worked. To a very considerable extent the distribution of ironworks was determined by the quality and availability of ore, and relict crater-like depressions are the roughly infilled bell-pits, originally some twenty feet deep.

A new phase in the wealden iron industry began with the introduction of the blast furnace from the Low Countries to Newbridge in the Ashdown Forest in 1496 by migrants from the Pays de Bray (the continuation of the truncated Weald into France) and with the successful 1543 casting of cannon by Ralph Hogge at Buxted. Continental technology put the Sussex Weald into the vanguard of the sixteenth-century iron industry, the first blast-furnaces in the Midlands not being built until after 1560. No Kent or Surrey ironmaster is known with certainty until 1550 but thereafter the iron industry spread into neighbouring parts of Kent and Surrey. This Sussex supremacy persisted (Table 4.3 and Fig. 4.3). The new furnaces and forges were sited on relatively swift streams to power large bellows or forge hammers. Water was diverted and impounded by building earthen dams ('bays') across the narrow valleys, to create long narrow hammer-ponds as reservoirs. Many of these are now dry but they remain among the most beautiful man-made features of the Weald (Crossley 1972b).

Growth came as a response to Henry VIII's military campaigns, to the ever-growing demands for bar- and cast-iron from the Crown, and to the growing population of London and other south-eastern centres. Pre-eminence arose largely from the nature of the Sussex Weald itself: its immense woods, including coppice, eagerly exploited by landowners such as the earls of Northumberland, the Sydneys of Robertsbridge, the Duke of Norfolk at Sheffield Park and the Crown in Ashdown Forest; the widespread availability of ironstone; water-power in the deep ghylls; and local labour with the skills of founders, finers and hammermen. Most of the ironworks were integrated works producing both pig and bar iron but a feature of the less-favoured districts of Surrey was the use of pig iron at forges imported from

Table 4.2   Recorded wealden ironworks, 1520–1717

Year	Furnaces	Forges	Total
1520	26		26
1548	53		53
1574	52	58	110
1653	36	45	81
(some works previously closed reactivated in the Civil War)			
1717	14	13	27

(Source: Cleere and Crossley 1985)

Table 4.3   Water-powered iron-working sites in the Weald

	Forges	Furnaces	Others	Total
Sussex	67	88	2	157
Kent	17	16	0	33
Surrey	12	6	0	18
Hampshire	0	1	0	1
Total SE	96	111	2	209

(Source: Cleere and Crossley 1985)

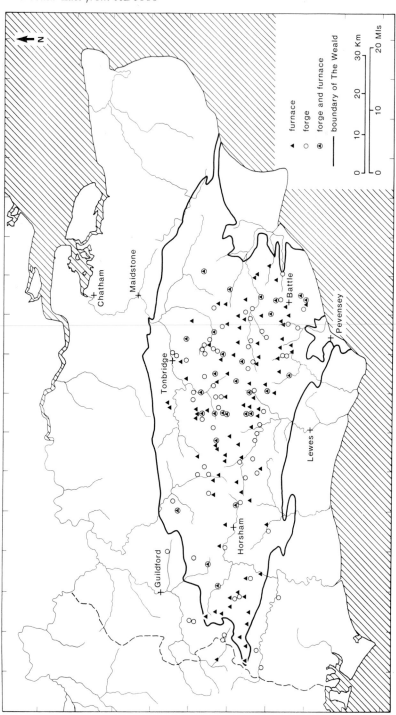

Figure 4.3 The wealden iron industry.

blast furnaces elsewhere. Such works were among the earliest closures with the stiffer competition from Staffordshire works in the seventeenth century. The industry produced many *nouveaux riches* who purchased former gentry estates. Leonard Gale the elder was a blacksmith's son from the Sevenoaks area who survived the plague which killed his parents and most of their children. Giving up his trade, he leased an iron forge in Worth Forest and subsequently became a partner with Walter Burrell in other ironworks. Prospering during the Civil War, Gale amassed a fortune. His son in turn had a university education, and using his father's legacy to purchase the Crabbett estate from the long-standing gentry family, the Smiths, he spent his life as a country squire and MP for East Grinstead.

The importance of Sussex iron-making should not obscure the rise of other water-powered industries, for example in the Tillingbourne valley of Surrey, where a miniature industrial *pays* included the manufacture of gunpowder at Wotton and Abinger by the Evelyns, and at Chilworth by the East India Company; and the production of brass and copper domestic goods from brassmills and wire-drawing plants, also at Chilworth and on the Evelyn estate (Fig. 4.4). By the 1650s water-powered sites in the Midlands were successfully competing in brass and copper consumer goods, and the market for the Tillingbourne products was undercut. A number of the mills, together with former fulling mills in this area, were turned over to the manufacture of paper, much of the raw material coming from the clothing industry (Brandon 1984b: 75–107; Crocker 1985; Crocker 1988).

The end of expansion in the eastern part of the Weald after *c.* 1585 and continuation of building ironworks in the Wey and Arun basins may

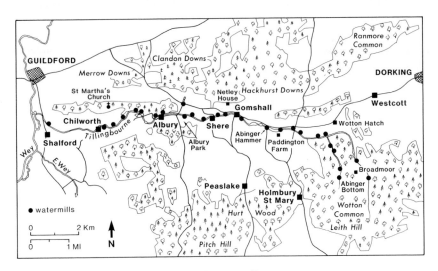

Figure 4.4 An industrial *pays:* the Tillingbourne Valley.

be explained by the passing of legislation in 1585 restricting the building of ironworks in the east of Sussex and adjoining parts of Kent to sites where ironworks had not previously existed, in the interest of conserving fuel. Special interest attaches to the ironworks of Witley and Thursley, Surrey, described on a lease of 1610 as being 'lately erected', for detailed leases have survived with inventories of the plant and tools in use. Anthony Smith's 1666 lease to William Yalden indicates that the ore was reduced into sows and pigs. The forge (hammer) contained two fires, the 'finery' and the 'chafery'. The sows were first converted at the finery into short thick blooms and then into longer ones called 'anconies'. At the chafery the roughened ends of the anconies were rounded off and the bars made ready for market (Straker 1931).

By 1560 coarse bottle-glass manufacture had become localized in the Surrey and Sussex Weald in the parishes of Wisborough Green, Alfold, Ewhurst, Chiddingfold and Kirdford. Rapid Elizabethan progress occurred in association with new methods of making window glass, green drinking vessels and apothecaries' wares, introduced from the Continent by immigrant craftsmen. Best known was John Carré of Arras who set up as a glassmaker at Fernfold *c*.1567 to make 'Normandy and Lorraine' glass and who was buried at Alfold in 1572. Glass-making demanded very highly skilled labour and the corresponding wages, together with beechwood and oak fuel, were the highest costs incurred. Nevertheless, the gross return from a glass furnace was very profitable, and certainly allowed the chief glass-makers to call themselves 'gentilhomme verrier' (Kenyon 1967, Crossley 1972a). The number of people employed directly was very small, although labourers and carriers might integrate their work with husbandry. Glass-making came to be dominated by the Norman, Isaac Bungar but his business success was short-lived because of technological change and monopolistic interference. The first patent granting a monopoly of coal-fired furnaces was granted to Sir Robert Mansell of Staffordshire in 1612 and after a fierce struggle Bungar was obliged to close down his last wood-fired furnace in 1618 (Kenyon 1967). A remarkable memorial to the industry are the small windows of Chiddingfold and Kirdford churches recently glazed with fragments of window glass discovered by Kenyon and other archaeologists. Peaking by 1600, glass manufacture was finished here by 1630, and the French moved away to the coal-fired works at Stourbridge or Newcastle-upon-Tyne.

Tudor and Stuart Population Change

The intersection of the many strands of economic, social, religious and political change in the region helps us to understand the population changes occurring between 1520 and 1660. This also had an intimate connection with the theme of changing house-building in the South East, then one of the most progressive regions in north-western Europe, and with Kent described by Leland as 'the key [quay] of al Englande' (Smith, L.T. 1963, IV: 57).

Nationally for one hundred years from the mid-sixteenth century, population doubled, representing a recovery from the late-medieval difficulties. However, regional variations in the timing and extent of population change were inevitable. Wrigley and Schofield (1981) based their work on a sample of 404 sets of parish registers, of which 57 were from the South East. Although west Surrey and south and west Sussex were under-represented and the Weald was over-represented, their figures portray broad demographic trends.

Within the South East, the rapidly growing population was beset with epidemics. Plague mortality was high in all the towns, killing 385 in Rye in six months in 1544 and 744 in five months of 1579. In August–October 1563, 191 people died in Hastings, and many more in Rye. In 1597 Hastings suffered its greatest losses of the sixteenth and seventeenth centuries, and 222 people died in Cranbrook, 181 of plague. Hastings was again hit in 1622–4, Rye in 1625, Hastings and Cranbrook again in 1638–40 (Gulley 1960: 184–8). The plague of 1665–6 struck severely, and even in the small market town of East Grinstead sums of money were 'collected on the first dayes in time of the plague for the releife of the infected' (WSRO PAR 348 1/1/1). Generally after 1550, with the exception of a few years, such epidemics declined in their intensity and population grew until the early to mid-seventeenth century, when the birth rate sagged, epidemics returned in greater strength and underlying death rates continued, thereby slowing up growth.

A slow rate of growth in the thirty years after 1640 was followed by about fifty years of actual population decline. Evidence points to a downturn of some magnitude between 1642 and 1676 affecting all regions except South London, although perhaps less severe in the western Weald (Turner 1978; Greenwood 1979: 39–40). Its causes are attributable in large measure to local reversals. The decline of rural industry in the Interior and the malaria experienced in the Marshlands were both locally-specific factors, to which should be added the depopulating impact of agricultural change in the Coastal Fringe; civil war uncertainties; the siphoning effect of London's growth; emigration to the New World; and the recurrence of disease which affected both fertility and nuptuality. The South East obviously shared the national demographic character of Tudor and Stuart England, while bringing to it the myriad local circumstances which existed (Dobson 1982).

Although Tudor and Stuart populations fluctuated markedly, internal regional redistribution was persistent. Urban populations generally increased throughout the region. Both Reigate and Horsham continued to grow in the later seventeenth century, although not all towns were growing at the same pace (see pp. 161–7). Some older coastal centres were now in irreversible decline, compared with the more thriving inland market towns, the new towns, and above all, with South London which grew almost entirely through in-migration. Plague and unsanitary conditions slowed growth unpredictably, especially hitting the ports and more densely-packed parts of the towns. And in the countryside, the impact of agrarian and industrial growth had markedly differential regional demographic results. It is to a consideration of these trends, largely excluded from Wrigley and Schofield's work, that we now turn.

Wealden population growth was constant though localized throughout the sixteenth century, apart from the main 'dismal peak' registered in the influenza outbreak of 1557–9. The lower degree of old manorial control, the existence of commons, the possibility of finding work amongst woods and industries, and the customs of partible inheritance and small farms which retained more youngsters in the area, added up to a strongly–growing population, through both natural increase and in-migration. Growth was particularly high in the eastern and north-eastern Weald around Cranbrook, compared with the north-west, where the chain of commonland between St Leonards and Waterdown Forest, allied with its remoteness, prohibited craft industry, agricultural employment and cottage settlement. Much of Tonbridge parish was still unpopulated within wood and parklands. Nevertheless, a comparison of taxpayers in 1524–5 with 1665 or 1670 shows that in 13 out of 16 wealden localities the number of taxpayers had risen by between 12 and 38 per cent. By contrast out of eight downland localities, six had fallen by between 13 and 44 per cent. In four of five localities combining Weald with marshland, there had also been a fall of between 16 and 31 per cent. Clearly the Interior, in producing a net population increase, was experiencing a quite different demographic history from that of the Coastal Fringe.

Natural growth (i.e. a surplus of christenings over burials) was a feature of all the eastern Weald, apart from partially urban Tenterden. The retention of many of its offspring was clearly one reason for growth. Another was the immigration of both refugees and specialist ironworking families. French immigrants were coming to Rotherfield, Maresfield and other High Wealden ironworking parishes by the 1540s, and by 1550 there were at least 300 immigrants working in the iron industry. John Carré and other French glassworkers arrived in the Kirdford area in the 1560s (Awty 1981; Kenyon 1967). More significant however, was the tramping of the poor. There were high levels of exemption from the 1670 Hearth Tax; while licences to parish officials to establish houses for the poor were made by 1641 to eight wealden parishes compared with just one downland parish. By 1638 Worth was 'full of poor people', and the increasing poor rate was affecting smaller farmers who were left with less to re-invest in their farming. The average poor rate per annum at Lindfield in 1595–7 was £9, rising to £60 by 1634–9, and to £115 by 1652–7. The problem of the poor in the towns has been mentioned previously (pp. 167–70), but the wealden situation was equally difficult. For some contemporaries there was a ready explanation for the state of unruliness which verged on biological determinism. Norden noted that 'The people bred among woods are naturally

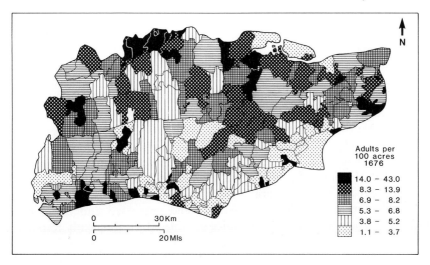

Adults per
100 acres
1676

14.0 – 43.0
8.3 – 13.9
6.9 – 8.2
5.3 – 6.8
3.8 – 5.2
1.1 – 3.7

0   30 Km

0   20 Mls

Figure 4.5 Population density in south east England 1676.
(Sources: MS Salt 33; Chalklin 1960; Cooper 1902)

more stubborn and uncivil than in the champion countries'. Aubrey noted that
woodlanders were 'mean people [who] live lawless, nobody to govern them,
they care for nobody, having no dependence on anybody'. Short-distance
but frequent movement characterized this population (Gulley 1960: 187–8;
Cornwall 1967; Brent 1973: 335; Short 1983; Zell 1985a and b).

Many new squatter settlements resulted from population growth. The
remaining wealden wastes, especially along the Forest Ridges, were especially
favoured, as were cottage communities at such places as Kennington Lees or
Stelling Minnis in the east and mid-Kent Chartlands. Godden Green (Seal) is
first recorded in 1516 (Everitt 1977: 27–8). Illegal wealden cottage building
prevailed to such an extent that between 1635 and 1641, 43 squatters were
cited in Quarter Sessions from the Sussex Weald, compared with two from the
marshland and just one from the downland. With cottages being constructed,
with partible inheritance offering the possibility of landholding, and with the
possibility of local work, marriages were contracted earlier in the Weald, and
data suggest a higher degree of marital fertility than elsewhere (Zell 1985b;
Brent 1973: 241–92). In the later sixteenth century it would also seem that
the rural Weald, in line with much of the south of England, was relatively
free from epidemics, and from about 1606–10 onwards, population growth
consistently outstripped that on the Coastal Fringe. More children surviving
and staying through to child-bearing age meant that between 1611 and 1640
population growth in the High Weald was about 19 per cent, compared with
3 per cent in the Low Weald, 7 per cent on the downland, and –12 per cent in
the Weald/marshland parishes. By 1676 there were high densities in the eastern
Weald where many parishes had over 8.3 adults per 100 acres, compared
with under 3.7 per 100 acres in the adjoining marshland (Fig. 4.5).

The contrast between champion and Weald mirrors similar contrasts elsewhere in England at this time in demonstrating the power of proto-industrial wood/pasture communities to grow. By the 1520s, despite about 200 years of gradual change, the population of the Coastal Fringe had been appreciably higher than that of the Interior (Cornwall 1976), but thereafter the processes quickened. Many contemporaries pointed to the loss of population on the Downs. There were significantly fewer hearths than elsewhere in 1664 along the North Downs from Addington 'aunciently . . . far bigger' westwards to Merrow and Compton, while migrants to Canterbury included many from the eastern Downs and Thanet. In east Sussex only eight downland parishes had more than 25 households in 1664–5. Hangleton and Sutton were effectively deserted except for their large farmhouses with living-in farm servants. Capitalist farmers purchased copyholds and engrossed and consolidated holdings, achieving internal economies of scale which frequently resulted in depopulation. Thus the 17 landholders in Rodmell in 1622 became 7 by 1700. The influence of London capital is exemplified by the London merchant who purchased Broughton Down, Jevington about 1654, bought out the pasture rights of the one remaining holder, leased out a small portion to him and kept the remainder under his sole control. Under such circumstances there could be little population growth (Brandon 1963: 201). Costs of fuel and food were also higher; there were smaller gardens and no commons or woodland except in parts of west Kent and west Sussex. Enclosure and resulting depopulation surfaces at Farningham in 1633 (Tate 1943) and while small gentry and husbandmen might survive precariously on 'the flinty fields of the downland', or on the 'stone shattery land' of the clay-with-flints (Everitt 1966; Georgical Committee, No. 30), incipient 'close' parishes were being formed by the progressive accumulation of land and power into the hands of relatively few people who, before the formulation of Poor Law structures, exercised semi-feudal control over their parishes and estates. The poor were consequently excluded very effectively, or introduced carefully only to relieve harvest bottlenecks (Short 1985: 311; Parton 1984: 155–60).

Since much of the marshland was incorporated into 'upland' farms and was really only used for fattening and rearing livestock, population dwindled alarmingly between the fourteenth and early seventeenth centuries. Romney Marsh was long known in addition as a 'sicklie and contagious place' (Univ. of Camb. Add Ms 2826), 'very aguish' with high mortality from malaria. By 1600 it had the lowest population density anywhere in the South East. The silting of New Romney and Hythe emphasized the decline, and there were as many as seven abandoned churches by 1670. By then the population had probably declined by about one-third since 1570, with only lookers, smugglers and 'mean peasants' left in parishes such as Brenzett or Appledore.

This demographic decline on the downland and in the marshland was the most extreme instance of south-eastern depopulation at this time. Elsewhere, many Coastal Fringe towns continued to grow (see pp. 158–67) despite the plague. The population of Guildford grew from *c*.1,300 in the 1560s to *c*.1,900 in the 1620s and 1630s. But by the 1660s this had been cut back to 1,700 owing to the incidence of plague, dysentery and possibly influenza. Epidemics at almost ten-yearly intervals depressed birth rates and added to economic problems as cloth-making declined in the early seventeenth century. In 1644 an application for £50 to one of the trustees of Trinity Hospital (George Abbot's foundation) to help with relief of the town's poor provoked the following response:

> When the town standeth so much in need, occasioned by an extraordinary hande, in respect of the warre which decayed all trade which makes warms of poor; in respect of the taxes which impoverish many that were formerly able to have relieved others; and in respect of the plague, which is so sore a visitation in its selfe ... I shall therefore give my full consent (in Bignall 1983: 113–21)

Around the coast, decaying seafaring towns such as Lydd, New Romney, Rye, Winchelsea or Sandwich lost population; while Deal, Dover, Milton and Faversham, as well as Chatham and the Kentish dockyard centres grew significantly. The population of Gravesend, for example, doubled from 1,000 to 2,000 during the seventeenth century (Chalklin 1965: 30–3). The older Coastal Fringe centres made halting progress. Population grew at Ashford, Canterbury and Maidstone, with Canterbury growing from *c*.3,000 in the 1520s to 7,000 in 1670. An influx of poor as well as Walloons largely

Table 4.4   Population of south-east England, 1676

Area	1 Population returned (16 yrs+)	2 Estimated Urban (16 yrs+)	3 Estimated Total pop (col. 1+31%)	4 % Urban	Notes
Sussex	52,001	8,733	78,121	17	
Rural Surrey	34,216	7,870	44,823	23	a
Thames-side Surrey	50,373	47,133	65,989	94	b
W Kent	35,799	17,111	40,897	48	c
E Kent	57,727	13,868	75,622	24	d
Total	230,116	94,715	305,452	41	

Notes: a Deaneries of Ewell and Stoke
       b Deanery of Southwark
       c Diocese of Rochester with estimate for Deanery of Shoreham
       d Diocese of Canterbury

It is assumed for the purpose of these estimates that where a parish is focused around a substantial town, which also contains rural areas, two-thirds of the population of that parish will be 'urban', the rest 'rural'.

(Sources: As for Fig 4.5)

accounted for this growth, since in common with many towns at this time, Canterbury could show little natural increase.

With overall urban growth, the proportion of population living in towns in the South East becomes a significant factor in understanding the rapidity of economic growth and hence social inequality in the region. Using calculations based on the 1676 Compton Census, an approximate total of 41 per cent of the population can be estimated as living in towns (Table 4.4). The urban proportion varied, with the Deanery of Southwark comprising most of London south of the Thames having 94 per cent of its population urban, compared with the 17 per cent so designated in Sussex. Kent east of the Medway and rural Surrey were very similar with about one quarter of their populations urban, compared with nearly half in Kent west of the Medway, which included the Thames-side growth areas. These estimates make allowance for omissions, the most serious being the entire Shoreham Deanery in Kent, and are based on the 31 per cent multiplier for children under 16 years of age as suggested by Wrigley and Schofield, rather than Chalklin's 40 per cent multiplier, now thought to be too high for the late seventeenth century (Wrigley and Schofield 1981: 218).

The population of Tudor and Stuart south-east England was a mobile, strongly differentiated one. Social cleavages, and to some extent social mobility, were increasing as wealth permeated from London and from indigenous agriculture and industrial concerns. A strong urban element provided a market and a dynamism that was lacking in other perhaps equally fertile regions, and population growth must therefore be seen as an independent as well as a dependent variable in unravelling the complex of social, economic and political forces at work in the region at this time.

Tudor and Stuart Housing

In both town and country, irrespective of overall population growth or decline, we also have abundant evidence of sixteenth- and seventeenth-century building activity. Styles, if not building materials, were different to those of the earlier periods and the income from farming, industry, trade and office-holding fuelled what used to be called 'the Great Rebuilding'. Whatever the detailed timing of this activity, the period from the 1520s to the 1640s was extremely important in building terms. Gulley noted that many more houses were built in the Weald between 1570 and 1640 than in any period of comparable length before or afterwards (Gulley 1961). But thereafter high taxation, political difficulties, and a downturn in population growth depressed activity. Mason has proposed that Hoskins' 'Great Rebuilding' in the Weald be re-aligned into two periods, one during the fifteenth century and one from 1570 to 1700.

But more recent work suggests that it is perhaps more appropriate to think in terms of a continuum from the medieval period onwards (Hughes 1988: 141–2; Machin 1977; Mason 1969). In some areas building may actually have increased in intensity *after* 1640 with a peak at the end of the seventeenth century.

The region possessed a full range of housing types from the great palaces at Nonsuch, Hampton Court, Oatlands or Richmond, through to the hall-houses of the gentry, parish clergy and yeomen, and the cottages of craftsmen and labourers. The great houses changed in tune with national social and architectural ambition, and the region contains many of the large new English buildings of the first half of the sixteenth century, displaying the wealth of the crown and the rising classes. The tendency towards greater comfort and privacy could also be accommodated. Tudor gatehouses appeared; complexes of courtyards, stables and outbuildings for servants were built, as at Petworth; and galleries, parlours and staircases were inserted alongside medieval halls. Brick came more fully to be used for building, and precise gardens were designed. By the 1570s there was not only the motive for such overt display of wealth in the relative stability of the later Elizabethan years, but also the space and materials created by the Dissolution. Materials from Abingdon Abbey were incorporated into Oatlands from 1538. Entertaining, often of the Queen herself, implied lavish rooms for guests and their retinues. Not all the houses of the elite were changing, of course. The Culpepers continued to live at Leeds Castle, and others continued in their late-medieval moated houses, such as Ightham. But this latter building contains a fourteenth-century hall, fifteenth-century gatehouse, early-Tudor chapel and a Jacobean drawing-room, and is representative of the piecemeal changes characteristic of the time (Chalklin 1965: 205).

At the summit of architectural splendour were the royal palaces. Sheen, destroyed by fire in 1497, was rebuilt and renamed Richmond after Henry VIII's former earldom. Two great courtyards now helped to make the palace a Tudor social and cultural centre. Hampton Court, built by Wolsey and given to the king in 1526, eclipsed Richmond and remained a royal favourite through to Charles II. Richmond was eventually sold in 1650 and almost completely dismantled shortly afterwards. Nonsuch (Cuddington), and Oatlands were also creations of Henry VIII, the former praised by Camden as 'built with so much splendour and elegance that . . . you would think the whole science of architecture exhausted on this building' (Camden 1977b: 18). Mostly built in the French style from 1538, and with French builders, the old village of Cuddington was moved aside to make room for its splendour, depicted in Hoefnagel's 1582 engraving with the appended tag *Hoc est nusquam simile* (Plate 4.6). Queen Mary allowed it to pass into the hands of the Catholic Earl of Arundel, whence it passed to Lord Lumley, who reconveyed it to Elizabeth in 1591. The Parliamentary survey of 1650 noted the three-storey 'stronge and gracefull' gatehouse, the large wainscoted rooms, the Court chambers,

197

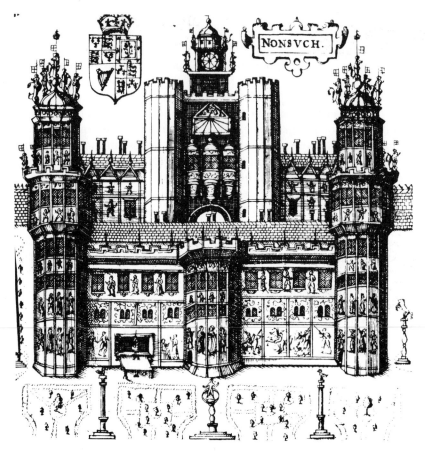

Plate 4.6 Nonsuch Palace built from 1538 on the site of the older village of Cuddington by command of Henry VIII, the palace passed in and out of Royal control in the sixteenth century. Charles II granted it to his mistress, the Duchess of Cleveland, who, from 1682 onwards, had the house demolished and materials sold, and divided the park into farms, which were 'plowed and broake upp . . . for great cropps of corne' thereafter (PRO E134 4 Anne Trin. 7). Little remains today but earthworks.

parks, gardens and art treasures. The house suffered in the Civil War period, coming afterwards into the hands of the Duchess of Cleveland, who oversaw its demolition in 1682.

The South East also contained many magnificent aristocratic houses, some of which were acquired by the Tudors in their consolidation of control. The royal mansion of Woking, for example, was the birthplace of Mary Tudor in 1514. Otford Palace had been transformed by Archbishop Warham in 1514–18 into an enormous house with nine towers and a splendour unparalleled in England until the building at Hampton Court. Henry VIII took control in 1537 until his death, after which time it fell into slow decay (Stoyel 1985: 259–80). The courtier Sir Richard Weston had Sutton Place built in the 1520s in brick and with a style redolent of the Loire, to which he had often travelled. An arched gateway, quadrangle and hexagonal towers marked new designs in mansions. Similarly innovative was Loseley, built in the 1560s from the stone of Waverley Abbey as the first H- or E-shaped plan in Surrey.

Cowdray, conservatively built in the 1530s was chiefly notable because it represented the progress of the Tudor mansion into the Interior. Income from wealden resources was channelled largely towards London, but some wealth was diverted for local mansions such as that of Sir William Fitzwilliam, treasurer of the King's Household and recipient of the Abbey of Durford in Rogate, where he built Cowdray. There were also the houses of Elizabethan courtiers such as Lord Buckhurst, on the northern Ashdown Forest slopes at the brick-built Old Buckhurst; parliamentarians such as Sir Walter Covert who built Slaugham Place (now ruined) in 1612; and many ironmasters and clothiers whose wealden houses, often with Renaissance details such as at Batemans (1634), incorporated the most recent architectural styles. They used (and sometimes re-used) local stone, timber or brick, and were set within gardens and parks which also reflected current landscape aesthetics.

Perhaps most characteristic of this period, however, were the alterations made to the houses of the lesser gentry and yeomen. The traditional timber-framed south-eastern hall-house continued to be built through to about 1530. But thereafter the larger houses had floors, chambers and staircases inserted in the open halls; rooms wainscoted; and glazed windows, chimney stacks and hearths added. If the chimneys were centrally placed, visitors could be shown either to the hall or the parlour, while economizing on fuel and giving a convenient prop for a staircase. Dormer windows were introduced to utilize roofspaces more efficiently, and outbuildings and exteriors were also improved. At Hendon House, Biddenden, a brick exterior of 1624 encased the early sixteenth-century timber structure. Weatherboarding and tiling probably increased in use, while new wings and new or refurbished barns were common. New houses were built without open halls and with integral chimneys. By these means the medieval wealden hall-house with its jettying of the solar and service bays at first-floor level so typical of the South East, was transformed, although its essential timber framing continued throughout the seventeenth century. Here was the local vernacular tradition, what Gertrude Jekyll writing of west Surrey termed 'the crystallisation of local need, material and ingenuity'. At Robertsbridge, West Horsley or Bramley such local survivals may still be seen. Older traditions lingered, especially in the countryside. In Sussex at least, conservatism in building design may have ensured something of a time-lag between the countryside to the north and south of the Weald. The Elizabethan Chiddingly Place and Wakehurst Place (Ardingly) both had Henrician details, although the latter dates from *c*.1590. It has been estimated that in the town of Horsham in the early seventeenth century, a little over half of the total housing stock would still have been medieval or early post-medieval. There would have been little new building in Horsham between 1540 and 1770, since there was already sufficient stock existing which could be modernized. In Kent, on the other hand, the early appearance of wash houses which otherwise were mostly seen in London, betokens early innovation, as does the appearance of Dutch gables which spread throughout north Kent but only marginally into the Weald (Nairn and Pevsner 1965; Hughes 1988: 18; Jekyll 1904: 5; Barley 1985: 696–766).

Scores of gentry and yeomen once living in wealden houses left inventories allowing glimpses of their accommodation. Many still retained well-built open halls with one or two-storeyed wings, and with close timber studding, until this gave way to larger panels (post and panel) at the end of the sixteenth century. Kitchens were not universal in the sixteenth century, but the multiplication and increased specialization of rooms was a feature, especially in wealthy north Kent. John Aiscough from the Isle of Sheppey (d. 1603) had a two-storey house which included a roof garret; hall, parlour and kitchen on the ground floor, together with larder, brewhouse and milkhouse; a downstairs bedchamber next to one for the maids; other chambers over the porch and the kitchen; and chambers for living-in farm servants over the outbuildings. The storage and processing of produce was becoming vital as larger farms became more specialized and commercialized. Butteries, boulting houses, cheese lofts and wool chambers become conspicuous. Edward Juppe of Horsham (d. 1643) had a parlour, kitchen, buttery, milkhouse and apple loft. He also possessed a bakehouse and 'another room' with cheesepresses, etc. (WSRO, Invs Horsham 1643). The galleries, social venues in the larger houses, were more workmanlike in the farmhouses. William Wethersole of Barham (d. 1649) had a hall, parlour, brewhouse, four bed chambers, a buttery, bunting house and a milkhouse, but also a gallery full of lamb's wool, sacks and hoops (KAO, PRC 11/16/101).

Husbandmen's houses were inevitably more modest. By the mid seventeenth century, halls if present, might still be used for cooking. There were fewer rooms of less specialized use, and rarely more than one chamber for sleeping. First-floor rooms might be reached by ladder rather than staircase well after 1660. With less access to markets and profits, the husbandmen did not possess the necessary capital to rebuild. If marketable surpluses fuelled rebuilding, then there would be no rebuilding of cottages. However, smallholders and craftsmen added shops on to these basic designs to supplement or sometimes profitably supersede their farming interests. Thomas Dix, a Lenham cloth worker in 1663 had a two-storey, seven roomed house and a shop with looms and a wood store. Finally, labourers and commoners might have single-cell, single-storey houses with hearths at the gable end, although many had virtual hovels or no permanent accommodation at all. Tents sheltered iron miners at Ashburnham in 1600, while turf-covered huts were used by generations of migrant charcoal-burners.

In the predominantly wooden world of the Tudors and Stuarts, houses were no exception. Most were completely or largely wooden, with oak favoured. The half-timbered wealden house might have a stone or brick base, but the use of such materials was largely reserved for the wealthy. Wattle-and-daub was used to infill between the timbers, although brick and stone might also be used. Impressive stone buildings include Wakehurst Place (1590, of High Weald sandstone), Streat Place (c.1607, of flint and Hythe Beds ashlar) and Brambletye (1631, also of wealden sandstone). Flint was widely available in the Coastal Fringe, but seldom penetrated far inland. Reed or straw thatch was the commonest roofing material, although tiled roofs were locally found as at Etchingham and Salehurst in the late 1590s, and oak shingles or Horsham Stone were reserved for roofs of prestigious buildings. The latter came from sandy outcrops in the Weald Clay around Horsham, but these enormous and heavy slabs were to be found as far north as Capel, as far east as Westham and Wartling, and as far south as Shoreham (Gulley 1961).

Chapter 5

Innovation and Stress, 1660–1837

Writing of Surrey and Sussex in 1829, Thomas Allen noted that 'From the Restoration to the present time little worthy of notice has occurred in either of the counties' (Allen 1829: 180). Leaving aside the fact that he was omitting the most dynamic of the south-eastern counties, Kent, it is still possible utterly to refute Allen's viewpoint. In rural and urban spheres alike this was a time of great change. Technical change embraced farming, manufacturing, and coastal and overland travel. Social instability, growing poverty and political change touched all parts, while London continued to spread its influence at an ever-greater rate. However, such change and innovation was interleaved with stress throughout the period, and the interaction of these two aspects also forms a theme for the chapter.

Regional Variation in Farming Systems

The concept of overall agricultural regions is now challenged. They are not 'natural' features of the agricultural scene and they vary between different observers. Regions should be devised to aid further understanding and interpretation, and in this text the regions largely follow geology, soils, drainage characteristics and other physical features. But although soils were of crucial importance, so too were the perceptions of changing technology, the cultural limitations of the social environment, and location with respect to market and to London in particular. Aubrey noted the unwillingness of farmers to experiment before the mid-seventeenth century because they did not wish 'to be more knowing than . . . neighbours and forefathers', while 'Twas held a sin to make a scrutiny into the ways of nature' (Aubrey 1718–19, V: 403).

Many interacting factors promoted the localization of husbandry practices. However, to escape from the circular and difficult arguments of the 'instance/counter-instance' variety which can bedevil the defining and use of agricultural regions, the following section is based on an analysis of over

800 south-eastern probate inventories from between 1640 and 1750. Such data have been used in the South East before, whether as intensive single parish studies (Kenyon 1955, 1958, 1960, 1961); as more generalized regional analyses based primarily on topographical frameworks (Cornwall 1953 *et seq.*; Brent 1973); sampling of inventories within regions (Chalklin 1965); or in-depth inventory analysis of one region (Zell 1985a and b). A full computerized analysis remains to be undertaken in south-east England. The main features of cropping and livestock production are shown in Table 5.1. It should be remembered throughout that an artificially static picture is being presented here, and that change will be analysed later.

The High and Low Weald

Cattle remained the support for farming in this pastoral area with greater numbers of cattle in the High Weald than anywhere else in the South East at this time. Each farm had its complement of four or five cows together with calves or weanlings, but there was little commercial production. Those living near towns such as Tunbridge Wells might sell some milk, cream or butter through the good offices of the 'artless damsels of the plain' (Aubrey 1718–19, II: 207–8) but marketable surplus in animal products was limited, in contrast to the wide market in fat cattle, entered into with London butchers and salesmen. Bullocks from South Wales were particularly favoured for fattening in the Weald, before being driven to fairs such as that at Islington, moved to Barnet in 1746.

By contrast, arable land was limited and acreages of wheat, oats and barley were circumscribed, although that for oats was actually the highest for all the regions – being used in human food and drink as well as for fattening horses and cattle, and being the most tolerant of the acidic soils. Peas and tares were also widespread as throughout much of the South East at this time. One speciality was hops, which were becoming scattered over the eastern and central Weald with the increasing consumption of beer in the later seventeenth century. By 1670 many isolated parishes had a thriving London trade. West Hoathly sent 15–20 cwt annually, and by 1708 there were at least 19 growers in the parish, although the largest garden was just six acres.

The Scarpfoot Zone

As an intermediate and diverse area between the Interior and downland, the Scarpfoot zone partook of characteristics common to both types of environment (see also pp 173–5). In Fig. 5.1 the entire zone has been differentiated into: the scarpfoot/Holmesdale zone proper of mixed farming and livestock (Zone VIII); lowland heath which was largely common grazings and cony warrens (Zone VII); the Petworth and Western Rother district of mixed sheep/grain, dairying, and orchards (Zone IV); the Vale of Ashford with mixed sheep/grain

Table 5.1 Principal crops and livestock of the agarian regions of south-east England, 1640–1750

High Weald			Low Weald			Scarpfoot Zone			Chalk		
crops	*av. area*	*%refs.*	*crops*	*av. area*	*%refs.*	*crops*	*av. area*	*%refs.*	*crops*	*av. area*	*%refs.*
wheat	10.4	81.7	wheat	10.5	91.2	wheat	22.2	88.1	wheat	25.6	91.0
oats	11.4	77.4	oats	15.7	84.7	oats	13.3	68.8	barley	25.8	87.0
grass/hay	–	74.2	grass/hay	–	73.7	barley	22.7	62.4	peas	7.8	67.0
hops	–	60.2	peas	5.1	48.3	peas	11.2	61.5	oats	10.3	62.0
peas	3.8	39.8	barley	6.6	29.6	grass/hay	–	59.6	grass/hay	–	36.0
barley	3.9	32.3	tares	2.9	21.2	tares	6.6	31.2	tares	3.9	

| crop refs/inv.=4.9 | | | crop refs/inv.=4.7 | | | crop refs/inv.=5.2 | | | crop refs/inv.=5.2 | | |

livestock	*av. nos*	*%refs.*	*livestock*	*av. nos*	*%refs.*	*livestock*	*av. nos*	*%refs.*	*livestock*	*av. nos*	*%refs.*
cows/kine	4.5	94.7	cows/kine	4.6	95.4	cows/kine	5.2	89.9	cows/kine	4.7	90.0
oxen	3.9	75.3	hogs	3.4	76.0	hogs	4.0	73.4	hogs	6.4	71.0
hogs	2.7	69.9	horses	2.2	64.1	horses	3.4		horses	3.4	64.0
horses	2.5	67.7	oxen	3.5		sheep	50.7	51.4	sheep	38.8	52.0
calves/w'lings	2.8	65.6	sheep	17.1	57.6	colts	0.8	45.0	colts	1.0	47.0
steers	2.1	57.0	calves/w'lings	2.4	54.4	pigs	2.9	43.1	mares	0.9	46.0

av. cattle	=	22.6	av. cattle	=	18.5	av. cattle	=	16.6	av. cattle	=	13.9
av. horses	=	3.9	av. horses	=	3.6	av. horses	=	4.8	av. horses	=	5.7
av. sheep	=	49.9	av. sheep	=	31.1	av. sheep	=	77.9	av. sheep	=	101.2
av. pigs	=	6.7	av. pigs	=	7.8	av. pigs	=	10.0	av. pigs	=	13.5

Notes: (a) 'av. area' is the area of crops on the ground divided by the total number of inventories.

(b) '%refs' is the number of times a crop or category of livestock is mentioned in the inventories.

(c) 'crop refs/inv.' is an index calculated by dividing the total number of different crops mentioned in the sample by the total number of inventories in the sample.

(d) 'av. nos.' of livestock. The total number of livestock divided by the total number of inventories in each sample.

(Source: Probate inventories (ESRO, WSRO, KAO, SRO, LPL))

and cattle fattening (Zone V); and mid-Kent with mixed sheep/grain, hops and orchards (Zone VI).

Obviously there was great diversity in cropping. Barley was more prominent than in the Weald, and rye and buckwheat were also to be found. Cereal acreages were also higher, although not as high as in the rest of the Coastal Fringe, as were those of peas and tares. Conversely, the area of grass and hay was probably less than in the Weald, except on the heathland commons. On the poorer soils there was also more woodland than nearer the coast, and more hops and fruit than on the chalk. Livestock were equally diverse. There was not the wealden emphasis on cattle, but numbers of sheep, pigs and horses were far higher. Both horses and oxen were used for draught purposes here, and indeed they were invoked in an attempt to delimit more precisely the boundaries of the Weald for purposes connected with tithe payment. In the 1630s Sir Roger Twysden had noted that:

> The Weald for softness of soil tilleth and laboureth with oxen unshod, the hill country [the downland] with horse and oxen shod,

Table 5.1   cont'd

Sussex Coastal Plain			North Kent			Marshland			London Clay/ Thames-side		
crops	*av. area*	*%refs.*	*crops*	*av. area*	*%refs.*	*crops*	*av. area*	*%refs.*	*crops*	*av. area*	*%refs.*
wheat	25.8	96.8	wheat	25.6	92.3	grass/	–	63.0	grass/	–	67.7
barley	22.1	85.7	oats	12.3	76.9	hay			hay		
peas	10.1	79.4	barley	12.2	66.2	wheat	7.2	60.9	oats	10.8	60.0
oats	8.9	61.1	peas	4.4	56.9	barley	5.2	39.1	wheat	8.6	49.2
grass/	–	51.6	grass/	–		oats	6.8	32.6	barley	13.5	40.0
hay			hay	10.8	47.7	beans	5.5	26.1	peas	7.3	38.5
vetches	6.8	45.2	beans			peas	3.8	23.9	beans	6.0	21.5

crop refs/inv.=5.7 crop refs/inv.=5.5 crop refs/inv.=2.8 crop refs/inv.=3.5

livestock	*av. nos*	*%refs.*	*livestock*	*av. nos*	*%refs.*	*livestock*	*av. nos*	*%refs.*	*livestock*	*av. nos*	*%refs.*
cows/	5.0	80.2	cows/	6.8	95.4	cows/	4.5	93.5	cows/	6.2	76.9
kine			kine			kine			kine		
horses	3.6	77.8	hogs	5.7	73.9	ewes	105.5	71.7	horses	2.5	60.0
hogs	5.3	70.6	horses	3.7	60.0	calves/			hogs	0.9	33.9
sheep	49.4	65.9	lambs	17.7	56.9	w'lings	2.5	65.2	mares	0.4	29.2
lambs	12.2	51.6	ewes	37.5	55.4	hogs	2.1	60.9	pigs	1.0	27.7
pigs	3.7	50.8	calves/	1.6	50.8	tegs	65.0	58.7	colts	0.4	26.2
			w'lings			colts	0.9				
						oxen	2.8	56.5			
						lambs	54.6				

av. cattle	=	15.2	av. cattle	=	17.7	av. cattle	=	22.5	av. cattle	=	8.1
av. horses	=	4.7	av. horses	=	6.8	av. horses	=	3.5	av. horses	=	3.6
av. sheep	=	85.4	av. sheep	=	147.6	av. sheep	=	300.3	av. sheep	=	13.9
av. pigs	=	11.6	av. pigs	=	12.6	av. pigs	=	5.2	av. pigs	=	2.5

Note: w'lings = weanlings

but between these two hills they use horse or oxen shod (Cambridge Univ. Add Mss 2825, 24)

In allocating the Scarpfoot Zone to the 'hill country' as we have done in this volume, as a consequence of its settlement history, we are thereby also following Twysden. This area, with its mixed and balanced agriculture, seen in the true scarpfoot zone along the base of the central Sussex Downs, was one of early settlement and open fields. Townships stretched from the top of the flinty downland, through Upper Greensand and Lower Chalk ledges, Gault clay vale, Lower Greensand ridge to the wealden clays.

The Downland

It is possible again to subdivide the south-eastern chalk into the North Downs Brown Earth soils with their stiff, clayey loams yielding 'stone shattery' land and woodland in the west; the more truly champion Kentish eastern downs and Thanet; the South Downs Clay-with-flint soils west of

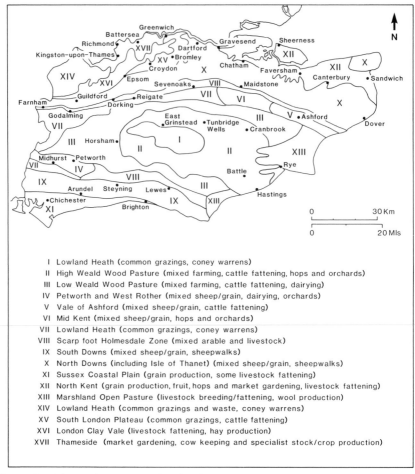

Figure 5.1 The South East: agricultural regions.

Findon, with more woodland; and the champion areas stretching eastwards towards Beachy Head.

Both wheat and barley were grown in larger quantities than in the Interior. The average area of both was over 25 acres while barley attained even more inventory mentions on the chalk than on the Sussex Coastal Plain. Not all soils were favourable for cultivation but fields were large and farms were being consolidated to give a most prosperous infrastructure for mixed farming relying heavily on good markets for cereals and sheep. Peas, oats and tares were also important; the first-named being frequently sown after barley, while tares were often sown for two years after barley and before wheat as a substitute for fallows (Young 1813: 102–6). The report to the

Georgical Committee in the 1660s from the area between Canterbury and Dover included the following observations:

> Barley is usually sown after wheat for it is a true observation that ground is much releived [sic] by the change of seeds . . . Peas and tares we sow upon the first plowing and commonly if the ground be light we sow peas under furrow . . . Oats are usually sown upon one earth . . . other graines are seldom used in these partes . . . We do use plowes with 2 wheeles and go with 4 horses in a plow, though about Sandwich and the Isle of Thanet where the land is of a gentler mould they go in barley season with but 2 horses in a plow. For meadow and pastures our country is little acquainted with them (Georgical Committee, No. 29).

In the same way that one must dispel the image of the chalk as treeless champion, so one must keep in proportion the extent of its sheep flocks. In eastern Sussex they were obviously large. Nathaniel Kemp of Preston (d. 1717) left 742 ewes, 440 tegs, 20 wethers, 35 'sheep' and 24 rams. In 1740 Nathaniel Webb of Falmer left 313 'sheep', 435 ewes, 90 old wethers, 250 tegs and 345 lambs (ESRO 1718/933; 1740/2807). Communal flocks were becoming rarer along the South Downs, although sheep leazes were attached to copyholds in most manors. Along the North Downs the importance of the common sheep flock varied. On the Surrey hills such flocks continued into the eighteenth century, with tethering and folding on the remnant intermixed strips. The local Banstead Downs sheep produced excellent mutton and house lambs for London. But overall the inventory sample showed the chalk to have only the third-highest average flock size, behind the marshland and north Kent.

The Sussex Coastal Plain

William Marshall proclaimed that there were few districts where he had seen less to mend than in the Sussex 'seacoast'. One of the most prosperous farming areas in Southern England, this was based primarily on deep, stoneless Brown Earths developed on Brickearth, interspersed with alluvial valley fills and coastal inlets. The sheep/corn husbandry had wheat and barley as its principal products. By 1640 a flexible ley system had evolved in both commonfield and severalty land, with grass leys being used for the fattening of sheep and bullocks. Wheat production was more widespread than in any other part of the South East, with acreages of wheat and barley surpassed only on the Chalk. Massive investment in arable equipment was a prerequisite. Richard Finers of Birdham in April 1710 had 100 acres of wheat and 36 acres fallowed for barley, together with four ploughs, probably of the one-wheeled variety, five harrows, six dung carts, four wagons, an 'oat cart', and two rollers. 'Long carts' and waggons were numerous here for the transportation of corn 40 miles overland to Farnham or to Dell Quay for seaward shipment to London, the West Country or the Continent. Mid-eighteenth century corn exports from Chichester equalled those of all other Sussex and Kent ports combined, and large granaries and tide mills were erected around the creeks of the Emsworth–Chichester area by the 1730s.

Between 1640 and 1750 this area displayed the most diverse cropping pattern in the South East (Table 5.1). Peas, oats and vetches figured prominently with the former sold at good prices in Havant for 'the fatning [sic] of the hoggs which come out of the forest' (PRO E134 6 Anne Easter 5, and Anne Mich 1). Clover, mixed corn, hemp, hops and fruit were also sold. The presence of the alluvial pastures ensured that cattle, sheep and pig numbers were also high. There were more cattle than on the Downs, but fewer sheep, horses and pigs. However, pigs and hogs were important, as in the Scarpfoot zone and the London Clay/Thames-side region; and bacon was plentiful from the mottled pigs grazing on tares or clover in the fields, brooks, or beech woods on the 'shravey' soils at the base of the downland dipslope. Sheep and lambs were fattened on alluvial grasslands and saltings for sale at Chichester and Arundel. Stinting rates were gradually reduced and common pasture rights were a source of dispute. A complaint against John Hale of Westhampnett in 1681 was that he put out nine score of sheep, often for the whole year on the commons of Singleton, East and West Dean, but that he could not maintain them on his own land, although he farmed over 300 acres of arable, with 60 acres in Westhampnett's common fields.

North Kent

Rivalling the coastal plain in diversity of cropping and productivity was the north Kent 'Watling street' zone. Soils ranged from fertile and retentive Brickearth loams between the Cray valley and Faversham to heavy wooded clays on the Blean, and light pebbly commons at Bromley, Bexley and Woolwich. But accessibility to the London market gave great intensity to farming – whether stock from the marshland or fruit, hop, cereal and vegetable production inland. Wheat acreages were comparable with the downland and coastal plain, and the area produced large amounts of malting barley by the second half of the seventeenth century. More than 6,000 qr of wheat, 4,000 qr of oats and 5,000 qr of barley and malt were exported coastwise from Faversham at this time, together with more than 2,000 qr of beans and peas (Andrews 1955). Large amounts of wheat and oats were also shipped via Herne from the heavier Blean area, while corn and malt were shipped from Sandwich.

Diversity also came from relatively large areas of fruit, hops and vegetables. By 1700 the modern distribution of fruit growing was apparent, together with prosperous market gardening areas at either end of north Kent at Gravesend and Sandwich. By 1660 there had been perhaps three generations of Flemish intensive seed and vegetable production around Sandwich, and intricate trading links had been developed with London.

Abraham Honess, 'gardener', died in Sandwich in 1692 leaving four cows, some pigs, 18 acres of cereals and fallow, and a further 26 acres of various crops such as turnips, parsnips, beans, canary seed, flax, and other seeds and peas. By 1660 Gravesend had acquired gardeners also, possibly from Greenwich, and by the 1740s the gardens supplied the surrounding towns and London with seeds and particularly with asparagus. Pehr Kalm remarked on the delightful countryside hereabouts, with earth walls along the Thames protecting farmland at high tide; haystacks of sainfoin; and large areas of wheat (three or four times that of barley and oats together). A little rye (for mixing with wheat for bread), together with buckwheat and luxuriant crops of tares were grown, while beans and peas were sown in rows. And between Gravesend and Rochester, were many cherry orchards sending fruit by the boatload to London (Lucas 1892: 344–76).

Cattle numbers were higher than in any other region outside the Weald and marshlands, at least before the spread of distemper from London and Blackheath in the 1740s. Numbers probably doubled during the seventeenth century, partly through the use of clover and sainfoin as fodder supplementation. Heifers and Welsh runts were fattened in the marshes, where the numbers of cows/kine were considerably greater than elsewhere. Extensive sheep flocks were also kept on the marshes, and flock sizes were second only to those of Romney and Pevensey. Charles Poole of Bapchild in September 1712 had a flock of 1,556, and John Randall of Harty St Thomas in 1713 had 1,742. Both men also had fleeces worth over £100 in this area which was building a reputation for its wool (KAO PRC11/71/218; 11/71/9).

Ploughing required a formidable amount of equipment on generally strong soils. Thus 'Plowes are usually very strong, for six horses in a plow, the beame made of the harte of oake about four or five inches square' and with 'wheeles as big as a pair of forewheeles for a coach' (Georgical Report No. 30). Nearly a century later, Kalm noted the use of three pairs of horses 'as large as the largest dragoon horse' being put into these Kentish turn-wrest ploughs, and sometimes five or six *pairs* of horses. Huge numbers of horses were thus retained here. Numbers of pigs were also relatively high, with many being kept here around starch factories or by distillers, where as many as 200–600 head were fattened on waste products and then sold to London butchers (Lucas 1892: 400–411).

The Marshlands

Lambarde quoted Hesodius to describe the Romney Marsh as 'evill in Winter, grievous in Summer, and never good', and offering 'wealth without health' (Lambarde 1970 repr.: 181). There was now little arable and the least diversity in cropping of anywhere in the region. Grass and hay dominated land use. In his note book in 1630 Twysden, referring to the marsh as a 'sicklie and contagious place', had advised his son to guard the marshland pastures, and to '. . . observe if he can whether it have been plowed or not for marshland will hardly ever recover ye auntyent goodnesse if it once have been broke up' (BL Add Mss 34, 163 f. 33).

Most of the pasture was in the hands of upland graziers and flockmasters. Thus by 1789 'the late arbitrary and tyrannical governor of Quebec', General Murray, then living at Beauport Park, near Hastings, had 500 acres of Romney marshland as part of his 1,667 acre estate, rented at £2 per acre compared with £1 per acre for arable land in the same area. Lookers were employed to protect the ewes and lambs. The general calculated that his annual profits were of the order of £1,700, which 'considerable profit depends very much on the union of two circumstances, the connection of an upland with a marsh farm; and sheep being the great dependence'. On the Sussex edge of the Romney Marsh such families as the Stilemans, Richardsons, Morphetts, Turks and Greenlands were famous for the sizes of their flocks, stretching to between 4,000 and 5,000 (Young 1789; Cozens-Hardy 1950: 45).

The basis of the Romney Marsh economy was the cover of rich perennial ryegrass, reserved almost exclusively for grazing. By 1660 distinct differences between fattening and breeding pastures were recognized. Twysden had advised the purchase of land 'such as will fat cattle not breed on younge', and Jones referred to 'the breeding land which is the general quality of the marsh . . . and the fatting land, which are the prime pieces and very rich' (Jones 1786). The main emphasis was the fattening of sheep, and an average flock of over 300 in inventories was more than double that of north Kent, which looked to the marsh for supplies, and 'as kind of nursery whence the Sheepey [*sic*] and other graziers of this county generally supply themselves' (Banister 1799: 426–8).

Young noted that Romney Marsh lacked fresh water and was devoted to sheep, while Pevensey Marsh possessed fresh water, and was given over to the fattening of oxen. But while the 'soil and rent are nearly the same . . . there are few fortunes made in the latter.' This analysis is not strictly accurate although the soils are both alluvial gley varieties, since there are detailed differences and fresh water was available around the edges of Romney Marsh. But it was certainly the case that the Pevensey Levels were devoted to cattle. 'Upland' estates in both Weald and downland relied on Pevensey marshland for fattening. By 1830, for example, the 6,000-acre Ashburnham estate had 1,500 acres of Pevensey marshland as an important adjunct to its larger farms (Short 1975: 157). Cattle numbers were approximately the same as in the High Weald, with significant numbers of calves/weanlings and oxen, the latter being fattened, rather than used for draught purposes since the arable area here was extremely limited. For the same reason, the number of horses was low, although the marshland was used for grazing younger horses.

Livestock fattening therefore imparted high values to areas otherwise deemed most unhealthy. Late eighteenth-century Appledore comprised 48 houses 'meanly built, and mostly inhabited by graziers, lookers and smugglers',

Plate 5.1 Battersea Fields: a watercolour by John Varley (1778–1842). The scene of the 1829 duel between the Duke of Wellington and the Marquis of Winchelsea, the area was converted in the 1850s to Battersea Park. Open fields and market garden specialists had previously used up much of this poorly-drained flat land, and the area had been of 'very evil repute', with the fairs being the resort of 'the roughest and most vicious characters of the neighbourhood' (VCH Sy iv: 9). A corn mill dominates the middle distance.

and such a description might fit Brenzett, St Mary in the Marsh, and many other small marshland communities (see p. 194) (Hasted 1797–1801, III: 122).

The London Basin

North of a line drawn approximately between Guildford, Epsom, Croydon and Greenwich were areas devoted to livestock fattening, hay production, cow keeping and a variety of specialist husbandries, including market gardening. Heavy London Clay gave rise to commons and poor grass, cultivable only with liberal dressings of chalk and London horse and cow manure. By contrast, the alluvium and low gravel terraces and brickearth along Thames-side were more prosperous, with remnant open-field strips worked by gardeners, farmer-fishermen, carriers and industrial labourers. Seventeenth-century Battersea presented a mixture of arable, grassland, market gardening, drained marsh pastures, and severalty nurseries (Plate 5.1). Such diversity owed much to the proximity of wealthy London tables, but Marshall regarded the farming as such to be unenlightened. Inventories of farmers, as opposed to gardeners, showed very high cattle numbers but low diversity of crops, with relatively few cereals, the average cropped areas of produce low, and with grass

211

or hay the most prominent item. Wheat and barley were the main cash grains, although oats for fodder were important.

Poor grass and meadows were relatively abundant. Meadows were let to cow keepers who used rotational paddock grazing to conserve grass until mid-winter stall-feeding became necessary. Hay was sent from Lee, Eltham and Deptford by water to London, most being purchased by the cow keepers. John Farrant of St Mary Newington in 1689 had a cow house with 40 cows, £92 worth of hay, but seemingly no land. Richard Latham from the same area in 1681 had 20 cows worth £50, hay worth £4, and was owed £1.6s for milk out of a total inventory of under £113. Standard equipment included carts and horses for retailing, together with milk vessels. Reginald Sargant of Putney (d. 1706) also kept six asses, which were driven from door to door to provide cleaner, though more expensive milk. The general hygiene of the milk was a problem and profits were badly hit in the distemper of the 1740s. Relatively high numbers of horses reflected the transport needs of London's population, while large numbers of hogs and pigs reflected the presence of distilleries, starch factories and dairying, all of which could use by-products to fatten pigs. But overall, livestock numbers were low, and when seen alongside a low diversity of crops, pointed to an undistinguished agricultural area by the middle of the eighteenth century (Short 1985: 288–91).

However, by 1700 market gardening and nursery production were well established among the open fields and growing suburbs, from Greenwich to Kew and Mortlake (see pp 182–3). Kalm noted that these growers 'mostly keep to something special'. Mitcham became a herb centre while other specialisms included the asparagus of Battersea, the watercress of Wandsworth, garden trees of Vauxhall, the osier beds of the Thames aits, and the plant centre at Putney. Not everyone specialized, but there was a considerable investment in crops and bell-glass, and the severe South London hailstorm in 1750 brought losses of over £4,000 to more than 40 growers. Four growers from St Mary Magdelene, Bermondsey, cited losses of over £230 each (SRO, QS 6/2 Midsummer 1750/62–106). But by experimenting with new crops such as tobacco or liquorice; by advocating setting or row culture, or digging and trenching, commercial horticulture played no small part in stimulating agricultural change in England.

Agricultural Change

The period from the Restoration to the accession of Victoria was one of great significance for the rural economy of the South East. Marked regional differences in the sixteenth and seventeenth centuries now gave way to more market-orientated, capitalized economies, with more standardized production and demands for cost-effectiveness and efficiency by the 1830s. The stimulus of urban markets and the proximity of the Continent induced a more intensive agriculture than in many other regions. Specialisms proliferated: hops and fruit, nursery and vegetable production, cow keeping or calf and lamb rearing. And equally finely tuned to market demands were the production of cereals, especially wheat and barley; the fattening of imported cattle, and the rearing and fattening of sheep.

Many interconnecting strands run through changes in south-eastern agriculture at this time. New techniques were allied to changes in agrarian structure, and with these twin forces the remaining marginal lands were tackled. It must always be remembered, however, that the 'improvement' of such land normally entailed the introduction of privatized commercial production into what had previously been a communal resource. Thus the enclosure and reclamation of the commons – whether large as at Ashdown, or smaller at Tooting or Epsom – entailed the replacement of often ancient rights of common usage by severalty farming. Such change was not always peaceful. Fences might be destroyed; illegal enclosure took place on Dorking Common in 1661; and attempts to privatize Ashdown resulted in the regulating of the forest and a commoners' protection society by the beginning of the nineteenth century (Cornwall 1953; Sy RO, QS roll, Midsummer 1661, n. 210).

Several types of environment were still marginal, and all were vigorously tackled. The long coastline, for example, still sheltered large areas of saltmarsh. Along the Sheppey coast land was leased in large blocks with appurtenant saltmarsh such as that belonging to the manor of Higham, owned by St John's College, Cambridge. The demesne was leased with 'commonings' in the saltmarsh for tenants and under-tenants, and by 1737 for each commoning a tenant might graze either five sheep or one horse or mare; or one cow or two 'twelve monthing' bullocks. For every offence against commoners' regulations 12d was payable, of which half went to the 'looker' and the other half was to be 'distributed amongst the poorest sort of people to whom the common doth belong equally according to their necessity'. However, there is evidence of the reclamation of the salt meads for arable land. A 1663 terrier mentions a 'peece of land in two severalls (now plowed) formerly course rushy land', and 'one piece of rushy ground lately broken up and called Barron Hillmarsh containing 12 acres . . . abutting on Highham Common'. A complex mixture of open field strips, severalty enclosures and marshland characterized the area. Although markstones had long been used, a 1762 surveyor was still unable to find many strips at Higham; but on the other hand at Lillichurch Farm on the estate, subdivision of large severalty fields was in progress, and he could note 'two pieces of land called Ridges, formerly in one piece now divided by a quickhedge containing together eighteen acres'. Long leases were being granted to substantial, innovatory tenants and reclaimers in this area, and by 1695, for example, tithes due to the vicar of Higham included those compounded for hemp, flax, hogs, 'st.ffoyle', rape and clover (St John's College Mss, Drawer 6575, 49 and Box 4/15).

However, around the coast not all was progress. The Isle of Sheppey marshes experienced bad floods in 1744 when it was written that 'the tenants of the Isle of Sheppey are so hurt by the sea water overflowing the marshes that they are likely to leave if the sea wall is not attended to soon' (ESRO, SAS RF 15/25). At Bracklesham Bay, West Wittering, the 1,000-acre estate of Cakeham Manor was exposed to 'blasts from the sea' and 'lyeth more exposed to blytes than some other lands thereabouts'. On one occasion at the beginning of the eighteenth century 'severall sheep going down to the sea shoar to feed on ye oar [seaweed] were drowned by ye sea coming in upon them' (PRO E134 Sussex 8 Anne Easter 20, 9 Anne Easter 17). Further east along the same coastline inundations and blowing sand affected other areas and communities constantly battled to maintain and protect their reclaimed land. Along the river valleys too, as at North Stoke on the Arun, there were regular floods in the 1720s, when meadow and feeding grounds were inundated and herds on occasion taken for keep into Arundel Park. In 1697–8 the Adur was subject to summer floods in the Bramber levels area near Steyning, so that 'many persons using and occupying lands in the said levell did that yeare lose all or the greatest part of their hay or grass intended to be made into hay' (PRO E134, 12 Geo I, Mich. 8; 11/12 William III, Hil. 2).

Marginal land existed most forcefully in the wastes and forests of Surrey and Sussex. Stevenson estimated about 5,000 acres of heath and rather more common in Surrey by 1807, while lowland heath covered the High Weald from St Leonard's Forest through Worth and Tilgate Forests, to Ashdown and Waterdown. Even during the boom Napoleonic war years there were few who attempted to cultivate the acidic soils and headwater ghylls of the Ouse, Medway and Mole. In 1973 the Rev. Arthur Young bemoaned the area, since it was 'a melancholy object to see forest, and commons and wastes, most of them highly improvable, within forty miles of the richest city in the World . . . for near forty miles in a line'. Instead these were areas of dwindling timber stocks, rabbit warrens or cottage smallholdings. The Ashdown Forest was affected by eighteenth-century pressures from the commoning of cattle, the cutting of turf and 'litter', and small illegal encroachments. As a reservoir of common land, the area was invaluable to rich and poor commoner alike. Young might inveigh against the tracts of waste, but the commoners were extremely concerned by the beginning of the nineteenth century to protect at least the Ashdown Forest from further enclosure (Stevenson 1809; Marshall 1818: 371; Young 1793).

On the wealden Forest Ridges, with over 7,000 acres of waste, the first grants on Heathfield Down were made in 1756–7, a year in which grain prices rose to over 50s per qr. By the 1780s 500 acres had been granted to 257 people in over 300 separate plots, and by 1840 over 2,200 people were living in scattered settlements along the ridge-top roads. Disputes occurred between landed families over title to manorial rights, such as that between the Ashburnhams and the Pelhams, which rumbled on into the nineteenth century. Here too the pre-capitalist economy revealed itself in disputes over commoners' rights to gather underwood for fuel. From Waldron Abraham Baley, steward to the Duke of Newcastle, recorded events in his correspondence:

> January 22 1763: In my walk over the woods I found that the people of Waldron had begun their old practices . . . and this day have sent Ranger to Horsham gaol [evidently to frighten the neighbourhood].
>
> January 31 1763: I have lately caught two others cutting grass to give to their cattle out of the woods felled last year . . . They are very poor and were very submissive . . . I have got a list of about ten poor wretches chiefly women and children that have been pilfering the woods this cold weather and intend having them all before a magistrate at the first proper opportunity and if I can prevail upon the justices to act as they ought shall get several of them whipped, the one man sent to the house of correction but I dont know that anything will be sufficient to keep them honest. They are a parcel of the most distressed and miserable objects I ever saw among the human species.
>
> May 13 1763: I have detected another wood stealer and have obtained an order to pull down his cottage (ESRO HA/310).

Such passages tell us much about the attitudes of the protagonists in this conflict. In June 1763 Baley was advertising a £50 reward for information on the setting fire to woods in Waldron; and the unfortunate Ranger was still held in Horsham gaol as a virtual hostage until the Waldron poor should renounce their underwood cutting. The poor also had to maintain Ranger's family. By October 1764 the parishioners were petitioning Baley for Ranger's release, and Baley noted that 'The Waldron people have lately been pretty quiet and I have great hopes that we shall now be able to keep them so'. At a time when the Fullers were taking some pride in their agricultural innovations and buying 'the latest treatises for the library at Rose Hill', the 'unspoken war against property' was also being conducted as a consequence of reclamation (Saville 1983; *Sussex Weekly Advertiser*, June 25, 1763; Worcester 1950: 144–71; Kirk 1986).

Not all this land was enclosed for farming. In the decades following the Restoration for example, Lord Montague prejudiced common rights to heath and turf on Pirbright Common by enclosing parts for peat digging, although timber was seen as the best possibility. However, the heirs to the 10,000 acres of St Leonard's Forest were accused by 1680 of mismanagement with:

> Waste and destruction made in the woodes and tymber there since the year 1672 by reason of the not encloseing the coppices or underwoodes after they were felled and taking in joycemt [agistment] cattell and keeping of sheep in the said forrest and woodgrounds soe cutt and by burning of heath for makeing better feed for the coneys, the young woods were dampnified and hindred in their growth (PRO E134, 36 Chas II, East 22).

Certainly there were areas where poor woodland management resulted in degradation. Large areas of St Leonard's Forest had been ruthlessly cut to feed about six iron furnaces in the late sixteenth century, and it was now reduced to a 'vast unfrequented place, heathie, vaultie, of unwholesome shades and overgrown hollows', with local tales of large serpents roaming free. Before the Civil War Sir Richard Weston had attempted to farm here among the commons and the small-scale enclosures made by part-time iron workers. Weston had advocated intensive sheep folding, denshiring, marling and the use of rotations which included flax, turnips, clover and lucerne. But 'it was a new, and foreign sort of husbandry, and therefore suspected' (Yarranton 1663: 4). The light Flanders soils where Weston had seen the techniques were very different to the 'extreme wet and gawled land' of St Leonard's Forest, and markets were inaccessible across the Weald Clay. Improvements were therefore modest. The 1655 Parliamentary survey also referred to the destruction of woodland, but the activities of the sequestration committee which took over the land from the royalist Westons exacerbated the losses. Witnesses in the 1680s remembered large amounts of cord wood being taken but with no subsequent encoppicing or fencing. And in the 1660s Sir Edward Graves, acquiring a life-lease of the forest, proceeded to deplete the remaining woodland without mercy. The last forge fell down 'for want of use' at this time, and during the 1670s beech timber was sold to timber merchants and taken out of the Forest as 'shovelltrees' or 'spadetrees' and planks. With no market for cordwood much of the underwood was spoiled. Fencing was maintained with difficulty, and the ever-encroaching heath was regularly burnt to allow the growth of feed for rabbits. By the late seventeenth century the forest was indeed regarded as a rabbit warren (Brandon 1963: 115–21; Gulley 1960: 48–60).

By the end of the eighteenth century little had changed in St Leonard's Forest. Together with Ashdown, Tilgate (the former Worth Forest) and Waterdown, there were about 25,000 acres awaiting 'improvement'. On the black sands and silty clays here even the enclosed land was used for rabbit warrens, returning rents of 1s 3d to 3s per acre, compared with an average £1 per acre for medium-quality farmland. Improvements were now attempted by Mr Bradford at Pippingford Warren, Ashdown; and by Mr Seaton in Tilgate but those by Marcus Dixon on 3,000 acres of St Leonard's had failed by 1793. Denshiring, followed by the sowing of turnips, rape, oats and clover had been tried, with sheep feeding off the turnips. But rabbit warrens and the cutting and crafting of birch brooms for sale in London appear still to have been the only commercial activities. By 1805 Dixon had died and his relatives were anxious to dispose of his lease. Arthur Young criticized the lack of improvement here, but before the 1840s little could be done without under-draining, and at the beginning of the nineteenth century most of the forest was as unproductive as at the beginning of the seventeenth.

The inherent infertility of these sandy wastes frequently re-asserted itself. The vicar of Godalming took William Perryer to the Court of the Exchequer since his tithes had been considerably cut by the substitution of coneys for sheep and cattle in the early 1670s. A similar case came from Lurgashall in the deep Weald Clay where several farmers were cutting and selling furze faggots in the 1660s, rather than the corn which they had sown previously (PRO E134, 28 Chas II, Mich 11; 23/24 Chas II, Hil 6). Much land would be broken up when prices permitted the hope of profit. Common sheepwalk at Sompting was broken up in 1711 by two farmers to give good crops of wheat over 60 acres of marginal chalk hills, and such land swayed in and out of cultivation throughout the period. Many smaller commons were tempting targets for 'improvement'. Swingfield Common was described as good land in the 1730s, but 'unused' because 30 commoners enjoyed rights over it. The enclosure of Tooting Common was held to be greatly to the benefit of the Duke of Bedford's tenants in the 1720s. Nevertheless, Wimbledon and Putney Commons were still 'flat and bare' when later visited by Pehr Kalm, used only for furze or 'abandoned to pasture' or otherwise 'under-used'.

Finally, parkland was converted wholly or partly to tillage in the seventeenth and eighteenth centuries, even at the height of parkland creation in the South East (see pp.238–48). Parts of Richmond, Nonsuch and Knole were turned to productive use. At Knole in 1705 the disparked lands had 'for severall years last past boar great cropps of corne, hay, clover and other tythable matters' for the tenants and under-tenants of the Duchess of Cleveland (PRO, E 134, 4 Anne, Trin 7). By 1750 there were nearly 400 acres of 'plain land' in the 1,000-acre park. When first taken into cultivation the yields might be high. One 1705 witness spoke of 7 or 8 qrs per acre on disparked land at Nonsuch, although the general level was between 1½ and 3 qrs but much obviously depended upon the skills of the husbandmen and the methods of improvement adopted.

Denshiring and liming continued steadily. At Arlington 60 acres of sheepwalk were denchered for wheat and barley in the 1690s, and the technique was being used at Pellingbridge Farm, Lindfield at the turn of the century. In the 1780s John Fuller was extending his Heathfield farmland onto former commonland by enclosing, denshiring, liming, and planting turnips on which sheep were folded prior to sowing with wheat, oats, rye or grass seed (PRO E 134, 6 Wm and Mary, East 8; Geo II, East 16; ESRO Fuller Ms 15/21).

Soil treatment rested largely on proven techniques but with refinements in the mixtures and amounts applied, and with care being enforced in many lease covenants. Liming was very necessary. Limekilns were fuelled with furze or heath faggots, and the use of lime or unburnt chalk was recognized as a major factor in the growing of crops on the Weald Clay or Lower Greensand. By the eighteenth century leases referred regularly to liming and it was allowed for in tenant valuations. The Purbeck limestone workings of the Earl of Ashburnham led to him being referred to by Arthur Young as 'the greatest lime burner in England', and numerous ruined workings are still to be seen on the former estate. The chalk escarpment, the main source of agricultural lime, is scarred by several hundred lime quarries, the most extensive and long-lived being the works at Dorking, Betchworth and Buckland on the North Downs, and at Amberley on the South Downs. The Surrey works are honeycombed with a dense network of shafts and underground galleries which came fully into production with the improved communications of the late eighteenth century. A theoretical ratio of about fifty wealden acres of farmland per limekiln is to be expected, as indeed is the case in Surrey, where ruined kilns have been most thoroughly surveyed (Plate 5.2).

Many husbandmen mixed or interchanged their fertilizers. Markham had advocated the interchanging of marl and lime in the Weald, a principle still applied by the 1760s. Depending on the locality, many other materials came to hand: sand and seaweed, woollen rags, ashes and iron-slag; malt-dust and ferns. Around Ashford 100 cartloads of dung per acre were sometimes spread, although the norm was probably nearer 30 loads, perhaps more for autumnal wheat sowing, but some leases specified considerably less. Marl was taken from communal pits on the Ashdown Forest, or from the corners of fields from the Weald Clay Paludina Limestone around Bethersden, the Coombe rock and brickearth of the Sussex Coastal Plain, or from the scarpfoot at Henfield, where it was freely available to tenants. William Topley believed the practice of marling to have been discontinued by the nineteenth century, but there seems sufficient evidence to believe that it continued intermittently and on a small scale long into the century. As late as 1825 it was being used, albeit unsuccessfully, at West Hoathly (Markham 1636; Topley 1876; ESRO Add Mss 3329–3401).

Crop and livestock husbandry similarly combined past practice with Restoration and Hanoverian innovation. Thus the use of either summer fallow or podware (or 'horsemeat' – combinations of peas, vetches and tares for livestock feed) was still very widespread. Folkestone estate leases from the 1720s and 1730s stipulated that land was to be sown with podware or left as 'summerland'. Elsewhere beans were sown in rows to facilitate hoeing. This practice was well established by 1650 on the sandy loams of West Surrey and the Sussex Coastal Plain, but elsewhere both beans and peas were still being broadcast by 1750. Around Goudhurst 'some beans were cultivated, part of which were dibbled in rows; horse and hand-hoeing are known but by no means practiced as in the other side of the county'. Horse-hoeing was used at Framfield during the late 1740s; was noted by Ellis in Kent prior to 1770;

Plate 5.2 George Scharf's sketch of flare limekilns with bottle-shaped chimneys on the North Downs *c*.1820. During the course of the seventeenth century, liming cold clays had replaced marling to some extent, and became the leading method for soil improvement on heavy wealden soils. This resulted in the working of huge chalk quarries on both North and South Downs, and the carriage by improved transport by road and water. Betchworth, near Reigate, and Amberley, near Arundel still characterise the relict features of this industry at the present day.

and was used in Thanet for wheat and barley by the 1790s. Early references exist to 'sowing with barley by horse' in 1653 at Puttenham, or to a 1697 'drill plough' at Richmond, but most innovations awaited enthusiasts such as Mark Duckett, the Esher inventor of ploughs, who began farming at Petersham about 1760.

The principles of alternative husbandry had been well-understood since at least the mid-fourteenth century (see pp 65–6), and were now improved by the use of new grasses, better sheep folding techniques, and the wider adoption of root crops. Flexible rotations of grass and cereals were being practised at Ashburnham and Kirdford by the 1680s and 1690s, demonstrating the adoption of methods advocated by Markham for the 'haizell moulds' of Kent. Thus neither the Rev. A. Young nor William Marshall could see any pre-ordained rotations by the end of the eighteenth century. Instead Marshall noted that men farmed 'by existing circumstances', and certainly in east Kent there was no 'mistic pivot'. On the Kentish Filmer estates 'rules for ordering cornland' in 1733 included sowing wheat or barley after summer fallow; peas, beans or tares; and oats or barley with clover seed or ryegrass. A general rotation of turnips/barley/beans or peas/summer fallow/wheat, was advocated here (KAO U120 A17 Filmer Accts).

References to water meadows are contained in the works of Weston and Twysden. In the Interior they were valued primarily as sources of hay and good fattening ground, Markham referring to better wealden pastures 'amended by irrigation of flouds, which there is called flowing and over-flowing'. Along the Western Rother near Petworth, common watermeadows were carefully regulated, and they existed also along the Lavant and in the Medway's headwaters at Crowhurst, Oxted, Godstone and Tandridge. Those at Lingfield and Edenbridge were being annually re-allocated by 1714. Seventeenth-century examples came from Chiddingstone and the Funk Brook at Bletchingley, and Marshall in 1818 noted that formerly irrigation in Surrey 'seems to have prevailed more'. However, water meadows provoked many conflicts. In a 1636 Cranbrook Session of Sewers Twysden 'spake with Mr Tuck . . . and complained to hym of stopping ye stream to my mylle by hys flowing hys meades wch he excused by hys mans negligence and yt he would not doe it but when it might not hynder ye mylle'. John Evelyn referred to the streams about Wotton as 'naturally full of Trouts, but they grow to no bigness, by reason of the frequent draining of the Waters to irrigate their lands' (Short 1985: 306).

The diffusion of new techniques was accompanied by the adoption of new varieties. Grassland management progressed rapidly so that by the late eighteenth century many could choose between the more familiar bents and ryegrasses; well-established clovers, sainfoin and trefoil; and perhaps the new lucerne. By the eighteenth century ryegrass leys were used in north and mid-Kent and the Weald, and a 1717 Lewisham lease specified the sowing of arable with 'ryegrass, clover or other seeds' four years from the end of the tenant's term. On the poorer sands of western Surrey bents were first grown at Send-cum-Ripley in the 1660s, and there were 19 acres being sown here by 1701.

In the wood/pasture areas clover was adopted enthusiastically. Many in the Low Weald were using seed imported via Maidstone by the 1670s; and on the western sands, in the Scarpfoot zone and in mid-Kent a process of adoption took place between 1650 and 1670. At Buckland, for example, the accredited innovator was William Stephenson from Betchworth who rented land in Buckland on which he grew clover in 1663 or 1664. From the 1670s clover cultivation spread to the South Downs, Western Rother, north-west and east Kent, and the Coastal Plain. The Kentish downland and London Basin were less receptive, with podware still being favoured on the flinty soils of the former, and abundant hay along Thames-side seeming to preclude innovation there. By 1690 Kentish seed was being grown for export, and many became buyers and/or sellers of seed depending on the quality of the season. Overall in south-eastern inventories the number of references to clover before 1660 was negligible, but grew so that clover featured in 28 per cent of all inventories by 1750 (Table 5.1).

Trefoil, sainfoin and lucerne all appeared at this time. By 1700 trefoil was also established on the downs for sheep feed and in Thanet instead of a fallow for wheat. In a 1722 Stalisfield lease Henry Wise was bound to leave at least twenty acres 'twice ploughed and fit to sow with wheat and clover or trefoil'. By 1750 it was ubiquitous on the Chalk in Kent. Early trials with sainfoin by Weston and others in the 1650s and 1660s were emulated during the 1670s, and the crop was widely established by 1700. At Eastry in 1708 about 500 acres were reputedly grown, and in north-west Kent Kalm noted in 1748 that '30 years back they had not known so much of it used as now'. In the 1720s large yields of hay were obtained on the Croydon downs for sale for the large London horse population, and the teams of horses working at the chalk quarries at Northfleet were also fed in this way. By 1805 sainfoin had become perhaps the most valuable grass in Kent (Boys 1805: 110). By 1733 lucerne was sown on the Filmer East Sutton estate, but the care necessary for its cultivation largely restricted it to gentlemen's gardens for the provision of horse fodder. Expansion occurred in the latter eighteenth century, Kalm noting of Gravesend that 'some have also now begun to sow lucerne but it is still uncertain how it will succeed' (Short 1985: 302).

The spread of root crops was far more hesitant. Turnips did not suit the Weald, London Clay, Clay-with-flints or marshland, and were consequently limited to market gardens except in the London basin where gardeners spread the crop to husbandmen. By 1700 turnips were being cultivated on the North Downs, mid-Kent and Bagshot Sands, and by the 1720s the root became commonplace on such lighter soils. Significantly perhaps, the large estates of Mereworth and Ashtead both grew turnips and both had East Anglian links. By the 1830s turnips were widespread on the lighter soils, with potatoes more in evidence in the Weald. The potato was a post-1750 entrant into south-eastern farming, via the London Basin gardeners. Marshall noted that 'until of very late years [it had not] been suffered to stir beyond . . . the garden, or hopground'. Some Irish imports by Lord Sheffield in 1765 were planted 'by a man who worked on the road' in the absence of any firm wealden expertise, but by the 1830s they too were established as part of normal husbandry practice.

Of the industrial crops, hemp and flax figured in seventeenth-century inventories, particularly from the Chalk, Coastal Plain and Low Weald, but the cessation of government encouragement, and covenants against exhausting crops in leases curtailed growth in the eighteenth century. The best known industrial crop in the South East was the hop, which showed a steady increase at this time. Mid-Kent was the main focus, but with the High Weald an important adjunct together with east Kent and the Farnham area. Around the latter town, superior quality hops had been grown on the narrow Upper Greensand belt in the former common fields since the sixteenth century. With Farnham an important corn market for London, hops fitted well into a marketing economy here, and Marshall later noted a great influx of people into the hop gardens at harvest time. Most of the hops were, in fact, marketed at Weyhill in Hampshire and thereby found their way to the West Country and Midland brewers (Brandon 1977: 90; Baker 1976).

All categories of livestock increased over the period. Improved animal husbandry, the use of reclaimed downland, woodland and heath for pasture, and fodder from new grasses and roots were all significant. And the main causal mechanism, at least in the absence of population growth on any scale between 1640 and 1750, was the constantly growing demand for food from London and the South East, together with some increase in living standards for the rising 'middling' families.

One important regional change at this time was an increase in numbers of horses in the Weald and Scarpfoot zone. Numbers of horses and oxen tended to move in approximately inverse spatial and temporal relationship, and the overall growth in horse numbers sets the stage for the discussions later in the eighteenth century by Arthur Young on the relative profitability of horses and oxen. In the South East, horse numbers were consistently below average in the High and Low Weald and the London Clay/Thames-side regions. In the latter area there is no inventory evidence for the use of oxen either, although the evidence for its use in the Weald for many generations after 1750 is well attested. By contrast horse numbers were always above the regional average in the downland and north Kent, compared with relatively low numbers of oxen.

However, there were few improvements, as opposed to numerical increases and regional fluctuations, in livestock before the late eighteenth century. Vast and motley cattle herds were driven into the South East, with most fatteners looking to the Cheshire, Staffordshire and Irish rather than to the native Sussex breed. Child had noted in 1651 that 'we are too negligent in our kine, that we advance not the best species, and better them'; and by 1737 John Fuller suggested the division of marshland among poorer wealden tenants who would be prepared to improve native breeds, rather than among graziers who imported the majority of their cattle. Crosses with Yorkshire stock by 1790 brought some popularity for Sussex-Teeswater cattle, but pure Sussex herds were still favoured by many of the larger landowners, such as Lords Egremont and Sheffield, although the most admired trait of these cattle was their draught prowess. Arthur Young thought that 'The Sussex are large enough at 5 years old for a pair of them to plough 18/20ths of all the fields of England, indeed any to be met with, except the heaviest and most tenacious clays' (Young 1789). In fact the Sussex were normally worked more gently in teams of up to eight since although trampling of the soil was a problem, a mature seven or eight-year-old ox would be worth about £16 – four times its value as a one-year-old.

There were few advances in milk production. Little entered the market and both quality and output were low and variable, although some cheese and butter was sold, particularly from the Sussex Low Weald in the eighteenth century. However, in northern Surrey Aubrey noted that 'they rob their cheese by taking out the butter for London, and they are miserably ignorant as to dairy' (in Mortimer 1707: 166). Around Gravesend the milk was strained in lead boxes, the cream skimmed off for pigs, but little cheese made. After about 1805 Alderney and Guernsey cows spread into Kent and Sussex, but of the latter county Youatt could still write in 1834 that 'there can scarce be said to be a decided breed for the dairy in any part' (Youatt 1834: 45; Lucas 1892: 370–1).

Sheep flocks also increased. Romney Marsh wool had become longer and coarser by this time, whereas that from the short-stapled fleece of the South Downs was valued almost as highly as Spanish wool by the beginning of the eighteenth century. Mutton, such as that from the small Surrey Downs and heathland animals, was also increasingly sought. From the end of the eighteenth century to the 1830s great advances were made in the two great sheep-producing areas: Romney Marsh and the South Downs. By the later eighteenth century the small, polled speckle-faced South Downs sheep was already well-known for its meat and wool. In 1761 John Ellman's father moved from Hartfield to Glynde, with John Ellman assuming the tenancy in 1780. Within ten years he had become one of England's leading sheep breeders, being mentioned for the first time in Young's *Annals of Agriculture* in 1789. His main achievement was to transform the Southdown from a folding animal into one giving a larger proportion of hindquarter mutton and an improved fleece. Rams and ewes were selected for breeding for the shape of their carcase and thick, curly and even wool; and Ellman's success was based on this careful attention. By the time of his retirement in 1829 he was internationally renowned (Plate 5.3).

The management of the Romney Marsh, or Kent sheep differed

Plate 5.3 John Ellman of Glynde (1753–1832). Straddling local, regional and national arenas, John Ellman was not only the most successful breeder of the Southdown sheep, but contributed regularly to the *Annals of Agriculture*. He was steward of the Trevor estate near Lewes, expenditor of the Lewes and Laughton Levels draining the lower Ouse, a founder member of the Sussex Agricultural Society and Smithfield Society, and Deputy Lieutenant of Sussex between 1814 and 1820. In 1821 he gave evidence, with his son, to the Select Committee on Agricultural Distress (BPP 1821, IX: 49–61,110–24). His tomb in Glynde churchyard has been excellently renovated at the expense of the Southdown Sheep society.

considerably. Whereas Southdowns were small, light-soil, arable-folding animals cared for by shepherds; the latter were larger, hardier and coarse-wooled, spending most of their lives on the marshland pastures tended by 'lookers', encompassing between 300 and 500 acres of marshland where rich perennial rye-grass was the key to success. David Jones noted that:

> ... about 30 years back they suffered the grass to grow long and rank, thinking they could never have too much grass for their stock ... but now they find that sheep do not require a long bite ... that they do much better by nipping it as it springs. They therefore keep more stock upon the land and feed it as close to the ground as they can without starving their sheep whereby the land carries more stock (Jones 1786: 5).

The great eighteenth-century emphasis on fattening entailed flock sizes as much as five times higher than elsewhere in the South East. The 'Kents' were widely renowned for their hardiness, early maturity, propensity to fatten, and good wool. The increasing emphasis on meat production rather than wool reflected the decline in wealden clothing demands. Nevertheless, Kent remained an important wool-producing county, with between one-third and one-half originating from Romney Marsh. Rye superseded Faversham as the main wool-exporting port after 1730 and its exports tripled from 1660 to the end of the eighteenth century, even allowing for an increase in the socially-acceptable 'owling' (export smuggling of wool).

South-eastern farming relied on inter- and intra-regional links. Larger enterprises combined 'upland' with marshland in varying ratios to reflect changing needs; downland farmers and marshland graziers rested their pastures by transferring sheep to the Weald during the winter and 'foreign' commoners moved stock long distances to use wealden commons such as the Ashdown Forest.

The region's links with the rest of England and Wales were complex. When in September 1747 movements of cattle were banned because of the cattle plague, Welsh and Scottish drovers *en route* to the South East were left stranded. A clerk of the peace in Surrey spent more than a day in examining owners and drovers and administering the ban, and over 8,000 cattle were scattered along the drove roads into or within the South East. In 1748 eight Welsh drovers were quarantined in Kent with substantial herds. In return, Kentish drovers were to be found in many other regions. Richard Gough in his *History of Myddle* notes the presence of unpopular purveyors in Shropshire who bought cattle for the king's household and who were 'likewise drovyers, who bought cattle [*sic*] in this country, and brought them into Kent to sell again', at a good profit. Agricultural workers might also travel long distances to work in the South East. Welsh women and girls came to Kent for the grain, hay, fruit and hop harvests. Londoners came to Kent for hop picking, while East Anglian harvesters regularly moved through the South East. References to Welshmen were numerous, since they were conspicuous with their own language, religion and manners; and visits to the cattle fairs were frequent. In October 1670 the East Grinstead parish register refers to the burial of a 'poor welshman'; to 'Thomas Probert a welshman' on 1 December 1686, and 'Robert Morgan a welshman' on 23 November 1698.

The cosmopolitan nature of south-eastern agriculture was further enhanced by the frequency of travel by landowners between London and their estates. The Duke of Newcastle held land in eleven different counties in the eighteenth century, but much of his time was spent at Halland (the Pelham base in Sussex) or at Bishopstone, his favourite hunting lodge, and from 1715 increasingly at Claremont near Hampton Court (Kelch 1974: 36, 49). Although the Duke was not himself a great agricultural improver, the possibilities of inter-regional diffusion of livestock and seeds was enhanced. The increasing possession of property by London-based nobility, gentry and businessmen also encouraged change. Even the seedsmen and nurserymen of London spent part of the year travelling around the country visiting customers, collecting orders and advising on garden improvements and design, in an age increasingly conscious of pleasure and kitchen gardens (Thick 1985).

Pockets of more isolated farming tradition undoubtedly lingered, but the overall impression for the period is one of the export of produce overland and coastwise, the importing of skills, seed and capital, and a sophisticated integration with national and international marketing. The extent to which the resulting rural prosperity was widely available within the region is one theme of the next section.

Agrarian Employment and Rural Stress

Improvements in the reclamation, reorganization and intensification of farmland were not shared equally, either spatially or socially. New crops and improved livestock might mean more work, but this was not necessarily the case. Instead, the triumph of fully-fledged capitalism in the south-eastern countryside brought with it increasing schisms within rural society. Profits accrued to few but stress came to many in the years leading up to Victoria's reign.

The expansion of cereal and sheep farming in the Coastal Fringe was achieved with economies of scale internal to the farm unit. Larger areas could be sown and harvested with no greatly increased labour input, and many downland farmers retained only minimal workforces, importing labour whenever necessary, and thereby externalizing and putting at a distance the burden for the care and upbringing of their labour force. Kingston Buci, for example, was farmed during the high-price years of the Napoleonic wars by Mr Gorringe whose 500-acre farm covered most of the parish. William Holloway, the historian of Rye, recalling the years about 1802 wrote that:

As there were not a sufficient number of labourers in Mr Gorringe's employ, nor in the parish altogether, the following plan was resorted to for supplying the deficiency. On Midsummer Day when the crop was sufficiently advanced in ear to enable a person to calculate on the quantity of straw to be cut, one or two men used to come out of the Weald, on the north side of the Downs, to agree with Mr Gorringe as to the number of men required to reap the wheat in due season and the price per acre. When the reapers were come they were lodged in an old farm house on the estate . . . When the men had cut the wheat they returned home to the Weald, in sufficient time to take part in the harvest there, which was some weeks later than on the south side of the Downs (Bagley 1962: 26–7).

As in earlier periods (pp.66 and 168–9), the tramping of poor families was constant, and probably increased with greater regional specialization. Competition for employment could be fierce. Nicholas Lutman, a Chichester timber hewer, recounted in 1710 that he had been employed as a 'monthman' (harvester) for four years at £2 per month at West Wittering in the Selsey · Peninsula. But in 1707 the bailiff had succeeded in importing cheaper harvest labour from Emsworth. By the mid-eighteenth century many large farmers were importing workers at cheaper rates than could be locally obtained, thereby also promoting small-scale migration.

One strong indication that the changes acted against the interests of the small farmer/labourer sector is that at this time it is precisely those areas of the South East experiencing innovation, capital inputs and reinforced marketing links which were losing population, either relatively or absolutely. In part, these trends were a continuation and indeed, an acceleration, of the process examined for the Tudor and Stuart countryside. The period from *c.*1660 to *c.*1720 was one of national population stagnation, but the demographic history of the South Downs at this time demonstrated a close correlation between agricultural 'progress' and population decline. On the North Downs champion countrysides were less evident but population densities were still low, and throughout the eighteenth century the Kentish Coastal Fringe freeholders were being bought out in the same way that the Sussex copyholders had been in the previous century. In Surrey, too, shrunken villages stretched from Addington through Warlingham, Chipstead, Headley, Mickleham, East Clandon, Merrow, Compton and Seale. Lysons noted that Addington, together with Morden, was one of the few parishes around London not to have increased its population significantly between the 1660s and the end of the eighteenth century. Edward Steele, in his parish notes made at the beginning of the eighteenth century remarked of Addington that:

> Allthough as I said 'tis now but of a small extent, yett the inhabitants talke much of a tradition (and not without some reason) beleiv'd amongst them, aunciently this towne was far bigger than now it is (Bodl. Ms Top. Gen e 80 f. 1).

As population fell the administrative and ecclesiastical framework disintegrated. The cost of living was dearer since there was less wood fuel to hand, fewer commons, smaller gardens to grow one's own food, and perhaps less time for the few estate-employed workers to spend there. Certainly there were few inducements to migrate onto the downland, even if that were possible.

The increasing south-eastern market orientation was therefore a mixed blessing. A handful of large sheep/corn farmers prospered, but the social distance between them and their smaller neighbours and labourers increased as the eighteenth century progressed. On many farms the system of living-in farm servants finished between the end of the Napoleonic wars and the 1830s, as fluctuating prices strained the farmhouse atmosphere. Thus even on what might be the only large farm in the parish, the workers might become day-labourers who could be laid off at short notice, and receive nothing in bad weather. Capitalist farming did not preclude living-in anywhere in the region, but when labour could be imported reasonably cheaply, the living-in servant often became superfluous (Short 1984b). A Frant JP noted the changes in 1834:

> Upon the poorer farms in Sussex the custom had almost ceased of domesticating the labourers. Upon the large South Down farms, it is done, but only to a limited and necessary extent. I have in my eye a few solitary incidences of all the labourers 'unmarried men' living with their employer, and I can well imagine the superior advantages of the old system . . . . The change, I presume, proceeded from the growing refinement, and greater affluence of the agriculturalists, in the last thirty years. Those new habits have now become fixed. From an excess of population which was not felt during high prices, the farmer can now command any labour when he wants it, without burthening himself permanently, with indoor labourers (*BPP* 1834: 470c).

This breakdown of social relations with depopulation was illustrated even more explicitly on Romney Marsh. Once again, there were no commons, few craft industries and little incentive to move in. By the 1660s St Mary in the Marsh contained 'not above fifty persons, all of mean quality, marsh lookers'. Broomhill parish was defunct, and low population densities characterized all the marshlands of Kent and Sussex (Chalklin 1965: 28–9; Brent 1973: 113, 227–92).

However, the Interior stood in contrast once again. Cloth and ironmaking had now declined, and glassmaking had already disappeared. But the woods and commons furnished materials which could be gathered, transformed and sold, either locally or in more distant markets. Cranbrook, the centre of wealden cloth manufacturing, with its outworkers and putting-out network, was not even classed among England's leading cloth towns by the mid-seventeenth century. Inter-regional competition from centres specializing in the 'New Draperies' as well as from urban clothiers at Sandwich, Canterbury and Maidstone, together with disputes over timber supplies, export restrictions and poor communications, all hastened the decline. Defoe wrote that the trade 'is now quite decay'd, and scarce ten clothiers left in all the county'; and although he noted the industry at Canterbury and Maidstone, even urban clothmaking and its linked trades fell away in the early eighteenth century, thereby depriving surrounding villages of outwork. By 1676 population densities were high in the Kentish clothmaking parishes (Fig. 4.5) but so too were emigration and unemployment, adding to the unrest created in these old centres of dissent. In the 1660s half the inhabitants of Cranbrook were too poor to be chargeable to the Hearth Tax, while in 1673 the inhabitants of Benenden complained of 'the great and general poverty in respect of the decay of the trade of cloth makeing with in the said parish, being the greatest support for most of the inhabitants' (Chalklin 1965: 121). Rough linen hop bags were the last product of the Cranbrook clothmakers. In Surrey only Godalming survived through to 1750 making kerseys, stockings and other cloths. Chichester kersey and broadcloth manufacture also lingered and Hasted noted woolstaplers at Cranbrook and Goudhurst in 1778, but no clothiers. Population densities remained high but the underlying rationale for population growth had gone.

More important generally for the Weald had been the iron industry. With relatively high demands for ordnance during the mid-seventeenth century the industry was still employing something over 1,500 people by 1664, falling to nearer 1,000 by 1717. A shift in emphasis away from bar iron to that of cast-iron objects including ordnance, had occurred from the mid-seventeenth century. Ordnance found a ready market with the Crown and the East India Company, and production became more stable in the first half of the seventeenth century, eventually overshadowing the production of pig- and bar-iron as competition for the latter increased from the Forest of Dean, from bar imported from Spain and Sweden, and from other water-powered tool makers, locksmiths and nailers in the Midlands. Thereafter wealden ironmasters concentrated on their gunfounding which was already established as the most important in the country. Partnerships had developed between London merchants, local gentry and ironmasters, and their employees included dynasties of skilled fillers, finers, hammermen and founders. There were also clerks, unskilled assistants, and large numbers of miners, colliers, woodcutters and carters, many of whom were also small farmers or farm labourers. By 1653 there had been at least 35 furnaces and 45 forges operating overall, falling to about 14 and 13 respectively by 1717, and to just three furnaces by 1787. The roads were deteriorating, water power was unreliable (as in the dry season of 1743–4), and there were localized timber shortages and competition for its use. Pressures varied from one ironworks to the next, but with declining ordnance demands from the Tower of London allied with eighteenth-century technical changes placing greater emphasis upon coal supplies, decline was inevitable. The industry resisted longest in the Eastern Rother/Brede heartland, owing to demand for ordnance during the emergencies of the Dutch wars, the war years of the 1740s, and the Seven Years

War (1756–63) but in the western and Surrey Weald labour costs and water shortages destroyed the industry. From 1764 Scottish Carron guns undercut wealden prices. The industry had probably been prolonged in the Weald for most of the seventeenth century by the Browne family of ironmasters (with works at Brenchley and Horsmonden) who clung to a gunfounding monopoly for the navy; and by the courtier Sackville Crowe with a similar monopoly for merchant ships.

In the last stages of the iron industry the Fullers of Heathfield and Waldron were among the leading manufacturers of cannon. John Fuller III at the Heathfield furnace was basically still using traditional sixteenth-century techniques of blast furnace operation and gunfounding. He stood the whole cost of digging and carting the mine, filling up the pits and levelling the ground; the extra costs of wood-cutting, cording, coaling, and carriage to the furnace. The final cost by the time they reached the furnace was higher than by using coke by as much as £5 per ton. His annual blasts were limited by the availability of water in the winter and spring. His cannon made the twelve-mile journey overland to tidewater at Lewes or to the Tonbridge navigation during the summer because the roads were impassable at other seasons. Not surprisingly, the wealden gunfounding industry collapsed in face of the Wilkinson patent for a stronger gun, a more accurate barrel and a process which made the use of hollow-casting obsolete (Tomlinson 1976). The end of the industry came before any demand for supplies for the French Revolutionary and Napoleonic wars could be envisaged, and the last furnace closed at Ashburnham in the significant war year of 1812. As with clothmaking, a high population density had developed through the possibilities of rural industrial employment, but the economic base was stripped away during the seventeenth and eighteenth centuries (Cattell 1973: 115–42; Short 1989).

Myriad woodland industries also provided wealden employment. No firm correlation is traceable between ironworking and deforestation, since both furnace and forge were generally fed from carefully managed coppices which were expanded rather than ruthlessly exploited by the later seventeenth century. The encoppicing of woodland, promoted by Evelyn's *Sylva*, became increasingly popular, but as iron output decreased, interest waned. As early as 1607 Norden had listed ten localities, mainly commonlands, where woodland had been devastated by demands for fuel, and Evelyn added his own criticism of the 'prodigious waste which these voracious iron [and glassworks] have formerly made in . . . the country of Sussex . . .' (Evelyn 1664: 231–8). In reality both destructive *and* ameliorative effects on woodland can be perceived and the conflicting accounts reconciled by realization that although the commons were largely stripped of usable wood for fuel, the enclosed severalty woodlands were carefully coppiced and managed (Brandon 1984b: 92–9; Rackham 1986: 90).

However, in such marginal environments livings could be made in smallholdings, in underwood industries, in turf or litter cutting and in stone quarries. On the Ashdown Forest by the beginning of the nineteenth century many families were dependent all or part of the year on the 6,400 acres set aside for common usage under the decree of 1693 which recognized areas of common and privatized land. Different groups had different rights and expectations. Forest common land could be used by the tenants of Duddleswell and Maresfield manors for example, who were permitted two loads of wood annually, fallen timber, brushwood, roofing ferns and mud for walls. Pasture was normally stinted at rates commensurate with the stock kept on the holding over the winter. 'Foreign' tenants were allowed fewer privileges, but there were also many non-commoners using the forest. An 1816 meeting inaugurated attempts by the commoners' association (mostly tenant farmers) and by the lord of the manor to restrict the cutting of turf and litter. However, opposition to such restrictions came from the cottagers and squatters on the forest edge who disregarded litter reservations or the impounding of illegally depastured cattle. A group of women in 1830 recovered the 'poor peoples' cattle from Nutley pound, and every winter seasonal litter cutting, legal or not, continued.

Robert Edwards, born in 1805, was the son of a man later to become woodreeve of the forest. In 1879 he remembered the activities associated with common rights:

> As far back as I can remember down to the present time all the commoners turned out their cattle and cut brakes and litter for fodder and turf and peat for fuel and heath for thatching and latterly for draining, that is to put on top of the pipes when laid in the ground. They had birch willow and alder for fuel and for stakes and binders for fencing. Marl has fallen into disuse at present by reason of a change of ideas as to its value as a manure.

Jesse Divall, born at Chuckhatch, Hartfield, remembered that at the age of 18 he:

> went to service with my uncle Thomas Divall at the Chuck Hatch and worked at tile making in the summer and at wood cutting and litter cutting in the winter . . . When I was about 24 I went to live with Mr Thomas Foster at Little Parrock Farm and worked for him for 5 years during that time after we had finished wheat sowing I used to go out on the forest and cut litter for him and helped bring it home . . . I also cut a little turf for him . . . [and] . . . a few brakes for him. He used to turn out young stock on the forest I used to drive them out (ESRO, Add Mss 3904–5; and transcript of evidence to Mr Raper, pp. 12, 23).

In such various ways Ashdown provided a living in an otherwise unpromising agricultural environment. Wherever open forest or heathland predominated, income from farmwork could be supplemented. Peat digging augmented squatters' smallholdings on the Bagshot Sands or Lower Greensand between Puttenham and Farnborough. Gorse and heather were taken from the London Basin commons, as at Blackheath, Hayes, Bromley, Chislehurst or Dartford

Heath. Gravel was extracted from Richmond Park with impunity after 1660. Northern Surrey witnessed many examples of eighteenth-century disputes between commonly understood rights of user and legally enforced protection of private property. Bagshot was a 'blacking' centre and feelings ran high also at Egham where deer were taken; at Farnham Old Park where there were disputes over commoners' rights; and also at Wimbledon and Richmond. Horace Walpole saw the latter as 'a bog, and a harbour for deer-stealers and vagabonds' (Thompson 1975).

Bromley Common, a locale for charcoal burners and commoners before the enclosures of 1764 and 1821, also illustrated another aspect of these residual environments, in many ways islands of an older culture caught up in one of the fastest-changing agrarian societies in the world, when in June 1652 John Evelyn was robbed here. Undoubtedly such areas sheltered many who could not have existed within the confines of respectable society. At Stelling Minnis on a small area of Kentish downland common Hasted saw 'numbers of houses and cottages built promiscuously on and about the Minnis (the common waste), the inhabitants of which are as wild, and in as rough a state as the country they dwell in' (in Everitt 1977: 4; Horsburgh 1971: 213).

Radical alternative societies made fleeting appearances in such places, including the Levellers in the 1650s on the Lower Greensand of mid-Kent at Charing Heath, Wrotham or Cox Heath; the Diggers at St George's Hill, Walton-on-Thames and at Cobham Heath; or the later millenarian-inspired followers of Courteney on the heavy Blean soils around Dunkirk. Equally radical were the many religious sects who found a niche in these marginal environments, such as the Muggletonians from the seventeenth century Kentish Weald; or the Society of Dependents (Cokelers) from the later west Sussex Weald (p. 320). The dissenting tradition, whether Lollard, Puritan or something more extreme, was persistent and rooted in the socio-economic structures as well as the soils of the Interior.

Smuggling and poaching were also locally sanctioned methods of supplementing incomes. The long and frequently poorly populated coastline of the South East offered many possibilities for illicit trading, and the Duke of Richmond complained in 1749 that 'the common people of this country have no notion that smuggling is a crime' (Rule 1979: 141). Indeed, it was claimed that carriers were so well paid that farm wages had to be increased to approach the guinea a week that could be earned working for a smuggling entrepreneur in landing and clearing a cargo. By the 1740s guerrilla warfare was being conducted around the Sussex/Hampshire borders. Whether seen either as brutal and intimidatory of local communities (the contemporary authorities' view) or as part of a defence of the local economy against commercial capitalism and an aspect of eighteenth-century class struggle, smuggling was rife. Centres such as Hawkhurst and Goudhurst lived, according to the Duke of Richmond, in an atmosphere of 'open defiance of the laws and all government whatsoever' (Rule 1979: 151; 1975). With secretive routes from the eastern Weald to the sea at Rye and Romney Marsh, the Hawkhurst gang became the most notorious of all the groups, and their activities were associated with house-breaking, threats, assault and murder, together with Jacobite and French connections. The gang was ultimately broken in 1749–50, largely through the personal enthusiasm of the Duke of Richmond. Altogether, 35 were executed and ten died in gaol. What was seen as a threat to governmental authority and income was repressed in a manner typical of much Whig legal savagery in the eighteenth century.

The severity of treatment for smuggling conviction was matched by that for poaching, which threatened property and was inimical to rural authority. Again, the Weald offered both the ideal environment and the socio-economic need for this 'social crime'. As with smuggling, so too was poaching seen as a rejection by working country people of ruling-class laws. Few actually possessed the right to hunt game, and penalties for transgression were severe, culminating in the protection of deer by the 'Black Act', which could result in transportation or death for offenders. Poaching was generally an individual activity, but there were loose associations and often a black-market trade which could be tapped. In early nineteenth-century wealden Burwash parishioners from a variety of social standings had reputations for poaching. One gamekeeper successfully prosecuted an average of two men per annum in the 1820s, but a 'poachers mutual aid club' probably operated to pay the heavy fines, allowing one poacher to pay a £50 fine in 1825, and then another £5 within the year for a similar conviction. As with smuggling, poaching could also shade from socially-acceptable crime into more unsavoury activity. There were several notorious families in Burwash, for example, who were regularly in receipt of poor relief but who also appeared frequently before the magistrates charged with a variety of offences, including theft and assault as well as poaching (Wells 1981: 524–5).

One other 'social crime' was marked in the Coastal Fringe rather than Interior, and this was 'wrecking'. The term covers a range of connotations from the deliberate luring of ships onto rocks to the casual picking up of articles cast ashore by the sea. The build-up of merchant shipping with wider colonial links brought something of a climax to such activity along the South Coast in the eighteenth century. At the beginning of the century the farming operations at Cakeham Manor, West Wittering, on a very exposed part of the Selsey Peninsula, were frequently hindered by numbers of wrecks and articles thrown onto the shore, such as the several casks of brandy in the winter of 1704/5. August 1705 produced another wreck which included bags of hops, brandy and sailcloth; in 1706 a three-masted 120-ton vessel came ashore, was purchased by the farm bailiff and broken up, the iron alone paying for the purchase, and the timber being used for local building work. In 1707 a large quantity of deal boards came ashore, and there were reportedly two or three other smaller vessels thrown onto the shore. These windfalls were obviously useful, but there were drawbacks too, and it was reported that in the winter of 1706 the hedges on the farm 'were very bad before the storm and made worse by the storms and trodden down after the time of storms by many people rideing [*sic*] upp and down there looking after wrecks' (PRO E 134 8 Anne, East 20). Even in 1839 there were reports of wrecking at Folkestone, Whitstable and Deal, with the inhabitants of the latter town assembling for plunder in 'every instance' of a wreck. Most were fishermen or farmworkers who were ensconced in a community tradition which sanctioned wrecking along with poaching and smuggling at a time when customary rights increasingly conflicted with legal controls.

Most such activities were essentially covert operations which, alongside arson and cattle-maiming, were endemic in poorer south-eastern communities. But in such downtrodden circumstances as the poor increasingly found themselves after the middle of the seventeenth century, there were signs of more blatant, overt protest as well. In the Coastal Fringe the concentration on corn production emphasized the seasonality of employment which caused many families to seek parish relief during the eighteenth century. At times of local scarcity the exporting of corn to London provoked disturbances in north Kent, while harvest failures were recurring problems provoking unrest from the 1690s onwards. Only the low prices 'depression' of 1730–50 can be seen as a period of relative plenty for the rural labourers, but by the 1790s there were years when weekly wages were insufficient even to meet the wheat component of a diet based largely on that product, and with nothing further to spend on other food, fuel, clothing and rent (Wells 1979: 118–121).

One answer to increasing poor relief demands was to adopt the Speenhamland system which supplemented wages from the parish rates, with the supplement varying with food prices. In Sussex, and in Kent to a lesser degree, the system became very expensive, and a range of other schemes was tried. At Hayes in 1800–01 bread purchased from communion funds was distributed to the poor after church; free clothes were given to large families and the very poor; a sack of potatoes was given to each family in autumn at half-price, together with occasional doles of skimmed milk, soup, coal and meat. Wages were maintained at the higher summer rates throughout the year, and women and children were found work. The finance for such charity came partly from the parish and partly from wealthier individuals. In such manner many parish populations 'depended ultimately for their survival, not on their employers, but on either the poor law authorities, or the charitable, and very often on both . . . the new dependence was seized on as a form of social control which assumed an unprecedented significance' (Wells 1979: 123). Control over the rural poor by church, squirearchy and farmers was therefore cemented.

The growth of population in the South East during the eighteenth century and through to the 1840s also helped to deprive the rural poor of any wage bargaining power. One of Malthus's great 'preventative checks' was also waning, for the threat of disease and plague had much abated, although influenza, typhus and typhoid continued to afflict some communities. In the 1670s and 1680s influenza hit both urban and rural areas with great force, with 1678–81 particularly bad in the South East. Weather conditions, malnutrition and overcrowding contributed to localized epidemics, particularly in the towns, which became only slowly more healthy as the eighteenth century progressed. But the region was spared from major famines at this time or from typhus epidemics; smallpox was controlled by inoculation fairly early on; while the squalor of the industrializing northern towns was absent. Severely malnourished communities were not common in the South East (Dobson 1987: 25).

But in the face of this eighteenth-century population growth the carrying capacity of the south-eastern countryside was being cut back. Increasing privatization of the land resources; a concern with external trade with London; depression in rural industry and economies of labour use in agriculture; and an increasing gulf between rich and poor brought social conflict to the surface on more than one occasion. Thus:

> In parts of the south and east two separate worlds faced each other, the one trying to impose its view of the countryside, justice and history on the other (Jones 1981: 569).

Although population growth was relatively slow between 1660 and about 1720, thereafter it began to increase. But in the Weald even the pre-1720 population was being maintained by a reduced industrial base. Thereafter came increased tension as small farmers faced escalating poor rates; as underemployment and unemployment rose, especially as discharged servicemen joined the workforce after 1815; and as the humiliations of the Speenhamland system of poor relief came more to be felt. The Weald was a powder keg, or as one seventeenth-century observer put it 'a dark country which is the receptacle of all schism and rebellion' (in Coleman 1951).By the 1830s the Weald surely had one of the highest proportions of paupers in the country.

The last great overt protest came in the 1830s as a regional movement of the utmost significance. This began with the 'Captain Swing' unrest, and was followed by a short-lived agricultural unionism during the mid-1830s, side by side with covert protests of all kinds; culminating in 1838 in the last rising of agricultural labour at Bossenden Wood, among the smugglers, woodcutters, poachers and small farmers of the Blean. The protests took various forms, and the objectives differed from place to place. In the highly productive rural capitalism of north and east Kent, machinery, mostly the hated threshing machine, was attacked. In mid-Kent, the Weald and parts of the South Downs, the riots were mainly to demand a fair and living wage, and frequently took the form of mass protest against the poor law officials or threatening letters to employers. In the far western coastal plain the protests were a mixture of machinery attacks and wage riots (Charlesworth 1983: 131–63; Reay 1988) (Fig. 5.2).

The greatest concentration of 'Swing' activity was undoubtedly in

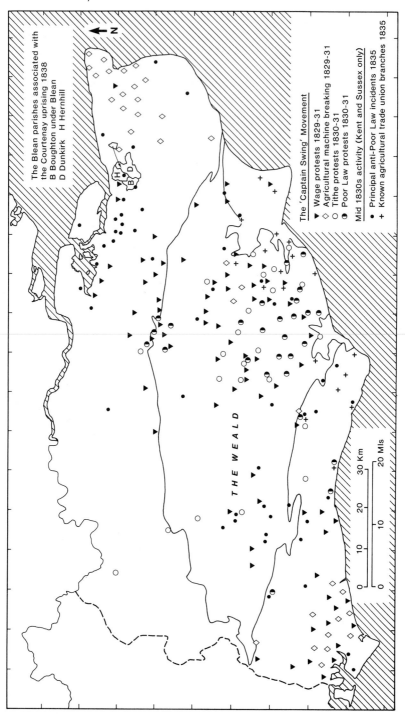

The Blean parishes associated with the Courtenay uprising 1838
B Boughton under Blean
D Dunkirk   H Hernhill

The 'Captain Swing' Movement

▶ Wage protests 1829-31
◇ Agricultural machine breaking 1829-31
○ Tithe protests 1830-31
◐ Poor Law protests 1830-31

Mid 1830s activity (Kent and Sussex only)

• Principal anti-Poor Law incidents 1835
+ Known agricultural trade union branches 1835

THE WEALD

Figure 5.2   Rural protest in south-east England in the 1830s.

the Weald, where overt protest, albeit somewhat inchoate, was again both necessary and possible: necessary because of the desperate unemployment situation there, and possible because there was frequently no great landowner who might spy on the protagonists and eject them from job *and* home simultaneously for the threat they represented to his authority. There were relatively few examples of the 'Swing' movement on the Downland therefore, compared with the Weald (Fig. 5.2). The movement began at Lower Hardres in east Kent in late-summer 1830 with both individual and collective protests against machinery; it moved quickly into the eastern Weald around Brede; and then spread across much of south-central England during November and December, before losing momentum. A secondary outbreak again saw east Kent as the scene of machine-breaking, fires and wage riots in summer 1831. The causes of such unrest were numerous and partly place-specific, but poverty was the backbone. Allied to this was the supposed role of catalysts such as Cobbett with inflammatory speeches, the presence of village radicals, and the possibility of meeting in the newly-opened beershops. News of riot spread along the main roads, especially the London roads, while the 'open' wealden parishes were larger, more egalitarian, contained more artisans, and had a long radical tradition in matters both spiritual and political. Many of these settlements (see pp. 319–22) were precisely those growing up loosely along the roadsides where news might arrive quickly. It is not surprising that the object of collective protest in the Weald was frequently the parson, rather than the major landowner. There were anyway fewer of the latter in the Weald, and the radical nonconformity of wealden chapel-goers would easily be channelled into anti-clerical protests, as they had been indeed in the same area in the sixteenth century. Indeed, dissenting ministers might act as spokesman for the people.

The protests are best understood perhaps, as the culmination of many difficult years; as the result of fear of unemployment; and as an expression of unease at the growing social polarity between rich and poor in the South East. Overt protest was possible in 'open' communities, and this certainly helps to explain the wealden concentration, but the action began outside the Weald in the Kentish Coastal Fringe, and the Bognor area also saw much rioting. Clearly the received conditions into which the riots spread may have influenced their success and extent, but there were conditions and changes which were perceived by the rural work-force all over the South East to be detrimental to their interests, and which finally sparked this last conservative effort (Hobsbawm and Rudé 1973; Charlesworth 1979).

Gardens and Landscape Parks

Its perceived beauty, comfort and accessibility has long made the South East a refuge. For this reason, designed landscapes, whether the ordered geometry of knots, parterres, gravel walks and topiary of the French and so-called Dutch styles, or the grandiloquent contoured lawns of Lancelot Brown have been celebrated elements in the regional character. Few early styles of gardening survive, and Walpole's prediction that the Brownian landscape would sweep across entire English countrysides, obliterating everything designed earlier, has been amply fulfilled (Walpole 1826-8, iv: 278–9). So all-pervading was the remodelling that mansions and their associated parklands and other ornamentations stamp a particular character on whole localities, and have transformed people's perception of them.

This creation of idealized eighteenth-century landscape was a more important process of change in the region than the contemporary improvements centred around the enclosure of agricultural land, which in the South East had been largely completed long before. Evidence of the great imparking movement survives in the remains of some two hundred pleasure grounds in Kent, with more than double that for each of the two counties of Sussex and Surrey, reflecting the remarkable development of large parks and freely-planted estates on the main London turnpikes. Although most of these versions of 'improved' landscape are now lost on account of their being built over or suffering from road construction, split ownership, agricultural use or sheer neglect, sufficient survives to give a semblance of the 'vast, created landscape, natural enough to our eyes, but in reality managed as much for picturesque appearances as for economic returns' (Hussey 1967 edn: 129).

Several inter-related factors help to explain the widespread diffusion of designed landscapes across the South East. The scenery provided variety and intricacy. In particular, the gently rolling contours, soft outlines, panoramic vistas, woodland and streamlets, together with the mild climate, lent themselves perfectly to the accomplishment of the Brownian ideal based on the Hogarthian serpentine 'line of beauty', and his three-dimensional curving line, winding and waving at the same time, the 'line of grace'. So minimal were the necessary alterations at many sites for this improved version of nature that Repton remarked of landscape art in Sussex as being 'only a question of whether you do not spoil nature's work' (Repton 1803, ii: 192). The soils have also been favourable to landscape gardening; the light sandy silts of the Lower Greensand providing a natural nursery for plants, as John Evelyn discovered at Wotton in the later seventeenth century, while the rank clays have always been associated with vigorous tree growth (Aubrey 1718–19: i). Moreover, South East England has always attracted an unusual number of wealthy and retired persons with the means to embellish their property according to prevailing tastes, whether established grandees who were Brown's clients, the *nouveaux riches* who tended to supplant them from the end of the eighteenth century, or the squirearchy and clergy who remodelled their grounds as enthusiastic amateurs. Another powerful factor in its pre-eminence in landscape design was its accessibility to London and the Court, and to the royal palaces of Hampton Court, Richmond, and later, Kew.

This town and country inter-relationship also affected the spatial diffusion of designed landscapes in the region. In considering a simple diffusion model, the roles of influential inventive individuals and of their imitators possessed of less originality need to be borne in mind, together with such factors as accessibility and site quality. Newton noted that the process of 'infection' involves three types of person; the original creative individual, from whom the idea is caught by second-rank artists who propagate it with a varying degree of inspiration among remaining adopters. The progress of a particular landscaping taste is influenced by such factors as income levels among the circle of imitators, distance from the radiating point and the strength of the original aesthetic impulse (Newton 1950: 140–5). Broadly speaking, it is possible to identify districts which may be termed 'source regions' of aesthetic innovation in which we can detect something of the interplay of mind upon mind. These were the sources of new and influential ideas on English landscape gardening which diffused to 'unimproved' districts, the choice of which was influenced by changing visual preferences in scenery as well as by economic and social factors such as lower land prices.

The first phase: the formal garden

The regional response to the new art form of the Renaissance garden is best seen at Hampton Court, which had been the source of its English inspiration. On a 2,000-acre site walled with red brick, two large deer parks and a great complex of gardens developed, incorporating such medieval features as mounts, walks, fountains, knots, topiary and arbours, all explicitly integrated into an architectural composition (Evelyn 1906 edn, ii: 188; iii: 267). Its creator, Henry VIII, also developed similar, if smaller, retreat gardens at Whitehall, Nonsuch and Oatlands. These Tudor gardens were the product of stylistic communication with France, including Francis I's Fontainebleau which, in turn, responded to impulses from Renaissance Italy. Examples of courtiers' mansions and gardens strongly influenced by the same movement include Richard Weston's at Sutton Place, the Boleyns' at Hever, the Sydneys' at Penshurst and the Sackvilles' at Knole. At Roydon Hall, a Tudor gazebo survives, and both here and at Hales Place are Tudor garden walls with octagonal turrets (Strong 1979).

The reign of James I had been marked by a new impetus in English garden design attributable to the arrival in England of Solomon de Caus, a French hydraulic engineer. Renaissance styles were given to Somerset House,

Greenwich and Richmond Palaces by means of elaborate fountains and grottoes and a more rigid geometry of parterres and avenues, replacing more haphazard medieval arrangements by a design conceived as a whole and architecturally related to the house. A still further Italianate advance was taken by the first 'English Palladio', Inigo Jones in the 1630s. He inspired gardens such as those at Wimbledon house, owned by the Cecils; Ham House, Twickenham Park, and a modernized Oatlands, home of Queen Henrietta Maria, which was gardened in a most avant-garde manner by the Tradescants. The landscaping of the 1630s at the Earl of Arundel's favourite country retreat of Albury in the Tillingbourne valley has been captured by Wenceslaus Hollar's etchings. A generation later the young John Evelyn, fresh from the Grand Tour, laid out with his brother's and nephew's aid a grand Italianate garden at Wotton, which still partly survives; and about 1670 reshaped Albury with magnificent stepped terraces, a canal, and formal avenues of Spanish chestnuts. This remains the finest survival of the region's formal gardens but even so its present aspect gives little idea of Evelyn's idea of Eden because of the devastation of many of the original features of his garden (Hunt 1986: 145–53).

Meanwhile, under the influence of Versailles, the diarist John Evelyn visited Hampton Court, but found far more delight in the smaller gardens attached to the newly-built courtiers' mansions such as Ham House:

> ... inferior to few of the best villas in Italy itself; the house furnished like a great prince's; the parterres, flower-gardens, orangeries, groves, avenues, courts, statues, perspectives, fountains, aviaries, and all this at the banks of the sweetest river in the world ... (Evelyn 1906 edn, iii: 18).

The influence of such gardens on the region's landed proprietors can be readily illustrated by reference to central and east Kent, with its wealthy squires and gentry. Nearly every parish church in the lower Medway valley, for example, is flanked by its Court lodge, rebuilt in brick and stone pediment in the late seventeenth and early eighteenth centuries when timber houses were disparaged. In Surrey Defoe noted that: 'The ten miles from Guildford to Leatherhead make one continual line of gentlemen's houses ... and their parks and gardens almost touching one another' (Defoe 1738 edn, repr 1927: 146). At Chilham Castle, remnants of formal parterres are still evident, and aerial photography elsewhere is bringing to light whole skeletal formal gardens overlain by naturalistic gardens in the second half of the eighteenth century, as at Chevening or Petworth (Plate 5.4) (Ogden and Ogden 1955).

Many of the evergreen plants required for the parterres and flowering 'wildernesses' of these formal gardens were cultivated and distributed from specialist nurseries in Thames-side Surrey and Middlesex. Perhaps as Sir William Temple noted they flourished there partly because of the 'heat-island' created by the extra warmth of the city fires. Certainly the purer air to the west of London would have been beneficial to horticulture. The Tradescant

Plate 5.4 An early eighteenth-century formal garden in Kent. The drawing is of Sir Arnold Braems's Bridge Place, near Canterbury, by artist–traveller Willem Schellinks (*c.*1661). The artist was a guest of Sir Arnold, a merchant of Flemish extraction living sumptuously in the style of an English country gentleman and patron of the arts. Bridge Place was then an old manor house with its own deer park, woodland, fish ponds, vineyard, orchards and pleasure grounds. The drawing shows part of Braems's garden, seen through an archway covered in vines. On the left, a fountain pours water into a circular pool. In the foreground, a formal garden of wide pathways edged with low stone walls, and behind, hedges of dark box, with plants in beds between, and cypresses placed at intervals. Across the back of the garden, topiary runs into a pavilion with a pillared entrance (Van der Hem Atlas of the National Library of Vienna; Journal of the Walpole Society, Vol. 35 1954–6, xviii–xix, 19).

nurseries at Lambeth were the most famous, being full of exotic plants from Africa, Asia and the Americas which they themselves brought back from their voyages of plant discovery. Many of their plants originated in Virginia where they had invested in land. Less important botanically, though even more important in terms of landscape, were the great nurseries established by Henry Wise and George London, the last of the great formalists, at Brompton which supplied plants to almost all the great southern houses. But most influential of all nurseries were the woods which John Evelyn planted at Wotton which were the subject of *Sylva* (1664), the first work published by order of the Royal Society, which successfully achieved its object of the rehabilitation of England's forests following the dangerous depletion of timber after the Civil War.

Evelyn's love of gardening and tree-planting was further developed at Wotton by his heir, Sir John Evelyn, who re-embellished the whole estate in an early-eighteenth-century version of Stephen Switzer's 'rural, extensive and forest gardening', a transitional, more flexible, form of landscape design between the formal and the succeeding naturalistic gardens. Here the controlling features were long avenues of fir between plantations of deciduous trees aiming at the distant South Downs, seen in the immense view from the summit of Leith Hill, a landmark on his estate (Christ Church Mss). Stansted, Sussex was another example of a vast geometrical exercise in forest gardening covering hundreds of acres with long avenues of magnificent beeches cut through woods bounding the sea. Their beauty *c.*1770 recalled to Walpole that the new mood in landscape under Kent and Brown seemed to 'have pushed too far', but he loved the 'noble air' of great avenues cutting through woods before entering the park, recalling to him 'such exact pictures of Claude Lorrain that is difficult to conceive that he did not paint them from this very spot'. Walpole's observations are a reminder that it was not only Brown's idealized landscapes that recalled to Georgians the landscapes of the Roman Campagna (Walpole 1826–8, iv: 271–2).

The second phase: the advent of landscape parks and ornamental farms

The first south-eastern landscape to become imbued with the romantic design movement was the Thames riverside between Chiswick and Windsor, where the first out-of-town mansions and gardens were built not only to take advantage of the perceived delights of a rural setting within easy reach of London, likened in beauty to Tempe itself, but because of the practical advantages of river transport. When William Gilpin rowed down the Thames between Windsor and London in 1746 he found handsome houses and delightful gardens, gilt barges, pleasure boats, sailing vessels and new bridges (V. & A. Mus. Mss H34). Seen through early eighteenth-century eyes these reaches of the Thames were England's Brenta or Tiber, perfectly suited for the idealization of newly-discovered pictorial qualities in landscape, and also answering to classical images of peaceful rural refuge from a latter-day Rome. From the seventeenth century, Twickenham increasingly became desirable, and by the early eighteenth century it was a fashionable riverside village and artistic and literary colony (Plate 5.5). Here the Augustan poet, Alexander Pope lived between 1719 and 1744, extolling gardening and rural self-sufficiency, the virtues of country existence and Nature's laws. His garden became famous for informal landscaping; and his grotto and Palladian villa – 'my Tusculum' he called it – publicized new interests in gardens which appeared natural, looked picturesque and had variety and contrast (Mack 1985: 358–87; 1969).

This wealthy riverside experienced an astounding creativity in gardening up to the 1730s which made it a primary 'source region' of new and influential ideas on English art and landscape. Here dwelt Lord Burlington, whose Palladian Chiswick House helped to establish the new style in England generally, as well as possessing the first serpentined river. There were also promoters of the new English landscape style such as Stephen Switzer, Batty Langley, John James, William Kent, Richard Morris, architects and landscapists; and the Duke of Argyll whose Whitton arboretum was one of the earliest collections of exotic trees. These world-famous innovations in design ended chronologically with Horace Walpole's Strawberry Hill, which became as important a model for the Gothic style as Burlington's Chiswick had earlier been for Palladian architecture (Brandon 1979: 171–2).

By the 1720s, however, there was already some spread of landscaping from the riverside towards the far edge of the Thames Valley and beyond, a trend probably accelerated by the land shortages reported by Walpole at the time. The earliest spread of 'improvement' was to the bordering heaths at places such as Esher and Cobham. Here two great estates were in contrasting mood; the Duke of Newcastle's Claremont radiated Claudesque scenery under Kent's, and later Brown's direction: while William Hamilton's Pains Hill, Cobham, included similar scenes but also was the origin of the 'savage garden', a forerunner of the nineteenth-century 'wild garden' (Plate 5.6).

By the middle of the eighteenth century the innovation of designed landscapes had spread still further outwards from London. One of the first of these re-modelled districts was the Vale of Mickleham in the Mole Gap between Leatherhead and Dorking, which was transformed from bare rabbit and sheepwalk as soon as the new Worthing turnpike reached the district in 1755. A quite different art form resulted from Philip Southcote's experiments with *ferme ornée* at Woburn farm near Chertsey. This was a farm-like way of gardening on a small property which, conceived on the principle of beauty in use, and being cheaper and more practical than a landscaped park, was to set precedents over much of the farmland of the South East with the coming of improved transport from the end of the eighteenth century. The stress on the free planting of trees around fields imparted a park-like appearance to farmland which rivalled in scenic charm the more contrived landscapes in the parks proper.

Plate 5.5 Peter Tilleman's view of the Twickenham waterside *c.*1717. The gleaming Thames winds in an exaggerated serpentine form through a grand vista of elegant Georgian waterside, a sign of the persistent westwards expansion of London. The white building is the Countess of Suffolk's newly-built Marble Hill House. Just beyond is Secretary Johnston's house with its new octagon room. Just behind are the two new speculative apartments in Montpelier Row with Montpelier chapel between the two. A glimpse of Pope's villa is caught in the distance. In the foreground is Cambridge House and Twickenham Park (both since demolished). In 1896 this view became the first protected landscape in Britain when the local councils combined to purchase land which was threatened with speculative development.

Plate 5.6 William Hamilton's landscape at Painshill, Cobham. This eighteenth-century painting reveals Hamilton's skilfully-designed landscape garden, evoking a series of moods and sensations by means of sudden changes of scenery, interspersed with architectural features. The whole garden was presented as a series of living pictures to be viewed as if one was walking around an art gallery, pausing at each painting (Forge 1986: 15).

The third phase: the natural landscape park

From the 1750s more of the South East was being brought within easy travelling distance of London by the new turnpikes and the new Thames bridges (253–9). At this time vast landscape parks in the Brownian manner were beginning to transform the landscape with their ideal of the natural English garden.

One of Brown's largest projects was Petworth, chosen by Horace Walpole in his treatise on gardening *c.*1770 as an excellent example of what English landscape was becoming, and perhaps the most perfectly preserved of all Brown's work. As Brown intended in 1751, deer come right to the windows of Petworth House across smooth lawns spreading over the site of once formal gardens. The park is diversified with Brown's famous artificial knolls, contoured and crowned with large circular clumps of beech. The third Lord Egremont (Plate 5.7) was the leading patron of Turner whose dramatic exaggerations of the park are among his masterpieces. Another of Brown's finest essays in English Palladianism was in 1769 at Claremont House, Surrey, for Lord Clive. The mansion was placed on an artificial mound in the centre of a large landscaped park, of which only the small portion around the lake now survives intact (Stroud 1974).

245

Plate 5.7 George O'Brien Wyndham, third Earl of Egremont. According to his great admirer, the Rev. Arthur Young, Lord Egremont conducted his Petworth estates 'upon a great scale, in the highest style of improvement' (Young 1813: 17). He was said to represent 'everything solid, liberal, rich and English' (Armstrong, J. R. 1978: 114). He financed the Rother Navigation as well as promoting agriculture by encouraging mechanisation, better husbandry and cultivation practices. J. M. W. Turner was resident, Capability Brown landscaped the park, and huge entertainments were hosted on great occasions. Such a 'Renaissance man' did not, however, fail to 'shovel out paupers' from his estates in the 1830s.

246

The later remade districts were still further afield, reflecting the deficiencies of roads before the new thoroughfares between London and the south coast were constructed, and also changing visual preferences for the Picturesque with its attraction for the intricate, wooded, country of the High Weald or the sandy heaths of west Surrey. Repton became the chief practitioner of the Picturesque from the late eighteenth century, and Bayham Abbey and Cobham Hall are his best surviving landscapes. In the 1820s landscaping spread ever further from London along the Brighton, Worthing, Portsmouth and Hastings turnpikes, accelerated by the industrialist *nouveaux riches* and the facility by which naturally beautiful landscape could be 'improved' with a minimum of expense. The distribution of designed landscapes and parks and villa grounds by 1820 was closely related to the turnpikes (Fig. 5.3). This strongly suggests that the carriage wheels of the new gentry pressed hard on the heels of the roadmakers. This roadside development of landscaped parks and *fermes ornées* was to be one of the first signs of the marked 'metropolitan' characteristics which the landscape of the South East was still further to acquire with the provision of railways (Brandon 1979: 174–6).

Turnpike Roads and Canals

Although the region lay athwart two of the busiest routes in the whole of England: from London to Dover and to Portsmouth, it nevertheless had little effective internal communication until after *c*.1750. One problem was the topography. On the drier ridges early road conditions were relatively favourable. Ogilby's *Britannia* (1675) described Watling Street between London and Dover as 'In general a very good and well beaten way, chiefly chalky and gravelly'. Yet in wet weather the deepest clay ways were impassable by horse, yet alone carriages or wagons, as Cobbett found at Ewhurst, Surrey (1930 edn, I: 198). Linking by-roads running down the chalk escarpments or the greensand uplands were hollowed out into deeply-rutted tracks along which the saddle-horse was normally the only practicable means of transport. Horse-riders often abandoned roads for a course over farmland. The atrocious roads near Epsom and Tunbridge Wells emptied the spas of their visitors in autumn. Regular carrier services were interrupted in winter, and thus many farmers were deprived of access to market towns.

Travel therefore demanded fortitude and patience, and was undertaken with a sense of adventure and foreboding. Walpole wrote in 1749:

> If you love good roads, good inns, plenty of postillions and horses, be so kind as never to go into Sussex. We thought ourselves in the northest part of England; the whole country has a Saxon air and the inhabitants as savage as if King George the Second was the first monarch of the East Angles. I have set up my staff and

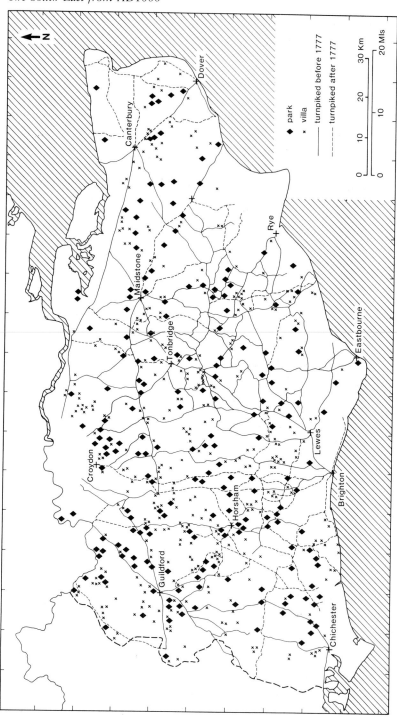

Figure 5.3 Gardens, parks and turnpike roads.

finished my pilgrimage for this year. Sussex is a great damper of
curiosity . . . (Walpole 1906 edn, ii: 178).

Three years later he had a terrifying experience descending Silver Hill
from a visit to Bayham Abbey, 'The roads grew bad beyond all badness, the
night dark beyond all darkness, our guide frightened beyond all fright-
fulness . . .' (Walpole 1906 edn, ii: 178).

By the mid-eighteenth century economic and social development called
for better communications, especially between London and the coast. Lack
of good roads prevented farmers from optimizing land use, and although the
wealthy had become travellers, their carriage-wheels found few smooth, hard
surfaces. Defoe noted in 1727 how corn in the Low Weald was 'cheap at
the barn because it cannot be carry'd out, and dear at the market because
it cannot be brought in'. The rise of Brighton and the other seaside towns
generated new roadmaking, as did the migration of newcomers, searching
for country houses and parks accessible to London. To this end, the various
turnpike trusts competed to provide the best surfaces, easiest gradients and
routes which were most direct and best provided with hostelries. By 1820
the best road system in Europe had been created, as noted by Byron, speeding
along the new turnpikes in north Kent after his long stay abroad:

> On, on! through meadows managed like a garden,
> A paradise of hops and high production.

He was sampling smooth coaching roads along which stages could reach
12 miles per hour! The inns at the Borough, Southwark, became packed
with carriers and their wagons making regular journeys from all over the
South East, creating the noisy scenes commemorated by Dickens (Fig. 5.3).

In Kent the first turnpike act was passed in 1709 for the improvement
of access to the Tunbridge Wells spa. By mid-century the Dover road had
been greatly improved and coaching inns such as the Royal Victoria and Bull
at Dartford, or the Rose at Sittingbourne, were thriving. By the end of the
century trusts were constructing roads with hard, rolled stone surfaces in the
manner of Telford and Macadam; and by 1837 there were 50 Kentish trusts
responsible for over 650 miles of turnpiking.

Surrey changes were even more dramatic. The dearth of roads was
replaced within a century by a virtually new system of direct trunk routes to
London and a close network of cross-country connections. The first stretch
improved was the ten miles between Reigate and Crawley authorized in 1696
as a saddle-horse road, although not upgraded for carriages until 1755. In
1820 the gradient of Reigate Hill was lowered by piercing the sand ridge at
Reigate, and instituting a more direct route between Sidlow Bridge and Povey
Cross. Other coaching roads ran through Surrey towards Brighton, such as an
alternative to the old way via Godstone, by the Epsom, Dorking and Horsham
turnpike opened through the Vale of Mickleham in 1755, and later improved
by abandoning the hilly Dorking–Coldharbour stretch in favour of the fine,

fast route over Holmwood (the present A24). The main alteration to the Portsmouth road was between Thursley and Hindhead in 1826, leaving the old track still evident near Thursley church. Another major new road was built under Acts of 1755–8 between Epsom and Guildford, running directly across fields and leaving the springline villages connected by the superseded loops of the old road. Its continuation to Farnham resulted in the 1758 abandonment of the steep grass-grown track, 'The Mount'.

In Sussex, successive improvements to the Brighton road opened up the Interior to full exploitation. Between the first Sussex turnpike in 1749 and the 1841 London–Brighton railway, the hub of the road network was Brighton, but each of the other resorts was eventually similarly served. The first of the new coach roads to Brighton was constructed through Cuckfield (the present B2036). In 1810 this was superseded by a shorter cut from Pyecombe to Bolney, avoiding Clayton Hill, the first successful crossing of the Weald Clay. The mail coach service was thereby speeded up, especially after the opening of the Reigate tunnel, but the fact that no regular mail coach service operated to Hastings before 1821 indicates the difficulty of extending coach travel.

Profound changes were wrought through the turnpikes. In districts well served by the roads agricultural rents escalated and under the impetus of late-eighteenth-century rising corn prices the Weald became a poor arable-farming area except on the remaining commons. In 1755 when the Horsham–Dorking driftway was turnpiked, rents rose from 7s to 11s per acre (Fuller 1953: 41). Fast coaches were important for the exuberant rise of resorts, and by the 1820s the fastest public coaches reached Brighton from London in less than five hours. It was even possible, as Cobbett noted with disgust, for 'dark, dirty-faced, half-whiskered tax-eaters' to commute from Brighton to London (1930 edn, I: 149). Country houses came within two or three hours of London and the new gentry spread out of the capital seeking 'improvable estates'. As early as 1825 Cobbett distinguished between the unselfconscious face of traditional wealden farming landscapes and the 'artificial' landscapes of the *nouveaux riches*. A day's journey across Surrey led him to conclude that tradition survived only along the rutted hollow-ways, unusable for carriages. Beside the London highroads the newcomers were expelling the yeomanry and rearranging landscapes for their own delight, activities associated in Cobbett's mind with the topsy-turveydom created by the repulsive eruption of the Great Wen:

> Those who travel on turnpike roads know nothing of England – from Hascombe to Thursley almost the whole way across fields or commons, or along narrow lanes. Here we see the people without any disguise or affectation. Against a *great road* things are made for *show* (1930 edn, i: 288).

The economic effects of turnpikes, however, should not be over-rated. Owing to the appalling local roads (by 1837 only 22 per cent of roads in

Sussex were turnpiked, for example) the land was still only half-cultivated owing to the expense of the carriage of lime, and neither could the excellent timber be exported. Farmers were also disadvantaged since wheat from the Dorking–Horsham area, for example, fetched lower prices at Horsham than at Guildford because Horsham had no water carriage, and fat steers walking to Smithfield in the traditional way lost 3–4 per cent in weight during the journey. The frequency of toll gates on the turnpikes also made carriage of bulky goods expensive (Malcolm 1805, I: 124).

It therefore became the avowed aim of improvers and canal-builders to provide for agriculture by bringing corn to market and carrying lime and other manures for farming. The 1791 Act authorizing the improvement of the Western Rother to Midhurst, and the prospectus for the Chichester canal (1817), expressly declared this as an aim. Another consideration was the strategic value of artificial waterways, as seen in the stillborn plans to link Portsmouth and London by the Grand Southern Canal, by-passing the North Foreland sea route, then prey to enemy shipping as well as storms. The Medway navigation had struck problems of viability in the late seventeenth century but thereafter in 1732 the Arun was improved to Arundel involving a direct cut to the sea at Littlehampton; and successive schemes embraced the Western Rother (1791), the Royal Military canal between Hythe and Winchelsea (1804), the Adur (1806), Ouse (1812), the Wey and Arun canal (1813), the Chichester and the Arundel and Portsmouth canals (1823). The third Earl of Egremont was particularly identified with such projects, and indeed with agricultural improvement in general. He personally financed the Rother navigation to serve his Petworth estate; and projected the west Sussex canals.

As Cobbett observed the canals had a brief heyday, and the restoration of peace in 1815 removed the immediate need for an inland water-route to London. From 1840 railways steadily sapped canal trade, as they did also that of the turnpikes, and one after the other they closed, leaving only the Chichester canal active by the 1870s. Imposing monuments of the old waterways include the Hardham tunnel, built in 1790 to avoid the wide meander of the Arun near Pulborough; and the Orfold aqueduct, which has partially collapsed, that took barges to Guildford and northwards to the Thames (Vine 1965; 1972).

Urban Change, 1660–1837: the Growth of South London

The expansion of Coastal Fringe towns, especially the seaside resorts, and the continuing growth of London were the key elements in urban growth at this time, and over much of the South East this expansion and rebuilding has left us with a pleasing Georgian legacy, from south London's busy streets to the peace of Chichester. Few towns offered industrial employment, which took second place to agricultural or urban service provision. The South East was now departing radically from the North and Midlands in terms of employment and industrial structures. By 1800 there were very few steam engines installed in the South East outside London; textiles employment had virtually finished by the 1830s; and there were no significant chemical works, engineering or heavy industries. Conversely the proportion of people in professional, domestic and personal services in Surrey and Sussex was only bettered by London and Middlesex. London's influence was, of course, paramount. By 1700 London handled 80 per cent of England's imports and 69 per cent of her exports. More members of the Stock Exchange, formally established in 1802, lived in the South East than in any other region, but provincial landed wealth was also drawn into the new houses and squares, especially to the west and north of the river. Defoe noted that London 'sucks the vitals of trade in the island to itself' (in Rudé 1971: 30). Its power was tightening on the region, and more city men, commuters, and London emigrés moved into the areas south of London as the eighteenth century progressed. And the villages beyond, with their own identities, were being fused into a common culture as London 'acted as a powerful solvent of the customs, prejudices and modes of action of traditional, rural England' (Wrigley 1967: 50). It is therefore appropriate to begin with the growth of what Raymond Williams has called the 'contradictory reality' of south London with its intense contrasts of wealth and poverty (Williams 1975: 179).

South London 1660–1837

After the Restoration the topographical development of London, the largest city in Europe, can be more accurately traced than hitherto because of the rise of mapping and surveying. William Morgan's *London Survey'd* (1681) went through several editions before John Rocque's detailed maps were published in 1746. The latter covered south London from Deptford to Lambeth and as far south as Walworth Common (Fig. 5.4 and Plate 5.8).

By the mid-eighteenth century the Ravensbourne still separated Greenwich from Deptford, and the penny toll across Deptford Creek still provided a barrier to movement. But the Deptford and Rotherhithe waterfronts were a near-continuous line of activity. Here were the Greenland Stairs, the Upper Wet Dock, and many victualling office warehouses. Timber yards, wharves and shipwrights' yards reached into Bermondsey where packed tenements jostled with St Saviour's Dock, tenter grounds, leather-dressers and tanners. By 1805 there were as many as 1,570 tanners in Surrey, most of whom probably worked around Bermondsey (Moore 1917: 5). To here also came the coals from Newcastle, noted by Aubrey. As the Borough was approached, the riverfront building line expanded southwards along the High Street from London Bridge in a maze of alleys, yards and tenements, more tenter grounds and some larger foundations such as St Thomas's (rebuilt as a

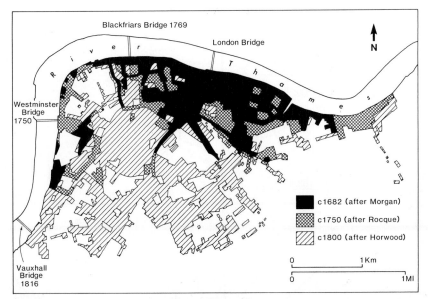

Figure 5.4   The growth of south London *c.*1680–*c.*1800.

---

hospital in 1701–6) and Guy's (opened in 1725 as a hospital for incurables) with their burying grounds. Buildings petered out as the Borough gave way to St George's Fields and Newington Butts. More wharves and timber yards stretched along the Thames towards Westminster Bridge (shown on Rocque's map but not actually open until 1750), but then gave way to open fields and gardens past Lambeth Palace and the Horse ferry (later replaced by Lambeth Bridge) as the ornamental lighting and fashionable walks of Vaux Hall Spring Gardens were approached – the south-westernmost extent of Rocque's map. Beyond this Aubrey in his 'Perambulations' between 1673 and 1692 had noted 'several handsome houses' in Wandsworth and Battersea, while Streatham was 'much frequented by the gentry and citizens of London' (Aubrey 1718–19, I: 130–5, 199).

Administratively there was confusion and corruption as London spread. The Bailiwick of Southwark was administered from the City, but its associated parishes were deemed to be in Surrey. County JPs, City Corporation and parish vestry all assumed some power. The old parish open vestries of metropolitan Surrey had been prone to disorder and corruption, and by the end of the eighteenth century many had been replaced for most purposes, by close or select vestries, dominated by 'exclusive and self-perpetuating oligarchies' (Rudé 1971: 132). Improvements such as paving, gutters, cleansing, and the numbering of houses came slowly. The number of different authorities was bewildering. At Lambeth the open vestry obtained an Act in 1810 for the administration of this rapidly-growing parish, but encountered no fewer than

Plate 5.8 South London, by John Rocque. The area encompassed by St George's Fields in the east and by the Thames to the north and west provides a glimpse into the heterogeneity of riverside South London *c.*1745. Lambeth Palace (Rocque's Lambeth House) was on a site originally acquired by Archbishop Baldwin in 1189–90, although the present building dates essentially from the mid thirteenth century. This was the most important building in a line of riverside development which also included timber yards and wharves, backed by tenter grounds and gardens, and through which threaded old walks and new turnpikes, such as that leading to the newly-built Westminster Bridge. Lambeth Marsh was an area of open fields, pasture and haunt for game before its enclosure in 1806 to facilitate the building of roads for the new Waterloo Bridge. At the corner of St George's Fields lay the notorious Dog and Duck, later the site of the Bethlehem Hospital. Between 1801 and 1831 the population of Lambeth and Vauxhall more than trebled, and by the middle of the nineteenth century this area was densely developed, with Waterloo Station occupying the area between Lambeth Marsh and College Street.

nine separate trusts dealing with lighting alone. There were thirteen trusts in St Mary Newington; but by contrast, the administration of Southwark ran over five parishes (Sheppard 1971: 24–30). In addition, Kent Street, the Mint and the Clink Liberty were still notorious, and between Lambeth and Rotherhithe 'loathsome ditches' still ran between the riverside and St George's Fields. In 1722 the area was described, probably by Defoe:

> These filthy places receive all the sinks, necessary houses and drains from dye houses, wash houses, fell mongers, slaughter houses and all kinds of offensive trades; they are continually full of carrion and the most odious of all offensive stench proceeds from them; also the other part of the said ditches westward as far as Lambeth, many of which lye a great depth in mud . . . the terror even of the inhabitants themselves . . . notorious fountains of stench, enough to corrupt the very air and make the people sick and faint as they pass by (in George 1925: 349).

In 1829 the Metropolitan Police Act established some semblance of law and order throughout London within a range of between four and seven miles of Charing Cross – the first step in coming to grips with the capital's expansion which had grown beyond the control of the old parochial authorities.

The opening of Westminster and Blackfriars bridges, the latter in 1769, stimulated development in Lambeth. Some older riverside slums were demolished although the replacement houses might also be wretched affairs. By 1811 the roads leading to the bridges were lined on either side with houses, and streets were being built onto St George's Fields into the area previously only occupied by the street known as Lambeth Marsh. Here the 'notorious Hedger of the Dog and Duck' had rented common land in 1789, paid a penalty of £500 for building, and built many small houses which were duly pulled down in 1811. The 'Dog and Duck', together with 'The Apollo Gardens' and 'Temple of Flora', all on St George's Fields were suppressed in the 1790s as 'notorious tea-gardens and places of amusement' – in reality centres for prostitutes and highwaymen. The social standing of the Lactarium in St George's Fields was apparently higher, with milk and syllabub being sold to discerning customers by the 1770s (George 1925: 81, 305, 349).

Growth in housebuilding and population in south London was halting and uncertain (Table 5.2). Most growth was still north of the river, or at Richmond, decently removed from London's workaday world. Indeed, the westward movement of fashionable London resulted in a redistribution affecting Southwark, such that its 1700 population of *c*.100,000 probably fell slightly by 1801. Numbers of houses fell in St Olave's in the eighteenth century, although there was still rapid growth in St George's. The number of houses further out in Surrey was clearly growing faster in the eighteenth century, possibly tripling, although from a lower base, compared with the overall doubling at Southwark. The latter's insalubrity was certainly not helped by the three water companies serving the area, who took their water direct from the Thames between Vauxhall and Southwark, and supplied a small amount of dilute sewage to households with a minimal amount of filtration. The Southwark area also contained perhaps 30,000 people with no supply at all, while many others drank water polluted by the industries

of the Wandle or Ravensbourne. Squalor and cholera were never far away in houses nestling among tanning, soap, candle, glue-making and fell-mongering workshops. Typhus raged through St George's and the Borough in 1817–18, assisted by the congregation of filth which accumulated too quickly even for the assiduous 'nightmen' to collect and dispatch by barge to the farmers and market gardeners of Kent and Surrey. And in 1832 (as again in 1848) the great London cholera epidemic first reached the capital at Rotherhithe, spreading through Southwark to Lambeth and other riverside areas (Plate 5.9).

The industrial character of the riverside was continued southwards along the Wandle. Here by 1805 there were no fewer than 38 factories for calico printing, bleaching, flour-milling and snuff manufacture along 12 miles of its length. During the early eighteenth century James Cranmer (Sr) was leasing ground near Mitcham containing 'colouring mills and whiteing ground'. His leases also mention copper mills, the grinding of dye-wood, and the manufacturing of oil (SRO, Acc 857). There were potters at Lambeth, including the Doulton works, while Coade stone, used for pottery and statuary, was manufactured on the site later used for the Festival of Britain exhibition of 1951. Innumerable breweries and distilleries included the well-known Beaufoys South Lambeth vinegar factory and the great Barclay, Perkins brewery, established at Southwark by 1814. London's engineering industry was also centred on Lambeth and Southwark. John Rennie, designer of Southwark, Waterloo and London bridges, had a works here; as did Joseph Bramah, the inventor of lock systems and the water closet; and Henry Maudesley, inventor of the hydraulic process, from *c*.1810. Cheap space and good transport links were important to those concerns, at a time before proximity to coal and iron was so vital for engineering.

South of the river, the presence of docks, timber wharves, alleys and slums in the East, compared with the superior social attraction of Lambeth and the river towards Richmond in the West, mirrored the better-known east/west division north of the Thames. Such divisions were further enhanced by the construction of more docks. Four companies were established by 1811 to build downstream from the Lower Pool and along Limehouse Reach. The Surrey Commercial Docks, opposite the Limehouse bank, took advantage of poorly-drained, flat and undeveloped land to enhance London's long-felt need for more port accommodation. The Legal Quays had not been increased since 1665, and despite the provision of Sufferance Wharves, where certain

---

Plate 5.9 Fore Street, Lambeth. Charles Booth, writing of the South London waterfront, noted how 'Poverty clings to the water' (Booth 1902: 3v: 161). Lambeth waterfront was the scene of many crumbling buildings such as these. Fore Street led to the archbishop's palace and Horse Ferry dock, the lucrative crossing place owned by the archbishops until the 1750 opening of Westminster Bridge (Manning and Bray 1814, 3: 463, 477). The street was finally swept away by the building of Bazalgette's Albert Embankment in the later 1860s.

Table 5.2 Population growth in south London c. 1620–1801

Parish	New houses built		Number of houses				Population		Av. number per house in 1801
	1620–56	1656–77	1708	1732	1737	1801	1710–11	1801	
Borough of Southwark									
St George	144	231	740	740 +	1,503	3,964	7,500	22,293	5.8
St John	–	–	–	–	1,255	1,566	–	8,892	5.8
St Olave	147	385	c.200*	3,000	2,012	1,374	17,400	7,481	5.5
St Saviour	339	–	c.2,500	–	2,554	2,661	14,004	15,596	6.1
St Thomas	160	–	c.300	c.130	229	180	–	2,078 †	11.6
Total			c.5,540			9,735			
Surrey									
Christchurch	–	109	c.800	c.1,000	1,011	1,586	3,102	9,933	6.4
Bermondsey	528	349	c.1,500	1,900	1,111	3,203	12,000	17,169	5.4
Lambeth	383	185	c.1,350	–	1,625	5,009	–	27,939	5.8
Newington	247	107	620	700	751	2,940	–	14,847	5.1
Rotherhithe	59	219	1,145	1,500	1,320	1,796	5,502	10,296	5.7
Total			c.5,415			14,534			

* This should almost certainly be 2,000. The original figure is from Hatton, *New View of London*, 1708.
† Excluding the 429 returned for St Thomas's Hospital.

The population figures for 1710–11 are based on a multiplier of six for the number of families.

(Source: George (1925) Appendix III: 414)

materials could be landed when a customs official was available, the total accommodation was little more than that of Bristol, despite still taking in about 70 per cent of Britain's imports by 1790. The West India Port Company developed nearly 300 acres in the Isle of Dogs and the Import Dock was opened in 1802, while further development at Wapping and Blackwall established the future Port of London.

Further south, London's influence was social, economic, spiritual, but not yet expressed in bricks and mortar. A two-mile walk southwards from the Thames would bring the traveller into countryside. But here the housebuilding boom of 1816–26 brought the capital to Clapham and Camberwell along short stage coach routes over the new bridges on the turnpikes. By 1801 such Surrey parishes as Putney, Clapham, Wandsworth, Streatham and even Richmond were included in the census return for London. Within its powerful ambit, only Croydon, and to a lesser extent Woolwich and Greenwich were able to offer any independent urban life. Woolwich, Deptford and Greenwich had long been important shipbuilding centres, although the latter had relied heavily on fashion, being to Defoe 'the most beautiful spot of ground in Great Britain'. The palace, hospital, park and observatory ensured success and attracted genteel residence for businessmen and naval officers. Croydon (population 6,000 in 1801) became the largest town anywhere near London north or south of the river, and was connected between 1803 and 1846 by the Surrey Iron Railway horse tramway to Wandsworth. Croydon reached out towards Carshalton, down the Wandle towards Mitcham, and also towards Rotherhithe after the 1809 construction of the Grand Surrey Canal link to Thames-side. London's turnpikes stretched out to Kennington, Newington Butts and Camberwell, allowing commuting by stage coach. Development was greatly conditioned by these roads and Kentish London's spread was more restricted since Kent did not develop its roads as quickly as did Surrey, looking as it did more to the river.

Some suburban villages provided environments whence came highly influential ideas affecting the cultural, religious and educational life of England. The village of Clapham (population *c*.2,700 in 1790), for example, was the home of several wealthy merchants by the late eighteenth century. Samuel and Richard Thornton lived in houses inherited from their father John, who had moved from Yorkshire with firm evangelical principles, bought the advowson of Clapham and built a new church in 1776 to see these views maintained. John Venn was appointed to the living from 1792 until his death in 1813. A third brother, Henry, lived at the manor house in Battersea Rise with the abolitionist William Wilberforce. All four were MPs. Also coming to live in Clapham was Charles Grant, later a director of the East India Company and an enthusiastic advocate of missionary work in the East; and Edward Eliot, brother-in-law of William Pitt and friend of Wilberforce. Also here were James Stephen, active abolitionist and solicitor; Zachary Macauley from 1802; and Lord Teignmouth, formerly Governor-General of India and later President of the British and Foreign Bible Society. These were the wealthy and influential members of the Clapham sect, revolving around Wilberforce and the evangelical church, and making Clapham the most influential parish in the country for about twenty years. Maintaining social distinctions, yet working hard for the poor, Venn became a model for churchmen up and down the country. In 1799 he founded the Society for Bettering the Condition of the Poor, and from the group also sprang Wilberforce's successful abolition of the slave trade (1807), factory legislation, penal reform, Catholic emancipation, and the abolition of press gangs and employment of chimney boys. The Church Missionary Society was founded in 1799, and the British and Foreign Bible Society in 1804. By the year of his death Wilberforce had achieved the abolition of slavery in the West Indies (1833) and the men 'by the intensity of their religious faith and of their zeal for good works provided the foundation for Victorian morality' (Sheppard 1971: 206).

Between the towns and the smaller villages, there was still much uncultivated heath and scrub, and by the 1820s open space still prevailed around Battersea Fields or on the Greenwich Marshes, as well as in the great array of commons between Woolwich and St George's Hill, Cobham. Towns such as Dartford with its powder and paper mills, Eltham, Streatham, Wimbledon or Kingston were still physically separate from the 'Wen'. Prosperous London tradesmen's families came to live in the outermost villages such as Stockwell, Lewisham, Brixton or Herne Hill.

The extent to which London grew in relative terms in the eighteenth century has been reviewed. Her share in foreign trade declined while provincial rivals grew with the Atlantic trade in particular; and her proportion of the total population of England and Wales stayed at around 11 per cent throughout the eighteenth century. But nevertheless the number of immigrants required to maintain this growth rate at a time of continuing high urban mortality still siphoned off much natural growth from the rest of the country. Provincial centres now began to challenge London for population attraction, but not in the South East, where only Canterbury and Chatham had populations of over 5,000 in 1700. Indeed, possibly a greater proportion than ever before of London's apprentices were coming from London and the Home Counties (Corfield 1982: 66–81).

Moreover, provincial produce still poured into the capital. With a population rising from 575,000 to 900,000 from the beginning to the end of the eighteenth century (of which 14 to 15 per cent was south of the river) the capital needed prodigious supplies of food and raw materials, much of which still came from the South East, despite the opening-up of trade links with Europe and the wider world. London's horses alone required huge amounts of hay and oats. Defoe noted that London was supplied with herrings, flat fish and mackerel from the south-eastern coasts; faggots and bavins for fuel came from Shooter's Hill; while Kent also supplied bullocks, corn, timber, Faversham and Swale oysters, cherries and apples. There were also paving stones from

Kent; capons, oats and meal from Croydon; vegetables from Lambeth; corn and meal from Chichester. Much of this trade came by the 'long sea' routes and the rivers to avoid the poor, crowded roads and the Newington Butts and Borough bottlenecks. In the later eighteenth century carriage of this produce into London was facilitated by the opening of Westminster and Blackfriars bridges, by the paving of streets after 1762, and by the innumerable turnpike improvements (pp. 247–51).

London's countryside was important not only for the food it produced and the space it provided for suburban expansion. It also symbolized wealth and privilege. By the 1660s above-average affluence was noticeable in the Hearth tax payments from Richmond, Barnes and Putney (Parton 1984) while eighteenth-century prestigious retreats included those of the Earl of Chesterfield at Blackheath, the Earl of Chatham at Hayes, or Lord Bolingbroke's ancestral home at Battersea. City merchants included Sir James Bateman at Tooting and Sir Theodore Jannsen at Wimbledon (Rudé: 1971: 56). Writers and artists escaped too: Samuel Johnson to the Thrales at Streatham Park or Reynolds to Richmond Hill. Visits to Epsom, Tunbridge Wells, Dulwich, Streatham and Sydenham Wells were popular, the latter for serious water-drinkers and the 'middle sort', the former for the aristocratic and gentry diversion. Vauxhall Gardens (known as Spring Gardens until 1785) was also very popular for balls, masquerades and other outings. In 1749 100 musicians played to 12,000 people, causing a three-hour traffic jam on London Bridge. Other popular pastimes included country cricket, and visits to Greenwich Whit Monday fair, Charlton Lady Fair, or that at Camberwell Green. Greenwich Park was a favourite Sunday excursion, as were St George's Fields before the 1768 enclosure. In July 1754 *The Connoisseur* noted of 'our common people' that since 'they all aim at going into the country, nothing can be a greater misfortune to the meaner part of the inhabitants of London and Westminster than a rainy Sunday' (Rudé 1971: 95).

Change in the Provincial Towns, 1660–1837

Much of the trade of south-eastern towns was bound in with London. The market towns continued to transmit rural produce to the capital, and to receive London goods in exchange. But such towns were also intimately related to the agriculture of their hinterlands. Farnham was, according to Defoe, 'the greatest cornmarket in England, London excepted'. The smaller market towns had more than half of their traders related to agriculture, as at Cuckfield, Battle or East Grinstead, while larger towns still had more than one quarter so employed (Cowley 1964: 185). Such transfers might still take place in open market squares, but now increasingly also in private meetings between producers and specialist middlemen and dealers. Corn exchanges and retail shops nevertheless grew apace. The latter, with barrel-shaped windows and relatively fixed prices, moved the process of exchange inexorably from its older periodic momentum into its modern, continuous context in the South East; although at first, as at Guildford, the shops were used by the wealthy, while the poor continued to use the markets.

The previous changing pattern of market towns and fairs has been noted (pp. 161–7), but such changes continued through into the eighteenth century. Some towns might appear 'solid' – as did both Horsham and Petworth to Cobbett – but these two towns were already diverging in their trajectories, with the former growing and the latter stationary. Those towns which were well-located on inland communications generally thrived, and were often remodelled with Georgian architectural frontages, as the high street at Farnham indicates. The number of south-eastern market towns remained roughly static at about 58 between 1690 and 1792 (Dyer 1979: 129). However, numbers of fairs did increase between the mid-seventeenth and mid-eighteenth centuries, with cattle and sheep transactions being especially significant. Kent and Sussex were the counties most heavily endowed with fairs of all southern England by 1756, and by 1792 there were 197 fairs in 119 places in Sussex alone. After 1820 this number declined as their *economic* functions (rather than social and cultural) were taken over by shops and market towns.

Chichester and Lewes, twin county market towns of Sussex at this time, illustrate the provincial market town as well as any others in the South East. The Rev. Alexander Hay in his *History of Chichester* (1804) stated that:

> The beast market, holden every second Wednesday throughout the year invariably, for black cattle, sheep and hogs, is by much the greatest of any in this or the neighbouring counties, that of London excepted. Not only the City, but the country around for many miles is supplied from thence. To it the Portsmouth butchers regularly resort – and not seldom the carcase butchers from London attend it. It is kept in the East Street the whole of which is occupied on market days, and more than half of the North Street (in McCann 1974).

A doubling in toll income was reported over the previous ten or eleven years. Chichester's role as a postal town and centre for mail deliveries in the late eighteenth century also promoted rural contacts. Wagons also went three times a week to London, and wool was brought in from the surrounding countryside for dispatch to London and thence to the northern textile industries. There were also five annual fairs and two weekly provision markets. The Napoleonic Wars gave added impetus to corn and cattle transactions and the Chichester markets were regulated and brought under one roof in 1808.

Lewes was a flourishing market centre. Here was a September sheep fair, Whitsun and Michaelmas cattle fair, August race meeting, and numerous inns and shops. A wool fair was established in 1786, and the market place moved from the High Street to a market area in 1791. Manufacturing was also represented by five breweries by 1823; tanyards, brick kilns, chalk pits; a small iron foundry and paper mill; and all were stimulated by the canalizing of the Ouse and the enlarging of Newhaven harbour. Baxter's the printers was established by 1802 and there was a small dockyard by the late 1830s. The Tudor High Street, with its houses on medieval undercrofts, was re-fronted with Georgian façades, indicative of an underlying prosperity much enhanced by the patronage of the Duke of Newcastle before his death in 1768. Here also were the Quarter sessions, militia musters, and the county gaol. The assizes, races and fatstock show constituted a fashionable season, while intellectual life was headed by Thomas Horsfield and the 1785 Library Society. Gentry such as the Dobells, Shelleys and Gorings came to pass the winter months in fashionable town houses (Brent 1985: 8–13).

This latter aspect of provincial life was a common feature of the larger towns. At Canterbury in the 1790s Hasted noted the races:

> attended by most of the Kentish gentry and a great number of people from the neighbouring parts; and this City being their usual rendezvous, it brings a vast concourse of them to it for the time, when there are assemblies, plays and other entertainments during the whole time of the race week (in Everitt 1979: 79–108).

By the 1820s, however, this role was in decline as the London season sucked in the leading families. But minor gentry and 'pseudo-gentry' persisted at Canterbury where 'many gentlemen of fortune and genteel families reside'. The Georgian country town was varied in its scope and quality of life, with cultural, intellectual and humanitarian activities for the wealthy, and a range of service and industrial employment, at least in the larger centres.

The fastest growth of all outside London was to be found at the coast. Following the mid-seventeenth century hiatus, commercial expansion could continue, and the region's ports and harbours grew in consequence. No provincial port could flourish here to match eighteenth-century Bristol or Liverpool, since London still accounted for 43 per cent of total English (legal) tonnage in 1709 and 31 per cent in 1792. Indeed, the combined tonnage of all the other south-eastern ports (including Southampton) amounted to just 5 per cent by 1709, falling to 4.6 per cent by 1792. Not all ports grew. Sandwich, referred to by Celia Fiennes in the 1690s as a 'sad old town' had a silted harbour; while Defoe noted the decay of ports such as Dover, Winchelsea and Rye. By contrast, Chatham and the lower Medway towns prospered greatly. Late-seventeenth century investment for the Dutch Wars continued, and out of a population of more than 5,000 in Chatham by 1700 there were perhaps as many as 1,000 working in the dockyard, itself possibly the largest industrial complex in England at this time (Reed 1983: 175). During the eighteenth century the populations of Chatham and Rochester doubled. The building and servicing of ships was all-important but Rochester nevertheless guarded its traditional market rights fiercely and in the 1760s the two towns were at loggerheads over proposals for joint street lighting and paving. In the early nineteenth century Chatham's wartime importance was again underlined by the building of barracks at Fort Pitt to the south; and by 1831 only Deptford and Greenwich in Kent were larger than the 27,300 population of the two towns combined.

The development of another type of south-eastern town, the inland spa, was also dealt with earlier (pp. 160–1). In the eighteenth century such towns became a key component of the entertainment circuit for the leisured classes. The early springs and wells close to London at Dulwich, Streatham or Epsom were now considered too close to the burgeoning capital, and it was Tunbridge Wells above all which received attention. While it could not rival Georgian Bath as a social attraction, Tunbridge Wells was close to London and received fast coach and mail services. On Mount Sion and Mount Ephraim housing grew. The promenade of the Pantiles was paved in 1700 and other additions included a cold bath (1708), assembly room, two libraries and a theatre (1770). Beau Nash was Master of Ceremonies by 1732, but the town, growing among commonlands, appeared to lack cohesion. Fanny Burney, *en route* for Brighton in 1779 wrote that 'The houses too, are scattered about in a strange wild manner, and look as if they had been dropt where they stood by accident, for they form neither streets not squares, but seem strewed promiscuously' (in Corfield 1982: 60). The peak of its fortunes as a social centre was reached in the mid-eighteenth century, and thereafter it was wealthy and retired residents who dictated its tone. By 1821 its population was less than 3,000.

One reason for the relative stagnation of the inland spas after the mid-eighteenth century was the vigorous competition forthcoming from the new seaside resorts – and from Margate and Brighton in particular. Brighton's fortunes had initially slumped considerably since 1660. At that time it had been the largest town in Sussex with a population of *c*.4,000; but its fishing industry was in serious decline. Indeed, by the 1720s Defoe referred to Brighton as: 'A poor fishing town, old built . . . the sea is very unkind to the town, and has by its continual encroachments, so gain'd upon them, that in a little time more they might reasonably expect it would eat up the whole town, above a hundred houses having been devoured by the water in a few years past.'

The declining demand for fish in European diets, maritime conflict in the Channel and North Sea, and local erosion of the foreshore combined to reduce population to *c*.2,000 by 1750. To some extent an increase in coastal trading, especially in coals, filled the gap, but the lack of a harbour and inland river link restricted progress, so that vessels berthed at Shoreham rather than Brighton. Of the 453 households in the town in 1744 about 75 per cent were exempted from the poor rate through poverty.

Cheap housing, underemployment and a lack of competition for capital were all background factors therefore, when Dr Richard Russell, a Lewes physician, began to extol the virtues of seawater for medical treatment in the 1740s. Seabathing was already established at both Brighton and Margate from the 1730s, but Russell's 1750 Latin publication, translated in 1752 as *A Dissertation on the use of seawater in Diseases of the Glands*, marked a real turning point in the town's fortunes. By 1780 resort facilities had multiplied, with assembly rooms (1754 and 1761); bathing machines; a library (1760); baths (1769 onwards); a theatre and chapel (1760s and 1770s). In 1766 it was remarked that 'By the means of his [Russell's] writings in favour of seawater, it has become one of the principal places in the Kingdom for the resort of the idle and dissipated, as well as of the diseased and infirm' (*Gentleman's Magazine* 1766: 59). By 1820 the Prince of Wales's Pavilion had been built and modified to its present Oriental design, and suburbs had spread north and east across the surrounding unenclosed open fields. Strips were developed piecemeal as streets of boarding houses, but there had also been more fashionable developments, such as the unified creation of Royal Crescent (*c*.1800), facing seaward for the first time in this old fishing town. The 1801 population was *c*.7,000, rising to 24,000 by 1821, and between 1811 and 1821 Brighton exhibited the fastest growth of any English town. From the 1820s further growth went eastwards in the form of the prestigious Kemp Town estate; westwards as a series of squares and crescents into Hove, as in the Brunswick and Adelaide developments; and northwards as more artisan housing behind the elegant façades and away from the sea front.

Proximity to London and Tunbridge Wells; access to Coastal Fringe capital; a lack of competition from alternative economic ventures; together with royal patronage helped Brighton to a flying start. In 1750 the populations of Brighton and Margate had been similar at about 2,000, but by 1821 the latter had grown to only 7,800 and the gap had widened appreciably. Margate's resort facilities were slightly older than those at Brighton. By the 1760s there were bathing machines, assembly room, baths, library, theatre and a Master of Ceremonies; all following on from Thomas Barber's advertisement placed in the 17 July 1736 edition of the *Kentish Post and Canterbury News Letter* advising clients of a sea water bath with 'convenient lodgings to be lett' (Scurrell *et al.* 1986: 3–27). Lower fares on hoys, and steamboat travel after 1814 also allowed poorer families to visit Margate, and it became the first popular seaside resort in England. Eighteenth-century prosperity was indeed built around the rather unfashionable hoys, or sailing packets as they were re-named after about 1804. The journey from London took between eight and 36 hours, depending on the state of tides and weather, but was cheap at 5s–6s per adult by the 1790s compared with an overland journey of 72 hours at 16s–19s. By 1815 it still took 11 hours for the overland journey, but in that year the first London–Margate steamboat service began. By 1824 *The Times* noted that 'The introduction of steamboats has given the whole coast of Kent . . . a prodigious lift' (Whyman 1981: 123). By 1831 about 120,000 passengers travelled annually from London to Margate in seven hours or less.

Day excursions became possible, and the heyday of the steamboat was reached during the 1830s, before rail travel took precedence and allowed Brighton to grasp the initiative in cheap excursions.

Although Brighton and Margate were clearly far ahead of any rivals, there were other growing Georgian seaside towns. By 1786 Hastings had become a summer resort for 'genteel company' and had bathing machines, reception rooms and gravelled walks (*Gentleman's Magazine* 1786: 649–51). By 1811 its population was 3,848, growing to 6,085 by 1821. The leisured classes were also attracted to smaller towns such as Ramsgate, Eastbourne, Bognor, Worthing, Folkestone and Littlehampton; while steamboats also served Gravesend, Sheerness, and Herne Bay. Broadstairs, Whitstable, Deal and Dover also assumed some significance. At Seaford a huddle of small houses, farmsteads and fishermen's huts was joined in the 1780s by Corsica Hall and Seaford House as the town began to project an image of health, quietness and retirement. In 1813 Shoberl wrote: 'Seaford has of late years attracted some visitors during the bathing season; three machines are kept, and hot and cold baths have been erected for their accommodation' (in Lowerson 1975: 9). These were joined by reading rooms and a marine terrace on the Steine, named in imitation of Brighton. To the west Hothampton was the ambitious scheme of the London hatter, Sir Richard Hotham, developed between 1784 and 1799 but a huge outlay received little initial response, and the development of this and other South Coastal resorts awaited the advent of railways in the 1840s (pp. 291–301). However, it is clear that at Margate and Brighton, and to a lesser extent at Gravesend and elsewhere, the initial impetus was a social and cultural phenomenon; that improved communications followed this trend and reinforced it, but had rarely initiated it.

Between 1660 and 1837 the pattern and texture of south-eastern towns changed. London pushed vigorously southwards and rising towns elsewhere eclipsed the stationary and the shrinking. New developments, whether associated with the needs of the state as at Chatham, or with cultural perceptions of recreation as at Brighton, emerged and are with us today. But many older towns, once important, were submerged and became sleepy backwaters as tourists and improved communications passed them by.

Plate 5.10a and 5.10b Hastings in the nineteenth century. These two watercolours taken from almost identical viewpoints record the rapid changes which took place in the townscape of Hastings between *c.*1840 and 1870.

Chapter 6

A Century of Change, 1837–1939

While no one would wish to belittle those changes occurring before 1837, there are few who could deny the enormous social, economic and regional impact of the Victorian, Edwardian and latter Georgian periods of our history. Here the south-eastern changes will be recounted in terms of population, rural, urban and industrial development. And once again we must acknowledge the forceful and continuing influence of London on the lives of south-eastern people.

Population Change

South-eastern population grew in line with national trends throughout the eighteenth century, with, if anything, a higher rate than many of the emerging industrial areas of the North and Midlands, thanks to the phenomenal expansion of London.

Population growth, steady and seemingly irreversible, has been constant from the first census in 1801 to the present day. In 1801 Kent among the counties of the South East had the highest population but was overtaken by Surrey by 1831. London-derived growth in the latter county continued until the abstraction of the London County Council area in 1888, which lowered the population of the newer, smaller Surrey to a level below that of Kent and Sussex. Growth began again however, and Surrey regained premier position by 1951. In 1965 the Greater London Council was formed, taking in a large part of Kent and Surrey (including the ancient county town of Kingston-upon-Thames) and by 1981 Surrey once more had a lower population than either Kent or Sussex (East and West combined).

Rates of population growth have been consistently higher than the national average (Fig. 6.1). From the 1740s through to 1840 high levels of rural fertility combined with high in-migration to the south-eastern towns. Between 1801 and 1851 all Registration Districts showed increases of at least 25 per cent, and much of the Interior showed 50 to 100 per cent increases, although the highest growth rates were around London, in north and mid-Kent and on the Sussex Coastal Plain, where there were 100 to 200 per cent increases.

By 1831 the highest population densities were in northern Surrey, Thames-side, and coastal Kent, extending to the Sussex border, in mid and west Kent at Tunbridge Wells (Fig. 6.2). Some densities were already very high. Camberwell's population had quadrupled since 1801, and that of Clapham had tripled, serving to bring Brixton (Eastern Division) Hundred to an overall density of over 1,400 people per 100 acres! That of the Borough of Southwark reached to over 15,000 per 100 acres! The growing towns of the Sussex Coastal Fringe were exemplified by Brighton's fourth ranking place in urban density behind Southwark, Dover and Woolwich. By contrast, values around or below the average obtained for much of the Weald. An area of somewhat higher densities did prevail around Frittenden, Hawkhurst, Salehurst and Ewhurst; while some market towns such as Tenterden, Uckfield or Battle also gave higher values to their respective Hundreds. The lowest densities were in two areas: the

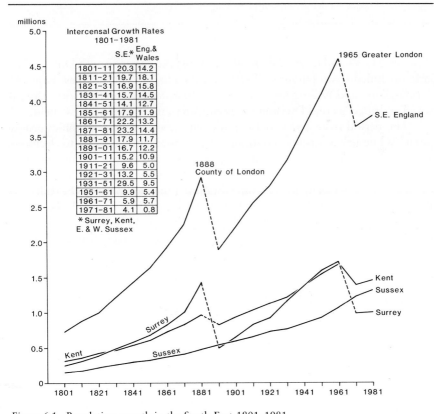

Intercensal Growth Rates
1801–1981

	S.E.*	Eng.& Wales
1801–11	20.3	14.2
1811–21	19.7	18.1
1821–31	16.9	15.8
1831–41	15.7	14.5
1841–51	14.1	12.7
1851–61	17.9	11.9
1861–71	22.2	13.2
1871–81	23.2	14.4
1881–91	17.9	11.7
1891–01	16.7	12.2
1901–11	15.2	10.9
1911–21	9.6	5.0
1921–31	13.2	5.5
1931–51	29.5	9.5
1951–61	9.9	5.4
1961–71	5.9	5.7
1971–81	4.1	0.8

* Surrey, Kent, E. & W. Sussex

Figure 6.1 Population growth in the South East 1801–1981.

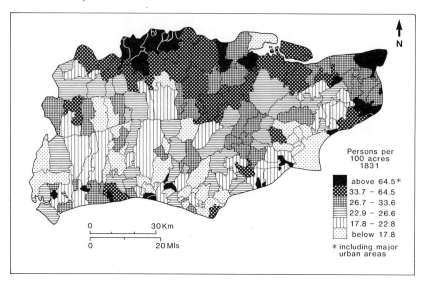

Persons per
100 acres
1831

above 64.5*
33.7 – 64.5
26.7 – 33.6
22.9 – 26.6
17.8 – 22.8
below 17.8
* including major
urban areas

0   30Km

0   20 Mls

Figure 6.2   Population density in South East England 1831.

Romney Marsh and in several Hundreds along the eastern South Downs. The latter included Dean Hundred (Patcham), Poynings, Totnore (West Firle and Beddingham) and Willingdon. The only comparable area on the North Downs was Tandridge Second Division between Caterham, Farley and Tatsfield.

The period from 1831 to 1851 was an important demographic turning point. While urban growth continued, rural populations began to decrease, relatively at first and then absolutely. The theme of rural depopulation is taken up later, but by 1851 at least 15 parishes in the eastern Weald registered population decreases in an arc from Goudhurst through Brede to Bexhill. The Registration District of Battle with above-average densities in 1831, had a density below that of the surrounding area by 1851, such was the impact of the decline. Romney Marsh in 1851 still had a relatively low population, but the same now could also be said for the Westhampnett and Westbourne Districts in Sussex and the Hoo District in north Kent on the Thames-side marshes.

Between 1851 and 1911 there were great changes. A rural exodus occurred, with indigenous working families leaving, and with their numbers being only partially replaced by urban newcomers. Some countrysides therefore experienced a net population decrease (Fig. 6.3a), as at Petworth for example in west Sussex, and Rye, Tenterden and Hollingbourne in the eastern Weald and mid-Kent. In contrast, many other communities were characterized by growth during the later nineteenth century. The majority were around the Coastal Fringe. The industrial areas of the lower Medway Valley showed

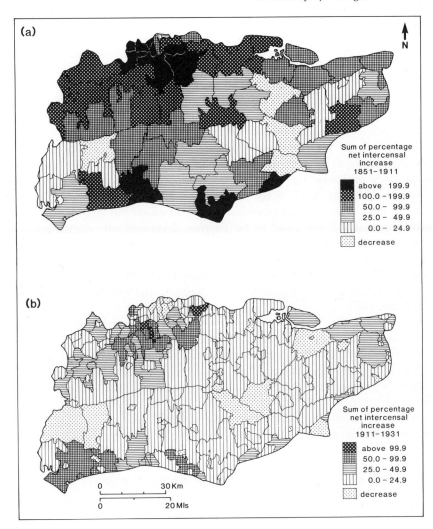

Figure 6.3   Population changes in South East England (a) 1851–1911 and (b) 1911–1931.

growth in the order of 50 to 200 per cent, with especially rapid growth between Queenborough and Aylesford. In east Kent there was growth at Faversham, Herne Bay, Margate and Folkestone. In Sussex, Eastbourne, Hastings and Steyning had increases of over 200 per cent between 1851 and 1911, while Worthing grew by over 100 per cent. Brighton grew more slowly than in its pre-Victorian boom years, but overflowed nevertheless into its surrounding villages. There was thus a twenty-fold growth at Preston between 1861 and 1901; three-fold at Hove; and a doubling at Portslade, Southwick and Kingston

271

Buci. At the formerly deserted settlement of Aldrington, with just seven people returned in the 1861 census, the population reached nearly 7,000 by 1901. Elsewhere, Bexhill quadrupled its population between 1851 and 1911, and there was growth also at Bognor, Littlehampton and Seaford.

Of course, the greatest population growth at this time was in south London. By 1901 Greater London accounted for 20 per cent of the population of the whole of England and Wales; and the central reaches of the south bank were very overcrowded. Densities rose to the 1880s, exacerbated by the many railway viaducts and embankments. And around this central area developed the south London suburbs. The invasion of north Surrey and north-west Kent constituted the major regrouping of population within the South East at this time. By 1911 the suburbs therefore stood out as areas of greater overall growth than either the countryside or Inner London. The population of the central area (north and south of the Thames) decreased only slightly between 1851 and 1891, but the percentage of London's total population living in the central area declined from 48 per cent in 1851 to 24.3 per cent in 1891, such was the strength of the suburban movement (Weber 1899: 463). The last intercensal gain for Southwark, Bermondsey and Lambeth was between 1861 and 1871.

After the Great War the expansion of London became even more pronounced. Between 1918 and 1939 the conurbation's area doubled as London accounted for more than one-third of the population increase of the whole of England and Wales. Most was directed towards the outer suburbs (Fig. 6.3b) through the creation of LCC housing estates and through the proliferation of semi-detached, nuclear family dwellings. Railway electrification and improvements in road transport encouraged the spread of commuting to much of the South East at this time, with most of the northern part of the region now pulled into the daily orbit of London. Between 1911 and 1931 the old County of London, including the south London riverside, lost more people by out-migration than any other county in the kingdom except for Durham, Glamorgan and Monmouthshire. By contrast the counties of Middlesex and Surrey gained far more than any other. Kent grew little through in-migration at this time, gaining less even than Sussex (Friedlander and Roshier 1966: 278).

Other increases were all around the Coastal Fringe. The east Kent resort areas now expanded with their London railway contacts and with the development of the east Kent coalfield. In general the theme of urban growth is strongly pervasive throughout the region from 1837 to 1939. Large parts of the coastline of Sussex and Kent became built over, while the 'great continent of suburbia' in South London spread inexorably across the London Basin and onto the North Downs in Surrey and west Kent. Many free-standing towns within the Interior also grew rapidly at this time, once again mostly governed by access to railway developments.

Table 6.1 depicts population in terms of five categories of town: resorts,

Table 6.1 Changes in the composition of urban populations in South East England, 1831–1931 (All figures are %)

	Kent 1831	Kent 1931	Sussex 1831	Sussex 1931	Surrey 1831	Surrey 1931	Total SE	
							1831	*1931*
Resorts	5.8	11.7	23.7	54.0	–	–	7.5	17.7
Ports/Industrial	23.2	25.7	2.0	5.8	–	–	9.4	11.3
Inland (Coastal Fringe)	9.7	10.3	9.4	3.5	10.1	41.1	9.8	20.1
Interior towns	2.6	5.1	6.9	5.4	–	–	2.5	3.3
London Suburbs	13.7	19.2	–	–	69.5	49.5	32.6	25.7
Rural	45.1	28.0	58.0	31.3	20.5	9.5	38.3	21.9
	100.1	100.0	100.0	100.0	100.1	100.1	100.1	100.0

Note: The figures for 1831 and 1931 are rendered strictly incompatible by the abstraction of the London County Council population totals from Surrey and Kent in 1888. The figure for the London suburbs for 1931 is thus for suburban population outside the LCC boundary. In 1888 approximately 1,500,000 people were transferred to the LCC from Surrey and Kent — 44 per cent of the population of south-east England at that time. The 1831 figures are for the old counties, stretching to the banks of the Thames.

(Source: Census Abstracts, 1831 and 1931)

ports/industrial, inland towns on the Coastal Fringe, Interior towns, and the London suburbs, as well as showing rural population. Overall figures for 1831 show most people still to be rural, followed by London suburban dwellers. The 1831 figures are for the ancient counties and thus include all Surrey and Kent up to the Thames. In 1931 the suburban and rural populations were still the largest, although reduced relatively. The inland towns of the Coastal Fringe on either side of the North and South Downs more than doubled their relative proportions, as did the resorts. The latter showed perhaps the most striking growth, gaining by over 160 per cent. However, the 1931 figures exclude the LCC statistics, and the 1931 suburbs as defined here are those outside the LCC boundaries. The importance of south London demographically is indicated by the fact that even at the 1888 creation of the LCC as much as 44 per cent of the south-eastern population was included within its new boundaries.

'All the same, London's creeping': the Growth of London South of the Thames

Thames-side in 1840

South London in the 1830s showed village, slum, palace and dockyard being gradually submerged beneath a tide of indifferent housing. But by 1840 the southern banks of the Thames still possessed extremely varied environments from Erith and Woolwich in the east to Kingston-upon-Thames in the west.

Between Erith and Woolwich, marshes still limited development except at the naval dockyard (closed in 1869) and the arsenal and garrison at Woolwich. To the west was fashionable Greenwich. Southwards the flat Blackheath Common was beginning to receive suburban terraces. Westwards again one came to populous Deptford with its shipbuilding and victualling yards, and upstream was the 1807 dockyard, later the Surrey Commercial Docks. Here the Rotherhithe community lived in a two-mile ribbon of cottages, wharves and warehouses. Marshy land again separated Rotherhithe from Bermondsey with its more specialized leather-processing industries, and leather market in Weston Street. Here was one of London's poorest rookeries – a fever-den, devil's acre or slum. Jacob's Island, south of Bermondsey Wall, was described in *Oliver Twist*

> tottering house fronts projecting over the pavements, dismantled walls ... chimnies half-crushed hesitating to fall ... windows broken and patched ... rooms so small, so filthy, so confined that the air would seem to be tainted even for the dirt and squalor which they shelter ... every repulsive lineament of poverty ... and every imaginable sign of desolation and neglect.

Southwark, still a bustling bridgehead with roads fanning from the Borough High street into Kent and Surrey, had ecclesiastics' town houses, inns, theatres, the King's Bench and the Marshalsea, Guy's Hospital and the hop exchange. The later building of the new London Bridge and Waterloo Station enhanced this nodality. Westwards grew Lambeth where the pleasure gardens and wealthy mansions were now being joined by humbler dwellings. Lambeth, Vauxhall and Kennington merged and grew towards Brixton and Herne Hill, the latter in 1841 'a spot bespangled with suburban villas, most . . . in the Italian style' (Cherry and Pevsner 1983: 328) (Plate 6.1).

Westwards again was Battersea, still distinct from Wandsworth and Putney, and still partly devoted to market gardening among open-field strips. By 1838 St Mary's church was the village nucleus, but in that year the London and Southwestern Railway opened their Nine Elms depot, bringing rapid industrial development to match that at Wandsworth. Westwards again the environment became more residential along the Upper and Lower Richmond Roads by the 1840s, later to be joined by Putney Hill and Heath. Grand Georgian villas characterized the Putney Park or Roehampton area, while in the northward sweep of the river to Mortlake the Georgian houses at Barnes were supplemented by Italianate villas at Castelnau after Hammersmith Bridge opened in 1827. At East Sheen and Kew country houses were built on the outskirts of Richmond Park, although royal interest in the Kew area was now finished, and Kew Gardens became a public institution from 1841. Upstream again, the Old Deer Park and Richmond Park, separated by Richmond itself, gave large open spaces. With its royal palace, deer park, Georgian architecture, and eighteenth-century tranquillity, Richmond was the antithesis of inner south London. Petersham and Ham, between Richmond and Kingston, and between the river and Richmond Park, were also fashionable, leisured and genteel. Finally, the medieval borough of Kingston, sheltered from London by woods on the slopes of Kingston Hill and Coombe, and by Richmond Park and Ham Common, looked southwards into Surrey rather than to London, and commuter development was deflected to Surbiton after 1840.

Thames-side social and economic differences were both enormous and growing. Palaces and the worst London slums were so close that one might have expected a large degree of class consciousness and conflict. Even before the barriers erected by the railways, South London was highly segregated into inner working-class or artisan sectors as at Bermondsey or riverside Lambeth; dockyard and wharfage at Rotherhithe or Woolwich; semi-rural villages at Putney or East Sheen; and aristocratic enclaves at Richmond and Greenwich. And weaving them all together were the Georgian terraces and early nineteenth-century semi-detached villas of the upper-middle and middle classes.

However, early-Victorian social segregation should not be over-emphasized. This was still a collection of loosely-connected villages outside Southwark; and economically it was an area of 'small masters' in a great variety of finishing and processing trades. Large factories, demanding unskilled or semi-skilled workers, did not dominate London as they did the northern industrial towns and there was a corresponding lack of effective unionization or working-class consciousness.

The Crisis of Inner South London, 1840–1880

Heterogeneous South London began to change almost at the time of Victoria's accession. Between 1840 and 1880 the urbanization of its villages quickened while the inner areas shared a societal and housing crisis common to most inner parts of the capital.

The great mid-nineteenth century British economic expansion was dependent upon, among other factors, an acceleration of foreign demand for British finished and capital goods, a well-developed financial and commercial superstructure, and a resultant broadening and deepening of industrialization. And at the junction of industry and empire was London, by 1840 focusing and symbolizing this expansion. The result for South London and its surrounding area was the creation of a demand for commercial and governmental offices, an expansion of docks and warehousing, and the advent of railway lines, stations and goods yards. The importance of access to such facilities entailed a rapid rise in central land values from renting land for businesses which completely eclipsed profits from the provision of land for housing.

This commercial transformation also entailed a demand for ever-increasing numbers of clerks, skilled, semi-skilled and unskilled workers, and many casual and poorly-paid. The day-time population of the City of London itself nearly doubled between 1866 and 1891. The crisis of Central London lay in the mis-match between this increasing demand for workers and the decreasing interest in the provision of housing. The area directly affected was relatively small – in the northward loop of the Thames between Deptford in the east and Lambeth in the west. But what happened here and across the river between 1840 and 1880 had enormous repercussions for the later history of the entire South East.

In Rotherhithe, Bermondsey and North Lambeth the rookeries became still more overcrowded. Between 1841 and 1851 London grew by over 21 per cent, the highest growth of the century, but there was no decentralization of industry and workplace, and much of the work of the poor had to be reached on foot. Housing in the surrounding villages was not designed for the poor, and was anyway inaccessible to them until cheaper fares became available after the 1870s. There was thus little alternative but to remain in the slums, trapped by the expansion of Britain's wealth which they helped to create but in which they could not share.

Plate 6.1 Acre Lane, Brixton, *c.*1820. George Scharf captures this now roaring town street when it was a rural lane, inhabited by nurserymen, cowkeepers, and smallholders. London families strolled into the fields to enjoy the views and fresh air on Sundays.

The obscure alleys and byways of riverside Southwark and Rotherhithe were thus densely crowded by mid-century. Population densities varied considerably between streets, partly due to interventions in the housing market. Street clearance was carried out in the building of Southwark Street in 1857–64 by the Metropolitan Board of Works. New thoroughfares, it was theorized, would expose the inhabitants to public scrutiny and those homes which were lost could now be replaced by new, healthy suburban dwellings, accessible by omnibus or railway. No alternative accommodation was thought to be necessary at the centre. The fallacy is now obvious, given the prevalence of casual work which demanded constant attendance, and the high price of fares, but it did have the merit of making parts of London *appear* more attractive – especially to capital.

At the same time as new roads were being sliced through working-class areas, the railway companies were competing to reach Central London. The resulting confusion of embankments, viaducts, goods yards, stations and approach roads cut the slums up into smaller, even more densely-populated streets. Thus the extension of the LCDR across the Thames to Ludgate, when combined with the making of Southwark Street, reduced the populations of St Saviour's, Christchurch and St Olaves parishes by about 9,000 (25 per cent) between 1861 and 1871. Neither scheme touched expensive properties such as the Barclay, Perkins brewery, but instead they displaced thousands of people. However no inconvenience was anticipated to the 'migratory artisans' who were thought to have much alternative accommodation in the Borough (Cannadine and Reeder 1982: 151).

The largest clearances resulted from ready agreements between the railway companies and the landowners, particularly the Church. The advance from Nine Elms at Battersea to Waterloo, involving the demolition of about 700 homes, or from London Bridge to Charing Cross and Cannon Street, was made over the property of the Bishops of Winchester, Rochester and London, and of the Archbishop of Canterbury. The surface railways removed the poor for the Church, which was perhaps something the Church itself found difficult. Overall, some 24,000 people were 'dishoused' in south London, mostly between 1840 and the 1860s. One of the last of the schemes was the LCDR Metropolitan extension of 1862–4 with four miles of viaducts, 346 arches and 24 wrought-iron bridges, bringing overcrowding and distress in the wake of demolition. The company still clung to the specious argument that those displaced could move into the new districts opened up by the line, but there were no workmen's trains on this line until 1865 (Course 1958: 225; Dyos 1982: 119–25; 1955: 11–21, 90–100; Kellett 1969: 256–9; Stedman Jones 1971: 159–78).

By the 1840s it was obvious to William Farr, and later to Dickens and George Godwin (in his *Town Swamps and Social Bridges*, 1859) that street clearance merely aggravated and transferred the problems. Other official responses included sanitary regulation and slum clearance, while private philanthropic actions included the provision of model dwellings and the Octavia Hill schemes. Unfortunately, one effect of the former schemes was to 'shovel out the poor' from one parish to the next, to demolish poor housing and often to sell the land for private development at some future date. Official approval and recourse was embodied in the Torrens Act 1868 and Cross Act 1875, which struck at concentrations of the poor, hitting 'costermongers, fish curers and thieves' in Southwark (Stedman Jones 1971: 202).

Philanthropic action tended not to help the very poor, since even this activity was supposed to make a profit of up to 5 per cent, and there was little chance of so doing by providing the very cheapest accommodation. Those would could pay rents were the better-off artisans, and not those dependent on seasonal and casual jobs. Six societies attempted to alleviate poverty in South London, but large families were often excluded from model dwellings, while the rules for living in the Peabody buildings seemed mostly designed to convert the working classes to more bourgeois morals.

By the later 1880s it became clear that despite these schemes, much of the more respectable 'labour aristocracy' was being forced into the slums alongside the very poor, casualized 'residuum'. Fears for the maintenance of social stability now emerged with possible alliances of criminal classes with respectable artisans. The process of 'embourgeoisement', the incorporation of the ideals and values of the dominant Victorian classes into the value systems of the skilled working elites, was a crucial and largely successful process, as demonstrated in Woolwich and Wandsworth at this time (Crossick 1978; Roebuck 1979).

The combination of structural change which caused the decay of heavier Thames-side industries, the 1880s trade depression, and the continuing housing crisis, indeed produced fear among many. The 'social explorers' encapsulated and exploited this fear, as in Greenwood's *Night in a Workhouse* (1866) based on Lambeth, or Sims' *How the Poor Live* (1889) describing the Borough and Mint of Southwark. Events approaching riot in central and south London stirred anxiety in February 1886 and liberal attacks on *laissez-faire* began to mount. Charles Booth's enquiries into London poverty were instituted among a general concern with the physical and moral degeneration of the urban poor. In 1889 the dock strike unionized unskilled workers but this was seen to be an effective means of incorporating the deserving poor, and threats of a labour aristocracy/residuum alliance now receded.

The South London Suburbs, 1840–1939

Expansion, 1840–1880

It has been argued that the towns of Deptford, Greenwich and Woolwich at this time can validly be seen 'as separate, identifiable communities, self-sufficient in their social relationships, and more complete in their social compositions than most parts of London' (Crossick 1976: 17). Internal residential and social segregation occurred as the three towns developed their own suburbs as they began to lose their 'old and respected inhabitants' from the 1850s. Deptford was 'uncommonly like a small country community' in the 1880s, still separated from London by acres of docks, railways and market gardens and with fertile mixed farming on its southern borders whence came rhubarb in abundance. Marshland and topography ensured a certain degree of isolation for both Greenwich and Woolwich, while further west a similar sense of community was retained at Wandsworth in the 1870s.

However, by the 1860s the suburban frontier had engulfed Tulse Hill, Camberwell, Peckham, Dulwich, Clapham and Streatham, conjoining to form part of Charles Booth's 'invertebrate . . . continent of suburbia'. Cheap terraces typified the areas immediately to the south of the slums, but such terraces were often incipient slums themselves almost as soon as they were built. But the cheap rents and their walking-distance to central London ensured a ready supply of tenants. Among them were women out-workers, Bermondsey leather workers, lightermen, watermen and printers. Areas such as Newington or Walworth had housed employers, clerks and artisans earlier in the century but by the 1870s they became overcrowded with casual and low-paid workers, 'dishoused' from the centre. Relatively large houses were turned into tenements and a whole host of local and non-local factors, including landownership policies, drainage, topography, and vestry attitudes, would then guide their path of social descent. These suburbs were 'settlement tanks for submerged Londoners' (Dyos 1982: 144) rather than receiving areas for provincial immigrants. Most were second or third-generation Londoners, and at Sultan Street, Camberwell in 1871, 60 per cent of the inhabitants were Londoners, mostly from the adjoining areas to the north. In 1871 661 people lived in 70 houses here, rising to 1,038 in 1881, an increase corresponding with a decline in numbers of skilled labourers present. Here was a slum in the inner 'walking' suburbs, as Camberwell changed from 'sought-after suburb on the edge of the country to integral part of the fully urbanised central metropolis' (Thompson 1982: 4).

Most of London's villages were overwhelmed economically, socially and physically after 1840. At Clapham by 1825 Clapham Park had been laid out by Cubitt for wealthy men and commuters (pp. 259–60) and by 1845 Thackeray, writing in *Punch*, could characterize Clapham as part of the 'cockney villa district' south of Kennington Common. Between 1863 and 1872 the Park Town Estate was built, effectively linking Clapham with Battersea. This was dairying and market gardening countryside, with meadows defined by marshy ditches or what Kingsley referred to as the 'flowery dykes of Battersea fields'. In 1865 Murray's *Handbook for Travellers in Surrey* noted that 'Battersea fields will soon be fields no more . . . (There) are to be built . . . nearly 3,000 "villa" and "cottage" residences – the projectors hoping to form in

Park Town, as it is to be called, a sort of southern Belgravia, though on a somewhat humbler scale' (Metcalf 1978: 11). Indeed the development was part of a grand scheme to link Clapham with Pimlico and Belgravia via the 1858 Chelsea Bridge, but the vast multiplication of railway lines and bridges of the competing LCD and LBSCR companies dampened the project. Instead inhabitants were drawn from the nearby Longhedge LCD railway works into an unexciting architectural maze which later absorbed Clapham into South London. By 1893 Clapham Common still had 'an inviting air of rusticity', and Clapham itself mounted concerts with its Philharmonic society and string quartets, lectures and readings. The wealthy had their own social groupings still, but much had inescapably changed since the heyday of the Clapham Sect (Fitzgerald 1893: 161–2).

Clapham, Camberwell and the riverside slums and industrial areas developed from older nuclei. Images of wholesale submergence in suburbia are therefore misleading. Internal ties remained important, and by the mid-nineteenth century at least, there were relatively few commuters, probably not more than ten per cent of the heads of household. At the end of the century an LCC investigation concluded that only one person in twelve used public transport of any kind to get to work although there was much walking to work, and strong cross-currents existed within the south London suburbs as well as towards central London. Older communities and social structures were certainly not overwhelmed by 1880.

Residential segregation was now apparent. South of the Thames an inner working-class commercial and poor residential zone emerged between Rotherhithe and Battersea, becoming increasingly expensive yet overcrowded as it was criss-crossed by the railways. Here there was better access to employment for all the family, cheaper food at the markets, and easier credit at pubs and pawnshops. Around this was a second zone, an inner working-class suburban zone which included older, more socially-heterogeneous villages. Between 1840 and 1880 the cheaper land between the villages was being built over for the receipt of 'respectable' working-class families from Inner London, and the wealthier residents were moving further south. The minutiae of class consciousness were important, and a third, outer zone could thus be distinguished, of wealthy residents who could afford to live at a distance from London at villages such as Wimbledon or Bromley.

It is to these outer suburbs that we now turn, and in particular to the pattern of suburban railway provision which was so important. The railway station was a necessary, though not sufficient explanatory factor in the transformation of villages into suburbs or dormitories. Before 1840 only the very leisured city workers could commute from this outer zone by private or short-stage horse-drawn coach. Fares were high and stages were precluded from operating within the paved area of central London by the Hackney cab monopoly until 1831. But by 1834 there were 376 licensed omnibuses operating to bring commuters from Greenwich and Camberwell. Greenwich also sent daily commuters by the steamboats, plying the Thames between Richmond and Woolwich, and which reached their maximum importance in the 1840s. But in December 1836 the first London steam-powered railway opened between London Bridge and Deptford, being extended to Greenwich in 1838. In 1839 the London and Croydon Railway joined the Greenwich for the last stretch to London Bridge, and by 1842 trunk lines to Brighton and Dover also used the lines. In the south-west the London and Southampton Railway opened its first line betweeen Nine Elms, Battersea and Woking in 1838, with trains to Southampton by 1840, and an extension to Waterloo by 1848 on a viaduct of 235 arches.

The decisions made in the boardrooms of the various railway companies accounted in large measure for the pattern of suburbanization which followed, although the alternatives offered to the boards by local landowners, local authorities, and national legislation were also important. Economic trends and the nature of the topography itself also set limits and costs to these massive operations. Frequently the railway was a genuine catalyst for future suburbanization. Elsewhere estate developers subscribed to new stations, as at Shooter's Hill, Eltham Park or Hither Green. In some cases railway companies gave season ticket concessions or free tickets for a period to newcomers taking up houses of specified values. The availability of housing as a key determinant of success was thus recognized by the railways. The LSW announced in 1859 that the principal occupiers of larger houses on the Kingston Hill estate would be granted a 10 per cent reduction in fares for seven years (Course 1962: 199; 1958: 312–29; Thompson 1982: 18–20). Other railways followed, rather than initiated new settlements, and many suburbs came to have more than one station, served by different railway companies. Croydon was a battleground for the LBSCR and SER almost from the beginning, and by 1876 had no fewer than eight stations with 300 trains daily.

At Bromley local landowners promoted the railway's arrival. In 1841 the population was 4,325, most of whom lived in the market town itself, although 'neat houses and villa residences' had been built on Bromley Common following enclosure in 1821. The Bishop of Rochester's palace and estate brought prestige and there was a thriving coaching trade. But in the 1840s arrangements were concluded for the sale of the palace; railway stations attracted development elsewhere; and tradesmen bemoaned its decaying residential and commercial functions. In 1856 a local committee (The Mid Kent Railway Company) was formed which agreed with the West End of London and Crystal Palace Railway, and with the East Kent Railway (later the LCD) to open a station at Bromley. This appeared in 1858, and the Bromley stretch became an integral section of the Dover–Victoria line.

The 7s 6d weekly fare to London Bridge precluded all but the wealthy from commuting from Bromley, but nevertheless a campaign was mounted for a branch line to serve the town. By 1871 many new villas had arrived and in 1878 a new branch line and station was built to join with the SER at Grove Park. By 1881 the population had reached 15,154, and was fictionalized by H. G. Wells in *The New Machiavelli* (1911, pp. 44–5). Wells referred to the invasion of a neat little market town by 'a mindless, wasteful, anarchy which was suburbia':

> The outskirts of Bromstead were a maze of exploitation roads that led nowhere, that ended in tarred fences studded with nails . . . and in trespass boards that used vehement language . . . It was a multitude of uncoordinated fresh starts, each more sweeping and destructive than the last, and none of them ever really worked out to a ripe and satisfactory completion. Each left a legacy of products – house, humanity, or what not – in its wake. It was a sort of progress that had bolted; it was change out of hand, and going at an unprecedented pace nowhere in particular.

In Bromley a combination of traders, commuters and property owners had attracted railway development, and thus more capital into the town. A vocal middle-class presence stimulated the Local Board, formed in 1867, to improve public health. And as the range of shops and services increased, so the still rural surrounds looked increasingly to Bromley as a centre. With a quadrupled population between 1840 and 1880, Bromley typified the transition from market town to suburb.

The South London suburbs show a mixture of voluntarism and realization of the forces of capital accumulation growing during the nineteenth century. The workings of the Inner London land market drove up land prices, forced change from residential to commercial use near the river, and split up old working communities. And despite attempts to improve slum areas and rehouse the poor, the middle classes were virtually powerless. But they could do something about their own places of residence, and villas were sought in the villages or on the old commons south of London. Privacy was now attainable in these single-family houses in a like-minded community, and work was now separated from domestic life in the complex commercial world of London. And in a world threatened by fears of the mob and social discord the safety of the suburb allowed the realization of the 'religious, moral and social aspirations' of the middle class. Where such powerful ideologies could be matched by a supply of cheap land, a wide range of building firms, and improved transportation the middle-class suburb evolved.

Suburban Expansion, 1880–1939

Before the 1880s there was little decentralization of working-class families from Inner London. But thereafter the picture changed. This should not be overstated, since 25 per cent of the working men included in a 1914 LCC survey still gave their reason for living in Southwark as having to live near

283

their work. By 1911 about 30 per cent of Southwark's population still lived in one- or two-roomed tenements, while Booth had found 47 per cent of south central London's population living at the poverty level. Overcrowding and slums were not easily eradicated.

In February 1865 the first workmen's trains south of the Thames ran on the LCD line between Victoria and Ludgate Hill via Brixton, Camberwell and Walworth. Henceforth such trains, together with trams, played a major role in the alleviation of overcrowding in inner London and in promoting suburban development through to at least 1914. The LCD also provided a cheap fares scheme for the Penge tenants of the Metropolitan Association for Improved Dwellings of Industrious Classes, together with one cheap train daily from south Camberwell to Ludgate Hill. After 1865 the LBSCR ran a similar train between New Cross and Liverpool Street, and the SER voluntarily issued workmen's tickets on the Woolwich line by 1868 (Dyos 1982: 87–91). Thus between 1860 and 1880 a limited attempt was made to enable the 'Lower middle class' to live in the suburbs, even before the Cheap Trains Act 1883 made such action compulsory.

Post-1880 suburbanization was distinctly uneven. Demand for better conditions and the supply of appropriate houses in South London was not altogether well matched. Investment in housing fluctuated both temporally and spatially as did the release of land and leasehold arrangements; and local authorities reacted differently according to local power structures, since not all suburbs welcomed an influx of working-class commuters. There was never the intensity that characterized London's expansion via the Great Eastern lines into Essex at this time, and while by 1905 the limit of travel on workmen's trains was more than 21 miles to the north-east, 12 miles to the west and 11 miles north, it was less than 9 miles southwards. Perhaps the only cheap fare scheme south of the Thames to work was the twopenny workmen's train on the south London line between London Bridge and Victoria via Brixton and Battersea (Dyos 1982: 97) where working-class accommodation therefore clustered. Most workmen could have afforded this fare at this time. The limits of the fourpenny return, probably the maximum payable by a workman, took in Tooting Junction, Crystal Palace, Putney and Southfields, Catford, Greenwich Park and Plumstead. Approximately a quarter of all suburban trains were now for workmen and many more now travelled in from a 12 to 15 mile zone.

The plight of some working-class households was also eased by limited decentralization of industry. Booth noted in 1902 that industrial centralization was slackening due to the expensive rents, and many employers wished to get out beyond the jurisdiction of the LCC and London rates. The lower Thames-side area began to attract engineering, oil and cake mills, and armaments at Erith; gasworks and power stations at Greenwich; together with the arsenal and associated military needs at Woolwich. New housing to cater for these workers grew up at Croydon and at Bexleyheath on the enclosed common to the north of Bexley village (Carr 1982: 212–67). In 1903 a local authority tramway opened between Bexleyheath and Woolwich allowing workers to reach Erith and Woolwich Arsenal early in the morning. Bexleyheath thus became a dormitory area for Thames-side workers, contrasting with the London-orientated middle-class suburb around Bexley village.

The cheapest form of public transport was the horse-drawn LCC tram, and this enabled many working-class families to move to the suburbs. By about 1900 trams operated along most radial routes as well as providing lateral connections. Working within a six-mile radius of Central London, they were cheaper and more convenient than the buses. By 1906 the London United Tramways Company was also operating an electric tram service to Kingston-on-Thames and Surbiton, extending to Merton in 1907. Elsewhere, as at Erith, Dartford, Bromley and Croydon, local councils operated trams, and an efficient LCC system spread from the initial line between Westminster Bridge and Tooting by 1915 (Jackson 1973: 26–41, 329–32).

South London therefore continued to spread between 1880 and 1914. Building occurred on the eastern side of Wimbledon; at Raynes Park; between Balham and Tooting along the tramway and thence to Streatham; and along the railway at Wallington, Carshalton, Sutton and Cheam, Coulsdon and Purley. The highest intercensal increase within the whole of London between 1901 and 1911 (156 per cent) was at Merton and Morden where old mills on the Wandle were now swamped by housing. Populations almost doubled at New Malden and Mitcham.

By 1914 the motor bus had eclipsed the tram as far afield as South Croydon. The railways responded by concentrating on middle-class commuter traffic in a 12–30 mile zone around London, and by the electrification of suburban lines where feasible. The LBSCR south London line was thus electrified in 1909, as were many others by 1912. The permissive effect of these improvements was enormous. However, to understand London's suburbanization the changes resulting from the 1890 Housing of the Working Classes Act must also be understood. This gave local authorities the power to acquire land compulsorily for additional housing, extending by 1900 even beyond their own boundaries. About twenty London authorities adopted the Act, but the most extensive use was that by the LCC at Tooting and Norbury. Between 1903 and 1911 the Totterdown cottage estate at Tooting was built with 1,299 houses and four shops. The estate was popular, with a good tram service, and a population of about 4,500 after the First World War. The first LCC 'out-county' estate was built at Norbury, south of Streatham and outside the LCC boundaries, between 1906 and 1910.

Thus in the period before 1914, a complex pattern of independent villages, semi-dormitory enclaves, and undifferentiated suburbia developed south of the Thames. Class status was closely related to distance from Inner London, with change vibrating along the transport routes. As Booth noted: 'Southwark is moving to Walworth, Walworth to North Brixton and Stockwell,

while the servant-keepers of Outer London go to Croydon and other places'
(Booth 1902, 3, iv: 166).

During the Great War there was little activity except for the rapid
building of the Well Hall estate at Eltham for munitions and arsenal workers in
1915, but after 1918 the suburbanization continued apace. The electrification
of the Brighton line in the 1930s, the building of LCC estates, and the growth
of private motor car ownership led to a doubling of the built-up area of London
between 1918 and 1939. Detached suburbs of London developed at such places
as Sutton, Cheam and Ewell. At the Clandons and Horsleys further west, the
inter-war changes came slowly. The parcel post came by rail rather than pony
and cart; mains electricity reached West Clandon in 1921; a library opened in
East Horsley in 1925; 12 council houses were built in East Clandon in 1926;
sewerage operations began in the Horsleys in 1937; and there were new private
housing estates and shops, traffic noise and pollution, and a spate of burglaries
in the new wealthy homes (Connell 1978: 45–51).

From 1918 Lloyd George's 'homes fit for heroes' slogan epitomized
a concern to provide decent accommodation for all. Relatively high living
standards within the South East led to an explosive demand for family houses
within commuting distance of London, and local authorities and private
developers feverishly endeavoured to fulfil this demand, on cheap land, for
which there was little agricultural interest. Thus by late 1922 Wandsworth
had acquired some 600 new cottages at Earlsfield, Upper Tooting, Tooting
and Southfields. The LCC, working under the Addison Act (1919) which
effectively subsidized local authority house building, was likened in 1938
to:

> A colonizing power, like Ancient Rome, pouring out the treasure
> and labour of her citizens in order to make homes for them in
> foreign lands (in Jackson 1973: 160).

Eight new cottage estates were built by the LCC between 1919 and 1938,
while three pre-1914 developments were completed (including Norbury) and
seven more were started. The St Helier's Estate astride the 1926 Sutton by-pass
contained about 40,000 people by the end of the 1930s; and at Downham,
Whitefoot Lane and Mottingham a combined population exceeding 30,000
also developed. This was to the south of Catford where the Bellingham Estate
had been started in 1920 with over 2,000 houses and flats built within three
years. To the west was the Castelnau Estate with over 600 houses in the late
1920s; and the larger Dover House (Roehampton) development with over
5,000 people by 1938. The magnitude of the local authority rehousing is even
more pronounced when one remembers that many other London authorities
were also active. Between 1919 and 1939 possibly as many as 250,000 people
came to live in council property south of the Thames.

The growth of private speculative building was enormously significant in
Kent and Surrey. Middle-class families escaping the worst of the depression,
thrived in an economy partly dependent on London and partly growing

through its own consumer durables, distributive, service and administrative jobs. From 1932 the building societies became more active in permitting the growth of owner-occupation, and demand soared. In the Greater London area by 1938 private firms had finished over 618,000 houses compared with a local authority total of 153,000 since 1918. Perhaps 2.5 million people would have been involved in this private building around London, with a large proportion south of the Thames.

The major inter-war growth areas here were Merton and Morden Urban District where the 1921 population of 17,532 grew to 68,980 by mid-1938, and Carshalton which grew from 13,873 to 59,510. On the claylands between Sutton and Kingston there was a great concentration of cheaper (under £1,000) housing; with more expensive properties further out around Epsom, Croydon, Effingham and on the heaths south of Esher and Weybridge. Bexley was transformed from a Thames-side dormitory looking to Woolwich into a 'metropolitan suburb' by the mid-1930s. The 1921 population of 21,104 grew to 77,020 by 1938. Growth at Chislehurst, Orpington and Sidcup came close behind.

The resultant landscape of outer London is well known. Formless and extensive suburbias grew piecemeal as whole areas were submerged beneath red-tiled roofs, mock-Tudor elevations, and redbrick or pebbledash walls. The focal points were shopping parades with flats above. By-passes attracted their own speculative housing, petrol stations, mock-Tudor pubs and factories; while middle-class dormitories infilled between the pre-1914 nuclei. Such 'ribbon development' came eventually to be seen as a great eyesore, but by the time that the 1935 Ribbon Development Act was passed much of the damage was done (Jackson 1973: 113).

By 1939 London stretched to a 12-mile radius around Charing Cross (Fig. 6.4). Its area had doubled since 1918, but its population had increased by only one-fifth, so low was the density of inter-war development. London's peak population was attained in 1939, while that of Inner London had been reached in 1901 and that of Outer London was to come in 1951 (Thomas 1970: 23–6). As with the inner suburbs before 1914, so too with the inter-war outer suburbs, there was a great variety of factors permitting or encouraging growth. However, improved transportation was very significant. By the mid-1920s there were by-passes around Kingston, Sutton, Croydon, Eltham, Sidcup, Bexleyheath, Orpington, Farnborough and Dartford, with more to come in the 1930s.

Other centres grew up around railway stations which had been subsidized by estate developers, as at Petts Wood (1928), Stoneleigh (1932) and Berrylands (1933). By this time nearly all the suburban lines of the Southern Region (formed in 1923 from the constituent companies south of London) had been electrified; while the underground opened as far as Morden by 1926. But trams still remained the cheapest form of transport, with workmen's fares remaining a significant feature throughout the 1930s.

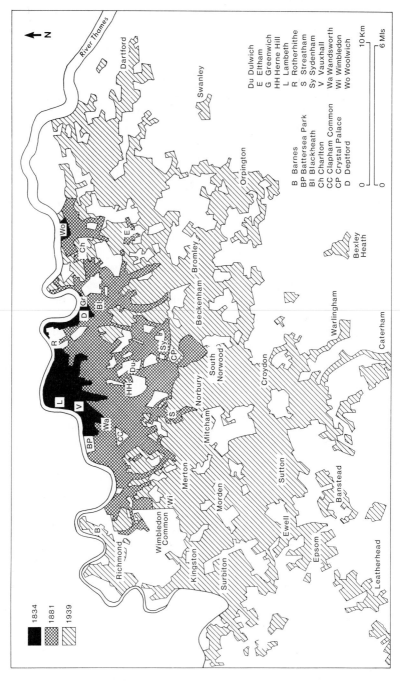

Figure 6.4 The growth of south London *c.*1834–1939.

The Control of Suburbia

Improved transport; easily-available land; the growth of large civil engineering and construction companies such as Costains, Laings, Wates and Wimpeys; coupled with the particular circumstances of London's burgeoning economic base, seemingly meant that the capital would ultimately cover all of south-east England.

However, with the 1889 formation of the LCC, the opportunity arose to re-examine piecemeal *laissez-faire* attitudes to growth. Organized communities or garden cities might combat urban sprawl, congestion, and London's substandard housing, health and amenities. In 1909 parliamentary recognition of planning came with the Housing, Town Planning, etc. Act which allowed local authorities to prepare plans for areas undergoing suburban growth. An Act of 1919 emphasized co-operation between authorities, and many plans were drawn up for the London suburbs. In 1929 county councils began planning in greater earnest, and from 1932 planning schemes were to be applied to all land, irrespective of whether it was scheduled for development or not.

By 1912 the *Spectator* had expressed public concern for the North Downs in Surrey where 'further placing of houses along the ridge can only spoil and disfigure the ridge as a whole . . .' (in Brandon 1977: 97). In the same year Colley Hill, near Reigate, was purchased by public subscription, as was farmland in the Wandle Valley earlier. The aesthetic and recreational values promoted by Meredith, Morris and Palmer were now bearing fruit. Walking and cycling became popular for suburban families who made excursions into the Surrey countryside armed with purpose-made Ordnance Survey maps and guide books (see pp. 307–8). Many wealthy landowners bequeathed their property to the nation, as at Box Hill in 1914, or Milford and Witley commons in 1921. Leith Hill was saved from development by a public appeal launched in *The Times* in 1929. And against this background of public concern co-ordinated planning began (Young and Garside 1982).

The LCC was very active. In 1927 the Greater London Regional Planning Committee was formed with representatives from local authorities within 25 miles of central London. In 1933 the committee's technical adviser, Raymond Unwin, proposed the formation of an open 'green girdle' to segregate old and new developments and to provide adequate recreation space. Changes of policy and financial constraints meant that his plans were not fully considered until just before the outbreak of war in 1939, but in the meantime a Green Belt Act was passed in 1938 to safeguard the open land acquired since 1935 by the LCC and other authorities, such as Nonsuch Park. As many as 97 Surrey and 22 Kent properties have passed into public ownership since 1935, most being purchased before 1947.

In many ways the legislation must be seen as a 'response rather than an anticipation of a landscape of disorder'. And although the pioneers of

London's drive into the south-eastern countryside, the 'plotlanders', were vilified by many contemporaries such as Thomas Sharp, others were more sympathetic. Clough Williams-Ellis likened the criticism to 'cursing a stricken family because in escaping from its burning home it trespassed over lawns and flower beds' (Hardy and Ward 1984: 39, 48).

The growth of south London between 1837 and 1939 was thus both vigorous and complex, threatening the North Downs by 1914. But private and public opinion was mobilized to halt the sprawl and to save the remnants of countryside. Although planning legislation at this time has been described as pitiful, and inter-war 'subtopia' has been universally condemned, two outcomes were clear. Firstly, many thousands of families were given the chance to find better living conditions than in central London, and secondly there was now a clear understanding of the need for regional planning mechanisms. For the first time in the history of the South East, public authorities were beginning to look at *regional*, rather than purely local problems.

The Development of the Resorts and Coastal Towns, 1837–1939

Urban growth was by no means restricted to South London, since an almost continuous line of development around the Coastal Fringe was traceable from the Thames to Selsey Peninsula. And as with South London, so too with the coastal towns, it was railway contact which facilitated development when prompted by a combination of local and national circumstances. It is therefore appropriate to begin with a review of the progress of the railways as they affected urban growth.

Railways to the Coast

The South East was not an ideal region for successful railway promotion. The population was not highly concentrated in large centres outside London and the topography was roughly at right angles to the projected railways, as with the turnpikes, rendering them costly. Industrial consumers and producers were not numerous, and water communication was already well established along the coastline.

Railway development therefore started modestly, but there were four local lines begun before the opening of the first trunk line. The horse-drawn Surrey Iron Railway, the world's first public railway, operated along the Wandle valley between Wandsworth and Croydon between 1803 and 1846. The first steam-powered passenger and freight line was opened in 1830 between Canterbury and Whitstable, with Stevenson's *Invicta* locomotive working the line for a while. The London and Greenwich Railway was opened to Greenwich in 1838, and the London to Croydon Line in 1839.

The development of the coastal towns is more closly related, however, to the 1839 advent of trunk lines. Almost simultaneously, three lines were promoted from London to major coastal points: Dover, Brighton and Southampton. The obvious route between London and Dover, the Watling Street alignment via Rochester, Faversham and Canterbury, was defeated by the barriers of the Medway, the Downs or by the refusal of the Admiralty to co-operate in the extension of the London and Greenwich Line before 1878. Instead the decision was made to cross the Downs north of Oxted and to follow a wealden route to Dover. The South Eastern Railway (SER) thereby ran through 'that part of Kent which requires opening', and there were possibilities of branch lines to Canterbury, Thanet, Hastings and even Brighton from this more westerly route. From London Bridge a shared line ran to Earlswood Common (later Redhill) and reached Tonbridge in 1842. By the end of the year Cubitt's six-mile long straight stretch of line reached Ashford, and in 1844 the line reached Dover via Folkestone. Thereafter branch lines were spawned to Tunbridge Wells, Canterbury (West), Margate and Hastings, and the line monopolized the region east of a line between Redhill, Tonbridge and Hastings by the 1850s (Fig. 6.5).

To the west, the London–Brighton line's six different proposed routes were whittled down to Rennie's 'direct route' by 1837. This line was built from the London and Croydon Line south of Norwood Junction, to reach Brighton in 1841. A branch from Brighton to Shoreham had previously opened in 1840, and a Lewes line opened in 1846. In that year the merger of the London and Brighton Railway with the London and Croydon created the London, Brighton and South Coast Railway (LBSCR). For the first time an effective link was made from one side of the Coastal Fringe to the other across the Interior, and the effect on both parts was to be dramatic. Further extensions reached Newhaven, 'The Liverpool of the South' in 1847, and Eastbourne via Polegate in 1849. An inverted 'T' pattern emerged in Sussex since coastal extensions east–west were relatively cheap. By November 1845 Worthing was reached, by 1846 Chichester, and 1847 Portsmouth.

The other basic south-eastern trunk line, later to become the London and Southwestern, opened throughout to passengers in 1840 via Woking to Southampton, although the 'Portsmouth direct line' via Guildford and Petersfield had to wait until 1859. The line was highly influential in the development of London's south-western suburbs, north of a line between Waterloo, Guildford and Farnham, but it had less influence over the south-eastern coastal towns.

After 1850 the coastal lines multiplied, new stations and junctions appeared, and competition reduced profits. The only new main line to emerge was the East Kent Railway, incorporated in 1853 to run from Strood on the Medway to Canterbury (East). This opened in 1860, bringing regular services from the new Victoria station along the old Watling Street approach. In 1859 the company became the London, Chatham and Dover (LCDR), with the latter town being reached in 1861, and thereby completing a rival route

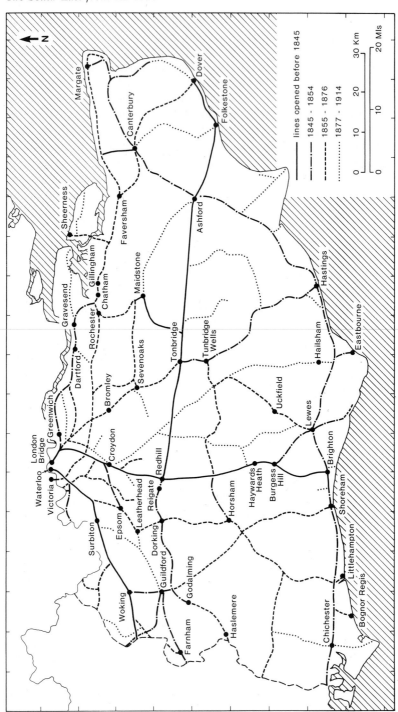

Figure 6.5 The growth of the railway network in the South East before 1914.

to that of the SER. A destructive feud ensued until the two companies were merged as the South Eastern and Chatham Railway in 1899, the year when the SER portrayed itself in its official guide as 'The Royal Mail route to Paris, India and the colonies' (Carrier 1937: 81).

Resort and Residential Development

In large measure, the nineteenth- and early twentieth-century urbanization of the coastline is the history of resort development. From Gravesend in pre-Victorian days around to the shores of Bracklesham Bay in the 1930s various attempts to provide for the seaside holiday have left their mark.

By 1837 sea bathing at Brighton had acquired a half-century of practice and a high degree of social prestige. In 1841 the combined population of Brighton and Hove approached 50,000 but their status was threatened by the advent of better communications, since Brighton's prestige had owed nothing to the railway. Instead, wealthy visitors gave way to London middle-class trippers and holiday-makers and thereafter until 1914 the town expanded largely through catering for the growing professionalization within the London orbit. To businessmen and their families were added annuitants, clerks and other white-collar workers. Except for the exclusive development at Kemp Town to the east of Brighton, growth pushed the built-up area westwards into Hove and Aldrington, and then northwards into Preston, West Blatchington and Hangleton. In 1873 the borough boundaries were extended to encompass much of old Preston, while Hove similarly acquired West Blatchington and Hangleton by 1923.

Two significant social changes were involved in the growth process. One was the development of a leisure industry and its migration seawards from Tunbridge Wells or Epsom. The second was the rise of a salaried middle class, whose growing real incomes matched London's growth at the centre of Empire. The institutionalization of Easter, Whitsun and Bank holidays in 1871, the granting of industrial holidays and the permissive role of cheap railway travel were also important. By the 1860s as many as 30,000 excursionists arrived on Whit Mondays to the 'Queen of resorts' although Queen Victoria herself had long since forsaken Brighton for Osbourne and Balmoral. The raffish tone of a popular trippers' resort came to mingle uneasily with the high moral and genteel tone demanded by propertied families, but Brighton, possibly alone among the south-eastern resorts, was large enough to accommodate most interests (Plate 6.2).

Once the railway arrived the functions of the resort might well be diversified by residential and industrial development. Thus Brighton, 'the West End maritimized' (Lowerson 1983: 222), developed inland on speculative building plots across former open field strips, with substandard housing being built around workshops or the new railway engineering works, which employed 3,000 people by the 1860s. Bad sanitation and poor health prevailed until the provision of adequate water supplies in the 1860s and the opening of the great Intercepting Sewer in 1874. Slums were already being demolished in the 1860s but overcrowding and common lodging houses (doss houses) went unregulated before the 1881 bye-laws (Fossey 1981: 53–9). Brighton had in 1911 one of the highest population densities for any county borough in England and Wales. By 1920 national attention was directed to the new garden suburb of South Moulscoomb, but this local authority initiative was a reaction to considerable local pressure from the unemployed, low-waged and demobbed military. In 1919 Brighton's mayor likened the town to 'a ragged garment with a golden fringe'. The combined population of Brighton and Hove exceeded 200,000 by 1939 as its industrial, service, residential and commuting functions multiplied and overtook its former leisure role. Inter-war suburbanization polarized between private developments at Rottingdean, Woodingdean, Ovingdean and Patcham, and working-class council housing at Whitehawk and Moulscoomb (Dickens and Gilbert 1981: 201–31).

The demand for leisure induced many contrasting resorts to grow after 1840. Before this time Gravesend and Margate had developed, based around steamboats and sailing packets from London. In 1842–3 over 100,000 visitors came thus to Margate, 'the goal of every young cockney's Sunday excursion' (Whyman 1981: 112). These too were therefore resorts which did not wait upon the railway for their success, although others in Kent certainly did. In 1842 and 1856 Margate acquired piers, and a pavilion in 1871. Although far smaller than Brighton, by 1851 there were 10,099 residents, rising to 20,057 by 1901.

As popular seaside resorts Brighton and Margate had no rivals in the South East. Both were moulded by events before 1837 but both reacted to transport improvements from the 1840s. Rail proximity made Brighton 'the lungs of the great Capital', and in 1845, after the LBSCR had arrived in Brighton but before the SER arrived in Margate, Mrs Elizabeth Stone commented that:

> It requires marvellous courage now to confess any interest in places so utterly discarded by fashion as are Margate and Ramsgate. They are still crowded, but by decidedly unfashionable people (in Whyman 1981: 133).

But there were other resorts nearby in Thanet which catered for different tastes. When Mr Pooter went on holiday, for example, it was to Broadstairs, Margate's more select neighbour around the North Foreland. Broadstairs grew from a medieval fishing community attached to St Peter's about one mile inland to experience population growth of over 80 per cent between 1801 and 1851. By 1837 Ramsgate was also challenging Margate for position as premier Thanet resort. Freehold building development had resulted in a spread of houses away from the existing harbourage so that by 1851 it ranked sixth in size among

Plate 6.2 The people's Brighton 1883. Late-Victorian views of Brighton are usually full of genteel-looking and very properly dressed strollers, equestrians, carriage-folk etc. giving an overwhelming impression of a high-class seaside resort enjoying itself decorously at the height of its prosperity and self-assurance. Uniquely, a Ditchling landscape artist, J. C. Dollman, kept a sketch-book of his holiday at Brighton in 1883 and this gives us a 'low life' glimpse of Brighton. From his cheap lodgings he and his friend sallied out to give us the excursionists' impression of Brighton (Sketch-book in the possession of Mr George Holleyman).

all English resorts, behind Brighton, Great Yarmouth, Dover, Hastings and Gravesend. Like these too, it did not rely purely on its resort functions, since it had long been an important agricultural exporting port. However, despite its music halls Ramsgate was not 'roaringly plebeian' (Walton 1983: 54, 251) and its growth faltered in the later nineteenth century.

Of the other Kentish coastal towns, only Folkestone and Herne Bay were really resorts. Dover, Gravesend and Deal certainly had continuing resort functions, but as the nineteenth century progressed they relied more heavily on other activities. Folkestone possessed a harbour for cross-channel boats, colliers and fishing boats, but from the 1820s it had become primarily a watering place. Building on long leases was encouraged and stimulated by the 1843 arrival of the SER. There was also the precedent set after 1838 by the layout of a high-class resort at Bournemouth. By the 1850s Lord Radnor in his 'pursuit of wealth and exclusiveness' had agreed a plan for development mainly aimed at the western end of the town – the West Cliff estate; with church, school and roads laid out and population growth assured. The 1851 population of 7,549 become 19,297 by 1881 and 33,502 by 1911. The greatest period of growth for this most genteel of the Kentish resorts was between 1851 and 1881, when it became a fashionable summer as well as winter convalescent spot.

The exclusiveness and prestige associated with pre-First World War Folkestone was not shared by the other new Kentish resort, Herne Bay. There was, however, one area of similarity since both were speculative ventures attracting resort and residential populations. But whereas Folkestone was projected by propertied gentry, Herne Bay resulted from the investment of capital by George Burge, contractor for the LCDR line to the Thanet resorts. From the 1830s a grid-iron street pattern was laid out one mile from the inland parent village of Herne, with assembly room, Hanover Square, promenade, 1837 clock tower, and pier. But although population grew by over 150 per cent between 1801 and 1851, the forecast prosperity never materialized. Among England's resorts Herne Bay ranked only 55th by 1911 with a population of 7,180. However Burge had been instrumental in pushing through a railway act and a station opened on the LCDR line in 1861 which was extended to Margate in 1863 and eventually the town did become something of a dormitory as London's commuting network spread in the 1920s. In the 1930s the Thanet Way also promoted car-based ribbon development, and Herne Bay became one of a series of resort and residential villages north of the Blean forest stretching towards Seasalter on the edge of the Graveney and north Kent marshes (Bishop 1973; Walton 1983; White 1982: 54, 216).

Equivalent stories of high growth rates and Victorian expectations can be found along the Sussex coast. By 1840 the resorts constituted a significant element in the local economy. While the 'vagaries of fashion and medical recommendation bulked disproportionately large' before 1840, thereafter it was the attraction of solid, residential middle-class families which became more important. At this time the resorts of Brighton and Hastings accounted for nearly two-thirds of the total urban population of Sussex. At Hastings the resort functions were enhanced following the building of Pelham Place and Crescent in the 1820s. These joined assembly rooms, library, baths, Wellington Square and purpose-built lodging houses to render Hastings an elite resort. The railway entered the Priory Valley in 1851 and debris from the tunnels and cuttings was used to build up the seafront, where later building would take place. Late-Victorian Hastings grew to the west of the Old Town, and included an 1880 Town Hall, an 1872 pier, and an Albert Memorial clocktower. To the west again arose St Leonard's. By 1840 the London builder James Burton and his architect son, Decimus, had established the centrepiece, St Leonard's Gardens, with highly-praised crescents of houses linking to an esplanade with assembly rooms, hotels and baths. Italian, Gothic and Lombard styles of architecture rubbed shoulders in this residential suburb, very similar in conception to Brighton's Kemp Town.

Other resorts had also accrued some late-eighteenth century prestige and development. At Worthing, the town had grown out of a rural seaside parish following the Improvement Act of 1803 and the visit of Princess Amelia in 1798. A solid middle-class clientele was firmly established here by 1840, by which time promoters and land speculators had ensured full resort facilities. From this date the town grew to encompass surrounding villages such as Goring, Tarring, Salvington, Durrington and Ferring.

It cannot be assumed, however, that such speculative growth was without hindrance. Several resorts promised much but yielded little financial return. At Bersted by 1784 Sir Richard Hotham, a wealthy London hatter, had begun the land acquisitions necessary to develop his dream of Hothampton. Before his death in 1799 Hotham had spent over £100,000 on his scheme, but despite visits from Princess Charlotte, only child of the Prince of Wales and Caroline of Brunswick, and later from Princess Victoria, in 1827 John Stuart Mill noted that Bognor was 'An insignificant village (but) full of abortive attempts to rival Brighton' (in Young 1983: 114).

By 1837 Bognor had a town hall and assembly room but very little else. A 'Bognor Improvement Company' had foundered and duties on imported coal remained the insalubrious financial mainstay, while a station was finally opened more than three miles to the north on the Worthing to Chichester section of the main line when it opened in 1846. Bognor's 'reputation of well-bred inertia' now came strongly to the fore, although external stimulus came from the development of the Goodwood races. By the 1880s the 'Glorious Goodwood' week gave an elegant impetus to the resort although royalty had now deserted the South East altogether. From a population of 1,399 in 1831 the town grew slowly to 3,290 by 1881.

In the 1850s the High Street was the only complete street in Bognor, with isolated houses or terraces within surrounding fields. But significant developments came with an 1864 rail link, an 1865 pier, a newspaper, and new terraces, squares and avenues to the west. In 1867 a local government board was formed which undertook the building of a sea wall, thereby also providing a promenade. Water supplies and drainage were also tackled, giving by 1893 'a quiet little place of eminent respectability and unimpeachable sanitary record' (in Young 1983: 156). Henceforth modest villas were the quiet style until the 1929 convalescence of King George V at Bognor left the town with the 'Regis' suffix and another revival of activity. In 1929 the West Bognor Estate Company was formed to develop Aldwick and Pagham, and superior mock-Tudor and Georgian villas appeared to the west. To the east of the pier meanwhile, smaller plots of land were being acquired by Mr Billy Butlin who became a local celebrity of the 1930s. A new type of entertainment, for different groups of people was about to burst on Bognor by 1939.

Bognor illustrates well the problems resulting from the interplay of the stimulus of fashionable visitors on the one hand, and the over-ambition of speculative developments on the other. As such, it has parallels with resorts such as Herne Bay or Seaford. The latter was by 1835 'a retired, but in many respects, an agreeable sea bathing place'. Seaford's railway link was completed in 1864, the same year as that of Bognor, and several schemes were promoted, led by Dr William Tyler Smith of London. But insufficient capital was available to both drain the marshy common and protect the town from the sea. The 1861 population of 1,000 increased only to 1,600 by 1911. The 'embryonic Brighton' had failed and retirement villas, convalescent homes and residential schools gave the town its flavour. As one bewildered commentator put it in 1876, 'somehow the railway has failed to develop it' (Lowerson, 1975; Lowerson and Myerscough 1977: 38–41).

If Brighton was the 'Queen of watering places', it was surely only correct that Eastbourne be dubbed 'The Empress of watering places'. It was the elegant and successful creation of the 7th Duke of Devonshire, one of the four great Sussex landowners. By 1840 there were already about 600 houses spread over four settlements within the parish – at Eastbourne itself, Meads, Southbourne and Sea Houses. The main residence was Compton Place which, together with two-thirds of the parish, about 2,600 acres, was under the ownership of the Cavendishes, Dukes of Devonshire. By 1849 the LBSCR had been persuaded to build an extension to Eastbourne from Polegate, and rapid development followed. In the early 1860s the Gilberts, the only other owners of property in Eastbourne, also laid plans to develop their property. Despite setbacks and recurrent over-ambitious property speculations, the population of the town reached 10,000 by 1871. During the 1870s and 1880s the national building boom was truly reflected in Eastbourne, so that by 1891 the population had reached 34,000, making Eastbourne the second-largest town in Sussex after Brighton.

By the 1880s 'cornfields and barns (had) given place to substantial shops and dwelling houses, almost from one end of the parish to the other' (in

Cannadine 1980: 246) and the 'Belgravia of Eastbourne', with wide, tree-lined streets and spacious villas, stretched from the seafront to Compton Place itself. Hotels, baths, pavilion, park and pier and full civic amenities accompanied this development, and in 1883 the town was incorporated, with the Duke's agent as first mayor. Despite slight recession in the 1890s and the death of the 7th Duke, growth remained rapid. With the 8th and 9th Dukes as mayors, the success of the town was founded on solid respectability. It was clearly now in the front rank of seaside towns but as such, it needed a large service sector to provide the necessary comforts. Invisible to the elite, the working-class residents of Eastbourne continued to be duly deferential. In 1913 one newspaperman noted that 'on the whole the people drag their chains with the utmost politeness' (in Cannadine 1980: 357–8). After 1914 the town changed very little in its exclusivity, with municipal councils replacing but echoing the paternalistic policies of the Cavendish family. The degree of control over social policy varied with time, but the tone set here by large landowners was certainly markedly different from that by businessmen.

However, tensions could arise between paternalistic developer and the local community, and they came acutely to the surface in the latest of the Sussex developments, at Bexhill. By 1840 the small village of Bexhill, belonging to the de la Warr family, had its theatre and circulating library, and was set for expansion with the arrival of the Brighton to Hastings railway in 1846 (Bartley 1971: 16–39). But as late as 1870 Lower noted that 'it is almost the only really available site on the Sussex coast that has not been turned into a "watering place", for which its natural beauty and healthful climate so eminently qualify it'. The familiar pattern of failed schemes then began with at least three local speculative ventures; but in 1880 the first de la Warr land came onto the market, and residential building began in earnest.

Between 1881 and 1911 population increased by a staggering 521.5 per cent, reaching 15,330 by the latter date. Indeed, it was the only south-eastern resort growing significantly at this time (Walton 1983: 68). Although rather too far from London to become a top-ranking resort, the enthusiastic promotion by the 8th Earl de la Warr, the 'maker of Bexhill', ensured success. In the 1880s and 1890s Bexhill-on-Sea gained a sea wall and esplanade, kursaal, cycle track, golf club and Sackville Hotel, the latter used by the Earl for his splendid *fin-de-siècle* parties. This social leadership once again set the tone, with the earl also chairman of the urban board and mayor in 1904 and 1905. Earl Brassey, related through marriage to the de la Warrs, served in 1908 and 1909, and the 9th Earl de la Warr served again as mayor in 1933–5. Bexhill provided a late flourish of the planned, holistic concept of a resort. It attracted the children of Imperial civil servants to the private schools in genteel surroundings. But success was crucially dependent on the spice of aristocratic individuality which had been provided by the de la Warrs.

Certain common features are apparent in resort development before

1914. Many grew initially as overwhelming and specialized suburbs of an older core, as did Bognor from Bersted, Herne Bay from Herne, Broadstairs from St Peter's, and Bexhill from its parent one mile inland. There were no totally new towns to compare, for example, with Bournemouth. The integration of accessible seafront, beach, and the combination of high and low ground and other topographical minutiae were of obvious significance. But more important in explaining success was landownership and entrepreneurial outlook. The aristocratic 'one-man towns' of Folkestone, Eastbourne or Bexhill set a certain tone from the outset, which was generally successfully maintained by later non-aristocratic local government boards and councils. In an age of emulation and social competition, the importance of landowning connections was prized, and when resorts enjoyed royal visits, whether to eighteenth-century Brighton or twentieth-century Bognor, development was greatly enhanced. By contrast the bourgeois resorts of Herne Bay or Seaford, however assiduously promoted, could not aspire to the same success. These also lacked another ingredient: an early start. Resorts such as Margate, Brighton, Hastings and Ramsgate had at least a half-century of development behind them at the time of Victoria's accession. Their accumulated expertise, prestige and physical expansion was thus only slowly overhauled by the more reputable newcomers such as Eastbourne and Folkestone. One further point on the importance of the railways – enough has been written here to demonstrate that their role was rarely a primary consideration. One can point to successful pre-railway resorts (Brighton, Margate), those rendered more financially viable by the arrival of the railway (Eastbourne), and those where railway access seemed immaterial for many years (e.g. Bexhill).

Ports and Industrial Developments

The ports and industrial towns of the South East have never fired the imagination in the way that the resorts have done, even though by 1831 their combined populations were higher than those of the resorts. Development owed much to seaward external linkage, rather than the railway network, which again therefore was not all-important in accounting for expansion.

Areas of late-nineteenth-century industrial expansion included the cement works on the coast between Dartford and Gravesend; paper manufacture in the lower Darent Valley; a variety of industries in the lower Medway; and brick and gunpowder manufacture south of the Isle of Sheppey. Between Dartford and Faversham there developed an industrial landscape and society quite different to its agrarian predecessor. In 1834 William Aspdin began the manufacture of Portland cement at Northfleet in a series of small cement works. The early Thames-side pits soon became uneconomic and were abandoned as the industry moved southwards, and at Swanscombe long rows of terraced houses were laid out in a grid-iron pattern for the cement workers as the population rose steeply.

At nearby Gravesend by the early 1840s the number of steamboat passengers alighting annually at the piers had passed the million mark. Water transport stimulated employment as the port attracted factories. Amon Wild designed a town hall in 1836, the Rosherville Pleasure Gardens were laid out in 1830 in an old chalk quarry and new houses, hotels, reading rooms and public baths appeared as the town flourished as 'half sea-port, half watering-place'. The industries included paper, lime, brewing and cement manufacture. However, it was the increase in sea bathing which was held to account for a combined population at Gravesend and Milton of 9,445. By 1931 the population was 35,495 and the nearly four-fold growth rate reflected the greatly increased industrial as well as commuting functions.

The River Darent was a focus for industrial development. Following the repeal of excise duty on paper, mills were established at Dartford in 1862, with paper production surging towards the end of the century. Here, and at Northfleet and Sittingbourne, logs and pulp were imported from the Baltic or Canada, and newsprint was sent to London. Growth at Erith occurred with the development of engineering and especially with the 1889 opening of the Maxim Nordenfelt Gun and Ammunition Company factory, which became Vickers in 1898. In the twentieth century, chemicals, gunpowder manufacture and large coal wharves all added to the Erith scene, while growth at Crayford came in the First World War with further expansion of Vickers armaments (Jessup 1974: 151–5).

The lower Medway was another urban/industrial growth area where Rochester, Strood, Chatham and Gillingham coalesced to form the largest urban agglomeration in the South East outside London. By 1911 both Chatham and Gillingham alone had populations well in excess of 50,000. Chatham's population reached 90,000 by 1901. Growth at Gillingham was particularly rapid from a population of 28,040 in 1891 to 52,252 by 1911. Downstream from Aylesford many industrial villages grew quickly in the later nineteenth century. The Medway had long been canalized but had attracted little London capital, and served mainly as a coal importing river with little industrial development until the mid-nineteenth century. Then the manufacture of Portland Cement provided many jobs, and population quickened at such places as Snodland, Burham, Halling, Frindsbury and Wouldham, (Preston 1977; Waters 1984).

Brickmaking and clay extraction flourished to the east of Gillingham at Lower Halstow, Newington and Sittingbourne on the brickearth soils. At Upnor and Snodland there were specialist barge-building concerns, constructing vessels to move the bulky materials. At Sittingbourne, paper mills had also been erected in the early 1840s, to be enlarged after the First World War. At Queenborough, old copperas works were superseded by noxious fertilizer and glue factories, together with tar distillation and gasworks. Snodland was also the location for a paper works, a gasworks and a bleaching powder factory. The industrial complexes also contained many seedcrushing and engineering works, the latter growing with the dockyards at Sheerness and Chatham. These two later concerns were probably the largest industrial employers in nineteenth-century Kent (Hood 1979: 291–8). On the Swale, sheltered by the Isle of Sheppey, Faversham also developed its coasting trade and by the nineteenth century production from gunpowder mills, brickfields and a large brewery gave it a flourishing economy.

This developing industrial coastline stimulated a remarkable railway 'feud' as companies competed to serve the area. By 1849 the SER line ran between Strood and London but in 1853 the East Kent Railway was permitted to build a line between Strood and Canterbury – the forerunner of the 1859 London, Chatham and Dover. After 1856 the cement and paper industries were helped by the opening of the Strood–Maidstone railway, but in the 1860s it was the LCDR line which increased Chatham's significance as a dockyard and military centre, and also stimulated development at Faversham. When the LCDR line to Whitstable was opened in 1860, Faversham became a railway junction, and the LCDR decided to situate its locomotive and carriage depots and repairs works here. The company became the second-largest employer in the town, after the Shepherd Neame brewery (Course 1958: 189; White 1982: 38). By contrast railway company developments on the Isles of Grain and Sheppey were not so successful. Sheerness-on-Sea failed as a new Victorian coastal resort, and the SER's 1882 Port Victoria on the Isle of Grain opposite and competing with Queenborough, closed in 1916. These failures were later echoed by the Southern Railway's failed venture at Allhallows-on-Sea, begun to emulate Westcliff-on-Sea in the inter-war period (Course 1958: 488).

Indeed, after 1914 industrial momentum slowed down. Many of the marginal cement concerns were closed following the formation of the Association of Portland Cement Manufacturers in the difficult years of the 1920s. Working was thereafter concentrated into four large works at Stone, Swanscombe and Northfleet. But the Isle of Grain now also became industrialized as oil storage plants and refineries were established. Paper-making continued to flourish, with mills scattered throughout the Medway, Darent and Cray valleys, as well as in large buildings at Erith, Northfleet and Gravesend. By the late 1930s such concerns as Gravesend's Imperial Paper Mill; Northfleet's Bowater's Paper Mill or Dartford's Daily Telegraph Paper Mills, dominated the scene (Carrier 1937: 58–60).

The industrial/urban complex developing along Lower Thames-side by the second half of the nineteenth century illustrates a number of points about

---

Plate 6.3 Dover Castle by J. M. W. Turner (published 1826). The view from the precipitous Shakespeare Cliff across the town, towards the castle. During the Napoleonic Wars these western heights were hollowed out with fortified trenches and caves, many of which are still intact under the 'dread summits of this chalky bourn' (*King Lear*, Act IV, Scene IV).

the nature of regional relations within the South East. Lower Thames-side was, of course, the successor as an industrial region to the now 'de-industrialized' Interior. The wealden armaments industry now found its more modern echo in the factories at Erith, Woolwich, Chatham and Faversham. And as the industries grouped along tidewater, they brought demands for transport, services and housing. Such development was stimulated by the advent of larger industrial plant, the locational freedom granted by the use of steam-powered engines, the ease of importing cheap foreign raw materials and proximity to London. And since much of the coastline was poor agriculturally, it was a cheap development for industrialists and railway companies.

After 1840 this industrial complex was also brought more firmly within London's residential grip. By 1939 electrified railways reached the Medway Towns, bringing much of the north Kent coast into daily contact with the capital. So industries came to mix, sometimes uneasily, with residential demands. The shift in political and demographic terms within Kent now became obvious. Before the 1832 Reform Act no borough west of the Medway had returned a member to parliament. But now both Greenwich and Chatham obtained seats, and the old eastern dominance was broken. By the mid-twentieth century west Kent returned more members than did east Kent, reflecting once again the growth of London out into the South East (Jessup 1974: 149–50).

The main commercial theme on the east Kent coast after 1840 was one of contraction into two towns, Dover and Folkestone. These two gradually absorbed the functions of nearby Deal and Hythe, neither of which recovered their Napoleonic Wars prosperity. Hythe declined throughout the nineteenth century, losing a seat in the 1832 Reform Act. Deal's 1811 population had been 7,351 but this had grown only to 8,004 by 1871. Its employment had rested largely upon the 'foying' concerns, refitting and supplying large vessels standing offshore in the Downs. But as ships grew larger they needed less provisioning and this, together with the lack of any harbour facilities, ultimately brought commercial decline (Whyman 1969: 129).

By contrast, Dover presented an example of cumulative growth accruing from its location as the nearest point on the coast to Europe. At the end of the eighteenth century Dover was the fourth-largest town in Kent and the Napoleonic Wars reinforced its strong garrison role. The fortifications remained impressive, and Cobbett was moved to point out characteristically in 1823 that on Shakespeare Cliff:

> More brick and stone have been buried in this hill than would go
> to build a neat new cottage for every labouring man in the counties
> of Kent and Sussex (in Whyman 1970: 42).

The combination of garrison town, seaside resort, port and harbour, and principal continental crossing point ensured a steady population increase in this pleasant town throughout the nineteenth century (Plate 6.3). Its 1801 population of 7,709 grew to 41,794 by 1901. Enhanced by the SER link in 1844, the LCDR link with Canterbury in 1861, and its telegraph station link with France in the 1850s, Dover's economy and nodal status continued to expand well into the twentieth century.

The industries of east Kent were not solely bound up with its ports. In the hinterland of Deal and Dover an industry unique in the South East was developing, for in 1890 the presence of coal was confirmed in an abandoned Channel Tunnel working. The first coal was produced from Shakespeare Cliff, Dover in 1912 after years of trial borings and difficulties over leasing and finance. In 1913 collieries at Tilmanstone and Snowdown began, to be followed by Chislet in 1918 and Betteshanger in the late 1920s. At least four other smaller inter-war collieries were opened but soon abandoned. The east Kent light railway network threaded through the coalfield, linking collieries to the Southern Railway and to the war-time supply port at Richborough. An aerial ropeway was erected in 1930 to carry coal from Tilmanstone to the wharves at Dover.

However, the coalfield faced both financial and technical difficulties. Small, unstable mining companies soon collapsed, as costs of obtaining the coal from beneath 1,000 ft of younger, water-laden rocks proved too great. Thus the Shakespeare colliery was sealed off in 1915. The production figures up to 1939 were in the order of 1.5 to 2.25 million tons, exceeding production from the Forest of Dean and Somerset, but not comparable with the larger northern and midland coalfields. The envisaged annual production of about 10 million tons was never realized, one reason being the failure to attract coal-using industries to the area. A planned iron-smelting works at Dover, for example, never materialized.

The absence of any local mining expertise entailed the importation of mining families into the area. Groups of cottages were built to be followed by planned, self-contained townships at Aylesham (to serve Snowdon colliery), at Elvington (for Tilmanstone) and Hersden (for Chislet). All these townships were at some distance from the pits, and only at Betteshanger is the settlement next to the colliery. In general, the coalfield failed to live up to expectations. The coal, lean-bituminous and semi-anthracitic, was not used locally, but was also expensive in London compared with imported coal. One result however, was that fears about the preservation of the rural character of the area proved unfounded. Although the townships are certainly very different from the local vernacular buildings, the surrounding east Kent countryside remained largely untouched (Millward and Robinson 1973: 179–83).

The Sussex coast did not share such industrialization. Problems of achieving and maintaining access to the sea were more complex because of persistent longshore shingle drift, while the railways acted not to reinforce locational advantages, as they generally had in north Kent, but to divert trade away from the sea.

Overall, this period witnessed the contraction of Sussex port commerce and industry into Shoreham and Newhaven, and also saw the changing relative importance of the two ports (Farrant 1976a: 97–120; and 1976b). By the 1840s Shoreham was the more important in terms of tonnage, with 36 per cent of the Sussex total. By 1850 Newhaven had replaced Rye as second-ranked port, but both Littlehampton and Chichester were relatively insignificant by mid-century. Rye lost a member of parliament in the 1832 Reform Act, but a modest coasting trade was maintained through fishing and flint carrying from the outport of Rye Harbour. Littlehampton, the outport for Arundel and a small resort, had a modest general cargo trade in coal and gravel which engendered wharves, shipyards and workshops; but by 1939 port traffic ceased altogether in the face of competition from its resort functions (White 1982: 102–3; Course 1958: 162).

Shoreham was the largest industrial/port complex in Sussex at this time. It had essentially been resuscitated by the growth of Brighton, which it served as an outport. The troublesome shingle bar across the mouth of the Adur had been pierced and the entrance stabilized after 1818. The lagoon behind the bar was canalized as far as Aldrington by the 1850s and the basin enclosed at its seaward end. By May 1840 the railway from Brighton had opened; a regular steamer services ran from Kingston to Dieppe; an important coal coasting trade was maintained; and a Portslade-by-Sea was envisaged. But there were setbacks. By 1847 the Kingston steamer service was switched to Newhaven, and Kingston thereafter concentrated on freight and on developing the modestly successful residential Kingston-by-Sea. Finally, Shoreham's coastal coal trade was badly affected by the 1862 switch to overland supplies to Brighton by rail from Deptford.

However, by the 1870s there were new gasworks at Portslade, with chemical works at the western end of the lagoon. Coal imports were increased to supply these ventures, and an electricity power station was built in 1902–6. In Portslade village John Dudeney had the large brewery building, Le Carbonne, erected in 1881. Although these industrial developments put paid to any hopes of successful resort growth at Portslade-by-Sea, there was continuous ribbon growth along the A259 in the twentieth century. In 1908–12 the LBSCR carriage and wagon works were transferred from Brighton to North Lancing, employing over 1,400 men by the 1930s, when there was also further expansion of gasworks and depot facilities at Shoreham, and the growth of yacht and launch construction. And on the Adur meadows Shoreham airfield was used by the military in the First World War and was then taken over by an aircraft manufacturer. But in 1933 it became a civilian municipal airport complete with a futuristic terminal and flights to the Isle of Wight, Deauville and the Channel Islands (Tonkins 1964: 247–51; Brookfield 1955: 35–50; Lowerson 1980b: 177).

Newhaven served the Ouse Valley as an outport and coal importing centre. The river was straightened and a large groyne, over 150 yards long, erected to stabilize shingle and to keep the harbour entrance open. In 1847 the railway spur from Lewes arrived and the LBSCR instantly transferred the Dieppe steamer service from Kingston to here. Henceforward much of the activity of the town centred on the packet steamers. The harbour was deepened in the 1860s, and an impressive breakwater erected in the 1890s. Newhaven dealt with cargo and passengers, mainly in the direction symbolized by the large London and Paris Hotel (demolished 1958) although diversification came with the later establishment of LBSCR and Southern Railway marine engineering.

In 1831 nearly 17 per cent of the South East's population lived at the coast, but by 1931 the figure was 29 per cent, rising still further by 1939. The successful resorts were clearly those at Brighton, Margate, Folkestone and Eastbourne. The successful ports and industrial centres were those of the lower Medway, Dover, Newhaven and Shoreham. The coast of Kent was more plebeian, industrialized and London-orientated than that of Sussex, with nearly five times as many people living in the ports and industrial coastal towns by 1931. Indeed, in Kent the balance of population had swung remarkably in favour of the ports over the hundred-year period. In Sussex, on the other hand, it was the resorts which showed phenomenal growth, accounting for over half the population of the county by 1931 (Table 6.1).

The Country Towns

The Inland Towns on the Coastal Fringe

In 1831 slightly more people lived in inland towns on the Coastal Fringe than in either resorts or ports. Before 1939 such towns experienced varied fortunes but by 1931 they claimed as much as 20 per cent of the region's population. In Kent such towns showed little relative growth, and in Sussex they underwent a dramatic relative decline to become the least important category of all by 1931. But in Surrey the towns between the Weald in the south and the LCC boundary in the north grew enormously.

Overall, inland towns which were near the coasts grew little in comparison with those on the coast itself. 'Sleepy hollows' served local needs and were subject to the vicissitudes of rural prosperity and depression, being both image and agent of the countryside (Lowerson 1983: 221–34). Many market towns now had a much reduced role.

Chichester and Lewes remained twin administrative centres, acting as county towns for East and West Sussex after the splitting of the county in 1888. By 1931 Chichester had grown to 13,912 from 8,152 in 1841 and Lewes to 10,784 from 9,199, hardly dynamic growth. Both received railway links in 1846, and Lewes became an important junction and the more go-ahead, with its iron foundry, printing works, breweries and tannery, among its administrative and juridical activities. In the important corn-growing Coastal Plain, Chichester was an ecclesiastical centre but also served as a corn market (the corn exchange being built in 1832); a retail market; and a livestock market, when the streets were foul with mud and when, as W. H. Hudson noted: 'bellowings, bleatings, and gruntings of the animals, and the smell of the same, filled the air'. But at other times, Chichester was very quiet, and Dean Burgon supposedly remarked that: 'half its citizens were fast asleep, and the other half walked on tiptoe so as not to wake them' (Lowerson 1980a: 165–6; McCann 1974).

Lower down the urban hierarchy, Steyning, Midhurst and Petworth stagnated gently. Petworth's population declined from 3,364 in 1841 to 2,503 in 1901, by which time the market was no longer recorded, and trade had decayed. In the 1820s Cobbett could write of its 'air of great strength . . . and durability'. By 1907 Midhurst possessed, in the form of its fictional counterpart Wimblehurst in H. G. Wells' *Tono-Bungay*, 'a clean and picturesque emptiness' (Cobbett 1930 edn: 161; Wells, repub. 1964: 65–6). When the castle and town of Arundel were transformed by the Duke of Norfolk in the 1890s it was significant that the money came neither from within the town, nor from the surrounding countryside, but from the Duke's coalfield interests. However, its population still declined from 2,803 in 1831 to 2,490 in 1931 (Plate 6.4).

The older Kentish market and administrative centres also experienced varying fortunes. Some were now threatened by the shifting emphasis towards London, which favoured north-west Kent and northern Surrey above all. Sevenoaks had grown from an 1831 population of 4,709 to 10,484 by 1931, although the SER official guide of 1859 had proclaimed that it was 'Near enough to London to keep it from decay and yet far enough to exclude an over-abundant measure of cockneyism' (in Course 1958: 202). Canterbury's population grew from 13,649 in 1831 to 24,446 in 1931. Milling, brewing, marketing and ecclesiastical functions occupied the city by the 1830s. Although several public buildings were erected at this time, mostly colleges and schools, there was no large population increase. This was in spite of the 1830 opening of the first English public railway between Canterbury and Whitstable to give

---

Plate 6.4 An aerial view of Arundel Castle. 'The traveller by train along the south coast of Sussex . . . is suddenly greeted by an improbable vision which combines Conway, Amiens and Claude Lorrain. The Downs roll back to reveal the careful eighteenth-century planting and model farms of a great estate, a red-roofed hillside town climbing to a ridge crowned by a huge French gothic Cathedral and a still more huge castle backed by a dramatically wooded park. As an overall landscape composition it is generally considered to be among the grandest and most successful creations of the Romantic imagination' (Robinson, J. M. 1982: v). The medieval castle had replaced Saxon Burpham as the central place for Roger of Montgomery's Rape of Arundel, but following the 1642 siege the castle was ruined. Nineteenth-century reconstruction began with a gateway of 1809 and extensions to the grounds in the 1830s. Apart from the keep, the gothic rebuilding bore little resemblance to its medieval predecessor.

the city access to the Thames estuary; the 1846 SER link with Ashford, and the rival 1861 LCDR link with Dover.

From the early nineteenth century Maidstone functioned as the county town of Kent. A Shire Hall and prison diversified the former economy which had revolved around brewing and paper-making. As a crossing point and Medway river port, transport interests were strengthened by the 1844 arrival of the SER. Motor engineering and foodstuffs processing were later added, and the 1831 population of 15,387 had grown to 42,280 by 1931, a growth rate more than double that of Canterbury. Even more striking was the growth of Ashford. From an 1831 population of 2,809 the market town had grown by 1931 to 15,248 people. Much of this growth – by far the greatest of the Kent inland Coastal Fringe towns – was traceable to the 1842 advent of the SER. In 1847 the SER moved its New Cross Gate locomotive works to Ashford, to be joined by the carriage and wagon works in 1850. An industrial new town was built, named Alfred's Town after the Duke of Connaught, who lived nearby. This company town was built alongside the works around a green and with public baths, inn and general store. The first housing was back-to-back and divided into flats, but rather better quality housing was added in the 1860s, together with a school and mechanics institute. New Town (as it came to be known) late expanded again with the 1913 transfer of workers from the Longhedge works at Chatham, when 126 new houses were built around the earlier development. (White 1982: 32–3; Course 1958: 39–40; Ashford Local History Group 1976: 15). Ashford's livestock market was also important, since by the late 1920s it had the largest turnover in the South East, drawing on large numbers of Romney Marsh sheep and wealden cattle. Its sales of store lambs were diffused throughout the South East (Min. of Ag. and Fish Economics Series 1929).

Surrey, 'the land of heart's desire', underwent the greatest transformation. From Haslemere to Farnham, Guildford, Dorking and Reigate, a chain of growth occurred. And on the southern edge of the London Basin there was similar growth at such towns as Woking and Leatherhead. In 1831 such towns had accounted for 10 per cent of Surrey's population, but by 1931 they accounted for over 40 per cent, nearly as much as the London suburbs up against the southern boundary of the LCC (Table 6.1).

Improved access by rail was a major factor. For some towns, such as Guildford, this reinforced and rejuvenated previously important marketing

---

Plate 6.5 Bank Holiday 1924: buses at Box Hill. Between 1919 and 1939 mid-Surrey was near enough to London for thousands to go on trains, buses, cycles, motor-cycles and in cars to enjoy its unrivalled facilities for recreation. Walkers preferred the remoter countryside of the North Downs ridgeway or the wooded Leith Hill district, but for the Cockney escaping from London for fresh air and a change of scene, Box Hill was then the limit of his ambitions. By 1924 fleets of special buses ran from all over south and west London on Bank Holidays. On the left is the Burford Bridge Hotel (British Transport Museum).

functions. For others, such as Woking or Redhill, it actually initiated urban society. Commuters and urbanites appeared, as at Farnham, where formerly 'prosperity hung on the seasons', but where now the glimpses and smells of countryside could be contrasted with 'the obtrusively new cockney villas' (Bourne 1913: 259–61).

Perhaps the best examples of railway creations are those of Redhill and Woking. In 1844 an important junction was made between the LBSCR and SER systems just north of Reigate at the lonely spot of Earlswood Common. With cheap building land available and with rail links to Ashford in one direction and Reading in the other, the junction soon grew to become Redhill. In 1849 a station was also opened at Reigate, bringing it within half-an-hour of London, and the two towns began to merge. North of the Downs in 1838 the London and South Western Railway opened a station at Woking Common on the banks of the Wey to serve Guildford. By 1858 the station was still in the midst of a solitary heath, but thereafter a grid-iron commuter settlement was established next to the village of Woking (now Old Woking), to be joined by expensive housing from the 1890s. Under the London Necropolis Act 1852, London citizens could be buried beyond the confines of the metropolis, and one quarter of the parish of Woking was purchased for this reason. The cemetery opened in 1854, and Brookwood station opened to serve it in 1864. Convict prisons and a lunatic asylum completed the strange mixture. What had been a parish of 1,975 people in 1831 became a town of 36,000 by 1931 and with electrification of the line, the volume of commuters steadily increased (Course 1973: 245–6).

Of the other rapidly-growing Surrey towns Guildford, Haslemere and Leatherhead were outstanding. The decayed market town of Haslemere had an 1831 population of just 849 people. Not until 1859 did the LSWR open a station here, but during the second half of the century the environmental quality of the Hindhead area was recognized, as many well-known Victorians came to acquire property nearby, including Tennyson and Shaw and an 'Arts and Crafts' movement was initiated (see p.346) (Rolston 1978: 97). In the twentieth century this artists' refuge was gradually submerged by commuters, a process hastened by the 1937 electrification of the Portsmouth line. By 1931 the population had grown to 4,340, although with the inclusion of neighbouring settlements, the census records it as 9,168. The whole area of former commonland towards Hindhead and at Grayshott, Shottermill, Churt and Thursley, was now being built over. Only the unusually high amount of National Trust property saved the area from even more amorphous and scattered development, and it was with the utmost difficulty that these Surrey towns retained their individuality.

Leatherhead grew equally rapidly from 1,724 in 1831 to 16,483 by 1931. Even in 1821 the Rev. James Dallaway could remark that the small town was:

losing its primary character and converting itself by a multiplication
of inconsiderable houses into an appendage of the enormous London
(in Brandon 1977: 89).

Its function as a Mole valley market town was enhanced by the manufacture
of bricks and tiles, but real growth came with the advent of the Epsom
and Leatherhead Railway and the LSWR in 1859. Increased commuting
possibilities were also opened up by the London-Guildford 'new line' of
1885 which passed through Leatherhead, and by the early electrification of
this line in 1925.

Links with London were therefore of the utmost importance to the
development of north Surrey. Most towns were commuter settlements from an
early date, but Guildford deserves special mention for its greater independence.
From an 1831 population of 3,924 it had grown to over 39,000 by 1939,
rejuvenated by the opening of the first station in 1845. Older industries such
as clothworking had lapsed; brewing and printing continued, but it was
principally an agricultural marketing town. The old market was held in the
High Street before its removal to North Street, and its ultimate banishment
altogether from the shopping area in the 1890s. The railway brought resident,
commuting and retired elements which tripled Guildford's population in the
second half of the century. Construction and motor car assembly were added to
its functions. A bypass was built between 1929 and 1934, using large amounts
of unemployed labour, and the speculative Charlotteville Estate of the 1860s
was followed by the spread of semi-detached housing through to 1939, limited
more by topographic difficulties on the steep chalk slopes than by any planning
constraints. The rapidity of population growth was recognized in 1927 by the
installation of the first Bishop of Guildford and in 1936 the foundation stone
of a new cathedral was laid on Stag Hill, although the cathedral itself was not
completed until 1961 (Chamberlin 1970).

Interior Towns

The Interior towns at this time represented by far the smallest category
of urban population. In 1831 they had accounted for just 2.5 per cent
of the south-eastern population, rising to 3.3 per cent by 1931. There
are, strictly speaking, no Interior towns in Surrey and only one, Tunbridge
Wells/Tonbridge (the census of 1831 still recorded them together) in Kent.
Maidstone, Interior in location, has already been discussed. It was thus in the
Sussex Weald that a number of small towns were to grow in the Victorian years.
But even here they were statistically insignificant, supplying in 1831 just 6.9
per cent of the county's population. By 1931 after considerable growth, they
had actually declined in relative terms to 5.4 per cent, being overwhelmed by
urban growth on the coast.

The one Interior town which was rather different was Tunbridge
Wells, which from the 1820s became a prosperous residential town. Its

Georgian architecture now mingled with substantial villas which merged the separate clusters of houses into one large settlement. The old spa centre at the Walks or Pantiles thus linked with Mount Ephraim, Mount Sion and Mount Pleasant, with the latter area in particular being favoured for commercial and housing development following the arrival of the SER in 1845. There had been no shortage of promoters for this line and both Tunbridge Wells and Tonbridge now grew vigorously. The 1841 population of the large parish of Tonbridge, which included both settlements, was 12,500 growing to 29,800 by 1871. Tunbridge Wells also gained links with the sea at St Leonard's by 1852 and Eastbourne in 1880–81, and could now provide access to resorts of sufficient quality to maintain its own elite aura.

In 1842 the SER had opened a station at Tonbridge five miles to the north of Tunbridge Wells. Originally 'Tunbridge', the settlement was now re-named so as to avoid confusion with its southern neighbour, an important decision since the station became the busiest on the SER outside London. As a station on the Redhill-Ashford Line, Tonbridge gained in significance with the opening of the more direct 'cut-off' from Deptford in 1868. This line penetrated the Chalk and Greensand escarpments and wove through 'a plethora of gentlemen's seats' (Course 1958: 159) and also opened up Sevenoaks to commuting. Originally a wealden market town, and with Medway trade down to Aylesford and Yalding, Tonbridge now grew around the station to the south of the river, separated by the floodplain from the old town and its castle. The 1851 population of 3,948 grew to 8,574 by 1871. But expansion here, in contrast with its more affluent neighbour, mostly emerged as unregulated rows, alleys and squares, often on the poorly drained floodplain. Not surprisingly, drainage issues were divisive within the town by the 1870s. Small traders made up a large proportion of the population and there were no wealthy landowners. Rates were already heavily felt, and it was not until after the 1875 Public Health legislation that provision for decent hygiene could be enforced (Barker-Reed 1982: 167–89).

Growth of the Interior towns therefore brought potential problems as well as wealth. Increased contact with the national economy stimulated social and spatial divisions which the rudimentary town councils found difficult to handle. The high-quality residential image of Tunbridge Wells was not matched elsewhere in the Weald, and it was the problems of neighbouring Tonbridge which were more akin to the experiences of several of the Sussex growth points.

There was certainly growth between 1831 and 1931. Older market towns such as East Grinstead, Hailsham, Horsham and Uckfield more than doubled their populations, while towns such as Burgess Hill, Crawley, Crowborough and Haywards Heath were created by purposive development on wealden commons. Administration lagged behind population growth, although census population figures are difficult to compare because these 'new' towns often grew at the edges of existing parishes. Burgess Hill, for example, grew at the junction of Clayton and Keymer; Crawley covered the small parish of that name as well as parts of Ifield and Worth; Crowborough was within Rotherfield parish; and Haywards Heath grew around a station set on heathland between Lindfield and Cuckfield. At East Grinstead, Horsham, Hailsham and Uckfield expansion similarly occurred on adjacent heathland. These centres had their unique aspects – Crowborough developed large, exclusive estates of housing; Horsham developed amidst an encircling ring of parklands, and Hailsham grew with the development of its ropeworks.

However, similarities in the growth of these towns can be noted. Firstly, all depended on the arrival of the railway to stimulate, if not to initiate, growth. Where local conditions favourable for growth occurred, the railway provided the link with London and the wider world which reinforced that growth. At Crawley, Haywards Heath and Burgess Hill it was the 1841 opening of the LBSCR (as it was to become) which overwhelmed old coaching functions and promoted growth. At Horsham growth was similarly stimulated after 1848, at Uckfield after 1858, at Crowborough after 1868, and at Hailsham after 1880.

A second similarity lies in the process of development. Commonland was enclosed and heathland purchased to facilitate the building of large estates without the piecemeal development on strip fields found nearer the coast. At Crowborough, the Beacon Hill and Crowborough Warren estates were built by the Connor brothers for retired businessmen or civil servants. At Crawley the 'new' town was built up alongside the railway by speculative developers by the 1870s, with the firm of Longleys coming into prominence thereafter. The enclosure of Hailsham common in 1855 brought builders from as far as Brighton or Hastings to buy former allotments. At Burgess Hill the enclosure of Keymer Common in 1828 similarly drew in speculative developers and businessmen, among them the Ellmans, the renowned sheep breeders from Glynde. The 1857 Clayton enclosure completed the process for Burgess Hill, allowing this area to become a 'very improving neighbourhood' among the farms and commons of the Low Weald. At Haywards Heath the 1861 enclosure of the common initiated a similar process, while villas could also be built on the nearby Boltro Farm estate (Short 1984a; Ford and Gabe 1981).

A third similarity was the prominence of local businessmen – especially builders and tradesmen – in local political life. Few of the towns had old-established resident gentry families. Therefore, when the newly formed parish council met at Crowborough in 1905 there were four tradesmen and five men representing building interests out of the 13 present. At Hailsham rope manufacturers, corn dealers, property developers, and representatives from the Church and professions guided the various town institutions before 1914. At Crawley it was the Longleys and Moses Nightingale, a corn dealer and son of the local brick manufacturer, who were most prominent (Lowerson 1980b). At Burgess Hill again it was brickmakers. The Norman family, with Sampson Copestake, combined Victorian philanthropy and self-interest on a variety of committees. As the town grew, so did the multiplicity of committees, and such men were brought ever more closely into tight networks of public and commercial power. The contexts for such exercise of power were the parish vestries and councils, the Rural Sanitary Authorities and District Councils, the Poor Law union guardians, the boards of education, the gas and water companies, and the agriculture marketing companies.

To some extent, these local committees also provided appropriate settings for the integration of 'pseudo-gentry' into their adopted communities. London financiers and bankers moved to the Crawley area; businesswomen 'Madam' Emily Temple and Lady Hastings brought prestige to Burgess Hill's development; while a great variety of merchant and finance capital found its way from around the world to the slopes of Crowborough. Hence, one final similarity can be discerned: there was an increasing social gulf opening up between wealthy newcomers and the older, locally-based community. While the 'colonization of the Weald' was predominantly a middle-class affair, the towns also had their artisan dwellings, often spatially distinct from the more affluent developments. Agricultural workers lived on the fringes of these towns, and thus Burgess Hill had its Ganders Row; Crowborough had its Jarvis Brook industrial area; while the working-class households at Hailsham were grouped on the edges of the old common and between the ropeworks, brickfields, and gasworks. The 'new town' at Uckfield to the south of the new railway link in 1871 had its Framfield Road, with households headed by labourers, tradesmen and industrial workers in the nearby brewery or brickyards (Pearce 1984: 203).

Not all ventures, of course, were successful. In the 1890s the Sussex Estates Company scheme at Crawley foundered for lack of capital; in the 1880s the Sackville Estate on newly-enclosed commonland at East Grinstead similarly faltered through to 1945; while cyclical over-provision of housing was commonplace at many other towns (Lowerson 1979). But overall, the romantic image of the Weald, doubtless stimulated by artists and writers, encouraged a veritable middle-class invasion.

Structure and Change in the Countryside

Although many saw the great changes of the period as bound up with urbanization, many retreated to the countryside in an attempt to keep the town at a distance. But even in the countryside there was a steady process of capital accumulation by cosmopolitan landowners and their tenants. National and international markets were joined and farming became more specialized, capital-intensive, cost-effective and efficient. But the success achieved by some was balanced by the failure of others. The first theme to be pursued therefore, is rural inequality and community contrasts, to be followed by a closer discussion of south-eastern farming and rural social change.

By the mid-nineteenth century various processes of change had created 'open' and 'close' parishes in the South East. The regional differences can be broadly signposted using J. M. Wilson's *Imperial Gazetteer of England and Wales* (1870) which gives details on landownership. Parishes were described as 'most or all in one estate', 'not much divided' or 'divided among a few' and these can be regarded as essentially 'close'. Alternatively they could be 'subdivided' or 'much subdivided' – in other words essentially 'open' (Fig. 6.6).

One point to emerge is that the balance of 'open' and 'close' parishes was essentially equal. The most extreme form of 'close' parish, where the land was 'most or all in one estate' (the estate village) amounted to just over 4 per cent, mostly on the North and South Downs, Sussex Coastal Plain and Lower Greensand/Scarpfoot zone. The less extreme version of the essentially 'close' parish were those 'divided among a few'. These constituted 42 per cent of the total but they were again relatively more important in the South Downs, Sussex Coastal Plain, Lower Greensand/Scarpfoot zone, and especially the North Downs and north Kent. In other words the essentially 'close' parishes in the South East were most frequently to be found in the Coastal Fringe. At the other end of the landownership spectrum were the essentially 'open' parishes. These were most significant in the High and Low Weald; but featured strongly also in the London Basin, Bagshot Sands, and on the Romney Marsh/Pevensey Levels, revealing a strong association between 'open' communities and wood/pasture Interior, underdeveloped environments. The *Gazetteer* is not an infallible source in detail but the broad regional trends are clear (Mills and Short 1983: 253–62).

The South Downs in particular was a countryside of 'close' parishes. Many were small in population and area, and completely dominated by individual families. The Gages owned 95 per cent of West Firle by 1840. The two parishes of Stanmer and Falmer were almost completely within the Earl of Chichester's estate centred on Stanmer Place. The absentee Earl of Abergavenny owned 94 per cent of Rodmell, the Earl of Liverpool 93 per cent of Tarring Neville, and the Trevors 75 per cent of Glynde. Large farms, held on long leases following centuries of engrossment and consolidation, were interspersed with the large houses of the squirearchy within their imposing parklands, perhaps landscaped by Brown or Repton. The scale and grandeur of the scene mirrored the conservative politics of deference and paternalism. Thus at West Firle 'the tone and tempo of village life was strongly shaped by the landowning class', while 'the array of visible and formal leisure activities was limited in the main to those sanctioned from above' (Griffiths 1976: 16). The number of cottages and the estate work-force were maintained at a low level so as to minimize potential costs of pauperism. An alternative explanation is that the Gages chose to sink their capital into their farming operations and tenantry obligations, rather than concentrate on cottage provision. Nevertheless, at West Firle, migrant harvest labour, with its potentially destabilizing effect,

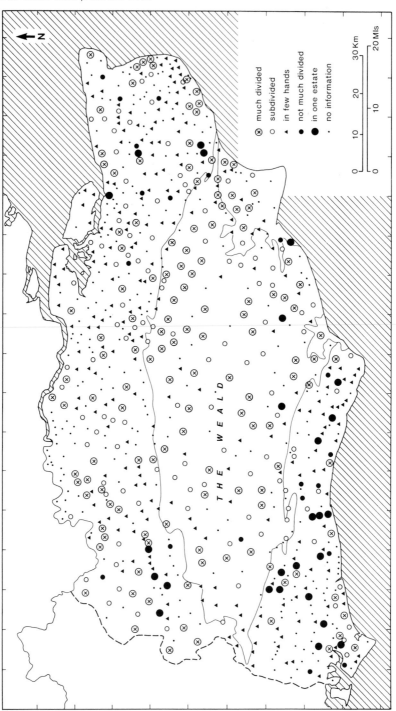

Figure 6.6 Contrasting patterns of parish landownership *c*.1870.

was rarely used. Instead a number of men, 'those who slept rough', were tolerated the year round, living geographically and socially on the edge of the community. They combined high degrees of skill with much routine drudgery and served to augment the local work-force at harvest times. Theirs was a cash wage but they were independent, and outside the paternalistic relations of the village.

However the 'close' parish is defined, whether in terms of restriction of settlement, concentrated landownership, or limited cottage provision, West Firle is a very good example. In other South Downland parishes, control by large tenants – 'the aristocrats of the farming community' (Wood 1938) – was equally keenly felt. At Kingston Buci, for example, there was really only the one farm in the entire parish, and many large downland farmhouses contained most of the farm labour force, often as living-in farm servants. Capitalist relations did not preclude the continuation of living-in where circumstances dictated (Short 1984b). Elsewhere, clergy control might be important where 'dispauperised parishes' were sought by means of various policies, including the encouragement of later marriages, or by simply making poor relief difficult to obtain. Landowners, tenant farmers and clergy produced a totality of paternalistic control which maintained 'the tissue of fear and gratitude that we call deference' (Hay 1975: 249). In such circumstances overt rural protest was rare. The farm and estate work-force was small, scattered and well-supervised. Church (Church of England) and Sunday school attendances might be monitored, and the voting patterns of the tenantry closely scrutinized. Magistrates in favour of game preservation were hard on poachers, and at West Firle, the latter, if caught, stood to lose jobs as well as cottages.

In west Sussex the downland was dominated by still more powerful landowners. From Goodwood Park, the Duke of Richmond owned more than 17,000 acres by 1873, worth nearly £20,000 in rent. Lord Leconfield at Petworth owned nearly 30,000 acres, while the Duke of Norfolk's 19,000 acres around Arundel were worth nearly £30,000. Elsewhere the four small parishes of East and West Clandon and East and West Horsley were dominated from the Palladian mansion of the Earl of Onslow at Clandon Park. At Chevening and Chilham owners re-aligned the old Pilgrim's Way to suit their own purposes while Capability Brown landscapes were fashioned at Chilham, Claremont and Danson Park, Bexley. The physical stamp of the 'close' village was thus ensured. At Kennington and Hothfield in Kent there had been evictions, resulting in journeys to work of four to six miles per day, and the destruction of houses, especially in east Kent, combined with a general population increase to create great pressure outside the 'close' communities.

The great contrast was to be found in the Weald. Now devoid of ironworks, glass and cloth, the woods and heathlands still attracted migrants. There were certainly large estates to be found, such as at Ashburnham, or that of the Abergavennys at Eridge Park, Frant, or Earl de la Warr at Buckhurst and Knole. But their estates were intermixed with smaller pastoral holdings. The dual employments of farmers, shopkeepers and tradesmen, carriers and woodcutters, etc., were also still a very real presence by 1840, despite Victorian assurances that the English peasantry had vanished. This large group of people were both marginal to, yet encompassed by, the capitalist permeation of the countryside in which they dwelt (Reed 1984: 53–76).

With land available and limited local powers to prohibit settlement, 'open' communities grew steadily, often spawning poorly-built cottages in profusion. At Chailey such activity nevertheless left a shortage of accommodation because although many cottages had been built by the 1860s at low rents, people held on to them and undertook long work journeys rather than leave, while others 'swarmed in from all around' (BPP XXVI, 1865). At least one attack of fever in Chailey in 1863 was attributed to the aggravations of overcrowding, and inevitable castigation came from contemporary observers. Richard Heath noted how:

> those who exercise the Christian ministry in the Weald complain of the apathy and stolid indifference of the people, of the rowdyism of the boys, and the immorality of both sexes. From all I heard it would be difficult to exaggerate the latter evil. Let no-one suppose however, that they are peculiarly corrupt. It is poverty, ignorance, and a low state of public opinion which is at the root of the evil (Heath 1978 edn: 186).

Nonconformity still thrived in such conditions, however. Sects such as The Dependents (Cokelers) had been founded by John Sirgood at Loxwood in the later nineteenth century, practising co-operation and communal living, and reaching more than 2,000 strong by his death in 1885. Other dissenting sects included the Huntingtonians from Cranbrook, Jezreelites, Latter-day Saints and Bible Christians. Their corrugated-iron sheds are still a familiar site across the Weald, as in the Heathfield area, and formerly they would have provided chapel-based community and friendship among migrant families (Everitt 1972). With wealden settlement more dispersed, an individualistic, semi-subsistence livelihood characterized such communities. At Nutley, on the fringe of Ashdown Forest:

> Numbers of little cottages may be counted below in the valley, each with cowhouse, garden, orchard, and one or two little crofts, green and flourishing, and all cribbed from the waste.

While:

> On the Forest reside numbers of those strange people who come down among the townsfolk in houses on wheels .... Their stock consists of toys, brushes and brooms of all kinds. From these secluded valleys issue, just before harvest, a motley group of men, women and children, all wending their way to the extensive corn tracts along the coast, and 'under the hills', intent

on earning as much as they can at harvesting, for to this they look
for their annual supply of clothes (*Brookes guide and directory for
Uckfield and District* 1888: 105).

The mobility of such people was characteristic of open communities.
Poor farming environments and small family farms combined with under-
employment by the 1830s to continue the tradition of south-eastern harvest
migrations. Such movements took place not only from the Interior Weald but
also from the 'miniature interiors' of the West Surrey heaths. The acidity of
the peaty-gley soils, their lack of minerals, and deficient drainage, gave rise
largely to 'cheerless unprofitable waste'. By the 1840s only just over half of
the Bagshot Sands were cultivated, and the area possibly had the poorest
soils in the South East (Ferguson 1979: 55). George Sturt (*alias* Bourne)
chronicled some of the working lives and movements of the heathlanders of
the Pirbright–Aldershot area. Men's work alternated between gravel-digging,
well-digging and maintenance, odd jobs in the local parks, carting timber and
sand or taking hops to Weyhill fair. Younger men still lived in service by the
1850s and there were regular hiring fairs at Basingstoke. Cows were kept
by some on the commons and small corn plots might even be attempted,
while women in this 'roughly-living set' collected rushes for hop tying. But
most found their work outside the parish. There were 'no rich farmers, no
employers of labour, to curb the rude independence of the inhabitants', and
consequently with no squire:

> ... the village is without those mellow traditions of respect
> for 'the gentry' which are preserved so religiously by those
> toothless old tea-drinkers in the books. It is no place for ladies
> like these ... (Bourne 1913: 62).

Bourne sympathetically recorded these nineteenth-century communities:
the basket-makers, horse-dealers, denizens of mud shanties and tents; and
'cunning' Jack Worthington, the fairground concertina-player and winter
gravel-digger. Frederick Bettesworth fondly recalled the harvesting journeys
with his wife to work for four to six weeks on the Sussex coast. They walked,
pushing their children in a handcart, across Hindhead, 'the haunt then of
outlaws and untamed folk, to meet whose attacks the harvesters travelled
with reaping-hooks bare and ready' (Bourne 1902: 129). The west Surrey
reapers travelled south in their hundreds in August, mostly to the coast between
Selsey and Littlehampton. The enclosure of their own commons, the breakdown
of the old poor law restrictions, and the introduction of the faghook into west
Surrey by mid-century all stimulated these movements from the Farnham
area. In Gertrude Jekyll's *Old West Surrey* (1904: 194–203) there are similar
references to the 'broom squarers' or 'squires' who worked in heather-thatched
sheds, to the heath fuel cutters, and to the hoop and wattle makers among their
woodland sawpits. In some genteel measure too, the watercolours of Jekyll's
acquaintance Helen Allingham also capture the 'cottage subjects' and their

heathy environment. Moving from Chelsea to Witley in 1881, she proceeded to emulate the work of Birket Foster in paintings such as 'A Witley Lane' or 'Night-jar Lane, Witley'.

Enormous localized variations could thus occur in rural society and economy. And the differentiation could be carried much further. Variations existed in Kent not only between 'wold' and 'weald', but also between the 'river' areas of the downland and the flintier upland wolds, a difference observable in land use and ownership throughout the south-eastern downland (Everitt 1977: 1–19). Such variations impinged upon all aspects of people's lives but it is to the differences in farming structure and their changes at this time that we now turn.

Agricultural Change, 1837–1939

The impacts of agricultural change, technical, economic and social, varied regionally. However, from about 1840 through to the early 1870s most of the South East enjoyed the so-called 'Golden Age' of high farming. In 1846 the Maidstone Farmers' Club resolved that:

> by the addition of more capital on a large breadth of the land in this county, the productive power of the soil might be greatly improved and the cost of production be diminished . . . through the means of tile draining, . . . increasing the size of enclosures . . . , and by grubbing hedgerow timbers (in Goddard 1974: 82).

Thanet was extremely prosperous farming land, and in 1833 it was observed by Mr Cramp in his evidence to a Select Committee that:

> The largest part of it is in the hands of the proprietors, men of property and capital . . . The soil is very fertile when capital is expended upon it, consequently it has not felt that general depression which has prevailed through other parts of the country (*BPP* V, 1833).

Despite the 1845 Corn Law Repeal, and a temporary depression in the early 1850s, Coastal Fringe farming was generally prosperous and largely given over to arable output in various mixed farming operations. Much of the South East was consequently strongly protectionist, and the Duke of Richmond was President of the British Agricultural Protection Society (Roberts 1979: 126). But centuries of capital investment now paid off, and many farmers prospered on the profits of corn and sheep husbandry. Large cereal yields came from the downlands, the Scarpfoot and the coastal brickearths of north Kent and south-west Sussex, with prosperity depending also upon judicious use of arable-fed downland sheep, imports of seasonal harvesting labour, capital inputs in the form of fertilizers or 'model farms', and proximity to growing markets. On the Coastal Plain enormous crops of wheat and barley were supplemented by the fattening of cattle and sheep on turnips and seeds. The Gravesend–Dartford market gardening area with its light, fertile soils on the lower dipslopes of the Chalk produced large quantities of early peas, turnips and corn for London. Between the Medway Valley and the Blean the north Kent fruit belt produced Kentish cherry, apple, plum, hops and small fruit, while the mid-Kent fruit belt around Maidstone – 'the garden of England' – produced great quantities of fruit and hops. At this time there was less fruit grown in east Kent (Stamp 1943: 613).

High prices could stultify farming or produce innovations. Caird noted with disapproval the four-field rotation and the heavy Sussex wooden plough still in use, 'which, for waste of opportunity, of power, and of time, could possibly not be matched in any other county in the United Kingdom'. But to the contrary there was also the successful Southdown sheep, now diffusing throughout the South East (pp. 223–4). By the 1830s the Southdown had achieved international repute. It fitted the need for cheap meat in the growing Northern industrial towns, the wool from the tegs was widely used for blanket-making or knitting, while the sheep still retained its folding qualities for the nightly improvement of fallowed arable on the lower downland slopes. Much of the newly-reclaimed high Chalk by the 1870s was actually given over to green crops and roots for the sheep. The importance of the shepherd at this time was never again to be surpassed, while the stories of the Sussex shearing gangs, each with its 'captain', still provide the material for Sussex country music today.

The Kentish downland mixed farming system was similar in many ways. Arable-fed Southdowns were important, since without them little profit could be expected from the thin soils. With their mixtures of arable and hops the Kentish downland farmers were prosperous. On the north and east Kent loams and dipslopes all farming was subsidiary to the 'round tilth' of beans, wheat and barley with an occasional fodder crop, but lacking any fixed rotation or fallow. Large Southdown flocks were to be found here also. John Boys of Betteshanger, author of the *General View* of Kent, kept about 1,000 with 400 breeding ewes. However, on the heavier soils of the west Kent downs the shepherd was a rarer sight, and Southdown and Wiltshire flocks were subsidiary to dairying or beef cattle. In Surrey wheat and barley were produced from the downland, although the farms were smaller than those on the Chalk of east Kent or Sussex, and Dorset and crossbred sheep were kept for folding, being purchased at Weyhill, and providing the small 'house lambs' produced from the Banstead area for London tables (Marshall 1818: 410–46).

In the Weald 'high farming' was subsidiary to animal husbandry. Leases, where granted, often contained covenants protecting the amounts of grassland and regulating arable crops. Consequently the area of wealden grassland actually grew at this time. For an incentive to market wheat from wealden farms, prices needed to be at 56–60s, a level only prevailing briefly in the 1850s and between 1866 and 1874. At other times oats provided a cheaper alternative.

Complementing the centuries of capital investment on the Coastal Fringe and its beneficial effects at this time, the effect of centuries of under-development in the Interior now brought condemnation from Victorian commentators. The subordinate role of arable farming entailed less interest in mechanized farming, and older Kentish wheel-ploughs, Sussex foot-ploughs and ox-harrows prevailed. Flails might still be used for threshing, although by the 1850s steam-threshing had become common elsewhere. Field size and morphology suited grassland, not arable farming, and altered little since landlords preferred to indulge their aesthetic and sporting interests in woodland rather than increase the prosperity of their tenantry. Steam-ploughing made little progress until the 1870s when some contractors were working in the western Low Weald. The soils – deficient in lime, phosphate and potash – were also problematic. Denshiring and the application of lime and marl were supplemented after 1840 by the 'artificials' and guano, but much awaited adequate drainage, and progress here was slow and patchy. Tile drainage was encouraged on some High Wealden estates such as Tilgate, Ashburnham or the Cornwallis estates in Kent, but the presence of ridge and furrow on the heavy Kent wealden clays illustrates the continuing use of surface drains (Mead and Kain 1976). After 1840 pipe drains were more effective, especially on the sands, but progress was still very slow (Hawes 1858: 188).

Caird summed up wealden farming:

> ... the farms are small, the land ill-drained, half-cultivated, and inadequately stocked ... too much occupied by wood, and cut up by overgrown hedgerows. The farmers as a class are unskilful and prejudiced in their methods of cultivation, and usually hold their farms on yearly tenures (Caird 1852: 126–7).

Leonce de Lavergne, in comparing the Weald to one of France's second-rate provinces wrote of the farmers as 'men without capital, and as ignorant as they are poor' (Lavergne 1865: 203). If a typical wealden farmer existed in the mid-nineteenth century, he would almost certainly have been a native of the area with scant knowledge of the outside world, farming perhaps 70 to 110 acres from year to year, but prepared to move to any adjacent holding to improve his conditions. Mobility detracted from farming prosperity, and farmers were keen to move to make a profit on ingoing and outgoing valuations associated with tenant-right, rather than by staying to develop a farm business (Short 1973; 1975).

One crop was grown too enthusiastically. The hop exerted an influence wholly unproportional to its acreage at this time, and was perceived as both the saviour and the blight of wealden farming. Between 1821 and 1874 the High Wealden acreage doubled, with the 1874 16,496 acres representing one-quarter of the entire country's production. Kent actually produced two-thirds of the national acreage at this time, with the area between mid-Kent and the High Weald as the centre. Wealden hop cultivation techniques lagged behind those of mid and east Kent, and hardier and coarser varieties were grown in very small plantations. Poverty was frequently seen as only being mitigated by a successful hop season. If the hops failed, rents might not be forthcoming (Harvey 1963).

Censure of wealden farming also extended to livestock. Sheep were not a major feature of the area other than in the fringes of the Romney Marsh, but the 'keep sheep' system was widely practised, whereby young sheep were over-wintered in the Weald from the Downs or marshes. Although this system was condemned as wasteful, it did at least provide wealden tenants with much-needed capital. However, cattle received more careful treatment. In the 1830s Thomas Childs of Michelham, followed by other tenant farmers, began to exhibit the native Sussex breed at national shows, and by 1878 a Sussex herd book was begun. But more fundamental was the mid-nineteenth century development of dairying. By 1870 the presence of urban centres and railway access gave the essential stimulus for commercial, rather than the older subsistence, dairying. Now 40 per cent of High Wealden cattle were dairy animals, and dairying had assumed a rural rather than urban aspect. West Country farmers arrived in the depression years to boost dairying further.

The onset of the depression came in the early 1870s when the large grain imports now possible under free trade and peacetime conditions in America and southern Europe, spread acute financial stress among arable farmers on the lighter soils of the South East. Gains accruing to livestock farmers through cheaper feed prices were soon nullified by lower prices for meat and livestock imports, and the worst years for agriculture in general were between 1887 and 1896, aggravated by severe drought in 1891–4.

By January 1880 large losses of ewes were recorded on the borders of Romney Marsh. There were short crops and low prices everywhere, especially for hops which had been badly affected by damp conditions. At public meetings throughout the South East there was talk of bankruptcy and of farms being let at a fraction of their old rents, while many were taken in hand. Landlords reduced their expenditure and gradually buildings, fences, ditches and hedges became neglected. One report stated:

> Farmers short of cash, many on the verge of ruin . . . the land around here more than half laid down (much of it dropped down) . . . whoever attempts to grow wheat at 30s a qr must linger out at last a wretched existence in the union house (*Sussex Agricultural Express* 2 November 1889).

Lightland farmers reduced sheep flocks and abandoned their poorest upland fields. At Ashtead and Headley the percentage of chalk cultivated fell from 63 per cent to 32 per cent between the 1880s and 1930s (Willatts 1933: 515–28). But many still could not survive and even north Kent farmers who concentrated on fruit and hops now faced the importation of almost one-quarter of Britain's hops and massive imports of French and Belgian fruit.

Coastal Fringe agriculture was badly affected by the depression but the effects were regionally differentiated. Areas with better communications, urban markets, or generous soils, such as east Kent, could diversify with intensive market gardening or fruit. In mid Kent hops and fruit also fared well, while the LCDR line to Sevenoaks and Maidstone allowed the marketing of vegetables, salad plants and potatoes, with tomatoes being grown under glass.

On the South Downs the effects were similarly variable. Many farms were sold off through pressures of cumulative debt exacerbated by Lloyd George's death duties and other financial legislation. A study of four estates in the Ouse Valley shows rents falling between 1880 and 1914. Three of the estates, the Abergavenny, Chichester and Wiston, held fast to the old sheep-corn husbandry, confidently expecting recovery. But by the mid-1880s their reserves had been undermined and no investment for agricultural change could be undertaken. By contrast the fourth estate, at Glynde, was less affected since its owner, H. B. W. Brand, speaker of the House of Commons, reacted swiftly to what he perceived to be a major structural shift in farming. He continued to invest; granted rent abatements, and built a creamery at Glynde quite close to the rail link to London, Brighton and Eastbourne thereby stimulating local dairying. The estate held together, in contrast to the others whose Ouse Valley components were decimated by 1919 (Farrant 1979: 155–70).

The Interior had, of course, never been 'highly farmed' in the manner of the Coastal Fringe. The effect of the depression was thus different again here. The conversion to permanent pasture was accelerated, so that by 1914 about 75 per cent of wealden farmland was under grass. However, this trend was composed of several elements. Grassland also increased because of conversions to building land. In 1869 the Earl of Abergavenny had been advised that his lands in Frant adjoining the 'villa residences' of Tunbridge Wells should be kept in grass, and that in letting any fields 'their ultimate building facilities must be borne in mind', since 'in a few years this land will be valued by the yard instead of by the acre'. The Earl proceeded to sell off much of this land for development. So there arose small areas of grassland pending development around Tunbridge Wells, Crowborough, Hastings, Burgess Hill and Haywards Heath, meeting a lively demand for hay for town horses and dairies. Rural depopulation (see pp.333–6 also accelerated the switch to grass through searches for less labour-intensive production or by minimizing the day-to-day upkeep of the farms.

As in north Kent, hops were seen, perhaps mistakenly, as saviours in the depression. Often only the smaller farms with hops could be let. Rudyard Kipling, moving to Batemans Farm, Burwash, put the case thus to Rider Haggard in a letter:

I shall probably lose much in getting the farm into shape because if I grub out the hops no-one will take it and if I don't I might as well keep a small Monte Carlo for hops are a demoralising gamble (in Cohen 1965: 49).

Many former hop gardens were in fact being planted up with fruit at this time, and the High Wealden fruit acreage doubled between the 1870s and 1914. The heartland was still the Kentish Weald, where hops, apples, cherries, blackcurrants and other fruit grew prolifically.

However, dairying also provided a generally sound alternative, diffusing into the more remote Forest Ridges and Ashdown area before the First World War. Herds were generally small, accommodation not always high quality, but income was forthcoming. The Glynde and Sheffield Park creameries gave milk contracts and there were cheese factories at Battle and East Grinstead.

The other major development at this time was far more localized. From obscure beginnings, poultry fattening had developed by the beginning of the nineteenth century, such that 'great stores of poultry' accumulated weekly at Horsham from the Weald Clay parishes of Kirdford and Northchapel, for conveyance by carrier to London. At about the same time the higgling (collecting) of chickens, and their fattening for market, was beginning in Heathfield and in the Interior behind Hastings. The growth of artificial fattening (cramming) has been dated to the early 1830s at Heathfield, and this area became a nucleus by the 1860s. The combination of small grassland farms with higgling and fattening in otherwise difficult ecological and socio-economic environments undoubtedly accounted for its popularity. Skim milk and fat was available from local dairying; there was shelter under the shaws; ample grass verges and commons for the coops; and a specialist London carrier service later taken over by the LBSCR. The depression acted as a stimulus. The numbers of fowls increased, there was investment in cramming machines, coops and incubators, while specialist crammers commanded good wages. There were no specialist poultry farms at this time, although poultry was frequently the most remunerative concern, shared also by many labourers and tradesmen (Short 1982: 17–30).

So the combination of hops, fruit, dairy farming and poultry production steered the Interior through the prolonged depression before the First World War. The changes in south-eastern farming between 1875 and 1914 are summarized in Table 6.2. Between these two years the LCC took a large slice of land out of 'historic' Surrey and Kent, most of which was urbanized. Thus the 1914 percentage figure for the crops and grass cover was slightly higher than that for 1875. More significant however, was the changed balance between arable and permanent pasture, with the latter increasing from 39 per cent of the area of crops and grass.

The war year 1914 brought no change to agriculture. Slow to respond, agricultural interests were not brought onto a war footing until the 1917 Emergency Regulations. Thereafter County War Agricultural Executive

Table 6.2 Land use trends in south-east England, 1875–1939

	Total area	Crops & grass	% Total	Arable	% Crops & grass	Permanent pasture	% Crops & grass
1875							
Surrey	483,178	298,009	61.7	190,318	63.9	107,691	36.1
Sussex	934,006	652,278	69.8	388,385	59.5	264,493	40.5
Kent	1,100,984	726,490	66.0	436,949	60.2	289,541	39.8
SE	2,518,168	1,676,777	66.6	1,015,652	60.6	661,725	39.4
1914							
Surrey	458,908	256,719	55.9	96,667	37.7	160,052	62.3
Sussex	928,735	651,116	70.1	227,102	34.9	424,014	65.1
Kent	973,846	732,179	75.2	293,596	40.1	438,583	59.9
SE	2,361,489	1,640,014	69.5	617,365	37.6	1,022,649	62.4
1918							
Surrey	458,908	255,456	55.7	111,920	43.8	143,536	56.2
Sussex	928,735	632,572	68.1	265,772	42.0	366,680	58.0
Kent	973,846	721,820	74.1	336,592	46.6	385,228	53.4
SE	2,361,489	1,609,848	68.2	714,284	44.4	895,444	55.6
1939							
Surrey	458,211	171,335	37.4	43,792	25.6	127,543	74.4
Sussex	928,735	530,842	57.2	134,723	25.4	396,114	74.6
Kent	972,940	637,570	65.5	253,915	39.8	383,655	60.2
SE	2,359,886	1,339,747	56.8	432,430	32.3	907,312	67.7

(Source: Ministry of Agriculture, Fisheries and Food: PRO MAF68 (June Returns))

Committees determined the regional and local direction of a plough-up campaign, tackling the poorest grassland first, which not surprisingly gave indifferent yields. The first Cultivation of Lands order was given in January 1917, to be followed by the Corn Production Act guaranteeing minimum prices for wheat and oats.

The overall impact on the Weald was that between 1914 and 1918 the arable acreage increased by about 50 per cent, with wheat most sought after. Unfortunately the plough-up campaign was mounted following decades of low investment and the targets were rarely achieved. Although wheat areas were doubled over most of the Weald, for example, only half the target was reached (Table 6.2). Dairy farms were immune from the plough-up, and although affected by shortages of fodder crops and cowmen, herd sizes in the Weald doubled or tripled, so herds of 60 to 100 became more common. Orchards and small fruit were also unaffected but hops were restricted to half the 1914 acreage, while pig and poultry populations were reduced sharply with restrictions on feedingstuffs.

Change was endemic but slow. In retrospect, perhaps the greatest impact within farming itself was the grudging acceptance of mechanization as an avenue to higher production, with reduced labour and horses. Although unreliable, the tractor gained in popularity. By November 1916 the 'Simplex', 'Mogul' and 'Bates' steel mule' were in use in the Lewes area, with 'Titans' being allocated by WAECs in 1917. By 1918 there were 10 applications for every available tractor, a dramatic reversal from 18 months previously, when they had been regarded with suspicion and ridicule. In the High Weald, the first tractor-ploughing competition was held in 1920 at Mayfield.

The years from 1918 to 1939 were possibly even more traumatic than those of the late-Victorian period. Agricultural prices rose to 1920 but were dramatically halved by 1922. The Corn Production Act was repealed and a decline ensued through the 1920s, emphasized by the 1929 slump. The area of arable in the South East was by 1939 at a lower ebb than in 1914, at less than a third of the total farmed area, and 1934 wheat prices were the lowest recorded since 1771. The depression affected the structure of farming everywhere, but there were three main inter-related changes; the 'silent revolution' in landownership; the loss of farmland to urban and other non-agricultural uses; and major changes in the uses of the farmland itself.

Structural change was widespread as the estates continued to be split up, and as farms were sold off to former tenants in the 1920s. On the downlands the changes were enormous. Around the formerly remote village of East Horsley on the Surrey chalk dipslope the Lovelace estate had been sold to Mr T. Sopwith (of the aircraft company) but by 1925 farms were being advertised as 'excellent sites for the erection of first-class houses' (Connell 1978: 70). At Shere, Reginald Bray looked to forestry and limited, high-quality housing developments to maintain his estate. Even the estate of Lord Onslow, president of the Board of Agriculture, came up for sale at Clandon from 1905. In Sussex the Stanmer estate, which had sold off outlying farms in 1912, was further decimated by the death duties needed in 1927 after the death of the 6th Earl of Chichester and his heir (Farrant 1979: 162-5). In Sussex as a whole between 1913 and 1927 the number of owner-occupiers tripled, and by 1941 43.5 per cent of Sussex farms were owner-occupied.

In addition the period saw much land taken from farming altogether. In the South East more than 270,000 acres vanished from cultivation between 1918 and 1939 (Table 6.2) and by the latter date only 57 per cent of the total area of Kent, Surrey and Sussex was being cultivated. The High Wealden reduction was from 64 per cent in 1918 to 58 per cent by 1939, representing a loss of about 20,000 acres or about 260 farms. In the Bagshot Sands area 28 per cent of the 1870 farmed area had gone to other uses by 1940 (Ferguson 1979: 61–7), and between 1905 and 1922 20 per cent of the entire region was offered for sale. Surrey now acquired the highest proportion of 'hobby farmers' in England.

More visually dramatic was the return to grassland, scrub and overgrown hedges. On the steep downland slopes of Surrey scrub vegetation gradually re-formed and the Clay-with-flints and downland tops were abandoned to heath or planted with coppice (Willatts 1933; 1937: 255–7). Only the combination of Middle and Lower Chalk, Upper Greensand and Bargate Beds formed a favourable arable area from Selborne to Farnham, Puttenham, Godalming, Bramley and Hascombe and again to the east of Guildford. The heavier clays, needing deep drainage and careful ploughing, were the first to go out of use in Surrey and throughout the region (Stamp and Willatts 1941: 392–7).

In the Weald an invasion of weeds and gorse was only too frequent. By the 1930s permanent pasture again covered over 80 per cent of the farmland. Dairying, poultry and pig-farming now re-emerged as the mainstays of farming, helped by the many different marketing boards established at this time. Many now turned to milk production from all-grass farms, using purchased concentrates. If the prewar period had marked the beginnings of large-scale interest in dairying, it was the inter-war period which established it as the lynch-pin of wealden agriculture. And poultry production became more complex as many small producers and fatteners entered in the depression, with ex-servicemen particularly prominent. Egg production increased in importance, co-operative marketing schemes replaced older, chaotic marketing strategies and motor transport rendered the higgler's former operations obsolete.

In general terms, elasticities of demand worked in favour of the Interior at this time. Regional dietary changes in the 1930s heralded a demand for more milk, eggs, butter, cheese and poultry, rather than bread and potatoes. And although external changes worked to homogenize agriculture to some extent, the regionalization of the various County Land Use Surveys of the 1930s still presented as many as 47 different land use regions in the South East. Under stress, the regional mosaic re-asserted itself.

330

Social Change in the Countryside

Here two interrelated themes of social and cultural change will be explored: firstly the loosening of the old deferential ties and consequent changes in rural social relations; and secondly rural depopulation.

The social, ideological and political hierarchy of the rural South East reflected economic structures. Overall after 1840 unemployment and poverty grew rapidly; wider education brought higher expectations; the railways allowed greater mobility; and urbanization brought its own problems. However, landowners 'lacked any dynamic, imaginative, or innovative approach that would solve their problems with an effectiveness that an age of progress, education and greater wealth expected' (Roberts 1979: 106–28). The landed patriarchy promoted for itself an unrealistic picture of harmonious, organic and unified communities under its care. The great landowners chaired the Quarter Sessions but their outlook was a static one which was essentially incompatible with many of the rural problems of the South East after 1840.

The lessening power of this old landowning group was not easily given up. Large houses, retinues and expensive lifestyles were still characteristic. Challenges to its authority came from the sometimes oppressive and new 'middling ranks of society'. Challenges also came from hard-pressed workers, and from the encompassing network of bureaucracy in central and local government, all of which acted 'to chip away at the wall of privilege and deference which had once surrounded the gentry' (Blackwell 1981: 184). When in 1839, for example, at a time of social stress, a rural police force was suggested, it was opposed by the Duke of Richmond, Lord Lieutenant of Sussex who attempted to prevent the Police and Lunacy Acts of 1839 and 1845 from applying in Sussex. The police force was in fact established originally in 1840 only in eastern Sussex, and not in Kent or western Sussex until 1857 (Allen 1982: 33; Roberts 1979: 125).

Alliances of landowners and tenant farmers controlled all the significant legal, governmental and social institutions. Each agricultural area was in Richard Jefferies's words 'a little Kingdom' with its market town 'capital' where farmers met to discuss common problems. Agricultural associations sponsored events and dinners where farmers established wage levels and working conditions and considered the need for defence associations against riot or agricultural strikes. Attitudes and habits changed little, despite the enormous upheavals after 1880. The concern for the community was expressed by a later Duke of Richmond in 1884:

> I look upon myself and the tenantry as members of one large vast, and . . . united family . . . It is my duty . . . to look after the interests myself personally, individually, of the humblest crofter on this estate as well as the wealthiest tenant (in Blackwell 1981: 194).

331

At Goodwood there was an estate nurse, annuities, pension and coal allowance for retired estate workers; cricket club and agricultural society, Church organization and local schools in 15 villages. The Goodwood kitchens doled out winter soup; the Petworth Park Friendly Society organized annual fetes, Lord Leconfield helped administer the almshouses, and there were jubilee treats and allowances for the needy. Local philanthropy continued to be an important aspect of regional life through to 1914, as was political influence, although this was eroded by a wider franchise and by elected local representatives. Some examples from Sussex will give the flavour of the resistance.

At the beginning of the period, in a rare annotated East Sussex poll book for 1832, various observations were made by the agent for one candidate. Around Horsham it was noted that the tenants of Mr Sergison of Slaugham were ordered to vote for Mr Curteis; at Dallington it was noted that Samuel Taylor and John Veness farmers and tenants of Lord Ashburnham 'would not like to go agt landlords wishes'. At Ticehurst, Thomas Barden, tenant of Samuel Baker 'would go as his landlord wish'd', while Thomas Jarvis and Thomas Judge were 'influenced by (their) landlord not to vote for Cavendish and Curteis'. The poll book is shot through with examples of social and economic influence being brought to bear on voting preferences (ESRO A 4570).

Secondly, Bertram, 4th Earl of Ashburnham was by the middle of the nineteenth century, revelling in a revival of medieval feudalism. His tenants supplied straw bales to Ashburnham Place, day-works were performed by their ox or horse-teams, and their very acceptance on the estate was dependent upon their political leanings. In October 1837 he wrote from London to his steward that:

> It would be well to make the same observation to him respecting *politics*, that you did to Wickham observing that tho' I do *not* interfere with the politics of tenants when I have found in possession of their farms, but I do consider myself *more* than at *liberty* and hardly *up than bound* to give a preference to those who are my way of thinking in such matters (ESRO Ashburnham Ms 1439).

Bertram maintained this attitude throughout his life. But after 1880 there is far less evidence of direct gentry involvement in politics. Traditional attitudes persisted, but political duties now consisted of organizing the local Conservative party, as did Edward Frewen at Northiam, George Shiffner at Hamsey and Lord Leconfield at Petworth (Blackwell 1981: 195).

After the 1840s self-help and self-reliance replaced paternalism as moral-economic codes, together with a wider philanthropic and bureaucratic social net. The new and mobile middle classes, much in evidence in the South East, did not fit easily with the landowning Tory High Church attitudes. Nowhere was it the case more than here that 'paternalism had to bow to

London immigrants' (Roberts 1979: 98). In general the wealthier county families were more immobile, certainly in Kent, where as many as 70 per cent of the 1840 squirearchy survived through to 1873 (Kain 1973). A large element of snobbery existed and newcomers, however affluent, were not always welcomed. Thus when the son of Thomas Brassey, the railway contractor and engineer, built Normanhurst in an 1867 French château style, the neighbouring Ashburnhams showed neither social nor political sympathy. And elsewhere there was local opposition within the community. In Lodsworth internal strife ensued from the arrival in the 1830s of Hasler Hollist, a lawyer at the Middle Temple. Arguments ensued over common rights, poor law administration, seating arrangements in the church, and the running of the village pub, whose name was changed from the Poyntz to the Hollist Arms (Reed 1982: 68–81).

The second theme is rural depopulation. The period was characterized by the out-migration of farmworkers which counterbalanced the in-migration by the ex-urban middle class. Before 1831 population growth had characterized most, if not all rural parishes, with increasing under-employment and poverty erupting into the 'Swing' violence and its aftermath in the 1830s (pp. 235–7). But after 1851 rural depopulation was the dominant trend.

However, between 1851 and 1911 demographic patterns were very mixed. In and around the growing towns and suburbs there was steady population growth due to in-migration. But overall decreases characterized areas such as the west Sussex downland, mid Kent and the eastern Weald. Constant loss, decade after decade, was the experience of much of rural Kent, of the eastern Sussex Weald and downland, and of Interior west Sussex. Losses, followed by later gains, were found in the rest of Sussex, while only Surrey, undergoing suburbanization, showed constant gains.

The factors behind these movements are familiar. A reduced demand for farm labour was coupled with growing demand for urban-industrial and service employment, and with a growing literacy and awareness of the wider range of urban amenities and higher wages. The outflow was correspondingly unbalanced, with younger people and especially females seeking urban employment.

Weekly agricultural wages in the South East, at about 8s 6d in 1850, rising to 12s in 1880, were about 1s below the national average, and well below those in the Midlands and the North (Allen 1982: 51). Wages undoubtedly improved in late nineteenth-century Kent, where the 1861 wage of about 12s per week already compared very favourably with the highest of the northern counties. The best rural wages in the region were those of west Kent, where fruit and vegetables were grown for London. The poorest were those of east Kent, the main corn-producing area, where the use of machinery undermined the labourers' bargaining position. In the mechanized mid-century 'Golden Age' labour demand seldom increased and the labourers' share of the increased profits was minimal. Nor were wages regular, since day and casual work had by now largely replaced living-in, rendering incomes precarious in the event of illness or bad weather (Short 1984b; Snell 1987: 67–103).

There were several processes by which people left the south-eastern countryside. In the 1830s the technique known as 'shovelling out paupers', as on Lord Egremont's estate, was frequently quoted. From here 1,800 were induced to emigrate to Canada and passages were filled firstly from those parishes where Egremont owned all or part of the land, for which he donated £10 per passage, through to more distant Pulborough where he was estimated to own one-thirty sixth of the parish. The Rev. Thomas Sockett, rector of Petworth and chairman of the local emigration society, calculated that the money directed to the relief of unemployment in Petworth fell from £1,401 to £426 by 1836, after 127 individuals in the parish had been so assisted. In addition there were emigrants from Dorking and elsewhere, sponsored by their parishes, who filled up the remaining berths on the vessels in 1832, a year of unprecedented emigration to Upper Canada. As well as cutting back on poor relief, the scheme also allowed for the removal of 'undesirables', such as when Hasler Hollist, squire of Lodsworth wrote in April 1838 that 'the notorious Charles Levett is willing to emigrate from the P(etworth) H(ouse) of Correction to Canada. Colonel Wyndham offers to subscribe towards getting rid of him . . .'. The same applied to Edward Birt, 'an idle and dissolute fellow' (Cameron 1973: 231–46; Reed 1982: 53,104).

The 1830s was a decade of protest and a deep if incoherent frustration with 'tiresome rural oligarchies of lesser men, to whom there was no traditional deference' (Lowerson 1982: 59 *et seq.*). Much violence was aimed at the New Poor Law and local wage levels (pp. 235–7). Poverty, isolation and the changing nature of social and economic relations fuelled the protest movement, and one reaction on the part of the authorities and landowners was to place families 'under new circumstances in a colony'. Between 1836 and 1847 2,240 people were sent overseas from Kent and 2,859 from Sussex. Most of this emigration was directly sponsored by wealden New Poor Law authorities before 1850, at which time the loss of rural population became manifest and labour shortages began to loom. In 1842 the Colonial Commissioners of Land and Emigration were also established, sending labourers mainly to Australia (Armstrong 1981: 129).

The main centres of protest in the 1830s were the eastern Weald of Sussex, the Kent/Sussex border and north Kent. Isolated from each other, they did not thrive, but continued nevertheless as pockets of radicalism throughout the nineteenth century. When the 'Revolt of the Field' began in earnest in the 1870s it was these areas once more which nurtured the Kent and Sussex Labourers Union. The Kent union was founded at Shoreham (Kent) in 1872 and led by Alfred Simmons, a Maidstone journalist. By the end of the year it was 6,000 strong and the following year it expanded into Sussex, becoming the Kent and Sussex Labourers Union. By 1878 it claimed 14,000 members. The union rapidly took on a social role in order to raise the status of the Kent workers. Simmons was more successful than his Midlands counterpart, Arch, following the lead of the urban trade unions and advocating a conservative attitude to strikes and conciliation. Within its first year the union gave emigration assistance to 86 members, and by 1874 Simmons reported having assisted 1,700 in the previous year. Migrants went to South Australia, New Zealand and Canada, and their letters fuelled the growth of the union. During the 1870s New Zealand took 3,900 assisted emigrants from Kent alone.

In January 1874 the *Dover Express* noted under the headline 'Kent agricultural labourers union':

> On Thursday evening an entertainment was given in the Corn Exchange, Maidstone, to 410 Kentish immigrants, on their departure to New Zealand, to which place they had been granted free passages through the instrumentality of the officers of the above union. On Friday the emigrants marched to the railway station, the High Street being crowded with spectators, and the party left for Gravesend (in *Cantium* 6, 1974: 83).

Similar scenes followed with the 1879 departure of the *Stad Haarlem* for New Zealand, with 400 emigrants coming from north Kent and the Lamberhurst area. One repeated observation here was that 'we should like to see our children better off than we have been' (Arnold 1974: 87). However, organized migration represented a minority of those leaving the south-eastern countryside. Everywhere there were subtle yet strong influences at work. Sturt referred to them in the context of west Surrey in 1913 as:

> Unsettled by education and by the influence of church and chapels, minds that would have gone empty, and souls that would have starved half a century ago, are being excited to ambitious dreams. Thus, from within, the push of never-felt needs is disturbing the outward life of the village (Bourne 1913: 85).

These 'ambitious dreams' might lead agricultural labourers or their sons to seek out work in nearby towns. The Metropolitan Railway Company at Ashford employed apprentices who were generally sons of farmworkers. In the 1890s population fell in 214 rural parishes of Kent, but far earlier in the century many south-eastern parishes had experienced losses. From the eastern Weald and all the parishes in the Bexhill area, as well as from parishes such as Newdigate in the Surrey Weald, the census enumerators recounted the depopulation. In 1861 unemployment was given as the cause of population decreases in High Wealden Rotherfield or Sedlescombe. In 1899 Charles Whitehead noted that:

> In the quiet country villages in . . . the Weald of Kent, if there are no waterworks, railways, light railways or similar works in course of construction, to compete with agriculture, the spirit of unrest moved the younger members of the labourers' families to leave their home for fresh fields and pastures new (Whitehead 1899).

So greatly had events changed within fifty years that by 1900 an East Sussex Farmers Club representative was in touch with the Irish Organization for the Importation of Irish Labour, to arrange the numbers of workers required (*East Grinstead Express*, March 1900). In 1901–2 Haggard noted the scarcity of younger and skilled workers on the downlands, and in the Weald the problem of obtaining men for milking. The pull of alternative employment, the Navy, the docks, towns or brickfields, meant that in Kent:

> No wages that employers can pay seem to be sufficient to induce the young men of Kent to stop upon the land, and when the old ones dies – what then? (Haggard 1906, I: 174.)

Rural depopulation thus became a real issue in the South East by the end of Victoria's reign. But despite the courses of action suggested, such as the provision of smallholdings; the extension of suffrage; or the improvement of communications, education and working conditions, depopulation continued in many areas throughout the early twentieth century, and indeed into postwar years (Fig. 6.3b). Images of an unchanging countryside were conjured by the artistic and middle-class newcomers, but underlying structural changes had already propelled the South East into a new era.

The Alternative World to London

The Beginnings of Tourism

Citizens of the first world capital to have grown so rapidly felt a great urge to renew contact periodically with the country or seaside. Hanoverian London had been relatively compact and coherent, enveloped in its fields and market gardens. This was the London so fondly praised by Charles Lamb and which inspired Dr Johnson's famous aphorism: 'He who is tired of London is tired of life'. Mid-Victorian London was, by contrast, virtually a new city that was 'more excavated, more cut-about, more rebuilt and more extended than at any time in its previous history' (Summerson 1973). In terms of physical growth London expanded from the 8.5 square miles on John Rocque's 1746 map, to about 22 square miles on John Cary's 1822 map, to some 50 square miles in 1851, and then continuously to more than 120 square miles in 1901 to over 200 square miles in 1939.

This sheer immensity dispersed people, distantly separated them from their places of work or of leisure, whether according to choice or not, and put up an unhealthy smoke canopy. *Pace* Dr Johnson, there was not in High Victorian London all that life could provide. As representative of late-Victorian London as was Dr Johnson of Georgian London was Sir Leslie Stephen, editor of the *Cornhill*, the most famous Victorian literary journal, of the *Dictionary of National Biography*, and father of Bloomsburyites Virginia Woolf and Vanessa Bell. For him, daily experience of London was an endurance test involving long journeys through crowded streets and compensating annual holiday and weekend breaks away from London as a restorative from the dirt and grind of the City.

Although parts of the South East from the mid-nineteenth century were to become *the* playground of Britain, the region was earlier, by reason of the badness of roads across the Interior, largely outside the polite bounds of established tourist routes. For this reason the Weald (apart from seaside Hastings) never established itself in the company of the Isle of Wight, the English Lakes, North Wales, the Peak District and Killarney as the early landscapists' preferred locales. Its earliest visitors were invariably dyspeptic travellers, so strenuously dwelling on the dirt and dangers of the roads that they had no appreciative eye for the beautiful scenery they were traversing.

Popular tourism came with the steam train and the paddle steamer. By the late 1850s the various railway companies were furiously competing with one another, with the result that the LSW and LBSCR excursion fares from London to Portsmouth and back were only 3s 6d and by 1862 bank holiday crowds at Brighton were lured with the advertisement 'Eight hours at the sea for half-a-crown'. From the beginning, the Brighton railway adjusted its timetables to permit passengers to travel between London and the seaside, or in the reverse direction, and back again, in a single day. The intervening countryside, hitherto almost inaccessible by road, was quickly exploited commercially by guidebook writers. As early as 1844 John Thorne's guide for walkers, the earliest literary production associated with the LBSCR, led city-wearied pedestrians across the nearest field from the exit to Balcombe station to 'one of the most fashionable notions of a thoroughly countrified English lane . . .'.

Before the scenery and climate of a district became popular holiday or residential factors its qualities had to be 'boomed'. Thus Martin Tupper wrote his historical romance *Stephen Langton* (1858) with the avowed intention of giving Albury near Guildford some 'special literary lift'. His novel was set in sites all now recognized as 'beauty spots' then virtually unknown to all but the natives, giving the author the same sort of satisfaction as that experienced by a seaside entrepreneur.

London's Playground and the Townsman's Rural Workplace

As one of England's most attractively varied countrysides, Surrey and Kent have long offered the best of *walking* within easy reach of London. Perhaps the first of modern walkers was poet and novelist George Meredith who as early as the 1860s was organizing high-spirited rambles to and from Surrey railway stations for London friends (Meredith 1970 edn: 76, 78, 82).

A new note is struck with the Sir Leslie Stephen's Sunday Tramps, a walking club of London intellectuals founded in 1878: as important a milestone in the sectarianism of the sabbath as in the history of leisure. The free-thinking Tramps included retired mountaineers like Stephen himself who had with advancing years come to regard the long uninterrupted stretches of the southern slopes and crests of the North Downs and the Leith Hill range as a geriatric substitute for the High Alps (Maitland 1906: 342, 357–62, 404).

By the 1880s country walking (and even more so the hiking movement of the 1930s) was largely urban in origin and outlook, and with the rise of the new professional and commercial classes, became a mass recreation as an antidote to 'city poison', providing opportunities lacking in everyday life; hard physical exercise in fresh air; a primitive and simple existence (walking being viewed as the modern equivalent of ploughing and fishing); and an occasion to restore broken contacts with 'mother Earth and unsophisticated nature'.

By the late 1920s adventurous hardy youths, connected with young workers' organizations and various Church and political bodies, became enthusiasts for shared aspects of the Simple Life such as community singing, organized games and camp life. Their reforming lifestyle was strongly encouraged by the Two Weeks' Holiday Movement and the shorter working hours of the 1930s. This coincided with the similar mass portent of urban civilization in Germany of the *Wandervogel*. In retrospect they provided a futuristic gleam of the 'Swinging Sixties' which was prematurely killed off by the Second World War.

Passion for the new sport of *bicycling* with the invention of the safety cycle in 1894 had even more momentous social and environmental consequences for the South East, for it saved many a remote pocket of southern England from genetic decay. All social classes took to the wheel but for working-class Londoners and those from larger towns of the South East it was the 'golden key' to the strange and half-forgotten countryside of childhood memory. The distribution of cycling clubs is in itself an index of urbanism: London in 1902 had no less than 274 clubs affiliated to the Cycling Association. Penny weeklies such as *The Rambler* and *The Wheelman* bore illustrated articles of the popular cycling country south of London. This mass use of major roads revived many inns to their former glory, including 'The Spread Eagle' at Midhurst, where H. G. Wells observed under-worked ostlers valeting customers' cycles. Cycling organizations acquired cheap premises at rest houses. Cafés and tea shops multiplied rapidly, especially after the First World War, with several in each of the most popular villages.

Another country recreation restoring the Londoner's physique and nerves was *golf*. Although an ancient game in Scotland, most of the few clubs surrounding London in the 1880s were modern. The doyen was the Blackheath golf club, oldest in England (Plate 6.6). The great upsurge in golf's popularity as a townsman's recreation brought a whole new generation of courses into being after the introduction of the rubber-covered ball in 1908. The most glorious golfing possibilities were among the fine views and challenging winds on the

Plate 6.6   The Blackheath golfer. The Royal Blackheath Golf Club was founded in 1766 and is England's earliest organised golf club. This portrait of William Innes by Lemuel Francis Abbot is also probably the first English painting of a golfer. Innes was a prosperous London merchant of Scottish descent. He wears the uniform of the club captain. His caddy, with a bottle of spirits at the ready, is a pensioner of the Royal Naval Hospital, Greenwich (Pilley 1988: 26–7).

coastal sandhills of Kent and east Sussex. For Londoners it was the Surrey sand and heather country that made the finest golfing country. Here the golfing boom was started when 'a few mad barristers' carved a golf course by main force out of miry and sandy waste near Woking.

The intensification of London life also created a vogue for *week-ending* among the rapidly-expanding middle classes. This habit had a long history among the wealthy. Defoe mentions City tradesmen who built 'Gentlemen's mere summerhouses or citizens' country houses whither they retire from the Hurry in Business and forgetting money to draw their breath in a clean air' (Defoe 1738 edn: 239). The first new social group to acquire the summer cottage-renting habit were landscape artists who, with new opportunities for travel provided by railways, preferred to paint in the green world beyond London. At the old wool town of Cranbrook, J. C. Horsley and the Hardy brothers enjoyed in the flesh one of the most successful fictional havens ever devised – Dickens's Dingley Dell of *Pickwick Papers* (1837). Meanwhile, the London to Portsmouth railway was so conveniently carrying artists to and from Witley, that the 1871 census attributed population increase in the sandy heathland to 'the attractions of the scenery, many artists having taken up residence in the district'. Here J. C. Hook, Whymper and Birket Foster were pioneers of a new colony (Plate 6.7).

Authors soon began to emulate artists in this summer habit. One of the earliest signs of the innumerable distractions of London life was the claim that books could not be written unless authors escaped from the city to write them. Among early refugees from London to west Surrey, attracted by the London to Portsmouth railway, were George Eliot and G. H. Lewes; Mrs Humphrey Ward, the distinguished Victorian novelist; Beatrice and Sydney Webb; William Allingham; Tennyson; Grant Allen; William Tyndale, the Victorian scientist; Stopford Brooke; young Arnold Bennett and Richard Le Gallienne.

Another close-knit group of intellectuals owing its origin to a railway was that of the Fabians and Russian emigrés at Crockham Hill on Limpsfield Chart, founded after the opening of the railway from London to Uckfield in 1898. Edward Garnett, Richard Heath, Henry Salt, Ford Madox Ford, E. R. Pease, Stephen Crane and others built new houses overlooking the exquisite panorama of the Weald where they were visited by Edward Thomas, D. H.

Plate 6.7 Clayton Adam's rendering of the Surrey Wild 1885. Adams had a studio on Coneyhurst Hill at Ewhurst, Surrey, which provided him with an eyrie overlooking the wealds of Surrey and Sussex. His landscapes epitomise the new outlook on nature as a restorative for jaded urban dwellers that is associated with the Victorians' sense of an increasing separation from their natural environment. Ruskin applauded the Surrey artist's choice of subjects: 'There are no railroads in it ... no tunnel or pit mouths ... no league-long viaducts ... no parks, no gentlemen's seats ... no rows of lodging houses ... none of these things that the English mind now rages after ...' (Cook and Wedderburn 1907, 33: 347).

Plate 6.8 Duncan Grant's studio at Charleston farmhouse, East Sussex. Charleston, the home of Vanessa Bell and Duncan Grant from 1916, became the country retreat of the Bloomsbury circle and a base for painting, interior decoration and garden sculpture which has been described as one of the most influential cultural households of the twentieth century. The studio was added in 1925. Duncan Grant retained it when a new one was built at the top of the house for Vanessa Bell, and worked there until his death in 1978. The fireplace was decorated by him *c.*1932. The decorations above the mantelshelf are *c.*1935. The glass-fronted cabinet once belonged to the novelist Thackeray, and by descent to Vanessa Bell. It contains glass and ceramics often used as still lifes by the Charleston artists. The screen was made in the Omega workshops in 1913 (Bell 1987: 69–74). Photograph by Howard Grey from *Omega and After: Bloomsbury and the Decorative Arts* (Thames and Hudson).

Lawrence, Prince Kropotkin, Stepniak, Montague Fordham and H. E. Bates. Octavia Hill, famous for her housing schemes under the inspiration of Ruskin, also acquired local cottages and let them furnished for week-ending by poorer Londoners.

The country cottage cult had a profound effect on building, interior decoration and social mores. 'Roughing it' without servants at a week-end cottage in a sort of bohemian freedom was very near to an earthly paradise. The better-off and therefore more emancipated, such as Fabian Edith Nesbit, bought 'aesthetic' utensils and furniture on William Morris lines from Heal's or Catesby's 'Country Cottage' range, and wore sack-like medieval dresses and

Jaeger suits. 'Not one solitary thing bore any relation to the city left behind – nothing to remind the occupant of the business lunch, the social scramble and the electric light type of existence' (Klickmann 1924).

In the inter-war years there was not a country lane in favoured parts of Surrey, Sussex or west Kent but resounded with the click of typewriters and hardly a village but in it novelists, poets, dramatists, critics, artists and university teachers outnumbered the permanent local population. At Shere, for example, Adrian Boult, G. M. Trevelyan, Clough Williams-Ellis, Edwin Lutyens, Wilson Harris (editor, *The Spectator*), broadcaster Raymond Gram Swing, poet Helen Waddell and artists Mary Freeman and Ethelbert White, among many others, rented summer cottages in the 1930s. The liveliest group of 'exiled' intellectuals were the Bloomsbury circle who included Virginia and Leonard Woolf, Vanesssa and Clive Bell, Duncan Grant, David Garnett and Maynard and Lydia Keynes, living in shabby but very easy surroundings in the beautiful setting below the Chalk escarpment near Lewes, from 1912. It was in the carefree garden of Charleston that Maynard Keynes wrote *The Economic Consequences of the Peace* (1919) and Lytton Strachey read aloud prior to publication *Eminent Victorians* (1918). Charleston farmhouse vividly expresses in its interior decoration, furniture and general atmosphere their pattern of life (Plate 6.8).

The '*Bungaloafing*' habit, mushrooming on patches of undeveloped land – shingle beaches, sand bars, coastal cliffs, riverside banks and also on downs and woods inland – is the most striking visible manifestation of the flight from urban living of the new middle classes. It also represents one of several attempts on the part of Victorians and Edwardians to recover simplicity. The movement developed from the 1890s when the new seaside colonies tended to be raffish, philistine and bohemian, and associated with the unchaperoned mixed-bathing type of existence which appealed to the more liberated but which was a kind of social behaviour then out of favour at established resorts such as Brighton and Worthing. The heyday of shanty towns coincided with the uproarious Edwardian period and the chic 'naughty' twenties.

Although shanty towns were widely condemned as a great anti-climax of ugly non-design, unjustifiably wasteful of land and often totally destructive of natural beauty, the newcomers did make a notable contribution to cheap holiday homes for mass consumption, economical to run, supremely practical and excitingly different. The favoured summer bungalow was built of two or more complete railway carriages of the pre-bogey wheel era with all their original doors and windows. These were joined with an asbestos or corrugated iron roof, so providing a large and lofty multi-purpose living-room bordered by kitchen, bathroom and bedrooms in the railway compartments. A verandah was commonly added on the front.

The earliest and largest of the shanty colonies was Bungalow Town, Shoreham. By 1901 it comprised more than 100 bungalows, a total that rose swiftly in the pre-1914 years to some 500 and reached 700 in 1939, this rapid

Plate 6.9 R. H. Carpenter's Lancing College Chapel. This vast and magnificent chapel matches the vision and love of architecture of the College's founder, Nathanael Woodard, curate of Shoreham. Dedicated to SS Mary and Nicholas, after the churches of Shoreham, it rises 90 feet high on the downland overlooking one of the finest views of the English Channel. The tapestries behind the altar were woven on the great loom of Merton Abbey, started by William Morris. The architecture was inspired by both medieval English and French Gothic and it is generally considered to be one of the finest church buildings of nineteenth century England (Handford 1931).

growth being associated with the 'discovery' of Shoreham beach by the Music Hall fraternity. The sense of easy comfort, a kind of infectious Wellsian sense of freedom induced by bungalow colonies, led to their spread all along the undeveloped parts of the coast, such as at Littleton-on-Sea, Camber Sands, between Portslade and Worthing, and then again intermittently westwards past Pagham and Selsey Bill (Hardy and Ward 1984: Worlters 1986).

The search for the 'Simple Life' has repeatedly enriched the cultural (if not the agricultural!) life of the South East because, as we have noted, the region has traditionally been perceived as an alternative world to London. Thus it has always possessed a concomitant of social nonconformity of one kind or another. From the 1890s up to 1939 this dissenting element expressed itself as a 'back to the land' movement, a re-affirmation of rural values on the part of those unable or unwilling to accede to the growing complexity, and what was judged the falsity, of modern urban life. Their principal objective was the moral, physical, political and economic regeneration of England through the revival of agriculture and country life, seen as destroyed by *laissez-faire* industrialism. But apart from simplifying life in healthy surroundings, Simple Lifers did not follow any one particular creed. One group comprised small producers with a blind attachment to William Cobbett's radicalism, seeking to purify themselves and enlarge their personalities by cultivating a self-sufficient plot. Others were collectivists and included disparate utopian socialists, Fabians, anarchists, quietists and pacifists, mingled with occultists, theosophists and spiritualists, striving to reduce the inequalities of life through a juster social state and challenging cultural mores and conventional Victorian ideas that 'progress' in the form of 'development' would by itself increase human comfort and well-being. As J. H. Plumb has observed: 'The dream of Elysian England has haunted English radicalism ever since William Cobbett inveighed against enclosure.'

'Simple Life' farming was most strongly developed on the more marginal soils of the clays and heaths where small farmers were in the 1890s still the largest, longest lasting, and deepest planted farming force in the South East. As late as 1857 people had still lived the self-supporting life that Cobbett had wished to see restored to all (Bourne *alias* Sturt 1905: 352). But most 'Simple Lifers' spent short-lived and disillusioned experiences, brought on partly by the falling prices of the years immediately before 1914 and the summer droughts of the early 1920s, but also through their own inexperience and mismanagement. Stuffing their minds with Ruskin and Tolstoy and equipping themselves with various cheap editions of the Open Road publishing house on Thoreau, Emerson and Carpenter could not resolve the problems arising from leaky roofs and patches of worn-out land, however extravagantly beautiful the country or extensive the view.

The wooded sandstone ridge of Limpsfield Chart housed the best-known colony of 'Simple Lifers'. From this incongruous setting on the fringes of London came publications that aimed at nothing less than the retrieval of a fast-dissolving rural culture. They include Edward Garnett's *The Imaged World* (1898), Richard Heath's solid *The English Peasant* (1893), a kind of modern Piers Plowman; Henry Salt's edition of Thoreau; and Montague Fordham's *Mother Earth* (1908) which, despite its title, outlined a realistic blueprint for the revival of agriculture, partially incorporated in legislation as the Wheat Act of 1931 and in government planning after the Second World War. The Limpsfield colony still lives in literature in Ford Madox Ford's *Simple Life Limited* (1909).

The Simple Life movement also gave the impulse to disillusioned urban dwellers to take up small-holdings in the South East. These were followed after the First World War by army pensioners and feminists. The idyll was also inextricably connected with the rural Arts and Crafts movement in the form of farmer-craftsmen, painters, book-binders, metal-workers, furniture-makers and sculptors. A colony of London craftsmen migrated to Steep near Petersfield in 1900 to found Bedales school on Art and Craft principles. A guild of handicrafts was also founded at South Harting by another group of London workers, including James Guthrie, Duncan Carse and Gunning King who worked in stained glass, metal, wood and leather. The Haslemere colony of weavers, embroiderers and other craftsmen included Romney Green, the famous furniture designer and joiner. Other similar colonies were founded at Amberley and Storrington and Shere. The most famous of these was perhaps at Ditchling, associated with the sculptor and calligraphist Eric Gill and his followers between 1907 and 1924 (Gill 1940).

The Country House Ideal

> Four postes round my bed,
> Oak beames overhead,
> Olde rugges on ye floor,
> No Stockbroker could ask for more
>
> Osbert Lancaster, *Homes Sweet Homes* (1948)

For several generations newly enriched professional, industrial and business leaders have had a historically inaccurate but comforting nostalgia for the southern English landscape as 'Olde England' where they could find a better quality of life – fewer people, unspoilt villages and countryside, invigorating air, stupendous views and prospects. The South East has a special place in this national psyche. Until nabobs went westwards along the M4 from the 1970s, parts of the region such as the Garden of Kent, the Surrey Hills and the South Downs were in the businessman's mind a great beckoning landscape of verdant charm.

Early founders of Britain's industrial bases in the Midlands and North, chose the South East as a place of retirement. These included Alexander Nasmyth who invented the steam hammer at Bristol but retired early to Penshurst to spend his leisure where rivets and cogwheels were unknown and Free Trader Richard Cobden who, once he had left Manchester, showed his suspicion of the city by protecting Midhurst against manufactories. Similarly Thomas Sheppard MP came from his Frome clothmaking concern to Folkington manor; a later owner was Gwynne, retiring from his West Midlands engineering business. The two sons of millionaire banker Frederick Huth built the huge Gothic Possingworth and Wykehurst. Surrey possessed a special magic, with its scenery as eventful as any disciple of the Picturesque could ever desire, and with silences and seclusion which turned Surrey into a chic upper-class residential area. It needed only one family to discover a secluded village and invite friends to spend the weekend to set off a chain reaction resulting in a number of large country houses springing up on its outskirts (Bird 1979: 11). In the exquisite scenery of the two adjoining parishes of Abinger and Holmbury St Mary, for example, new mansions were owned by the heads respectively of the Castle Shipping Line, Doulton's Lambeth and Wedgewood potteries, Stephen's inks, Guinness, Brooke Bond Tea, and accountants Price Waterhouse; together with the then Lord Chief Justice, High Court judges, ex-colonial administrators, doctors, and artists and architects. Ten large country houses were built in the space of twenty years. Joldwynds (the home of the Queen's occulist) had 26 bedrooms. All possessed extensive gardens and landscape parks planted with the then popular exotic trees such as monkey puzzles, ginkos and Himalayan rhododendrons. Such houses demanded a large amount of domestic labour, and while many households brought down their staff from London at weekends, there were many jobs available for local people, particularly as gardeners. Waterhouse's Feldemore, for example, had a staff of 11 gardeners and nine domestic servants. Cottages were built in villages to house staff not accommodated in the servants' quarters, shopkeepers migrated to set up business, and churches, chapels and schools were erected (Waterhouse 1988).

In Victorian and Edwardian Surrey the continuous stream of wealth and piety pumped by *nouveaux riches* into the formerly thinly peopled and poorly endowed countryside carried the new movement of church building and restoration to an intensity hardly equalled in any other part of England. Cracklow's famous views of Surrey churches in 1823 (Cracklow 1979), show that rural Surrey possessed hardly any large parish churches, unlike many parts of Kent and Sussex where wealth from the wool and iron industries had resulted in church rebuilding in the fifteenth and later centuries. Typically, Surrey churches were dilapidated patchworks of varying periods, owing partly to the badness of local stone, partly to neglect and partly to injudicious repairs which that neglect had brought. Often of considerable charm, they were deemed to be no credit to an Age of Prosperity and Progress. Even by Cracklow's day some medieval churches had been completely rebuilt, for example, Holy Trinity, Guildford, and the parish churches of Chertsey, Egham and Mitcham: Shalford, Long Ditton and Walton parish churches were rebuilt twice. Very few Surrey churches survive unaltered and many were completely rebuilt in mass imitation of the greater medieval churches of thirteenth-century France or of the Stone Belt of England, as Ruskin had urged. These were paid for by the new country-house owners and their families. The archaeological loss from insensitive so-called restorations was tremendous. The history of Reigate parish church is typical. In Woodyer's 1845 'restoration' a fine fifteenth-century window in the nave was replaced by a commonplace Decorated one, an anachronism confusing the history of the church. The interior monuments were treated with a similar disregard; and as a consequence of the decay of the local sandstone ashlar the most exposed walls, and a doorway and even window were coated with stucco. Gilbert Scott junior's thorough restoration of 1873 was necessary to make the church once more worthy of its site. He rebuilt the noble arcades of *c.*1200 stone by stone and refaced the tower in Bath stone.

In Sussex the losses from 'restoration' were also great. Fernhurst, Loxwood and Plaistow, all demolished, are shown in early watercolours as timber-framed in the same style as surrounding farmhouses (Plate 2.4) (Smith 1979). Other simple little buildings before the advent of *nouveaux riches* included Albourne, Balcombe, Crawley, Crowborough, Elstead, Wivelsfield and Woodmancote. Harsh restorations abound. Lindfield monuments were treated with no regard for propriety or respect of antiquity (Lower 1870). Philip Webb decried the 'witless fiddling' of Slater's drastic 1856 restoration of Burwash. William Morris vainly protested at the spoliation of the dramatic axial design of the Templars' church at Shipley by the addition of a north aisle in 1893 to the design of J. L. Pearson. For the restoration of Findon church, Morris supplied decorated tiles for Sir Gilbert Scott's heavy restoration, before the great rift developed between them that led to the founding of the Society for the Protection of Ancient Buildings in 1877. This society had an early triumph at New Romney where a ferocious 'restoration' was abandoned in the light of its protest, but it failed to have any influence at New Winchelsea where Webb found glorious tombs 'being shamefully scraped. Too late now to smash the head of either parson or architect against the angle of them.' (Brandon 1981: 4). In compensation, the South East was also to gain from some magnificent Victorian church-building (Plate 6.9).

In this way whole districts were 'gentrified' and manicured leaving few traces of the old rural population. On the flanks of Leith Hill the population was said to be 'the least advanced' in the southern counties, being 'the worst type of heathmen', smugglers, fugitive settlers, squatters and commoners. In wealden Sussex, Burwash was described by Lower as notorious for the lawless 'lower part' of its population but 'opulent families attracted to the beauty of the situation are choosing this for their homes'. Burwash Down, once dreaded, was now 'a little centre of civilization'. Similarly, Crowborough was being rescued 'from heathendom to a more Christian condition of things', while Waldron was 'favoured with the presence of several persons of influence and wealth who have completely changed its character'. In respect of Kent, Everitt has calculated as many as 9,000 such 'pseudo-gentry' resident by 1870, and this

Plate 6.10 The sumptuous interior of William James's West Dean mansion. Edwardian West Dean was a by-word for modernity, opulence, comfort and convenience. It was so over-blown that Lutyens designed Monkton higher up in the Downs as a holiday home for Mrs James and the children. This became the home of Edward James, the surrealist collector. Shown in the photograph is the Library extended into a former drawing room. The pair of Corinthian columns mark the former division of the rooms. The Jameses were on close terms with the Prince of Wales (later King Edward VII) who stayed at West Dean for Goodwood Races because the Duke of Richmond, his former host, had objected to two ladies in his entourage (Aslett, 1982).

suggests a possible 20,000 such families throughout the region (Everitt 1974: 170).

An evaluation of the new order produced by such new arrivals argues that a 'wealthy landowner understanding the economics of agriculture, a farmer, master of his practice, a village not over-populated, with pure water, decent houses, allotments and a school, made up the most successful experiment in social organization that England had so far seen' (Young 1936: 145). But this social upheaval, some of it meretricious, did not go unchallenged. It was at the price of uprooting the old social order and destroying much of the traditional landscape.

The glutting of parts of the South East with commonplace parks and jumbled gardens was one source of criticism. This type of landownership was fostered by sharply falling prices for poorer agricultural land and woodland in the depression from the 1870s. Whole areas came instead to be used for ornament and game conservation, with a cow or blade of corn hardly to be seen, to the puzzlement of foreign observers such as Kropotkin (1974 edn: 53). Such third- and fourth-rate landscape parks were created almost continuously along the main highways between London and the coast, notably around Brighton, where their mock-country appearance was really a form of suburbanization. 'The contribution of the average English landscape park to the landscape is notable only for its dullness and monotony' complained *The Spectator* (1897).

By the Edwardian period communities might suffer because of the fashion of letting country houses to wealthy city men who had no real knowledge of or sympathy with the neighbourhood. It was remarked of this practice that 'The formerly real bond of connection between a landlord and his tenants had then ceased to exist except on a very few estates' (Nevill 1907). This can be illustrated with reference to Rickettswood in Charlwood, rented in the summer months by civil engineer Lord Rendel: 'Rickettswood was a closed Rendel community. It had almost no rural contacts with the surrounding countryside. No vicar called. It did not visit neighbouring houses, nor was it visited. Nor did it deserve to be. It was self-sufficient' (Stocks 1970: 39).

In the era of 'Land of Hope and Glory' country houses and gardens took on an extravagant and ostentatious swagger which by their presence disturbed the economic and social balance of whole countrysides. Such plutocrat owners, satirized by H. G. Wells in *Tono Bungay* (1907), were real enough. To William James, heir to American fortunes, a country house meant the enormous mansion at West Dean, built originally in the castle style of James Wyatt, but re-modelled by Ernest George and Peto in 1891–3 and set in an 800-acre downland estate (Plate 6.10). When electric light was installed 364 incandescent bulbs were needed. A hydraulic lift and an automated steam laundry were among the sophistications (Aslett 1982: 16–27). Even more opulent was William Astor's Hever built from a fortune in American property and fur. Astor built 45 guest-rooms resembling a Tudor village as a separate wing to his restored castle, which became a 'miniature Metropolitan Museum of New York'. The lake and Italian garden occupied 800 men over a period of two years.

Writers in each generation vainly railed at these social changes. As early as the 1820s Cobbett observed that frock-coated farmers in Surrey only survived along rutted hollow-ways unusable to carriages. His most sinister figures were the 'Jews and Jobbers' buying up Surrey farmhouses and building and furnishing in new-fangled styles, 'Parlours, aye, with a carpet and bell-push too', where once had been traditional oak tables, bedsteads, chests of drawers and clothes chests (Cobbett 1930 edn: i, 276). Ruskin in 1870 was horrified at the rapidly growing Surrey 'cocktail belts' which were forcing up land rents, and increasing farmers' difficulties. Newcomers

Plate 6.11 A poster for the London underground railway advertising the Surrey countryside, 1925. Ethelbert White's joyous poster is an imaginative rendering of the landscape near Shere, where he lived in a caravan. The wooded North Downs, the Vale of Holmesdale and the sandy heathlands can be broadly identified but the artist spirits an exaggerated wilderness out of what wooded nature survived, and avoids any suggestion of work, as befitted a protected paradise in the urban imagination.

who induced the parish to make up green lanes, thereby increasing the rates, added another nail to the farmer's coffin (Brandon 1979: 176). George Sturt (Bourne) of Farnham lamented the readiness in the 1890s 'to sell or break up or cut down or level away anything on any sites' and the growing demand for land by speculative builders which was pushing up land prices to such an extent that commons were being enclosed and sold off in convenient building lots (Bourne 1956 edn: 74–5; 1967 edn: 611–12, 696–7, 789–90). He also deplored 'the educated, the propertied, acting towards the uneducated and unpropertied without understanding'. He saw the middle classes wanting to civilize the worker, to 'do him good' and wanting '. . . to make him more like themselves and yet keep him in his place of dependence and humiliation' (Bourne 1956 edn: xiii).

The Victorian passion for collecting might also be allied with semi-anthropological studies of the wealden natives. This can be seen, for example, in the collecting of folk song and music, begun by the Rev. John Broadwood and his niece Lucy in the Surrey/Sussex borderlands in the 1840s and 1850s. By 1903 Cecil Sharp and Ralph Vaughan Williams were collecting in the same area, and in 1912 the latter told an audience that:

> I am like a psychical researcher who has actually seen a ghost, for I have been among the more primitive people of England and have noted down their songs (in Gammon 1980: 80).

The rural working classes were being sought out as musical noble savages in an area three hours from London. Other collectors followed, including Carey to the west of Petworth, Butterworth throughout much of Sussex, and Percy Grainger (Gammon 1985).

Yet in its more inspired forms the resurgence of landscaping and domestic building represented one of the most vital forces in English contemporary culture (Stamp and Goulancourt 1986: 13–43). Some of the new ideas in gardening and landscape design were anticipated by William Wells (1766–1847) of Redleaf near Penshurst whose re-introduced flowers near the house, 'natural' rock gardens, specimen exotic trees, and ferns were widely imitated. George Devey's revival of Kentish vernacular half-timbered houses for Wells was also to prove a watershed in house design. Subsequently William Robinson and Gertrude Jekyll drew on the effects of informal planting of hardy plants, shrubs and trees. Their 'wild' or 'woodland' gardens and herbaceous borders in keeping with the house and its setting mark a new stage in the apprehension of nature by landscape gardeners who were also naturalists and artists in outlook. It was also seen as an antidote to modern industrialism. Robinson's *Wild Garden* (1870), *The English Flower Garden* (1883) and his numerous gardening magazines spread his ideas on informal, naturalistic plantings which were unconsciously an updated and more radical statement of the Picturesque principles of Uvedale Price (Hussey 1967 edn: 184). Robinson's own landscaping was at Gravetye near East Grinstead where he resisted imparking and instead embellished his estate with woodland plantations and such other ornamentation as was compatible with farming. The germ of his ideas is found in Addison's famous pronouncement that 'by planting, a whole estate might be thrown into a kind of garden' (Robinson 1911). 'Wild' gardening caught on and traces of Robinson's influence occur all over the South East. Most affected was the triangle bounded by Horsham, Lewes and Tunbridge Wells where wealthy business people modified entire parishes into one continuous 'wild' garden, notably Messel of Nymans, Loder of Leonardslee, Stephenson Clarke of Borde Hill and Soames of Sheffield Park.

The other major innovation in gardening was Gertrude Jekyll's influence, claimed by Hussey to be as widespread as was Capability Brown's on account of the popularity of her *Wood and Garden* (1899) and *Home and Garden* (1900) with suburban gardeners. Miss Jekyll's inspiration came from Robinson but she also emulated all the Arts and Crafts ideals of William Morris, becoming in effect, 'a one-woman version of the famous Firm'. For her colour sense she owed much to Brabazon, the Sussex watercolourist. And the most powerful impact on her work was the 'genius' of her local west Surrey landscape with its heaths, woods, fields and cottage gardens popularized by Birket Foster, Helen Allingham and Ralph Caldecott (Jekyll 1904: viii–x). By the nineteenth century some of the cottage gardeners were gentry such as Miss Mitford of *Our Village* (1832) but most were agricultural workers such as Old Grover, whose garden figures in Sturt's journals, or those whose gardens were earlier admired by Cobbett (1930 edn: 81, 547). Jekyll restored the labourer's cottage flowers to favour among the gentry in place of carpet-bedding. The summit of her achievement was the collaboration with her cousin-architect Edwin Lutyens. Between them they devised 27 gardens between 1890 and 1900 and a further 30 in the following decade for Lutyens's revivalist houses, and in all Miss Jekyll undertook over 300 gardening commissions.

The revival of Kent and Surrey vernacular building from the 1860s, a reaction to country houses poorly-designed without regard to site or locality, rendered the South East the most accessible and richest source of 'Old English' homes (Fig. 6.7). George Devey's assistant, C. F. Voysey, who attached great importance to simple outdoor life, built in the traditional vernacular style and was 'fortunate in finding enough vegetarians and Fabian socialists to keep him in business'. More importantly, the cottages and other rural buildings near Penshurst sketched by the young Norman Shaw and William Nesfield in the 1860s became the model for the new domestic architecture which Shaw called the 'Old English' style. One of his earliest houses was built for Horsley at Cranbrook who paid for it out of the profits of his invention of the Christmas card. Other Shaw houses such as Leys Wood near Groombridge (1868–9) and the nearby Glen Andred set a new tone for years to come.

Philip Webb's bricked Red House for William Morris at Bexley in 1855, was another influential design. Although Webb shrank from and

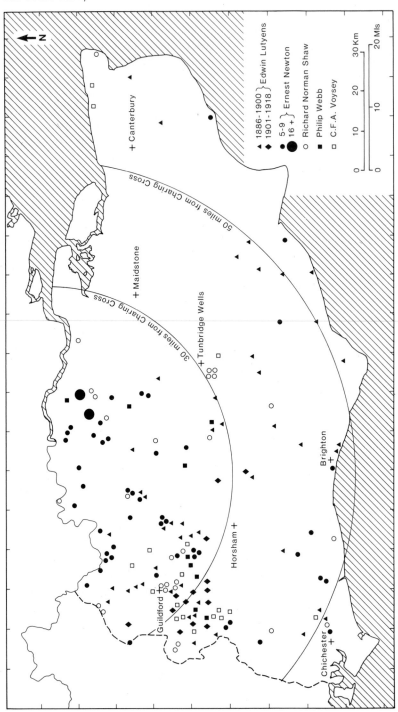

Figure 6.7 The last country houses in the South East.

eluded both wealth and fame, his country houses such as Coneyhurst and Standen were widely admired for their inventive use of traditional building crafts and his sympathetic relation of new building to its setting. At Standen Webb unaffectedly used a harmonious variety of local materials and building techniques; while the light, uncluttered and airy rooms were in complete contrast to standard Victorian interiors. Webb also inspired Lutyens, greatest of the revivalists. Through his cousin Gertrude Jekyll, Lutyens was educated in the picturesque Arts and Crafts traditions of the late nineteenth century and learnt to work in traditional Surrey materials in the 'thorough and honest spirit of old days'. Lutyens's Munstead Wood (for Miss Jekyll herself), Orchards, Goddards, and Tigbourne Court, captured and quietly dramatized 'Old English' feeling. His ideas were spread by Edward Hudson of *Country Life* who so greatly shared Lutyens's vision that he became the promoter of the Edwardian dream house for country living.

Between the two World Wars a debased mock-Tudor style acquired a cherished place in commuters' hearts. A rash of Osbert Lancaster's 'By-pass Variegated' and 'Stockbroker's Tudor' spread with a phoney rusticity from the countryside to the leafier suburbs. Houses, pubs, shopping parades and even cinemas and churches were built in 'Tudorbethan' style, which Barron unashamedly promulgated for country living in *The House Desirable* (1929). This has chapters entitled 'New "Old" Houses'; 'The Art of building with Antique Oak, Bricks and Mossy Tiles'; and 'Modern Houses which look centuries old'. Such houses, as at West Chiltington and Storrington, with eccentric heavy oak joinery such as 'half-timbered airing cupboards' and thatched garages, so faithfully imitate the wealden fifteenth-century hall house that they are now being passed off as the real thing.

Rural Ideology for Urban Needs

As London increasingly took on the cosmopolitan, nondescript air of a modern international metropolis, the changes stimulated a complete transformation of the feelings of its citizens for the surrounding rural environment. The south-eastern countryside became a means of satisfying their spiritual as well as physical needs (Plate 6.11). This was a purpose for which it was well suited, with a neat, ordered and variegated charm, part wild, part cultivated, and its spaciousness with a touch of the sublime. It thus bred sentimentality for the countryside, sitting alongside the deep sense of estrangement from natural life in London; heightening perceptions of the South East and making cockney visions of the countryside fantastically green:

> No wonder our country was supernaturally beautiful. It has London for a foil and background. It was not like ordinary country. The sun there was permanently bright. There was something unusual in the green of its grass, the caw of the rooks in April, in the singing of the mistle thrushes, in the little round islands of wood upon the

> ploughland . . . separated by great distances and great enchantments
> from the rest of the world . . . (Thomas 1913: 67–8).

Foreign observers such as Lavergne who saw nothing out of the ordinary failed to appreciate what a tremendous difference London made to the perceived freshness of the air and the beauty of the views (Lavergne 1865: 202).

Apart from a few attempts at verse by local landowners and antiquarians the South East does not really come into English literature until it was 'discovered' by urban visitors. In the years before the Second World War Sussex and Kent were the most preferred locations of 'country writers', media-symbol operators and landscape painters (Brandon 1984c: 53–74). Behind this concentration is the centralization of wealth and opportunities in London which has traditionally drained the brightest intellects towards the metropolis. Partly for this reason the numerical share of persons in the arts and sciences who have worked in the South East is greater than that of any other part of England (Doyle 1888; Ellis 1927 edn: 37).

The region became the main powerhouse for the 'second and minor Romantic Movement' which helped to change the way the new readership, drawn from the suburbanized white-collar class, perceived the countryside (Wiener 1981). Extreme attachment to the countryside is also expressed in landscape painting which turned the Weald into a vast open-air studio, and botanists have drawn abundantly upon its diverse plant habitats (Fig. 6.8). This nostalgia culminated in the disenchantment following losses on the battlefields of World War One, giving rise to the wave of rural writing in which the region's writers cherished a traditional rural world which seemed to be passing away with industrialization.

The South East became emphatically part of writers' and artists' England and figured in the English imagination as a snug retreat from the harsh realities of a racked and tortured world. 'Short story writers leapt from behind hedges. Minor poets dropped from the trees like ripe fruit. Philosophers, sociologists and artists ran like rabbits about the woods' (Chesterton 1904 edn). In few parts of England was feeling for the soil as a factor of production or knowledge of farming as a way of making a living so lost under a welter of sentiment for country life. Urbanized people apparently had no notion of what agriculture as an economic and social system involved (Brogan 1943: 235–6). Even today, after fifty years of industrialized farming, Sussex remains mildly implausible to the visitor as a working landscape: 'You feel that the sheep and cattle have been stationed in the fields rather like the animals turned out to graze in eighteenth-century landscape gardens, merely to give scale to the prospect' (Keates 1988).

The response of the regional writers and artists to the countryside of the South East was generally like that of an exile who was a habitual week-ender oscillating between departure and return. His city, as T. S. Eliot remarked, was 'that of the man who would flee to the country, his country that of the

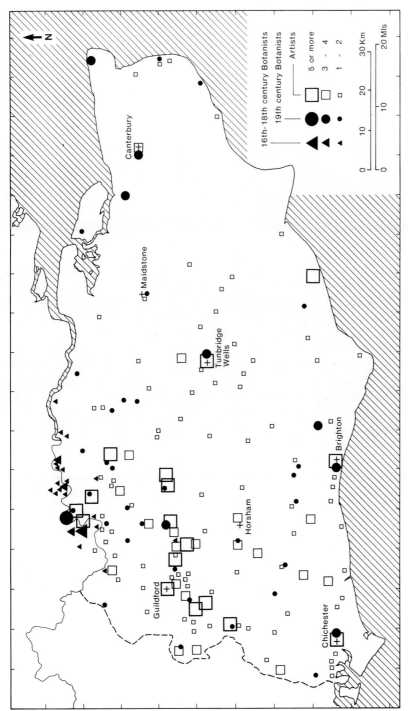

Figure 6.8 The locations of botanists and artists in the South East.

man who must tomorrow return to town' (Monro 1933: v). This love–hate relationship between city and country was constantly relevant in a writer's or artist's creative life. The regional environment became almost wholly external, a thing to feel, observe and measure and a thing to act and react upon, but rarely to absorb or be fully absorbed in, as in the painting of Eric Ravilious (Constable 1982). Like any other Eden it was indiscriminately over-praised, over-written and over-painted on the basis of a fleeting type of experience. The preference for weekend to weekday values is one of the principal themes of Monro's verse. The line from his *Week-end*, 'The train! The twelve o'clock for paradise' was published as a motto in 'country writing' for the urban reader (Mendel 1925). In short, the South East to the urban mind became a 'Region of dreams and Trifles of no consequence', as expressed by Vita Sackville West's opening line to *The Garden* (1940): 'Small pleasures must correct great tragedies'. The essence of the regional literature is thus its lightness, and its lyrical watercolours generally are in similar vein. At its most banal the repetitive stream of innocuous *belle-lettrism* and its equivalent in landscape painting has the soul of a picture postcard with chronometers eternally halted somewhere around 1914. Yet at a higher level, the South East produced a school of poets able to talk to a wider public, so building up a stock of good minor poetry when some of the major poets suffered from isolation. Belloc's verse is one of the most sustained achievements (Belloc 1954).

Whatever one's assessment of the literary and artistic qualities of this outpouring, the region's imaginative history is a social phenomenon of which the regional historian needs to take account, for it is an invaluable source of material for changes in attitudes to the environment formed early in megalo-politan civilization. Its essence has been a Romanticism which inspired a love of the land, of southern England as 'Old England', a respect for old traditions and old buildings in the face of industrialism and materialism which seemed to be destroying both countryside and society. The themes tend to be social and sporting and the summer pleasures of seaside and countryside, but the southern English manner of responding to the natural environment has also drawn abundantly on natural history, rural affairs and country folklore, gardening and conservation. Much of the writing is in imitation of the most celebrated of all the worshippers of the *genius loci* of the South East, the naturalist Gilbert White of Selborne. As early as the year of publication of the *Natural History and Antiquities of Selborne* (1788) it was presciently recognized that future generations of urban dwellers would see in the parson's new modes of thought and observation endless opportunities for leisure themselves, so 'counteracting the allurement of the metropolis' (*Gentleman's Magazine* 1789, 59, i: 60–1). Successor naturalists such as Edward Newman ('Rusticus' of Godalming), Denham Jordan of Dorking ('Son of the Marshes'), William Harrison of Ightham, George Bourne of Farnham, and Tickner Edwards of Burpham, among numerous others, have amply fulfilled this prophecy. As significant as Gilbert White's *Selborne* in its effect in establishing a vogue in rural literature was Mary Russell Mitford's *Our Village* (1832), followed by sketches of life in her country town of Reading in *Belford Regis* (1835). Both were pioneers in the idealized writing of the countryside as a place of retreat which has ever since dominated the rural writing of the South East. Sport and outdoor pastimes which have so wholeheartedly been pursued in the South East for centuries enter into regional literature in various ways. The most famous of the fictional cricket matches are those between the All Muggletonians and Dingley Dell in Dickens's *Pickwick Papers* (1837) and those of Hugh de Selincourt's novels set at Storrington and in A. C. Macdonnell's *England their England* (1933). Walking has a rich crop of literature, as provided by E. V. Lucas's anthology *The Open Road* (1899) or Belloc's *The Four Men* (1904); while the bicycling stories of H. G. Wells release urban lower-middle and working classes from their appalling lack of social and educational opportunities into the self-educative novelty of London's countryside.

Moments of Change, 1837–1939

Regional evolution proceeds slowly, responding to long-term structural changes in both local and national economy and society. Moments of change are thus difficult to recognize, and to pinpoint particular years as heralding change is often to give such years symbolic rather than actual significance. The year 1837 itself ushered in no change. Neither did 1846, with the repeal of the Corn Laws, have any immediate impact. However, both years were part of an important demographic turning-point, during which rural depopulation began to take place. In the same vein, the mid-century 'golden years' cannot be dated precisely in the South East, and the onset of the Great Depression cannot be put more accurately than into the early 1870s.

Other than 1939, perhaps the years 1914–18 are the most significant pivot of change. Agriculture was changed economically; the great estates which framed agrarian structure were decimated; and society, both urban and rural, was irrevocably changed. The impact of the Great War in the South East has been traced for agriculture, but it is important also to touch on its social impact. The South Country of Edward Thomas or Richard Jefferies was never to be the same again.

The summer of 1914 saw crowded beaches as usual, but when war was declared on August 14, troop trains began to compete with the specials for the Brighton races. Recruitment meetings were held, and Kitchener's army was encamped at Shoreham, Seaford and Bexhill in Sussex, ready to end the war by Christmas. Many parts of the South East collected for, and took in, Belgian refugees. At Plumpton and East Chiltington, the Roll of Honour included six men serving in the Royal Navy and 60 in the Army, mostly in the Royal Sussex Regiment. A concert at Plumpton school was held to help the Red Cross cottage hospital at East Chiltington, a local event which must have been repeated many times across the country. At Plumpton, music and songs, together with the musical tableau 'Britannia's sons' raised a good sum of money. In many instances the patriotic fervour was encouraged by the evocation of the English countryside. The 'Georgian' poets drew heavily upon the south-eastern and Home counties for their settings, and soldiers embarking for the front had their last glimpse of England in this region. The Kentish countryside seemed unreal just before Flanders, as it did to Siegfried Sassoon, waiting to cross, and hearing the faint thud of the guns in France (Sassoon 1960 edn: 257; Howkins 1986).

Nevertheless, much of the social and economic impact by-passed the rural South East. Some businesses, such as the Thames-side armaments factories, expanded, while others were adapted to war-time production. More women volunteered or were drafted in to work. Airfields, both emergency and equipped, were established at places such as Shoreham and Ford in Sussex. Hospitals to receive the allied wounded were converted from schools or other large buildings such as the Royal Pavilion at Brighton. After 1916 conscription took more young farmworkers to the front; food queues were seen in genteel Hove and in 1918 there were hunger marches in neighbouring Brighton. Women, schoolboys, scouts, and prisoners of war helped with the harvesting, although Lloyd George still singled out Sussex as being too conservative in its attitude to women workers (*Sussex Express* 28 December, 1917).

The end of the war was marked by civic celebration in 1918 and 1919. But the sense of loss and change was all-pervasive. Most villages erected their war memorials and few families were unaffected by casualties. The huge war memorial in Burwash stands as testimony to such loss and it is scarcely surprising to find that by 1921 Sussex, for example, had nearly 4,000 fewer men of the appropriate age group than it had in 1911 (Lowerson 1980a: 170–3), and this was despite the presence of army corps on the Ashdown Forest.

Men had fought and experienced a wider world, and such experiences were now brought back to south-eastern villages and towns. In January 1918 labour unrest took the form of a strike by Brighton locomotive workshop employees and railway workers. In January 1919 7,000 soldiers awaiting demobilization marched on Brighton town hall. Work and adequate housing were now seen as immediate necessities for the returned fighters. Change was in the air, and social welfare legislation was enacted to meet the demands of reproducing the south-eastern labour force, spurred on by a fear of 'Bolshevism'. Neither adequate housing nor plentiful jobs had in fact been achieved, even in the South East, by 1939, as south-eastern men and women prepared once again to defend their shores against invasion.

Chapter 7

'Megalopolis Denied': The South East Since 1939

> There's no space. I never saw a more spreading lot of animals
> in my life, all in the wrong places.
>
> A. A. Milne, *The House at Pooh Corner*

Although the Second World War was really a continuation of the First,
dramatic advance in aerial warfare made its effects on the region's civilian
population radically different. Within minutes of the declaration on 3
September 1939 the wail of air raid sirens symbolized a region, again
the 'cornerstone of England', on front-line war alert. Yet not until the
Germans occupied France and the Low Countries in May 1940 did they
secure the necessary bases to force the Channel. This led to the famous
Battle of Britain over Kent and the Thames estuary in August and September
1940, which saved Britain from Nazi occupation, owing to the resistance of
Royal Air Force fighter pilots operating against the Luftwaffe from airfields
at Tangmere, Kenley, Biggin Hill and Hornchurch. This proved to be one of
the decisive battles of the war, when 'never in the field of human conflict was
so much owed by so many to so few' (Plate 7.1). Biggin Hill lost 400 of its pilots
and destroyed 1,400 enemy aircraft within three months (Wallace 1957: 287;
Blaxland 1981).

After the retreat of the British Expeditionary Force from Dunkirk in June
1940 the danger of invasion was as acute as it had been in 1803. The coast
of Kent and Sussex was sealed off as a War Zone and general access to it was
prohibited for more than four years. Along the beaches steel scaffolding and
barbed wire were put up to discourage enemy landings. Guns were installed
at commanding points around the coast, anti-tank ditches were dug around
key towns, part of the population was evacuated, and at strategic points all
over the region concrete pill boxes were built which remain as reminders of
Hitler's War just as the Martello towers are of Napoleon's (Jessup 1974). In his
defensive, anti-invasion role, the then major-general Montgomery demolished
hundreds of the shanty bungalows of Shoreham and places west of Brighton, a
ruthlessness amply justified by the knowledge gained after the war that on 16

361

Plate 7.1 Former Battle of Britain pilots at Biggin Hill commemorating the many sorties they made in Hurricanes during the autumn of 1940. RAF Biggin Hill closed down in 1988, and pilots' logs, medals and mementos in various local pubs now form the main link with this critical phase of the Second World War.

July Hitler had ordered an amphibious assault on Britain involving landings on either side of Beachy Head (Fleming 1957; Hamilton 1981: 410–13). German troops were to push forward to hold bridgeheads from Brighton through Uckfield, Tenterden, Ashford and the coast at Thanet and, once established, to cover the whole of the South East before attacking London, a strategy broadly similar to that of William the Conqueror in 1066. These German preparations were compared by Churchill to 'the days when the Spanish Armada was approaching the Channel ... or when Nelson stood between us and Napoleon's Grand Army at Boulogne' (Churchill 1949: 300).

With the failure to gain air superiority as an indispensable prelude to invasion, the German Luftwaffe switched to bombing English cities. The almost ceaseless Blitz on London and its suburbs in the autumn of 1940 resulted in the loss of more than 22,000 lives and destruction and damage to over three million homes. And after the failure to knock out London it became the turn of Canterbury, Dover, Chatham and other coastal towns to suffer bombing which continued, on and off, throughout the war. A war diary kept by a solicitor in a Sussex coastal town recorded no less than 800 air raid alerts in the first four years of the war.

362

From mid-1944 until the end of the war London and the South East again came under heavy aerial bombardment, this time from unmanned missiles ('doodlebugs' or 'flying bombs') launched from the French and Dutch coasts, and later, from rockets (V2s). Over 3,000 flying bombs rained on London and its suburbs in five weeks. Parts of Sussex and Kent became known as 'bomb alley' because they lay along the route of flying bombs falling short of their target of London. Guns stationed on the North Downs, and later on the coast, together with a balloon barrage deployed south and south-east of London accounted for many of the bombs. Despite these precautions Croydon was the worst hit of the outer south London boroughs and Wandsworth, Mitcham and Epsom, for example, also suffered severe loss of human life and property. Chuter Ede of Epsom noted in his diary that 498 bombs had fallen on Epsom in seven weeks, killing 409 persons among a total of more than 5,000 casualties (BL Add Ms 59699 f. 24). London with its eighteen miles width and 24 miles depth was a perfect target for such inaccurate bombardment, until relief from the V2s came with the capture of the launching stations in The Netherlands late in 1944.

In the concluding stage of the war, the South East became an indispensable springboard for the seaborne allied assault upon Europe in June 1944. Country houses and their estates were commandeered for Canadian troops; remote rural areas were supplied for the first time with piped water and electricity; new roads were constructed and many byways metalled. In the months up to 'D-Day' thousands of army vehicles were stored under camouflage, as on the north-bound carriageway of the A24 near Dorking (BL Add Ms 59699). Extensive areas of the wealden heaths were used as military training grounds. At the ports, hundreds of landing craft, barges and torpedo boats were built and petrol pipe lines laid from the Isle of Wight to Normandy and later from Dungeness to Calais. A major deception that the main assault would be across the Straits of Dover involved fleets of dummy ships in the Cinque Ports and simulated concentrations of troops in parts of Sussex and Kent. The actual Anglo-American invasion force was an immense armada of upwards of 4,000 ships and several thousand smaller craft which made a rendezvous off the Isle of Wight.

During the postwar era the South East has changed more rapidly and radically and with greater consequences than ever before. With the decline of the industrial North and Midlands, it has been Britain's most economically advanced and successful region (but by the standards of an economically unsuccessful country), and its overwhelmingly middle-class and white-collar workers are wealthier, healthier, better educated and earning more Gross Domestic Product per head than those elsewhere in the country. One calculation has suggested that the 1988 changes in levels of tax paid by the highest earners have resulted in the South East, with 30 per cent of the national population including London, gaining no less than 57 per cent of the cuts. Of the £2 billion tax cut, £1.2 billion went to the South East, widening growing regional disparities still further (*The Times* 1988: 9 June, 4g; 2 July, 2c).

Despite regional planning in favour of controlling and dispersing London for the sake of the older industrial regions of Britain, the South East has become in postwar years the most prosperous and sought-after corner of England both as a place to live and work in, and for recreation and leisure. London continued to grow at an alarming and accelerating rate in the 1950s and 1960s, largely resulting from an enormous growth in service industries including those in public administration. This led to a concentration of jobs in central London necessitating long-distance commuting from dormitory villages. Rising standards of living above the national average and wider car ownership brought congestion to towns and roads, which was alleviated to some extent by the surge of new building required for the planned movement of people and jobs out of the capital into the suburbs and beyond to small and medium-sized towns in the South East. Since the late 1960s this process, together with a general urge of the more affluent to move out into green countryside, has resulted in professional, managerial and white-collar workers flocking out of London into the rest of the South East. The region is now cumbered by towns such as Frimley, Woking, Guildford, Maidstone, Tunbridge Wells and Ashford, which in the 1960s were intended to assist the escape from London, but now in their enlarged form are creating in their turn a new need of escape (Plate 7.2).

The primary fact about the South East since the War has been the dominance of London. Most of the South East now lies within the mounting pressures of the web of wider London far exceeding in area the physical conurbation that Patrick Abercrombie strove to halt (Abercrombie 1944). Meanwhile, the English Channel looks narrower each year so that the metropolitan South East is becoming a part of the major European growth-zone that stretches from Manchester to the Ruhr. Further vast changes which will raise problems for the regional economy and for the environment of the region as a whole are imminent from the pull of Europe and the completion of the Channel Tunnel – which is moving forward at the rate of 20 ft an hour as this is being written. It is too early to forecast the appearance of the South East landscape in twenty to thirty years' time. Some idea of it is contained in Peter Hall's 1963 vision of life in which Edward Dymill living near the entrance to the Channel Tunnel in

---

Plate 7.2   Modern urban sprawl. This view of Woking evokes the expression 'rurban' coined in 1931 for the kind of human settlement that was neither town or country but a hybrid of the two, sprouting pseudo-Tudor cottages more frequently than trees. This was a half-realisation of H. G. Wells' prediction in *Anticipations* (1900) that '... The city will diffuse itself until it has taken up considerable areas ... The country will take to itself many of the qualities of the city. The old antithesis will indeed cease, the boundary lines will altogether disappear; it will become indeed merely a question of more or less population'.

Kent catches the 8.28 Boulogne-London express (already filled with French commuters) and picks up a pool car at Brixton to carry him to his south London office (Hall 1969: 148).

Another envisaged urban future is where:

> we shall live in a Kentish wood but work in Westminster, hop over to Paris for shopping or Amsterdam for a concert, run down to the coast for sailing or over to Le Touquet for a little golf and gambling. The modern middle-class mobility that generates a creeping urbanisation which is stretching infrastucture to its limits and creates neither pure town nor pure country and has left behind in decaying Inner London a highly immobile population of the old, the unskilled, the poor and the blacks. There will be no future for the South East apart from roaring roads, the rending scream of jetliners and landscapes of steel and concrete unless regional planners turn their attention to ensuring that London and other cities, and not merely the spaces between cities, provide a fitting environment for the people of all classes, incomes and degrees of mobility (Elkins 1973: 70).

The stunning redevelopment of London's Dockland is one sign of this new preoccupation.

This latest chapter in the story of the region has involved distinct historical processes operating at diverse levels and speeds. In the medium term, the dispersal of London has had the main impact on the region, but the once-buoyant economic opportunities are now being more and more qualified by congestion and pollution. Indeed, as early as 1965 the South East was identified as one of the world's problem regions (Brett 1965). Consequently, a strong backlash has arisen against the planning and development nostrums of the 1960s. Another rapid alteration has been the complete character change Brighton and other seaside resorts have undergone, with a decline in demand from holiday-makers bringing better-balanced employment, including the conference business (Plate 7.3). In all change some things remain the same. This is true of a long-term perception, the vision of the South East as a 'land of milk and honey' still being evoked among the urbanized middle classes whose preference is to live in a Barratt home in commuter countryside, rather than in a flat in Inner London. This continues to be, and will remain in the foreseeable future, the most potent of all viewpoints transforming the region's landscapes, population, styles of life and political ideology.

Nevertheless, from the early 1970s to the mid-1980s the South East ceased to be a region of great dynamism. In the planners' eyes it was 'Britain's tarnished golden corner' which was losing its economic superiority in some respects to other regions of Britain such as East Anglia and the Bristol district, as well as internationally (Hall 1976: 228–31). In 1976 Britain stood seventeenth in the table of incomes among 49 EEC regions and has since slipped even lower. This was due in part to regional consequences of the arrested economic growth in Britain with the rise in oil prices in 1973 but another fact was the great internal battle

Plate 7.3 Brighton's largest postwar development: the marina. Is the Channel coast destined to become a developer's paradise, ringed by marinas and luxury yachts? Brighton Marina Village is being built in the late 1980s on a spectacular waterfront overlooking the Marina, an artificial yacht harbour conceived by Henry Cohen, a Brighton businessman, in the 1960s. The principal harbour works were completed in 1980 with two breakwaters enclosing 126 acres providing moorings for 2000 boats. A temporary sea wall was built in order that construction could commence in open sea conditions. Shops, boutiques, a hypermarket, bars, bistros and restaurants, together with hotels, apartments and flats will make it one of Europe's largest leisure developments in the 1990s.

(which still continues) within the region between those wanting growth and those fearing change. Since the War the proportion of the population in the South East concerned about the quality of life rather than the 'economic rat race' has shifted heavily in favour of the former. Recent years have seen the rise of strong anti-populationist views and a general revulsion against growth and its consequences. There is now a striking emphasis on rural living, with less emphasis on an evanescent style of living and more on permanent values in

367

society and the environment. The as yet unbuilt-over South East is seen as part of the green world of rural England in contrast to the black world of industry. The South East in fact is a classic example of a region becoming post-industrial and even post-agricultural, where a decreasing number of men and women are concerned with the production of goods and an increasing number with things of the mind and spirit (Nossiter 1978). Ultimately these contemporary values held in the South East have come to dominate the consciousness of many persons all over Britain (Dahrendorf 1982: 43).

Behind these attitudes is the dream of a medium-sized house and garden in attractive scenery. The village has survived architecturally, but not socially. The 'new countrymen' are persons whose livelihood is made in the towns but who commute to rural peace in the evenings or at weekends. They are supplemented by those who retire to the country after a lifetime of work in town and increasing numbers of people with holiday or second homes. The latter are a growing breed in the wake of greater prosperity, shorter working hours, soaring property values in London and the prevalence of the 'good life' idea. They are forcing up the price of rural housing far beyond the means of local persons who need to work in the countryside. With the lack of affordable homes for the lower-paid, genuine villagers are so rapidly becoming an addition to the list of rare breeds themselves that rural residents drive more than ten miles to the nearest town to collect their cleaning ladies and window-cleaners. These are not the only social groups affected; neither teachers nor policemen can afford to buy new houses in the south-east countryside. Will country living remain fashionable when there is no-one left to do the chores?

This present-day conviction that it is in the countryside rather than in the city that life is lived to its fullest extent poses huge problems for the protection of what countryside is left in the South East. Inherent in this viewpoint is the inconsistency noted by that most appreciative of visitors, Nirad Chaudhuri, between the general lament at the industrialization of the landscape and the silence about the industrialization of society and human personality from which it cannot be separated. Why do they want a *plebs urbana* to live in an Arcadia? (Chaudhuri 1959: 212). Such 'polite' communities are a powerful political force who as soon as installed in their rustic dream home jealously protect their position against the threat to change the *status quo*. This NIMBY attitude is resulting in a clash of interests between those who have adopted the countryside for what it is and those who were born there and need to change it if they are to have a chance to stay. It is unclear whether government attempts to galvanize the region into 'high-tech', post-industrial dynamism will succeed (already parts of the region have one of the highest concentrations of high technology in Britain) or whether the inhabitants will turn their face from the present to the past and witness the 'museumization' of the South East into a giant theme park.

The problem of London's growth into one of the half-dozen largest cities of the world has made the contemporary South East a classic example of a 'planned scape'. The need to control and disperse London for reasons of growth and space triggered off the development of physical planning curbs in the South East with the use of the Green Belt. This curbed the outward growth of London and saved Surrey from suffering wholesale disfigurement as merely a vast commuter dormitory. Unhappily the Belt includes a medley of land uses, many existing before its designation, producing a 'strange hermaphrodite sort of landscape, half country, half town, of extremely doubtful value to Londoners or anyone else' (Hall 1974: 2, 52–8). The Green Belt should not be allowed to buckle but it must be rid of the charge that it is social engineering discriminating against the deprived Inner London population who need more public access to the countryside. Special protection has also been given to areas of exceptional landscape beauty (Plate E.1, p.374). Areas of Outstanding Natural Beauty include some five-sixths of the total land surface of the South East and include the Surrey Hills, the cockney's traditional playground, the small 'water park' around Chichester Harbour, the rounded hills of the South Downs and the wooded humps of the Kent Downs and the High Weald and the Kentish Garden of England (Fig. 7.1). Unfortunately, the coastline has been so damaged that little constitutes an area of high landscape value. The designation of the South Downs as an Environmentally Sensitive Area should encourage the restoration of more traditional farming practices.

Although the image of the South East is of a comfortable and prosperous region, this conceals an enormous diversity of population and living conditions. A 'Domesday 1990' would disclose at one extreme the inner London 'spectral city of night shelters and crumbling squats, down-at-heel bed-and-breakfast hotels and damp alleys' and distressed areas of Brixton. At the other extreme is the Stockbroker or Cocktail Belt of Surrey and north-west Kent, 'a land of large drives and even larger houses. The land of cocktails and G. & Ts and the natural habitat of the Mercedes, BMW and Range Rover set' (Hamnett 1984: 534–8). Less arcadian reaches abound, for example, shabby and sleazy back-streets in Brighton; the decaying industrial areas along the Thames estuary and the New Enterprise Zone of the Medway towns; the Wandle Valley west of London where industrial hideousness is still at its most irredeemably banal; and the M25, Britain's busiest motorway, which has rapidly developed a reputation as its most dangerous. The relative deprivation of Romney Marsh (the last remaining undeveloped part of the South East, now the South East's only Rural Development Area), and the New Town of Crawley (disastrously sited adjacent to Gatwick, London's second airport, developed after Crawley was built) are also further evidence of the mixture of incomes, occupation and social classes. Remarkable diversity exists even between neighbouring settlements. For example, Reigate has been described as a 'genteel world of bijou cottages, kept gardens and bedizened ladies discreetly buying gin at Cullens', whereas Redhill is represented as 'in essence a car park, or series of car parks, strung together with links of smouldering rubble and ragwort, buddleia

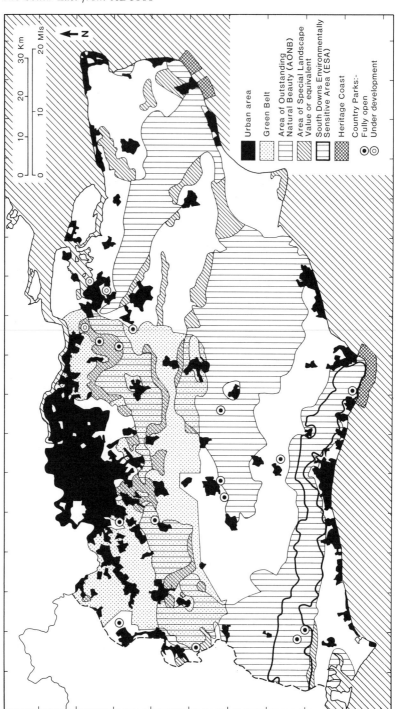

Figure 7.1 The protected landscapes of south-east England.

and willowherb', the two worlds meeting together because children from both places attend the same schools (Mackay 1986). Among the region's delightful anomalies is Chichester, the 'entire ancient city not much larger than many a suburban village' and Lewes, an agreeable and often beautiful hill-town. Neither of them are museums but instead are busy centres of commerce and public administration and still regional capitals serving local people as they have been over millennia. With their conscious use of indigenous building materials and harmonious architecture, they are now seen as good examples of modern urban living.

Despite the over-spilling of London and other towns, the fields, woods, heaths and landscaped parks of the South East can still challenge comparison with any other part of Britain for a richly-varied scenery and a fascinating diversity of wild life. Yet the intensification of agriculture and the social pressures of the past thirty years have inevitably systematically impaired both townscape and countryside. Man's power to alter landscape has grown enormously and wholly outstripped his wisdom. The agricultural environment has been substantially damaged by the increasing use of chemical sprays, the removal of hedges and the ploughing up of old grassland and draining of ponds. This process began with the rapid reclamation of idle farmland to overcome the threat of enemy submarines in the Second World War when both downland and wealden pastures retreated before the plough. In the latter area farmers had walked away from their land in the 1930s, leaving machinery to rust, until re-discovered lying in scrub (Gunner, Pers. Comm.). Although postwar destruction has been less than in the cereal-growing prairies of East Anglia and elsewhere, in general one is obliged to agree with Rackham that 'almost every rural change since 1945 has extended what is already commonplace at the expense of what is wonderful, or rare or what has meaning' (Rackham 1986: 28). The emergency war-time plough-up was thereafter maintained in the protected economic climate after the war, and the downland in particular was transformed into a grain-producing area of international importance. Between 1980 and 1985 alone 2,800 miles of hedgerows were lost in the South East: a sad testimony to the efficiency of the region's farmers and their responsiveness to government incentives. More problem rural areas may soon be created by the decision to curtail agricultural production. The most highly productive and fertile parts of the South East seem likely to continue to prove profitable, but the Weald, where land has traditionally gone into and out of agricultural production with the longest-term cycles of agriculture, poses future problems.

In the short term, the most dramatic change occurred at 0300 hours GMT on October 16 1987 when a great storm gusting at more than 100 mph laid waste much of the countryside. The region has relied for much of its beauty during the past fifty years on over-mature trees in an overgrown landscape garden now bursting like a pulpy, over-ripe fruit. The tremendous catastrophe of the great storm has now radically altered whole landscapes. Parkland of Capability Brown and others of two centuries ago and the woodland gardens created at the close of the nineteenth and early twentieth centuries were almost totally flattened or changed virtually out of recognition. This has brought home the extent to which the present is indebted to the legacy of past landowners and it presents a challenge to design a new rural heritage along lines more appropriate to modern budgets and contemporary ideas of beauty, worthy of the region's physical attractiveness for twenty-first century England. Such a 'brave new world' on old foundations would transform the reality without shattering the dream and emphasize continuity rather than a break with the past. The greatest challenge for the future 'is to find ways of accommodating economic growth and development in ways that conserve resources and protect the environment' (Dept of Environment 1986).

As enemy aircraft flew over south-eastern villages in the Second World War, Virginia Woolf stumbled upon the historical truism that English history is not only of great, cataclysmic events, but also of the underlying continuity in regional life that flowed on largely unchanged in between. This perspective on history which was first introduced as the theme of her last novel *Between the Acts* (1941), will be cordially endorsed by the regional historian. The authors of this book have been at pains to stress how correct was her vision.

Epilogue

Changing Regional Relationships over the Last Millennium

As relationships between people are the cornerstones of relations between regions, so regional differences respond to, and are indeed created out of social, economic, cultural and political differences. Regional differences in turn shape the lives and societies that inhabit them, thereby setting up a two-way interrelationship between people and place. These relationships and landscapes, fashioned to fit the needs of each age, are passed on and reformulated by successive generations. This is as true of the eleventh century South East as of today.

Throughout this volume much has been made of the essential difference in the South East between the Interior and the Coastal Fringe. This has re-emerged at every period, and can be seen as a deep force within the region, mingling with other processes which are more specific to particular periods. Thus early-medieval expansionism, late-medieval retrenchment, early-modern industrialization, or more recent agrarian change all initiated their own modifications, which were 'of their time'. All were to some degree related to forces which emanated from *outside* the South East, but all came to rest on the Interior/Coastal Fringe dichotomy, which in turn shaped their impact on the region.

This deeper structure should not be thought of as some force outside man's control. Instead, the essential differences are the product of myriad human decisions, some weighty, some ephemeral and inconsequential, which have together reinforced the regional contrasts over the last millennium. In Chapter 1 some basic physical differences in topography and soils were outlined, and yet one constant theme in this volume has been not the physical impact on regional structures, but the human impact. Indeed it is possible to note that local differences in such things as soil fertility, closely related as they are to drainage improvements, manuring, cropping and capital inputs, which are in turn dependent upon human social and economic structures, are thus inherently *socially-created*.

At each stage in the evolution of the South East therefore, we have traced the essential differences between Coastal Fringe and Interior. Through

a variety of intertwined institutions and processes the regional differences of the last millennia have emerged, creating inequalities which had begun in the prehistoric and Classical ages and continued into feudalism. These inequalities therefore certainly did not begin with capitalism, but with the transition from feudalism, they were increased. The comparative advantage gained by the Coastal Fringe in agricultural productivity resulted in profits which fuelled expansion, consolidation and engrossing, as it was caught up in an agrarian capitalism geared closely to the demands of external markets, and London in particular.

However, in the Weald, centuries of agricultural neglect had produced a socio-economic structure and landscape setting which was ironically ideal for early capitalist investment. Money came in from London merchants and bankers, as well as from local magnates. But even at its height of wealth from rural industry in the sixteenth century, the Interior was storing up problems for the future. The industrial base was cut away in the two centuries following, leaving it as a de-industrialized area by the Victorian period (Short 1989). South-eastern industries moved to tidewater or towards London – back to the Coastal Fringe at north Kent and Thames-side in particular. With farming structures and techniques lagging behind those of other parts of Britain, under- and unemployment, seasonal and permanent, brought stress, 'social crime' and violence to the Weald in the years immediately before Victoria's accession.

Ironically once again, it was the very fact of its less-developed environment in the nineteenth century, together with its location on London's doorstep, which ushered in the next round of investment, as the Weald became gentrified with villas, mansions and parks. The social cleavages resulting from this juxtaposition of classes within the south-eastern countryside gradually gave way to a process of nineteenth- and twentieth-century 'cultural homogenization' (Hechter 1975: 164), brought about by increased state schooling, Church teaching, improved communications and the urbanization of parts of the Interior near the railways. The Weald ultimately became respectable as 'Hodge' became educated and mobile. But the Coastal Fringe remained dominant, and still does today. Decisions on the wealden future are taken at London or the county towns of Kingston, Maidstone, Chichester and Lewes. Not one of the south-eastern county towns is within the Weald. The Interior is therefore seen, depending on the historical moment, as a reservoir for commuters' homes; poor land which can be used to develop a new town (Crawley);

Plate E.1 Pooh's bridge, Gill's Lap, Ashdown Forest. A. A. Milne was inspired by Ashdown Forest to write the children's books about Christopher Robin, Winnie the Pooh and the rest, which are now internationally known. In 1987 East Sussex County Council refused British Petroleum's application to drill oil near here. In 1988 the eleventh Earl de la Warr sold the Forest to the East Sussex County Council, part of the purchase money being covered by public subscription.

an area for 'key settlements' and to develop light industrial workshops; or as urban recreation space, with the High Weald accorded AONB status in 1983.

Many processes are therefore identifiable as acting within the theatre of the South East. The results of these core processes of inequality: under-development, internal colonization, proto-industrialization, engrossment and depopulation, de-industrialization, urbanization and gentrification, to list some of the more important ones, were equally varied. But by incorporating them into a holistic concept of regional dependence and dominance it is possible to see that features, seemingly unconnected, are in fact the product of an underlying structural unity. Such disparate phenomena as downland hill forts, Saxon *denns*, medieval assarts or deer parks, the wealden iron industry or the detached suburbanization from London, all have their place, as shown in Fig. 1.3 (p. 15).

If regional history is to develop, such holistic concepts are necessary. In their absence, regional geography fell into a morass of poorly-related detail and description from which it is only now being rescued. Regional history must be able to develop and convey a complete and dynamic understanding of the regional complex: to interrelate the development of *pays* and to understand that the actors and their stage come together to make regions man-made artefacts, both in their boundaries and contents. In a region as old-settled and dynamic as the South East such an underlying structure is vital, but the idea is surely just as applicable to any study of regional history.

Bibliography

Abbreviations

Ag.Hist.Rev.   Agricultural History Review
Ant.   Antiquity
Arch.Cant.   Archaeologia Cantiana
BL   British Library
BPP   British Parliamentary Papers
CBA   Council for British Archaeology
CCE   Centre for Continuing Education, University of Sussex
Econ.Hist.Rev.   Economic History Review
ESRO   East Sussex Record Office
KAO   Kent Archives Office
LPL   Lambeth Palace Library
PRO   Public Record Office
SRO   Surrey Record Office
Surr.Arch.Coll.   Surrey Archaeological Collections
Suss.Arch.Coll.   Sussex Archaeological Collections
V. & A.   Victoria and Albert Museum
VCH Kent   The Victoria County History of Kent
VCH Surrey   The Victoria County History of Surrey
VCH Sussex   The Victoria County History of Sussex
WSRO   West Sussex Record Office

List of Unprinted Sources

British Library
British Library Additional Mss (BL Add Ms).
Bodleian Library, University of Oxford
Topographical Mss

Cambridge University
Additional Mss (Twysden's *Remembrances*)
Christ Church College, Oxford
Christ Church manorial Mss
Evelyn Mss
East Sussex Record Office
Ashburnham Mss
Ashdown Forest Case (Raper Books of Evidence)
Danny Mss
Fuller Mss (HA/310)
Probate Inventories
Poll Book 1832 (A 4570)
Kent Archives Office
Filmer Accounts (U120 A17)
Probate Inventories (PRC)
Lambeth Palace Library
Probate Inventories
Merton College, Oxford
Merton College Mss
Public Record Office
Exchequer Depositions (E134)
Ministry of Agriculture, Fisheries and Food June Returns (MAF 68)
Royal Society
Royal Society Mss: Classified Papers 1660–1740, X, Reports 28–30. (Georgical Committee)
St John's College, Cambridge
St John's College manorial Mss
Surrey Record Office (Kingston)
Quarter Sessions Rolls
William Salt Library, Stafford
MS Salt 33 (Late-eighteenth-century copy of the 1676 Compton Census)

The place of publication is London unless otherwise specified.

Abercrombie, P. (1944) *The Greater London Plan.*
Aberg, F. A. (1978) *Medieval Moated Sites*, CBA Research Report.
Albery, W. (1947) *A Millennium of Facts in the History of Horsham and Sussex 947–1947.* Horsham.
Alcock, L. (1962) Settlement patterns in Celtic Britain, *Ant.*, 8, 51–5.
Aldsworth, F. G. (1979) 'Three medieval sites in West Dean parish', *Suss.Arch.Coll.* 117, 109–24.
Alexander, J. and Binski, P. (1984) *The Age of Chivalry: Art in Plantagenet England, 1200–1400.*
Allcroft, A. H. (1923) *Downland Pathways.*

Allcroft, A. H. (1930) *Waters of Arun.*

Allen, S. (1982) Poaching and the game laws in East Sussex, 1830–1880, unpublished M. A. diss., University of Sussex.

Allen, T. (1829) *History of the Counties of Surrey and Sussex.*

Andrews, J. H. (1955) The trade of the port of Faversham 1650–1750, *Arch.Cant.*, **69**, 125–33.

Armstrong, J. R. (1978 edn) *A History of Sussex*

Armstrong, W. A. (1981) The Workfolk, in Mingay, G. E. (ed.) *The Victorian Countryside*, 491–505.

Arnold, R. (1974) The revolt of the field in Kent 1872–1978, *Past and Present*, **64**, 71–95.

Ashford Local History Group (1976), *Ashford's Past at Present*. Ashford.

Ashworth, G. J. (1967) Some aspects of the historical geography of Central Surrey: a study in economic change, unpublished. M. Phil. thesis, University of Reading.

Aslett, C. (1982) *The Last Country Houses.*

Aubrey, J. (1718–19) *The Natural History and Antiquities of the County of Surrey.*

Awty, B. G. (1978) Denization returns and Lay Subsidy Rolls and sources for French ironworkers in the Weald, *Wealden Iron Research Group*, **13**, 17–19.

Awty, B. G. (1981) The continental origins of wealden ironworkers, 1451–1544, *Econ.Hist.Rev.*, **34**, 524–39.

Bachrach, B. S. D. (1985) Some observations in the military administration of the Norman Conquest, *Proceedings Battle Conference*, **8**, 1–25.

Backhouse, J., Turner, D. H., and Webster, L. (eds, 1984) *The Golden Age of Anglo-Saxon Art, 966–1066.*

Bagley, W. (1962) The life and times of William Holloway, Historian of Rye, *Suss.Arch.Coll.*, **100**, 24–45.

Bailey, K. A. and Galbraith, I. G. (1973) Field systems in Surrey; an introductory survey, *Surr.Arch.Coll.*, **69**, 73–87.

Baker, A. R. H. (1963) The Field systems of Kent, unpublished Ph.D. thesis, University of London.

Baker, A. R. H. (1964) Open fields and partible inheritance on a Kent manor, *Econ. Hist. Rev.*, **17**, No. 1, 1–23.

Baker, A. R. H. (1966) Some evidence of a reduction in the acreage of cultivated land in Sussex during the early fourteenth century, *Suss.Arch.Coll.*, **104**, 1–5.

Baker, A. R. H. and Butlin, R. A. (1973) *Studies of Field Systems in the British Isles.*

Baker, D. A. (1976) Agricultural prices, production and marketing, with special reference to the hop industry 1680–1760, north-east Kent, unpublished Ph.D. thesis, University of Kent.

Balchin, W. G. V. (1940) Past sea levels at Dungeness, *Geographical Journal*, **96**, 258–85.

Ballard, A. (1910) The Sussex coastline, *Suss.Arch.Coll.*, **53**, 5–25.

Ballard, A. (1920) *An Eleventh-Century Inquisition of St. Augustine's Canterbury*

Banister, J. (1799) *A Synopsis of Husbandry.*

Baring, F. H. (1898) The Conqueror's footprints in Domesday Book, *English History Review*, **13**, 17–25.

Barker, E. (1948–50) Sussex Anglo-Saxon charters, Parts 1–3, *Suss.Arch.Coll.* **86**, 42–101; **87**, 112–63; **88**, 51–113.

Barker-Reed, M. (1982) The public health question in the nineteenth century; public health and sanitation in a Kentish market town, Tonbridge, 1850–1875, *Southern History*, **4**, 167–89.

Barley, M. W. (1985) Rural housing in England. In Thirsk, Joan (ed.) *The Agrarian History of England and Wales vol. v (ii) 1640–1750*, 697–766. Cambridge.

Barley, M. W. (1986) *Houses and History.*

Bartley, L. J. (1971) *The Story of Bexhill.* Bexhill.

Barton, M. (1937) *Tunbridge Wells.*

Beier, A. L. (1986) Engine of manufacture: the trades of London. In Beier, A. L. and Finlay, R. (eds.), *London 1500–1700: the Making of the Metropolis.*

Bell, Quentin (1986 edn) *Bloomsbury.*

Bell, Quentin, *et al.* (1987) *Charleston.*

Belloc, H. (1954) *Complete Verse.*

Beresford, M. (1966) *New Towns of the Middle Ages.*

Beresford, M. and Hurst, J. G. (1971) *Deserted Medieval Villages.*

Bettey, J. H. (1986) *Wessex from A.D. 1000.*

Bignall, J. R. (1983) Epidemics in Tudor and Stuart Guildford, *Surr.Arch.Coll.*, **74**, 113–21.

Binney, M. (1988) Herstmonceux castle, *Landscape*, **5**, 31–5.

Bird, M. (1979) *Holmbury St Mary: One Hundred Years.* Holmbury.

Bise, Gabriel (1978) *Gaston Foix's Hunting Book.* Geneva.

Bishop, C. H. (1973) *Folkestone: the story of a Town.* Folkestone.

Bishop, T. A. M. (1938) The rotation of crops at Westerham, 1297–1356, *Econ.Hist.Rev.*, **9**, 38–44.

Blackwell, P. (1981) An undoubted jewel: a case study of five Sussex country houses, 1880–1914, *Southern History*, **3**, 183–200.

Blaxland, G. (1981) *South-East Britain: Eternal Battleground.* Rainham.

Blome, R. (1673) *Britannia.*

Blomfield, R. (1940) *Richard Norman Shaw, R. A.*

Blunt, W. (1917) *History of the Crabbet estate in Sussex.*

Booth, C. (1902) *Life and Labour of the People in London. Third Series: Religious Influences, vols IV and V. Inner South London.*

Boulton, J. (1987a) Neighbourhood migration in early-modern London. In Clark, P. and Souden, D. (eds) *Migration and Society in Early-Modern England*, 107–49.

Boulton, J. (1987b) *Neighbourhood and Society: a London Suburb in the Seventeenth Century*, Cambridge.

Bourne (Sturt), G. (1902) *The Bettesworth Book*.

Bourne (Sturt), G. (1905) Seventy years ago, *Longman's Magazine*, **45**, 347–58.

Bourne (Sturt), G. (1913) *Lucy Bettesworth*.

Bourne (Sturt), G. (1956 edn) *Change in the Village*.

Bourne (Sturt), G. (1967 edn) (ed. Mackerness, M. D.) *The Journals of George Sturt*. (2 vols.) Cambridge.

Boys, J. (1805) *A General View of the Agriculture of the County of Kent*.

BPP (1833) Report from the Select Committee on Agriculture, V, 5457–5771. Evidence of Mr. J. Cramp.

BPP (1834) Report of the Royal Commission on the Poor Law, XXVII, Appendix C.

BPP (1865) Seventh Report from the Medical Officers of Health to the Privy Council, XXVI, Report of Dr H. J. Hunter, Appendix 6, 126–302.

Brandon, P. F. (1962) Arable farming in a Sussex scarpfoot parish during the late Middle Ages, *Suss.Arch.Coll.*, **100**, 60–72.

Brandon, P. F. (1963) The common lands and wastes of Sussex, unpublished Ph.D. thesis, University of London.

Brandon, P. F. (1969) Medieval clearances in the east Sussex Weald, *Trans. Institute British Geographers*, **48**, 135–53.

Brandon, P. F. (1971a) Late medieval weather in Sussex and its agricultural significance, *Trans. Institute British Geographers*, **54**, 1–17.

Brandon, P. F. (1971b) Demesne arable farming in coastal Sussex during the late Middle Ages, *Ag.Hist.Rev.*, **19**, 13–34.

Brandon, P. F. (1971c) The origin of Newhaven and the drainage of the Lewes and Laughton Levels, *Suss.Arch.Coll.*, **109**, 94–106.

Brandon, P. F. (1971d) Agriculture and the effects of floods and weather at Barnhorne, Sussex, during the late Middle Ages, *Suss.Arch.Coll.*, **109**, 69–93.

Brandon, P. F. (1972) Cereal yields on the Sussex estates of Battle Abbey during the later Middle Ages, *Econ.Hist.Rev.*, **25**, 403–20.

Brandon, P. F. (1974) *The Sussex Landscape*.

Brandon, P. F. (1977) A History of Surrey. Chichester.

Brandon, P. F. (1978) The Andredesweald, in Brandon, P. F. (ed.), *The South Saxons*, 138–59. Chichester.

Brandon, P. F. (1979) Designed landscapes in South-East England, *Trans. Institute British Geographers*, Special Number No. 10.

Brandon, P. F. (1981) Philip Webb, the Morris circle and Sussex, *Sussex History*, 2, 8–14.

Brandon, P. F. (1982) A twentieth-century squire in his landscape: Reginald Bray of Shere, Surrey, *Southern History*, 4, 191–220.

Brandon, P. F. (1984a) *The Tillingbourne river story*. Shere.

Brandon, P. F. (1984b) Land, technology and water management in the Tillingbourne valley, Surrey, *Southern History*, 6, 75–107.

Brandon, P. F. (1984c) Wealden nature and the role of London in nineteenth-century artistic imagination, *Journ.Hist.Geog.*, 10, 53–74.

Brayley, E. W. (1850) *A Topographical History of Surrey*. (5 vols).

Brent, C. E. (1973) Employment, land tenure and population in eastern Sussex, 1540–1640, unpublished D. Phil. thesis, University of Sussex.

Brent, C. E. (1976) Rural employment and population in Sussex between 1550 and 1640, *Suss.Arch.Coll.*, 114, 27–48.

Brent, C. E. (1978) Rural employment and population in Sussex between 1550 and 1640, Part ii, *Suss.Arch.Coll.*, 116, 41–56.

Brent, C. E. (1985) *Historic Lewes: official guide*. Lewes.

Brent, J. A. (1968) Alciston manor in the Middle Ages, *Suss.Arch.Coll.*, 106, 89–102.

Brett, L. (1965) *Landscape in Distress*.

Briault, E. W. H. (1942) *The Land of Britain: Sussex (East and West)*.

Bridbury, A. R. (1973) The Black Death, *Econ.Hist.Rev.*, 26, 577–92.

Bridbury, A. R. (1977) Before the Black Death, *Econ.Hist.Rev.*, 30, 393–410.

Britten, J. and Boulger, G. (1931) *Index of British Botanists*.

Brogan, D. W. (1943) *The English People: Impressions and Observations*.

Brookes' Guide and Directory for Uckfield and District (1888).

Brookfield, H. C. (1952) The estuary of the Adur, *Suss.Arch.Coll.*, 90, 153–63.

Brookfield, H. C. (1955) Three Sussex ports 1850–1950, *Journ. Transport History*, 2, 35–50.

Brooks, N. P. (1981) Romney Marsh in the early Middle Ages. In Rowley, T. (ed.), *The Evolution of Marshland Landscapes*. Oxford.

Brooks, N.P. and Walker, H. E. (1978) The authority and interpretation of the Bayeux Tapestry, *Proceedings Battle Conference*, 1, 1–34.

Brown, A. (1977) London and north-west Kent in the later Middle Ages: the development of the land market, *Arch.Cant.*, 92, 145–56.

Brown, R. Allen (1976 edn) *English Castles*.

Brown, R. Allen (1981) The Battle of Hastings, *Proceedings Battle Conference*, 3, 1–21.

Brown, R. Allen (1984) *The Norman Conquest*.

Brown, R. Allen (1985 edn.) *The Normans and the Norman Conquest*.

Buckatzsch, E. J. (1950) The geographical distribution of wealth in England, 1086–1843, *Econ.Hist.Rev.*, 2nd ser. 3, 180–202.

Burleigh, G. R. (1973) An introduction to deserted medieval villages in east Sussex, *Suss.Arch.Coll.*, 91, 45–83.

Burleigh, G. R. (1974) Medieval earthworks at Arlington, *Suss.Arch.Coll.*, **112**, 80–4.

Burleigh, G. R. (1976) Further notes of deserted and shrunken medieval villages in Sussex, *Suss.Arch.Coll.*, **114**, 61–8.

Butcher, A. F. (1974) The origins of Romney Freeman, *Econ.Hist. Rev.*, **27**, 16–27.

Butcher, A. F. (1977) Sandwich in the thirteenth century, *Arch.Cant.*, **93**, 25–31.

Butcher, A. F. (1979) Rent and urban economy: Oxford and Canterbury in the later Middle Ages, *Southern History*, **1**, 11–44.

Caird, J. (1852) *English Agriculture in 1851–2.*

Camden, William (ed. Copley, G. J. 1977a) *Camden's Britannia: Kent.*

Camden, William (ed. Copley, G. J. 1977b) *Camden's Britannia: Surrey and Sussex.*

Cameron, W. (1973) The Petworth emigration committee: Lord Egremont's assisted emigrations from Sussex to Upper Canada, 1832–37, *Ontario History*, **65**, 231–46.

Campbell, B. M. S. (1983a) Agricultural progress in medieval England, *Econ.Hist.Rev.*, **36**, 26–46.

Campbell, B. M. S. (1983b) Arable productivity in medieval England, *Journ.Econ.Hist.*, **43**, 379–404.

Campbell, B. M. S. (1988) Towards an agricultural geography of medieval England, *Agric.Hist.Rev.*, **36**, 87–98.

Cannadine, D. (1980), *Lords and Landlords: The Aristocracy and the Towns, 1774–1967.* Leicester.

Cannadine, D. and Reeder, D. (1982) *Exploring the urban past.* Cambridge.

Cantor, L. (1982) *The English Medieval Landscape.*

Cantor, L. (1983) *The Medieval deer-parks of England: a Gazetteer.* Loughborough.

Cantuarensis or Dorovorensis, Gervasius (1932 edn) *Of the Burning and Repair of the Church of Canterbury in the year 1174.* Canterbury.

Carr, M. C. (1982) The development and character of a metropolitan suburb: Bexley, Kent. In Thompson F. M. L. (ed.), *The Rise of Suburbia*, Leicester.

Carrier, E. H. (1937) *The Inner Gate.*

Cattell, C. S. (1973) The historical geography of the wealden iron industry, unpublished M.A.diss., University of London.

Chalklin, C. (1960) The Compton Census of 1676: the Dioceses of Canterbury and Rochester, *A Seventeenth Century Miscellany. Kent Records XVII.* Maidstone.

Chalklin, C. (1961) A seventeenth century market town: Tonbridge, *Arch.Cant.*, **76**, 152–62.

Chalklin, C. (1965) *Seventeenth Century Kent. A Social and Economic History.*

Chalklin, C. (1974) The making of some new towns c.1600–1720. In

Chalklin, C. and Havinden, M. (eds), *Rural Change and Urban Growth 1500–1800.*

Chamberlin, E. R. (1970) *Guildford: a biography.*

Charlesworth, A. (1979) *Social protest in a rural society: the spatial diffusion of the Captain Swing disturbances of 1830–1831.* Historical Geography Research Group monographs 1. Norwich.

Charlesworth, A. (ed.) (1983) *An Atlas of Rural Protest in Britain 1548–1900.*

Chartres, J. (1985) The marketing of agricultural produce. In Thirsk, Joan (ed.), *The Agrarian History of England and Wales vol. v (ii) 1640–1750.* 430–9. Cambridge.

Chartres, J. (1986) Food consumption and internal trade. In Beier, A. L. and Finlay, R. (eds), *London 1500–1700: the Making of the Metropolis.* 168–96.

Chaudhuri, N. R. (1959) *A Passage to England.*

Cheal, H. (1921) *The Story of Shoreham.*

Cherry, B. and Pevsner, N. (1983) *The Buildings of England: London 2: South.*

Chesterton, G. K. (1904 edn) *Tremendous Trifles.*

Church, R. (1955) *Over the Bridge.*

Churchill, Winston S. (1949) *The Second World War: Vol. 2 Their Finest Hour.*

Churchill, Winston S. (1954) *The Second World War: Vol. 6, Triumph and Tragedy.*

Clark, C. (1980) Battle *c.*1100: an anthroponymist looks at an Anglo-Norman new town, *Proceedings Battle Conference*, 2, 21–41.

Clark, F. L. (1960) The history of Epsom Spa, *Surr.Arch.Coll.*, 57, 1–41.

Clark, P. (1972) The migrant in Kentish towns 1580–1640. In Clark, P. and Slack, P. (eds), *Crisis and Order in English Towns 1500–1700: Essays in Urban History*, 117–63.

Clark, P. (1977) *English Provincial Society from the Reformation to the Revolution.* Hassocks.

Clark, P. and Clark, J. (1983) The social economy of the Canterbury suburbs: the evidence of the census of 1563. In Detsicas, A. and Yates, N. (eds), *Studies in Modern Kentish History*, 65–86. Maidstone.

Clark P. and Slack P. (1972) *Crisis and Order in English Towns 1500–1700: Essays in Urban History.*

Clark, P. and Slack P. (1976) *English Towns in Transition, 1500–1700.*

Clarke, P. and Stoyel, A. (1975) *Otford in Kent: a History.*

Cleere, H. and Crossley, D. C. (1985) *The Iron Industry of the Weald.* Leicester.

Clifford, C. A. (1982) Ship money in Hampshire: collection and collapse, *Southern History*, 4, 91–106.

Clough, M. (ed.) (1964) *The Book of Bartholomew Bolne.* Sussex Record Society, 63.

Clough, M. (ed.) (1969) *Two Fitzalan Surveys*, Sussex Record Society, 67.

Cobbett, William (1930 edn) (eds Cole, G. D. H. and M.) *Rural Rides.*

Cockburn, J. S. (1975) *Calendar of Assize Records: Sussex Indictments, James I.*

Cohen, M. N. (1965) *Rudyard Kipling to Rider Haggard: The record of a friendship.*

Coleman, B. I. (1983) Southern England in the census of religious worship, 1851, *Southern History*, 5, 154–88.

Coleman, D. C. (1951) The Economy of Kent under the later Stuarts, unpublished Ph.D. thesis, University of London.

Coleman, D. C. (1963) *Sir John Banks: Baronet and Businessman.* Oxford.

Coleman, O.(1960–1) *The Brokage Books of Southampton, 1443–4,* Southampton Record Series, 4–6 Southampton.

Collier, Basil (1962) *The Battle of Britain.*

Connell, John (1978) *The End of Tradition: Country Life in central Surrey.*

Constable, Freda (1982) *The England of Eric Ravilious.*

Cook, E. T. and Wedderburn, A. (eds 1907) *The Works of John Ruskin,* 33.

Cooper, J. H. (1902) A religious census of Sussex in 1676, *Suss.Arch.Coll.,* 45, 142–8.

Cooper, W. D. (1866) Participation of Sussex in Cade's Rising, *Suss.Arch.Coll.,* 18, 17–36.

Corfield, P. (1982) *The Impact of English Towns 1700–1800.*

Cornwall, J. (1953) The agrarian history of Sussex, 1560–1640, unpublished M.A. diss., University of London.

Cornwall, J. (1956) *Sussex Lay Subsidy Rolls, 1524–5.* Sussex Record Society, 56.

Cornwall, J. (1960) Agricultural improvement 1560–1640, *Suss.Arch.Coll.,* 98, 118–32.

Cornwall, J. (1967) Evidence of population mobility in the seventeenth century, in *Bull.Inst.Hist.Res.,* 40, 143–52.

Cornwall, J. (1975) The Ecclesden outrage: a fresh interpretation, *Suss.Arch. Coll.,* 113, 7–15.

Cornwall, J. (1976) Sussex wealth and society in the reign of Henry VIII, *Suss.Arch.Coll.,* 114, 1–26.

Corporation of London (1878) *Analytical Index to the Remembrancia 1579–1664.*

Course, E. (1958) The evolution of the railway network of South East England, unpublished Ph.D. thesis, University of London.

Course, E. (1962) *London Railways.*

Course, E. (1973) *The Railways of Southern England: the Main Lines.*

Cowley, G. O. (1964) Sussex Market Towns, 1550–1750, unpublished M.A. diss., University of London.

Cozens-Hardy, B. (1950) *The Diary of Sylas Neville.*

Cracklow, T. (1979) (ed. Gravett, K. W. E.) *Views of Surrey Churches.*

Crocker, Alan (1988) *Paper Mills of the Tillingbourne.* Oxshott, Surrey.

Crocker, Glenys (1985) *A Guide to the Chilworth Gunpowder Mills*. Surrey Industrial History Group. Guildford.

Crossick, G. S. (1976) Social structure and working-class behaviour: Kentish London 1840–1880, unpublished Ph.D. thesis, University of London.

Crossick, G. S. (1978) *An artisan elite in Victorian society: Kentish London 1840–80*.

Crossley, D. W. (1972a) The performance of the glass industry in sixteenth-century England, *Econ.Hist.Rev.*, **25**, 421–33.

Crossley, D. W. (1972b) A sixteenth-century Wealden blast furnace at Panningridge, Sussex, *Post.Med.Arch.*, **6**, 42–68.

Crossley, D. W. (1981) Medieval iron smelting. In Crossley, D. W. (ed.) *Medieval Industry*. CBA Res. Rep. 40.

Cunliffe, B. W. (1980) The evolution of Romney Marsh; a preliminary statement. In Thompson, F. H. (ed.) *Archaeology and Coastal Change*, Society of Antiquaries, 37–55.

Curzon, Lord (1926) *Bodiam Castle*.

Dahrendorf, Ralph (1982) *On Britain*.

Darby, H. C. (1977) *Domesday England*.

Darby, H. C. and Campbell, E. M. J. (1962) *The Domesday Geography of South-East England*.

Davis, J. F. (1966) Lollard survival and the textile industry in the South-east of England. In Cumming, J. G. (ed.), *Studies in Church History*, **3**, 191–201.

Davis, J. F. (1983) *Heresy and Reformation in the South East of England, 1520–1559*, Royal Historical Society.

Defoe, Daniel (1738 edn, repr 1927) *A Tour Through The Whole Island of Great Britain*.

Department of the Environment (1986) *Circular 14/86*.

Dickens, P. and Gilbert, P. (1981) Inter-war housing policy: a study of Brighton, *Southern History*, **3**, 201–31.

Dobson, M. (1982) Population, disease and mortality in South East England 1600–1800, unpublished D. Phil., University of Oxford.

Dobson, M. (1987) *A Chronology of Epidemic Disease and Mortality in Southeast England, 1601–1800*. Historical Geography Research Series 19.

Dobson, R. B. (1977) Urban decline in late medieval England, *Trans.Roy.Hist. Soc.*, **5**, 1–24.

Douglas, D. C. (ed.) (1944) *The Domesday Monachorum of Christ Church*.

Douglas, D. C. (1964) *William the Conqueror*.

Douglas, D. C. (1969) *The Norman Achievement, 1050–1100*.

Doyle, Conan (1888) The geographical distribution of the educated elite in England, *Nineteenth Century*, **24**, 184–95.

Drewett, P., Rudling, D. and Gardiner, M. (1988) *The South East to AD 1000*.

Du Boulay, F. R. H. (1959) Late-continued demesne farming at Otford, *Arch.Cant.* 73, 116–24.

Du Boulay, F. R. H. (1966) *The Lordship of Canterbury; an essay in Medieval Society.*

Du Boulay, F. R. H. (1974) The Assembly of an estate; Knole in Sevenoaks, *c.*1275–1528, *Arch.Cant.*, **89**, 1–10.

Dulley, A. J. F. (1966a) Four Kent towns at the end of the Middle Ages, *Arch.Cant.*, **81**, 95–108.

Dulley, A. J. F. (1966b) The level and port of Pevensey in the Middle Ages, *Suss.Arch.Coll.*, **104**, 26–45.

Dulley, A. J. F. (1969) The early history of the Rye fishing industry, *Suss.Arch.Coll.*, **107**, 36–64.

Dunbar, J. (1966) *A Prospect of Richmond.*

Dunlop, John (1964) *The Pleasant Town of Sevenoaks: a History.*

Dyer, A. D. (1979) The market towns of southern England, *Southern History*, **1**, 123–34.

Dyos, H. J. (1955) Railways and housing in Victorian London, *Journ. Transport Hist.*, **2**, 11–21, 90–100.

Dyos, H. J. (1977) *Victorian Suburb: a study of the growth of Camberwell.* Leicester.

Dyos, H. J. (1982) Some social costs of railway building in London, in Cannadine, D. and Reeder, D. (eds.) *Exploring the Urban Past*, 119–25. Cambridge.

Eddison, Jill (1983) The Settlement of Romney Marsh: some aspects re-considered, *Arch.Cant.*, **99**, 47–58.

Elkins, T. H. (1973) *The Urban Explosion.*

Ellis, Havelock (1927 edn) *A Study of British Genius.*

Evelyn, John (1664) *Sylva, or a Discourse of Forest Trees.*

Evelyn, John (ed. Dobson, A. 1906) *The Diary of John Evelyn.*

Everitt, Alan M. (1957) *The County Committee of Kent in the Civil War.* Leicester.

Everitt, Alan M. (1966) *The Community of Kent and the Great Rebellion 1640–60.* Leicester.

Everitt, Alan M. (1967) The marketing of agricultural produce. In Thirsk, Joan (ed.), *The Agrarian History of England and Wales, vol. iv 1500–1640,* 466–592. Cambridge.

Everitt, Alan M. (1969) *Change in the Provinces: the seventeenth century.* Leicester.

Everitt, Alan M. (1972) *The Pattern of Rural Dissent: the Nineteenth Century.* Leicester.

Everitt, Alan M. (1974) Kentish Family portrait. In Chalklin, C. and Havinden, M., (eds) *Rural Change and Urban Growth, 1500–1800.*

Everitt, Alan M. (1976) The making of the agrarian landscape of Kent, *Arch.Cant.*, **92**, 1–31.

Everitt, Alan M. (1977) River and wold; reflections on the historical origin of region and *pays, Journ.Hist.Geog.*, **3**, 1–19.

Everitt, Alan M. (1979) County, country and town, *Trans. Royal Historical Society*, **29**, 79–108.

Everitt, Alan M. (1986) *Continuity and Colonization: the Evolution of Kentish Settlement.* Leicester.

Farrant, J. (1976a) The seaborne trade of Sussex, 1720–1845, *Suss.Arch.Coll.*, **114**, 97–120.

Farrant, J. (1976b) *The Harbours of Sussex 1700–1914.* Brighton.

Farrant, J. (1985) The Rise and decline of a South Coast seafaring town: Brighton 1550–1750, *The Mariner's Mirror*, **71**, 59–76.

Farrant, S. (1978) John Ellman of Glynde in Sussex, *Ag.Hist.Rev.*, **26**, 77–88.

Farrant, S. (1979) The management of four estates in the Lower Ouse Valley (Sussex) and agricultural change, 1840–1920, *Southern History*, **1**, 155–70.

Ferguson, M. H. (1979) Land use, settlement and society in the Bagshot Sands region, 1840–1940, unpublished Ph.D., University of Reading.

Fergusson, P. (1984) *Architecture of Solitude: Cistercian Abbeys in Twelfth-Century England.*

Fielding, A. J. (1981) *Place, work and folk: a study of the development of Crowborough, Sussex,* Geography Research Paper, University of Sussex.

Finlay, R. and Shearer, B. (1986) Population growth and suburban expansion. In Beier, A. L. and Finlay, R. (eds), *London 1500–1700: the making of the Metropolis*, 37–59.

Finn, R. Welldon (1971) *The Norman Conquest and its Effect on the Economy, 1066–1086.*

Fisher, H. A. L. (1934) The development of the London food market, *Econ.Hist.Rev. Old Ser.*, **5**, 46–54.

Fitzgerald, P. (1893) *London City Suburbs as they are Today.*

Fleming, Lindsay (1959) Lessay Abbey, mother-house of Boxgrove Priory, *Suss.Arch.Coll.*, **98**, 119–29.

Fleming, Peter (1957) *Invasion 1940.*

Fletcher, A. J. (1975) *A County Community in Peace and War: Sussex, 1600–1660.*

Flinn, M. W. (1959) Timber and the advance of technology: a reconsideration, *Annals of Science*, **15**, 109–20.

Ford, W. K. and Gabe, A. C. (1981) *The Metropolis of Mid-Sussex: A History of Haywards Heath.* Haywards Heath.

Forge, F. (1986) *Painshill.* Esher, Surrey.

Fossey, K. (1981) Slums and tenements 1840–1910. In Farrant, S., Fossey, K. and Peasgood, A., *The Growth of Brighton and Hove 1840–1939.* CCE.

Friedlander, D. and Roshier, R. J. (1966) A Study of internal migration in England and Wales: Part I, *Population Studies*, **19**, 239–79.

Fuller, G. J. (1953) The development of roads in the Surrey and Sussex Weald and coastlands between 1700 and 1900, *Transactions Institute of British Geographers*, **19**, 37–49.

Furley, Robert (1871–4) *A History of the Weald of Kent*.

Gammon, V. (1980) Folk song collecting in Sussex and Surrey 1843–1914, *History Workshop Journ.* **10**, 61–89.

Gammon, V. (1985) Popular music in rural society: Sussex 1815–1914, unpublished D. Phil. thesis, University of Sussex.

Garrad, G. H. (1954) *A Survey of the Agriculture of Kent*.

Gelling, Margaret (1988 edn) *Signposts to the past; Place-Names and the History of England*.

Gem, R. (1984) An early church of the Knights Templars at Shipley, Sussex, *Proceedings Battle Conference*, **6**, 238–46.

George, M. D. (1925) *London life in the eighteenth century*.

Gill, Eric (1940) *Autobiography*.

Given-Wilson, C. (1987) *The English Nobility in the Middle Ages*.

Glasscock, R. E. (1965) The distribution of lay wealth in Kent, Surrey and Sussex in the early fourteenth century, *Arch.Cant.*, **80**, 61–8.

Goddard, N. (1974) Kentish farmers' clubs in the mid-nineteenth century, *Cantium*, **6**, 80–3.

Golding, Brian (1981) The coming of the Cluniacs, *Proceedings Battle Conference*, **3**, 65–77.

Goring, J. (1978a) The riot at Bayham Abbey, June 1525, *Suss.Arch.Coll.*, **116**, 1–10.

Goring, J. (1978b) Wealden ironmasters in the age of Elizabeth. In Ives, E. W. *et al.* (eds), *Wealth and Power in Tudor England*, 204–27.

Gravett, K. W. E., (1967) Merstham limeworks, *Surr.Arch.Coll.*, **64**, 124–47.

Gray, H. (1915) *English Field Systems*.

Green, R. G. (1968) *The Soils of Romney Marsh*, Soil Survey, Harpenden.

Greenaway, G. W. (1961) *The Life and Death of Thomas Becket*.

Greenwood, J. (1979) A lost seventeenth-century demographic crisis: rural Surrey, *Local Population Studies*, **23**, 39–40.

Griffiths, A. and Kesnevova, G. (1983) *Wenceslas Hollar: Prints and Drawings*.

Griffiths, N. (1976) Firle: Selected Themes from the Social History of a Closed Sussex Village, 1850–1939, unpublished M.A. diss., University of Sussex.

Gulley, J. L. M. (1960) The Wealden Landscape in the Seventeenth Century and its Antecedents, unpublished Ph.D. thesis, University of London. (2 vols).

Gulley, J. L. M. (1961) The Great Rebuilding in the Weald, *Gwerin*, **3**, 1–16.

Gurney, J. R. (forthcoming) The County of Surrey and the English Revolution 1640–60, unpublished D. Phil. University of Sussex.

Haggard, H. Rider (1906) *Rural England: Being an account of Agricultural and Social Researches carried out in the years 1901 and 1902.*

Hall, A. D. (1913) *A Pilgrimage of British Farming 1910–12.*

Hall, A. D. and Russell, E. J. (1911) *A Report on the Agriculture and Soils of Kent, Surrey and Sussex.*

Hall, P. (1969) *London 2000.*

Hall, P. (1974) *The Containment of Urban England.*

Hall, P. (1976) The South-East: Britain's tarnished golden corner, *New Society*, 228–31.

Hallam, H. E. (1981) *Rural England, 1066–1348.*

Hamilton, Nigel (1981) *Monty: The Making of a General.*

Hammersley, G. F. (1977) The charcoal iron industry and its fuel, *Econ.Hist.Rev.*, **26**, 593–613.

Hamnett, C. (1984) Life in the Cocktail Belt, *Geographical Magazine*, **56**, 534–8.

Handford, R. (1931) *A History of Lancing College.*

Hardy, Dennis (1979) *Alternative Communities in Nineteenth Century England.*

Hardy, Dennis and Ward, Colin (1984) *Arcadia for All; the Legacy of a Makeshift Landscape.*

Hare, J. N. (1981) The buildings of Battle Abbey, *Proceedings of Battle Conference*, **3**, 78–95.

Harris, T. M. (1985) Government and urban development in Kent: the case of the Royal Naval dockyard town of Sheerness, *Arch.Cant.*, **101**, 245–77.

Hartlib, S. (1651) *His Legacie, or an enlargement of the Discours of Husbandrie Used in Brabant and Flanders.*

Harvey, Barbara, F. (1966) The population trend in rural England, 1300–1348, *Trans.Roy.Hist.Soc.*, fifth ser., **16**, 23–42.

Harvey, D. (1963) Locational change in the Kentish hop industry and the analysis of land use patterns, *Transactions Institute of British Geographers*, **33**, 123–44.

Harvey, J. (1973) The Putney Nursery: an early plant centre, *Surr.Arch.Coll.*, **69**, 135–42.

Hasted, Edward (1797–1801, repr. 1972) *The History and Topographical Survey of the County of Kent.* Canterbury.

Hawes, S. (1858) Notes of the Weald Clay of Sussex and on its cultivation, *Journ. Royal Agric. Soc. England*, **19**, 182–98.

Hay, D. (1975) Poaching and the game laws on Cannock Chase. In Hay, D., Linebaugh, P. and Thompson, E. P. (eds) *Albion's Fatal Tree*, 189–253.

Hearne, T. (1720) *Textus Roffensis.* Oxford.

Heath, Richard (1893, repr. 1978) *The English Peasant; studies, historical, local and biographical.* Wakefield.

Hechter, M. (1975) *Internal Colonialism: The Celtic Fringe in British national development 1536–1966.*

Hill, D. (1978) The origin of the Saxon towns in Sussex. In Brandon, P. F. (ed.) *The South Saxons,* 174–89.

Hilton, R. H. (1969) *The Decline of Serfdom in Medieval England.*

Hobbs, M. (1987) The Restoration correspondence of Bishop Henry King, *Suss.Arch.Coll.,*125, 139–53.

Hobsbawm, E and Rudé, G. (1973) *Captain Swing.*

Holden, E. W. (1963) Excavations at the deserted medieval village of Hangleton, Part I, *Suss.Arch.Coll.,* 101, 154–82.

Holden, E. W. (1965) Slate roofing in medieval Sussex, *Suss.Arch.Coll.,* 103, 67–78.

Holden, E. W. (1989) Slate roofing in medieval Sussex: a reappraisal, *Suss.Arch.Coll,* 127.

Holden, E. W. and Hudson, T. P. (1981) Salt making in the Adur Valley, *Suss.Arch.Coll.,* 119, 117–48.

Holmes, U. (1959) The houses of the Bayeux Tapestry, *Speculum,* 34, 179–83.

Homans, W. M. (1949) The founding of New Winchelsea, *Suss.Arch.Coll.,* 67, 22–41.

Hood, M. A. (1979) The historical geography of the river Medway navigation, unpublished Ph.D., University of London.

Hood, M. A. (1981) *Politics and navigation on the Medway in the seventeenth century.* Bedford College Papers in Geography.

Horsburgh, E. L. S. (1929) *Bromley, Kent from the Earliest Times to the Present Century.*

Hoskins, W. G. (1976) *The Age of Plunder: the England of Henry VIII, 1500–1547.*

Howard, H. E. (1935) *Finances of St. John's College, Cambridge 1511–1926.* Cambridge.

Howkins, A. (1986) The discovery of rural England. In Colls, R. and Dodd, P. (eds) *Englishness: Politics and Culture 1880–1920,* 62–88.

Hudson, T. P. (1980) The origin of Steyning and Bramber, Sussex, *Southern History,* 2, 11–30.

Hudson, W. (1919) On a series of rolls of the manor of Wiston, *Suss.Arch.Coll.,* 53, 143–82.

Hughes, A. (1988) The evolution and ownership of timber-framed houses within the old parish and market catchment area of Horsham, *c.*1300–1650: a socio-economic survey, unpublished D. Phil. thesis, University of Sussx. (2 Vols.)

Huish, M. B. (1890) *Birket Foster.*

Huish, M. B. (1892) *Happy England, as painted by Mrs. Allingham.*

Hull, F. (1966) *The White and Black Books of the Cinque Ports*. Historical Manuscripts Comm.

Hunt, John Dixon (1986) *Garden and Grove: The Italian Renaissance Garden in the English Imagination, 1660–1750*.

Hurst, J. G. and D. G. (1964) Excavations at a deserted medieval village, Hangleton, Part 2, *Suss.Arch.Coll.*, 102, 94–112.

Hussey, Christopher (1950) *Sir Edwin Lutyens*.

Hussey, Christopher (1967 edn) *The Picturesque*.

Hussey, Christopher (1967) *English Gardens and Landscapes, 1700–1750*.

Jackson, A. A. (1973) *Semi-detached London*.

Jefferies, R. S. (1975) The Alice Holt medieval potters, *Surr.Arch.Coll.*, 70, 25–46.

Jekyll, G. (1904) *Old West Surrey*.

Jekyll, Frances (1974) *Gertrude Jekyll*.

Jessup, Frank W. (1974) *A history of Kent*. Chichester.

Jones, D. (1786) A letter sent in 1786, transcribed as 'Sheep on Romney Marsh in the Eighteenth Century', *Occasional Paper of Wye College* (1956). Wye.

Jones, David (1981) Rural crime and protest. In Mingay, G. E. (ed.) *The Victorian Countryside*, 2, 566–79.

Jones, D. K. C. (1980) *The Shaping of Southern England*.

Jones, G. Stedman (1971) *Outcast London*. Oxford.

Jones. G. R. J. (1961) Settlement patterns in Anglo-Saxon England, *Ant.*, 35, 221–232.

Jones, G. R. J. (1971) The multiple estate as a model framework for tracing early stages in the evolution of rural settlement. In Dussart, F. (ed.) *L'Habitat et les Paysages ruraux d'Europe*, 251–67. Liège.

Jones, G. R. J. (1979) Multiple estates and early settlement. In Sawyer, P. H. (ed.) *English Medieval Settlement*, 9–34.

Jordan, W. K. (1961) Social institutions in Kent, 1480–1660: A study of the changing pattern of social aspirations, *Arch.Cant.*, 75, 133–8.

Kain, R. J. P. (1973) The land of Kent in the middle of the nineteenth century, unpublished Ph.D. thesis, University of London.

Keates, J. (1988) *Times Lit. Suppl.*, 732.

Kelch, R. A. (1974) *Newcastle: A Duke without Money: Thomas Pelham-Holles 1693–1768*.

Kellett, J. R. (1969) *The Impact of Railways on Victorian Cities*.

Kenyon, G. H. (1955) Kirdford Inventories, 1611–1776, with particular reference to the Weald Clay farming, *Suss.Arch.Coll.*, 93, 78–156.

Kenyon, G. H. (1958) Petworth town and trades, 1610–1760, *Suss.Arch.Coll.*, 96, 35–107.

Kenyon, G. H. (1960) Petworth town and trades, 1610–1760, part II, *Suss.Arch.Coll*, 98, 71–117.

Kenyon, G. H. (1961) Petworth and trades, 1610–1760, part III, *Suss.Arch.Coll.*, **99**, 102–48.

Kenyon, G. H. (1967) *The Glass Industry of the Weald.*

Kerridge, E. (1967) *The Agricultural Revolution.*

Kirk, J. C. (1986) Colonists of the waste: the structure and evolution of nineteenth-century economy and society in the Central Forest Ridges of the Sussex Weald, unpublished M.A. diss., University of Sussex.

Klickmann, F. (1924) *The Flower Patch among the Hills.*

Kropotkin, Peter (ed. Ward, C. 1974) *Fields, Factories and Workshops.*

Lacey, H. M. and U. E. (1974)*The Timber-framed Buildings of Steyning.*

Lambarde, W. (1576, repr. 1970) *A perambulation of Kent: Containing the Description, Historie, and Customes of That Shire.*

Lavergne, L. de (1865) *The Rural Economy of England, Scotland and Ireland.*

Lehmann, H. I. (1973) The history of Epsom Spa, *Surr.Arch.Coll.*, **69**, 89–97.

Lennard, R. V. (1959) *Rural England, 1086–1135.*

Lethaby, W. R. (1979) *Philip Webb and his Work.*

Lewis, W. V. (1932) The formation of Dungeness foreland, *Geogr.Journ.*, **80**, 309–24.

Loftie, W. J. (1883) *A History of London* (2 Vols).

Longworth, Ian and Cherry, John (1986) *Archaeology in Britain since 1945.*

Lower, M. A. (1870) *A Compendious History of Sussex* (2 vols).

Lowerson, J. L. (1975) *An embryonic Brighton? Victorian and Edwardian Seaford.* CCE.

Lowerson, J. L. (1979) Building on East Grinstead Common, *Bulletin East Grinstead Society*, **27**, 5–8.

Lowerson, J. L. (1980a) *A Short History of Sussex.* Folkestone.

Lowerson, J. L. (1980b) *Crawley: Victorian New Town.* CCE.

Lowerson, J. L. (1982) The aftermath of Swing: anti-poor law movements and rural trades unions in the South East of England. In Charlesworth, A. (ed.) *Rural Social Change and Conflict since 1500*, 55–83. Humberside.

Lowerson, J. L. (1983) Resorts, ports and "sleepy hollows": Sussex towns 1840–1940. In Geography Editorial Committee, *Sussex: Environment, Landscape and Society.* Gloucester.

Lowerson, J. L. and Myerscough, J. (1977) *Time to spare in Victorian England.* Hassocks.

Loyn, H. R. (1966) *Harold son of Godwin.* Bexhill.

Loyn, H. R. (1982) *The Norman Conquest.*

Lucas, J. (ed.) (1892) *Pehr Kalm's Account of his Visit to England.*

McCann, T. J. (1974) *Restricted Grandeur: Impressions of Chichester 1586–1948.* Chichester.

McGrath, P. V. (1948) The marketing of food, fodder and livestock in the London area in the seventeenth century, with some reference to the sources of supply, unpublished M.A. diss., University of London.

Machin, R. (1977) The Great Rebuilding: a reassessment, *Past and Present*, 77, 33–56.

Mack, M. (1969) *The Garden and the City*.

Mack, M. (1985) *Alexander Pope; a Life*.

Mackay, Shena (1986) *Redhill Rococo*.

Macray, Reverend W. D. (1891 and 1894) *Calendar of charters and documents relating to the possessions of Selborne and its priory preserved in the muniment room of Magdalen College, Oxford*. Hants. Record Society, London and Winchester.

Maitland, F. W. (1897) *Domesday and Beyond*.

Maitland, F. W. (1906) *Life and Letters of Leslie Stephen*.

Malcolm, J. (1805) *A compendium of Modern Husbandry*.

Malmesbury, William of (ed. Stubbs, W. 1887–9) *Gesta Regum*. Rolls Series 90 (2 vols).

Manning, O. and Bray, W. (1804–14) *The History and Antiquities of the County of Surrey* (3 Vols).

Manning, R. B. (1969) *Religion and Society in Elizabethan Sussex*. Leicester.

Markham, Gervase (1636 edn) *The Inrichment of the Weald of Kent*.

Markham, Gervase (1638 edn) *Farewell to Husbandry*.

Marsh, Jan (1982) *Back to the Land*.

Marshall, W. (1798) *The Rural Economy of the Southern Counties* (2 Vols).

Marshall, W. (1818) *The Review and Abstracts of the County Reports to the Board of Agriculture*, Vol. 5.

Martin, David (1974a) *Historic Buildings in eastern Sussex*, vols. 1–4 (ongoing).

Martin, David (1974b) Chateaubriand, Burwash, *Suss.Arch.Coll.*, 112, 21–9.

Martin, David (1978) Portland Cottages, Burwash, *Suss.Arch.Coll.* 116, 14–20.

Masingham, Betty (1960) *Miss Jekyll; A Portrait of a Great Gardener*.

Mason, J. F. A. (1964) The Rapes of Sussex and the Norman Conquest, *Suss.Arch.Coll.*, 102, 68–93.

Mason, R. T. (1957) Fourteenth-century halls in Sussex, *Suss.Arch.Coll.*, 95, 71–93.

Mason, R. T. (1969 edn) *Framed Buildings of the Weald*.

Mason, R. T. (1975) The dating of timber-framed vernacular architecture in Sussex, *Suss.Arch.Coll.*, 113, 1–6.

Mason, R. T. (1978a) Alciston Court: a manor of Battle Abbey, *Suss.Arch. Coll.*, 116, 159–62.

Mason, R. T. (1978b) Single-aisled halls in Sussex, *Suss.Arch.Coll.* 116, 155–8.

Mate, Mavis (1983) The farming out of manors: a new look at the evidence from Canterbury Cathedral Priory, *Journ.Med.Hist.*, 9, 331–43.

Mate, Mavis (1984) Agrarian economy after the Black Death: the manors of Canterbury Cathedral Priory, 1348–91, *Econ.Hist.Rev.*, 37, 341–54.

Mate, Mavis, (1985) Labour and labour services on the estates of

Canterbury Cathedral Priory in the fourteenth century, *Southern History*, 7, 55–68.

Mayhew, G. J. (1982) Religion, faction and politics in Reformation Rye: 1530–59, *Suss.Arch.Coll.*, **120**, 149–60.

Mayhew, G. J. (1987) *Tudor Rye*. Falmer.

Mead, W. R. and Kain, R. J. P. (1976) Ridge-and-furrow in Kent, *Arch.Cant.*, 92, 165–71.

Melling, E. (1965) *Kentish Sources, V: Some Kentish Houses*. Maidstone.

Mendel, V. *et. al.* (1925 edn) *The Week-End Book*.

Meredith, G. (ed. Clive C. L. 1970) *The Letters of George Meredith*.

Metcalf, P. (1978) *The Park Town Estate and the Battersea Tangle*. London Topographical Society, 121.

Mill, J. S. (1951 repr.) Account of a Tour in Sussex in July 1827, *The Worthing Parade*, 1, 159–83.

Mills, D. R. and Short B. M. (1983) Social change and social conflict in nineteenth-century England. *Journ. Peasant Studies*, 10, 253–62.

Millward, R. and Robinson, A. (1973) *South East England: the Channel Coastlands*.

Mingay, G. E. (1963) *English Landed Society in the Eighteenth Century*.

Ministry of Agriculture and Fisheries Economic Series (1929) *Markets and Fairs in England and Wales, Part IV: Eastern and Southern Markets*.

Monro, Alida (ed.) (1933) *Collected Poems of Harold Monro*.

Moore, H. Keatley (1917) *Surrey Deeds in the Reference Library at Croydon: a Catalogue*. Croydon.

Moore, J. S. (1965) *Laughton: A study in the Evolution of the Wealden Landscape*. Leicester.

Morris, John (ed.) (1975) *Domesday Book: Surrey*. Chichester.

Morris, John (ed.) (1976) *Domesday Book: Kent*. Chichester.

Morris, John (ed.) (1976) *Domesday Book: Sussex*. Chichester.

Mortimer, J. (1707) *The Whole Art of Husbandry*.

Mortimer, R. (1981) The beginning of the Honor of Clare, *Proceedings Battle Conference*, 3, 119–41.

Mousley, J. (1955) Sussex gentry in the reign of Elizabeth, unpublished Ph.D. thesis, University of London.

Murray, K. M. E. (1935) *The Constitutional History of the Cinque Ports*.

Myers, A. R. (1972) *London in the Age of Chaucer*.

Nairn, I. and Pevsner, N. (1965) *The Buildings of England: Sussex East and West*.

Nesfield, W. E. and Shaw, R. Norman, Sketch-book (Archive Roy. Inst. Brit. Arch.).

Nevill, D. (1907) *Personal Memoirs*.

Newton, E. (1950) *The Meaning of Beauty*.

Norden, J. (1610 edn) *The Surveyor's Dialogue*.

Norman, P. (1901) The accounts of the overseers of the poor of Paris Garden, Southwark, 17 May 1608 to 30 September 1671, *Surr.Arch.Coll.*, **16**, 55–136.

Nossiter, B. D. (1978) *Britain: A Future that Works.*

O'Connell, M. (1977) *Historic Towns in Surrey.* Surrey Archaelogical Society.

Ogden, H. V. S. and Ogden, M. S. O. (1955) *English Taste in Landscape in the Seventeenth Century.*

O'Grady, Sister M. (1987) Aspects of the Development of the Eastry Estate, 1350–1836, unpublished Ph.D. thesis, Council for National Academic Awards.

Otter, Sir John (1925) *Nathaniel Woodard.*

Park, D. (1983) The Lewes Group of wall paintings in Sussex, *Proceedings Battle Conference*, **6**, 200–23.

Parkin, E. W. (1984) The ancient Cinque Port of Sandwich, *Arch.Cant.*, **100**, 189–216.

Parton, A. G. (1967) A note on the open fields of Fetcham and Great Bookham, *Proc. Leatherhead and District Local History Society*, **3**, 25–6.

Parton, A. G. (1984) The Hearth Tax and the distribution of population and prosperity in Surrey, *Surr.Arch.Coll.*, **75**, 155–60.

Pearce, S. A. (1984) The impact of the railway on Uckfield in the nineteenth century, *Suss.Arch.Coll.*, **122**, 193–206.

Peckham, W. D. (1925) *Thirteen Custumals of the Sussex Manors of the Bishop of Chichester.* Sussex Record Society, 31.

Phythian-Adams, C. (1979) *Desolation of a City: Coventry and the Urban Crisis of the late Middle Ages.* Leicester.

Pilley, R. (1988) *Golfing Portraits.*

Plantagenet Edward, Duke of York (1909 edn) *Master of Game.*

Postan, M.M. (1972) *The Medieval Economy and Society.*

Preston, J. M. (1977) *Industrial Medway: an Historical Survey.* Rochester.

Rackham, Oliver (1986) *The History of the Countryside.*

Reay, B. (1988) The last rising of the agricultural labourers, the battle in Bossenden Wood, 1838, *History Workshop Journal*, **26**, 79–101.

Redwood, B. C. and Wilson, A. E. (1958) *Custumals of Sussex Manors of the Archbishop of Canterbury.* Sussex Record Society, 57.

Reed, M. (1982) Social and Economic Relations in a Wealden Community: Lodsworth, 1780–1860, unpublished M.A. diss., University of Sussex.

Reed, M. (1984) The peasantry of nineteenth-century England: a neglected class?, *History Workshop*, **18**, 53–76.

Reed, Michael (1983) *The Georgian Triumph 1700–1830.*

Reed, Michael (1986) *The Age of Exuberance 1550–1700.*

Reid, I. G. (1958) *The Small Farm on Heavy Land.* Wye College, Dept. of Agric. Econ. Wye.

Renn, D. (1968) *Norman Castles in England.*

Repton, H. (1803) *Observations on the Theory and Practice of Landscape Gardening.*

Rigold, S. E. (1966) Some major Kentish timber barns, *Arch.Cant.*, 81, 1–30.

Rigold, S. E. (1978) Structures within English moated sites. In Aberg, F. A. (ed.) *Medieval Moated Sites*, CBA. Res. Rep. 17, 29–36.

Roberts, D. (1979) *Paternalism in early Victorian England.*

Robinson, J. M. (1982) *The Dukes of Norfolk: a Quincentennial History.* Oxford.

Robinson, J. M. (1987) Medieval deer parks, *National Trust Mag.* 231.

Robinson, W. (1911) *Gravetye Manor.* Gravetye, Sussex.

Roebuck, J. (1979) *Urban Development in Nineteenth-century London: Lambeth, Battersea and Wandsworth 1838–88.* Chichester.

Rolston, G. R. (1978) *Haslemere.* Chichester.

Round, J. H. (1899) The settlement of the South East. In *Commune of London and other Studies*, 1–27.

Rowley, Trevor (ed.) (1981) *The Origin of Open Field Agriculture.*

Rudé, G. (1971) *Hanoverian London 1714–1808.*

Rule, J. G. (1975) Wrecking and coastal plunder. In Hay, D., Linebaugh, P. and Thompson, E. P. (eds) *Albions Fatal Tree*, 167–88.

Rule, J. G. (1979) Social crime in the rural South in the eighteenth and early nineteenth centuries, *Southern History*, 1, 135–53.

Sackville-West, V. (1946) *The Garden.*

Saint, Andrew (1976) *Richard Norman Shaw.*

Salzman, L. F. (1910) The inning of Pevensey Level, *Suss.Arch.Coll.*, 53, 32–60.

Salzman, L. F. (1921) *The Cartulary of Sele.* Lewes.

Salzman, L. F. (1931) The rapes of Sussex, *Suss.Arch.Coll.*, 72, 20–9.

Salzman, L. F. (ed. 1932) *The Cartulary of the Priory of St. Pancras at Lewes, Part I.* Sussex Record Society.

Salzman, L. F. (1953) The property of the Earl of Arundel, *Suss.Arch.Coll.*, 91, 32–52.

Salzman, L. F. (ed.) (1955) *The Ministers' Accounts of the Manor of Petworth, 1347–1353.* Sussex Record Society 55.

Sassoon, S. (1960 edn) *Memoirs of a Fox-hunting Man.*

Saul, Nigel (1986) *Scenes from Provincial Life: Knightly Families in Sussex, 1280–1400.* Oxford.

Saville, R. V. (1983) Gentry Wealth on the Weald in the eighteenth century: the Fullers of Brightling Park, *Suss.Arch.Coll.*, 121, 129–47.

Sawyer, P. H. (1965) The Wealth of England in the eleventh century, *Trans.Roy.Hist.Soc.*, 5th series, 15, 145–64.

Sawyer, P. H.(1976) *Medieval Settlement: Continuity and Change.*

Sawyer, P. H. (1978) *From Roman Britain to Norman England.*

Schofield, R. S. (1965) The geographical distribution of wealth in England, 1334–1649, *Econ.Hist.Rev.*, 18, 483–510.

Scurrell, D., Stafford, F. and Whyman, J. (1986) *Margate: a resort history.* Margate.

Searle, E. (1963) Hides, virgates and tenants: settlements of Battle Abbey, *Econ.Hist.Rev.*, **16**, 290–300.

Searle, E. (1974) *Lordship and Community: Battle Abbey and its Banlieu, 1066–1538.* Toronto.

Searle, E. (1980) The abbey of the Conqueror: defensive enfeoffment and economic development of Anglo-Norman England, *Proceedings Battle Conference*, **2**, 154–64.

Sheail, J. (1972) The distribution of taxable population and wealth in England during the early sixteenth century, *Trans. Institute British Geographers*, **55**, 111–26.

Sheppard, F. (1971) *London 1808–1870: the infernal Wen.*

Sheppard, J. B., (ed.) (1887–8) *The Letter Books of the Monastery of Christ Church Canterbury.* Rolls Series, 85, ii.

Short, B. M. (1973) The agriculture of the High Weald of Kent and Sussex 1850–1953: a study in the application of multivariate statistics in historical geography, unpublished Ph.D., University of London.

Short, B. M. (1975) The turnover of tenants on the Ashburnham estate, 1830–1850, *Suss.Arch.Coll.*, **113**, 157–74.

Short, B. M. (ed.) (1980) *The String Town; Hailsham, 1870–1914.* CCE.

Short, B. M. (1982) The art and craft of chicken cramming: poultry in the Weald of Sussex 1850–1950, *Agric.Hist.Rev.*, **30**, 19–30.

Short, B. M. (1983) *The Geography of Local Migration in Sussex, 1500–1900.* Geography Research Paper, University of Sussex.

Short, B. M. (ed.) (1984a) *'A very improving neighbourhood': Burgess Hill 1840–1914.* CCE.

Short, B. M. (1984b) The decline of living-in servants in the transition to capitalist farming: a critique of the Sussex evidence, *Suss.Arch.Coll.*, **122**, 147–64.

Short, B. M. (1985) South-East England: Kent, Surrey and Sussex. In Thirsk, Joan (ed.) *The Agrarian History of England and Wales, Vol. v (i), 1640–1750.* 270–313. Cambridge.

Short, B.M. (1989) The de-industrialisation process: a case study of the Weald 1600–1850. In Hudson, P. (ed.) *Regions and Industries: a new perspective on the origins of Britain's Industrial Revolution.* 156–74, Cambridge.

Simmons, J. (1978) *The Railway in England and Wales 1830–1914.* Leicester.

Sinclair, D. J. (1964) The growth of London since 1800. In Clayton, K. M. (ed.) *Guide to London Excursions*, 11–19.

Smail, H. (1941) *The Worthing Map Story.* Worthing.

Smail, H. (1944) *The Worthing Road and its Coaches.* Worthing.

Smith, Ann (1963) Regional differences in crop production in medieval Kent, *Arch.Cant.*, **78**, 147–60.

Smith, H. (1982) 'William Daniell's Brighton', *Country Life*, 7 January.

Smith, L. T. (ed.) (1963) *The Itinerary of John Leland*, Vol. 4.

Smith, R. A. L. (1943) *Canterbury Cathedral Priory.*

Smith, Verena (ed.) (1979) *The Sharpe Collection of Watercolours and Drawings, 1797–1809.* Lewes.

Snell, K. D. M. (1987) *Annals of the labouring Poor.* Cambridge.

Stamp, G. and Goulancourt, A. (1986) *The English House, 1860–1914.*

Stamp, L. D. (1943) *The Land of Britain: Kent.*

Stamp, L. D. and Willatts, E. C. (1941) *The Land of Britain: Surrey.*

Stevens, K. F. and Oldig, T. E. (1985) *The Brokage Books of Southampton for 1447 and 1527–8.* Southampton Record Series, 28.

Stevenson, W. (1809) *A General View of the Agriculture of the County of Surrey.*

Stewart, Ian (1978) The Sussex mints. In Brandon, P. (ed.) *The South Saxons* 89–137.

Stocks, Baroness M. (1970) *My Commonplace Book.*

Stow, J. (1603, repr. 1971) (ed. Kingsford, C. L.) A Survey of London, Vol. 2.

Stoyel, A. D. (1985) The lost buildings of Otford Palace, *Arch.Cant.*, **100**, 259–80.

Straker, E. (1931) *Wealden Iron.*

Streeten, A. (1980) Potters, kilns and markets in medieval Sussex; a preliminary study, *Suss.Arch.Coll.*, **118**, 119–24.

Strong, Sir Roy (1979) *The Renaissance Garden in England.*

Stroud, D. (1974 ed.) *Capability Brown.*

Summerson, Sir J. N. (1973) *The London Building World of the Eighteen Sixties.*

Sutermeister, H. (1976) Burpham: a settlement site within the Saxon defences, *Suss.Arch.Coll.*, **114**, 194–206.

Switzer, S. (1742 ed.) *Icnographia Rustica.*

Tate, W. E. (1943) A hand-list of English Enclosure Acts and Awards, part 17: Open fields, commons and enclosures in Kent, *Arch.Cant.*, **56**, 54–67.

Tatton-Brown, T. (1984) Three great Benedictine houses in Kent: their buildings and topography, *Arch.Cant.*, **100**, 171–88.

Tatton-Brown, T. (1988) The Anglo-Saxon towns of Kent. In Hooke, D. (ed.) *Anglo-Saxon Settlements*, 213–32.

Taylor, Christopher (1972) Medieval moats in Cambridgeshire. In Fowler, P. J. (ed.) *Archaeology and the Landscape*, 237–49.

Taylor, Christopher (1983) *Village and Farmstead.*

Tebbutt, C. F. (1981) Wealden bloomery iron-smelting furnace, *Suss.Arch. Coll.*, **119**, 57–64.

Thick, M. (1985) Market Gardening in England and Wales. In Thirsk, Joan (ed.) *The Agrarian History of England and Wales, Vol. v (ii), 1640–1750*, 503–32. Cambridge.

Thirsk, Joan (ed.) (1967) *The Agrarian History of England and Wales, Vol. iv, 1500–1640.* Cambridge.

Thomas, D. (1970) *London's Green Belt.*

Thomas, Edward (1913) *The Happy-Go-Lucky Morgans.*

Thomas-Stanford, C. (1910) *Sussex in the Great Civil War and the Interregnum 1642–1660.*

Thompson, E. P. (1975) *Whigs and Hunters: the Origin of the Black Act.*

Thompson, F. M. L. (1982) *The Rise of Suburbia.* Leicester.

Thorpe, L. (1973) *The Bayeux Tapestry and the Norman Invasion.*

Thrupp, S. (1969) Aliens in and around London in the fifteenth century. In Hollaender, A. and Kellaway, W. (eds) *Studies in London History*, 419–27.

Titow, J. Z. (1972) *Winchester yields: A Study in Medieval Agricultural Productivity.* Cambridge.

Tittensor, A. M. and Ruth M. (1985) The rabbit warren at West Dean near Chichester, *Suss.Arch.Coll.*, **123**, 151–81.

Tomlinson, H. L. (1976) Wealden gunfounding: an analysis of its demise in the eighteenth century, *Econ.Hist.Rev.*, **39**, 383–99.

Tonkins, W. G. S. (1964) Shoreham Harbour, Sussex, *Geography*, **49**, 247–51.

Topley, W. (1876) *The Geology of the Weald.*

Tout, T.F. (1917) Medieval town planning, *The Bull. John Rylands Lib.*, 1–33

Turner, D. H. *et. al.* (1980) *The Benedictines in Britain.* British Library Board.

Turner, D. J. (1966) A moated site near Burstow Rectory, *Surr.Arch.Coll.*, **63**, 51–65.

Turner, D. J. (1977) Moated sites in Surrey: a provisional list, *Surr.Arch.Coll.*, **71**, 89–94.

Turner, Derek (1978) A lost seventeenth century demographic crisis? The evidence of two counties, *Local Population Studies*, **21**, 11–18.

Underdown, D. (1971) *Pride's Purge: Politics in the Puritan Revolution.* Oxford.

Underdown, D. (1985) *Revel, riot and rebellion: popular politics and culture in England 1603–1660.* Oxford.

Urry, William (1967) *Canterbury under the Angevin Kings.*

Urry, William (ed. Butcher, A. 1988) *Christopher Marlowe and Canterbury.*

Veale, E. M. (1969) Craftsmen and the economy of London in the fourteenth century. In Hollaender, A. and Kellaway, W. (eds) *Studies in London History*, 133–54.

VCH, Kent, II (1926)

VCH, Surrey, I (1902); II (1905); IV (1912).

VCH Sussex, II (1907).

Vine, P. A. L. (**1965**) *London's Lost Route to the Sea.* Dawlish.

Vine, P. A. L. (1972) *The Royal Military Canal.* Newton Abbot.

Vinogradoff, P. (1908) *English Society in the Eleventh Century.*

Wagner, A. R. (1959) The Wagners of Brighton, *Suss.Arch.Coll.*, **98**, 35–57.

Wallace, Graham (1957) *R.A.F. Biggin Hill.*

Walpole, H. (1906 edn) (ed. Cunningham, P.), *Letters of Horace Walpole,* Edinburgh.

Walpole, H. (1826–8) *Anecdotes of Painting in England.*

Walter, J. and Wrightson, K. (1984) Dearth and the social order in early modern England. In Clark, P. (ed.), *Rebellion, Popular Protest and the Social Order in Early Modern England,* 113–19. Cambridge.

Walton, J. (1983) *The English Seaside Resort: a Social History 1750–1914.* Leicester.

Ward, E. M. (1922) *English Coastline Evolution.*

Ward, E. M. (1934) The river Limen at Ruckinge, *Arch.Cant.,* 45, 129–32.

Ward, G. (1936) The *Haeselerse* charter of 1018, *Suss.Arch.Coll.,* 78, 19–29.

Waterhouse, E. (1988) (ed. Jones, E.) *The Memoirs of Edwin Waterhouse.*

Waters, M. (1984) Dockyard and Parliament; a study of the unskilled workers in Chatham Dockyard, 1860–1900, *Southern History,* 6, 123–38.

Webber, K. (1980) *The Peasants' Revolt.*

Webber, R. (1968) *The Early Horticulturalists.* Newton Abbot.

Weber, A. F. (1899, repub. 1963) *The Growth of Cities in the Nineteenth Century.* New York.

Wells, H. G. (1907, repub. 1964) *Tono Bungay.*

Wells, R. A. E. (1979) The Development of the English Rural Proletariat and Social Protest, 1700–1850, *Journ. Peasant Studies,* 6, 115–39.

Wells, R. A. E. (1981) Social conflict and protest in the English countryside in the early nineteenth century: a rejoinder, *Journ. Peasant Studies,* 8, 514–30.

Wheatley, Ronald (1958) *Operation Sea Lion.*

White, Rev. Gilbert (1816 edn) *The Natural History and Antiquities of Selborne.*

White, H. P. (1982) *Southern England: a regional history of the railways of Great Britain,* 2.

White, J. T. (1977) *Down and Weald: Kent, Surrey and Sussex.*

Whitehead, Sir C. (1899) *A Sketch of the Agriculture of Kent.*

Whyman, J. (1969–70) Rise and decline: Dover and Deal in the nineteenth century, *Arch.Cant.* 74, 107–37; 75, 35–54.

Whyman, J. (1981) Water communications to Margate and Gravesend as coastal resorts before 1840, *Southern History,* 3, 111–3.

Wiener, M. J. (1981) *English Culture and the Decline of the Industrial Spirit, 1850–1980.* Cambridge.

Willatts, E. C. (1933) Changes in land utilisation in the Southwest of the London Basin 1840–1932, *Geographical Journ.,* 82, 515–28.

Willats, E. C. (1937) *The Land of Britain: Middlesex and the London Region.*

Williams, Ann (1981) Land and power in the eleventh century; the estate of Harold Godwinson, *Proceedings Battle Conference,* 3, 171–87.

401

Williams, R. (1975 edn) *The Country and the City.*

Wilson, A. E. (1961) *Custumals of the manors of Laughton, Willingdon and Goring,* Sussex Record Society, 60.

Wilson, D. M. (1985) *The Bayeux Tapestry.*

Wilson, J. M. (1870) *The Imperial Gazetteer of England and Wales,* (2 vols).

Winbolt, S. E. (1933) *Wealden Glass.*

Witney, K. P. (1976) *The Jutish Forest: A Study of the Weald of Kent from 450–1350 AD.*

Witney, K. P. (1982) *The Kingdom of Kent.* Chichester.

Witney, K. P. (1988) The economic position of husbandsmen at the time of the Domesday Book: a Kentish perspective, *Econ.Hist.Rev.,* **37**, 23–34.

Wood, E. S. (1965) A Medieval glassworks at Blunden's Wood, Hambledon, Surrey, *Surr.Arch.Coll.,* **62**, 54–79.

Wood, Margaret (1981) *The English Medieval House.*

Wood, William (1938) *A Sussex Farmer.*

Wooldridge, S. W. and Linton, D. L. (1933) The loam terrains of South East England and their relations to its early history, *Ant.,* **7**, 297–310.

Wooldridge, S. W. and Goldring, F. (1953) *The Weald.*

Worcester, D. K. (1950) East Sussex landownership. The structure of rural society in an area of old enclosure, 1733–87, unpublished Ph.D. thesis, University of Cambridge.

Worlters, N. (1986) *Shoreham's Bungalow Town.* Shoreham.

Wrigley, E. A. (1967) A simple model of London's importance in changing English society and economy, 1650–1750, *Past and Present,* **37**, 44–70.

Wrigley, E. A. and Schofield, R. S. (1981) *The Population History of England 1541–1870.* Cambridge.

Yarranton, A. (1663) *The Improvement Improved, by a Second Edition of the Great Improvement of Lands by Clover.*

Yates, E. M. (1975) The *Meare* marsh of Merston, *Suss.Arch.Coll.,* **113**, 118–23.

Yates, N. (1986) The condition of Kent churches before Victorian restoration, *Arch.Cant.,* **103**, 119–25.

Youatt, W. (1834) *Cattle.*

Young, Rev. A. (1789) A Tour in Sussex, *Annals of Agriculture,* **11**, 170–304.

Young, Rev. A. (1793) A Tour through Sussex, *Annals of Agriculture,* **22**, 202–334; 494–631.

Young, Rev. A. (1813) *General View of the Agriculture of the County of Sussex.*

Young, G. (1983) *A History of Bognor Regis.* Chichester.

Young, G. M. (1936) *Victorian England: Portrait of an Age.*

Young, K. and Garside, P. L. (1982) *Metropolitan London: Politics and Urban Change 1837–1981.*

Zarnecki, G. (1951) *English Romanesque Sculpture, 1066–1140.*

Zarnecki, G. (1978) Romanesque sculpture in Normandy and England in the eleventh century, *Proceedings Battle Conference*, 1, 168–79.

Zell, M. (1985a) A wood-pasture regime: the Kentish Weald in the sixteenth century, *Southern History*, 7, 69–93.

Zell, M. (1985b) Population and family structure in the sixteenth century Weald, *Arch.Cant.*, 100, 231–57.

Index

Numbers in italics indicate a reference to a plate, figure, or table